SOMETHING ABOUT THE AUTHOR®

Something about
the Author *was named
an "Outstanding
Reference Source,"*
the highest honor given
by the American
Library Association
Reference and Adult
Services Division.

ISSN 0276-816X

SOMETHING ABOUT THE AUTHOR®

**Facts and Pictures about Authors
and Illustrators of Books for Young People**

volume 174

THOMSON

GALE

Detroit • New York • San Francisco • New Haven, Conn. • Waterville, Maine • London

THOMSON

GALE

Something about the Author, Volume 174

Project Editor
Lisa Kumar

Editorial
Amy Elisabeth Fuller, Michelle Kazensky, Mary Ruby

Permissions
Robert McCord, Barbara McNeil, Tim Sisler

Imaging and Multimedia
Leitha Etheridge-Sims, Lezlie Light

Composition and Electronic Capture
Tracey L. Matthews

Manufacturing
Drew Kalasky

Product Manager
Peg Knight

LIBRARY OF CONGRESS CATALOG CARD NUMBER 62-52046

ISBN-13: 978-0-7876-8798-4
ISBN-10: 0-7876-8798-7
ISSN 0276-816X

This title is also available as an e-book.
ISBN-13: 978-1-4144-2938-0, ISBN-10: 1-4144-2938-X
Contact your Thomson Gale sales representative for ordering information.

Printed in the United States of America
10 9 8 7 6 5 4 3 2 1

Contents

Authors in Forthcoming Volumes

Below are some of the authors and illustrators that will be featured in upcoming volumes of *SATA*. These include new entries on the swiftly rising stars of the field, as well as completely revised and updated entries (indicated with *) on some of the most notable and best-loved creators of books for children.

Chris Abouzeid ∎ An award-winning fiction-writer whose stories and poetry have appeared in literary journals such as *New England Review, Southern Review,* and *Other Voices,* Abouzeid moved into children's literature with the novel *Anatopsis.* An updated fantasy, his novel follows the adventures of a thirteen-year-old immortal princess who has magical powers as well as a burdensome destiny: to take over control of the family's corporate kingdom, Amalgamated Witchcraft Corporation.

*Meg Cabot ∎ The prolific Cabot, whose frothy fiction is popular among teen girls, has earned a reputation for capturing the essence of the way adolescents think and talk in her many young-adult novels. She is best known as the author of *The Princess Diaries,* which focuses on a gawky Manhattan teen who suddenly finds herself living in the limelight after her estranged father returns as European royalty. In addition to sparking a novel series that follows Cabot's likeable protagonist through her high-school years, *The Princess Diaries* was also adapted as a popular feature film.

*Russell Freedman ∎ The author of more than forty nonfiction books for children over a career spanning four decades, Freedman has been honored with several major awards. His Newbery Medal-winning *Lincoln: A Photobiography* was the first to showcase the author's creative mix of text and image; other award-winning historical works by Freedman include *The Wright Brothers: How They Invented the Airplane* and *Eleanor Roosevelt: A Life of Discovery.* With topics ranging from famous teenagers to animal behavior, his books are noted for their understandable and entertaining presentation of detailed facts.

Maureen Garvie ∎ An editor and writing instructor at Queen's University in Kingston, Ontario, Canada, Garvie writes teen novels such as *Lake Rules,* as well as historical novels that bring North American history to life for younger readers. Her novel *George Johnson's War,* co-authored with friend Mary Beaty, follows the coming of age of a young man of mixed British and Native American heritage, as he tries to navigate social prejudice and growing political antagonism on the eve of the American Revolution.

Josef Holub ∎ Holub is the author of the critically acclaimed young-adult novels *The Robber and Me* and *An Innocent Soldier,* the latter an exploration of the horror of war as seen through the eyes of a sensitive teen. Although literary success came late for Holub—who has worked as a mason, a mail carrier, and a village mayor in his native Germany—he published his first novel at age sixty-seven, and has gone on to win several awards, including the Zurich Children's Book Prize.

*Annette Curtis Klause ∎ A professional librarian, Klause broke new ground in young-adult literature with *The Silver Kiss,* a vampire love story that, while graphic in its content, was praised by critics as a darkly seductive thriller with a positive message. Her more recent novels, which include *Alien Secrets, Blood and Chocolate,* and *Freaks: Alive, on the Inside!,* have sparked some measure of controversy due to their violence and sexual content. In response to criticism, Klause has said of her writing that she hopes to change the way readers look at themselves and remind teens that they have the right to be different.

Tracy Lynn ∎ Lynn, one of several pen names of Elizabeth J. Braswell, is the author of several popular young-adult novels focusing on mature teen-related themes, among them *Snow* and *Rx. Snow* is an imaginative retelling of the story of Snow White, while in *Rx* Lynn brings to life the world of a high schooler whose addiction to prescription drugs draws her into criminal activity. Using other pseudonyms, Braswell has penned novels in the "Nine Lives of Chloe King" and "Big Empty" teen novel series, and is known under her real name as a video-game producer and the author of short fiction.

Beau Riffenburgh ∎ Riffenburgh is an author and historian specializing in polar exploration. A member of the Scott Polar Research Institute at the University of Cambridge and the editor of *Polar Record,* he is the author of several highly regarded academic works, as well as *Shackleton's Forgotten Expedition: The Voyage of the Nimrod.* This popular account follows the British-sponsored Antarctic expedition fronted by legendary explorer Ernest Shackleton from 1907-09 which, while overshadowed by the explorer's subsequent exploits, resulted in the discovery of the South Magnetic Pole.

Michele Serros ∎ A poet, novelist, and short-story writer, Serros has produced several critically acclaimed books that emphasize Latina culture, among them *How to Be a Chicana Role Model* and *Honey Blonde Chica.* In addition to her writing, she also tours with Lollapalooza as a road poet, has been a radio commentator, and worked on the staff of television's *The George Lopez Show.* Serros has been praised by several critics for sharing with readers the difficulties young Latinas face in forging an identity within America's Anglo culture.

Michael Winerip ∎ An award-winning journalist who covers education for the *New York Times,* Winerip has also produced several books as an outgrowth of his work. *9 Highland Road* is a profile of an endangered group home in a Long Island suburb, while the middle-grade novel *Adam Canfield of the Slash* introduces readers to the complexities of the newsroom as two middle schoolers work to ensure freedom of the press but ultimately find themselves in hot water with school administrators and parents.

Introduction

Something about the Author (*SATA*) is an ongoing reference series that examines the lives and works of authors and illustrators of books for children. *SATA* includes not only well-known writers and artists but also less prominent individuals whose works are just coming to be recognized. This series is often the only readily available information source on emerging authors and illustrators. You'll find *SATA* informative and entertaining, whether you are a student, a librarian, an English teacher, a parent, or simply an adult who enjoys children's literature.

What's Inside *SATA*

SATA provides detailed information about authors and illustrators who span the full time range of children's literature, from early figures like John Newbery and L. Frank Baum to contemporary figures like Judy Blume and Richard Peck. Authors in the series represent primarily English-speaking countries, particularly the United States, Canada, and the United Kingdom. Also included, however, are authors from around the world whose works are available in English translation. The writings represented in *SATA* include those created intentionally for children and young adults as well as those written for a general audience and known to interest younger readers. These writings cover the entire spectrum of children's literature, including picture books, humor, folk and fairy tales, animal stories, mystery and adventure, science fiction and fantasy, historical fiction, poetry and nonsense verse, drama, biography, and nonfiction. Obituaries are also included in *SATA* and are intended not only as death notices but also as concise overviews of people's lives and work. Additionally, each edition features newly revised and updated entries for a selection of *SATA* listees who remain of interest to today's readers and who have been active enough to require extensive revisions of their earlier biographies.

Autobiography Feature

Beginning with Volume 103, many volumes of *SATA* feature one or more specially commissioned autobiographical essays. These unique essays, averaging about ten thousand words in length and illustrated with an abundance of personal photos, present an entertaining and informative first-person perspective on the lives and careers of prominent authors and illustrators profiled in *SATA*.

Two Convenient Indexes

In response to suggestions from librarians, *SATA* indexes no longer appear in every volume but are included in alternate (odd-numbered) volumes of the series, beginning with Volume 57.

SATA continues to include two indexes that cumulate with each alternate volume: the Illustrations Index, arranged by the name of the illustrator, gives the number of the volume and page where the illustrator's work appears in the current volume as well as all preceding volumes in the series; the Author Index gives the number of the volume in which a person's biographical sketch, autobiographical essay, or obituary appears in the current volume as well as all preceding volumes in the series.

These indexes also include references to authors and illustrators who appear in *Gale's Yesterday's Authors of Books for Children, Children's Literature Review,* and *Something about the Author Autobiography Series.*

Easy-to-Use Entry Format

Whether you're already familiar with the *SATA* series or just getting acquainted, you will want to be aware of the kind of information that an entry provides. In every *SATA* entry the editors attempt to give as complete a picture of the person's life and work as possible. A typical entry in *SATA* includes the following clearly labeled information sections:

PERSONAL: date and place of birth and death, parents' names and occupations, name of spouse, date of marriage, names of children, educational institutions attended, degrees received, religious and political affiliations, hobbies and other interests.

ADDRESSES: complete home, office, electronic mail, and agent addresses, whenever available.

CAREER: name of employer, position, and dates for each career post; art exhibitions; military service; memberships and offices held in professional and civic organizations.

MEMBER: professional, civic, and other association memberships and any official posts held.

AWARDS, HONORS: literary and professional awards received.

WRITINGS: title-by-title chronological bibliography of books written and/or illustrated, listed by genre when known; lists of other notable publications, such as plays, screenplays, and periodical contributions.

ADAPTATIONS: a list of films, television programs, plays, CD-ROMs, recordings, and other media presentations that have been adapted from the author's work.

WORK IN PROGRESS: description of projects in progress.

SIDELIGHTS: a biographical portrait of the author or illustrator's development, either directly from the biographee—and often written specifically for the *SATA* entry—or gathered from diaries, letters, interviews, or other published sources.

BIOGRAPHICAL AND CRITICAL SOURCES: cites sources quoted in "Sidelights" along with references for further reading.

EXTENSIVE ILLUSTRATIONS: photographs, movie stills, book illustrations, and other interesting visual materials supplement the text.

How a *SATA* Entry Is Compiled

SATA editors examine a wide variety of published sources to gather information for an entry. Biographical and bibliographic sources are consulted, as are book reviews, feature articles, published interviews, and material sometimes obtained from the biographee's family, publishers, agent, or other associates. Whenever possible, the author or illustrator is sent a copy of the entry to check for accuracy and completeness.

Entries that have not been verified by the biographees or their representatives are marked with an asterisk (*).

Contact the Editor

We encourage our readers to examine the entire *SATA* series. Please write and tell us if we can make *SATA* even more helpful to you. Give your comments and suggestions to the editor:

Editor
Something about the Author
Thomson Gale
27500 Drake Rd.
Farmington Hills MI 48331-3535

Toll-free: 800-877-GALE
Fax: 248-699-8070

Something about the Author Product Advisory Board

The editors of *Something about the Author* are dedicated to maintaining a high standard of excellence by publishing comprehensive, accurate, and highly readable entries on a wide array of writers for children and young adults. In addition to the quality of the content, the editors take pride in the graphic design of the series, which is intended to be orderly yet inviting, allowing readers to utilize the pages of *SATA* easily and with efficiency. Despite the longevity of the *SATA* print series, and the success of its format, we are mindful that the vitality of a literary reference product is dependent on its ability to serve its users over time. As literature, and attitudes about literature, constantly evolve, so do the reference needs of students, teachers, scholars, journalists, researchers, and book club members. To be certain that we continue to keep pace with the expectations of our customers, the editors of *SATA* listen carefully to their comments regarding the value, utility, and quality of the series. Librarians, who have firsthand knowledge of the needs of library users, are a valuable resource for us. The *Something about the Author* Product Advisory Board, made up of school, public, and academic librarians, is a forum to promote focused feedback about *SATA* on a regular basis. The nine-member advisory board includes the following individuals, whom the editors wish to thank for sharing their expertise:

Eva M. Davis
Youth Department Manager,
Ann Arbor District Library,
Ann Arbor, Michigan

Joan B. Eisenberg
Lower School Librarian,
Milton Academy,
Milton, Massachusetts

Francisca Goldsmith
Teen Services Librarian,
Berkeley Public Library,
Berkeley, California

Susan Dove Lempke
Children's Services Supervisor,
Niles Public Library District,
Niles, Illinois

Robyn Lupa
Head of Children's Services,
Jefferson County Public Library,
Lakewood, Colorado

Victor L. Schill
Assistant Branch Librarian/Children's Librarian,
Harris County Public Library/Fairbanks Branch,
Houston, Texas

Caryn Sipos
Community Librarian,
Three Creeks Community Library,
Vancouver, Washington

Steven Weiner
Director,
Maynard Public Library,
Maynard, Massachusetts

something about the author

ARNOLD, Caroline 1944-

Personal

Born May 16, 1944, in Pittsburgh, PA; daughter of Lester L. (a social worker) and Catherine Young (a social worker) Scheaffer; married Arthur Arnold (a neuroscientist), June 24, 1967; children: Jennifer Elizabeth, Matthew William. *Education:* Grinnell College, B.A., 1966; University of Iowa, M.A., 1968.

Addresses

Home and office—10353 Rossbury Pl., Los Angeles, CA 90064. *Agent*—1076 Eagle Dr., Salinas, CA 93905. *E-mail*—csarnoldbooks@yahoo.com.

Career

Freelance writer and artist. Art teacher and substitute teacher in Yellow Springs and Xenia, OH, 1968-69; New York Hospital, New York, NY, secretary, 1969-70; Rockefeller University, New York, NY, laboratory assistant, 1971-72, 1972-76; University of California—Los Angeles, laboratory assistant, 1976-79; University of California—Los Angeles Extension, instructor in writers' program, 1982—.

Member

Society of Children's Book Writers and Illustrators, PEN, Southern California Council on Literature for Children and Young People, Children's Literature Council of Southern California.

Caroline Arnold (Photograph courtesy of Caroline Arnold)

Awards, Honors

Outstanding Science Trade Book citations, National Science Teachers Association/Children's Book Council (CBC), 1980, for *Five Nests* and *Electric Fish*, 1982, for *Animals That Migrate*, 1983, for *The Biggest Living Thing* and *Pets without Homes*, 1985, for *Saving the Peregrine Falcon*, 1987, for *Genetics, Trapped in Tar, Koala, Kangaroo, Giraffe*, and *Zebra*, 1988, for *Llama, Penguin*, and *A Walk of the Great Barrier Reef*, 1989, for *Tule Elk, Hippo*, and *Cheetah*, 1991, for *Flamingo* and *Snake*, 1992, for *House Sparrows Everywhere*, 1995, for *Rhino* and *Lion*, 1997, for *Bat* and *Fox*, 1998, for *Hawk Highway in the Sky*, 2004, for *Uluru*, and 2005, for *Pterosaurs, Rulers of the Sky in the Dinosaur Age;* Children's Science Book Award honorable mention, 1983, for *Animals That Migrate;* Golden Kite Honor Book, Society of Children's Book Writers, 1984, for *Pets without Homes;* nonfiction award, Southern California Council on Literature for Children and Young People, 1985, for *Too Fat? Too Thin?;* Booklist Children's Editors' Choice, 1985, *School Library Journal* Best Book designation, and American Library Association Notable Book designation, all 1985, and special achievement award, PEN Los Angeles Center, 1986, all for *Saving the Peregrine Falcon;* Best Children's Books and Films selection, American Association for the Advancement of Science, 1987, for *Trapped in Tar* and *Koala*, 1988, for *A Walk on the Great Barrier Reef*, 1990, for *Orangutan* and *Wild Goat*, and 1999, for *Bobcats;* John Burroughs Nature Award, 1988, for *A Walk on the Great Barrier Reef;* Orbis Pictus Award for Outstanding Nonfiction, National Council of Teachers of English, 1989, for *Cheetah* and *Hippo;* School Library Journal Best Books designation, 1992, for *The Ancient Cliff Dwellers of Mesa Verde*, and 2001, for *Easter Island;* Notable Children's Book in the Field of Social Studies designation, National Council for the Social Studies/CBC, 1999, for *Children of the Settlement Houses*, 2001, for *Easter Island*, and 2004, for *Uluru; Washington Post* Children's Book Guild Nonfiction Award, 2005, for body of work; Parent's Choice Gold Award, 2006, for *The Terrible Hodag and the Animal Catchers.*

Writings

JUVENILE NONFICTION

Five Nests, illustrated by Ruth Sanderson, Dutton (New York, NY), 1980.

Electric Fish, illustrated by George Gershinowitz, Morrow (New York, NY), 1980.

(Self-illustrated) *Sun Fun*, Franklin Watts (New York, NY), 1981.

Sex Hormones: Why Males and Females Are Different, illustrated by Jean Zallinger, Morrow (New York, NY), 1981.

Animals That Migrate, illustrated by Michele Zylman, Carolrhoda (Minneapolis, MN), 1982.

What Is a Community?, illustrated by Carole Bertol, Franklin Watts (New York, NY), 1982.

Where Do You Go to School?, illustrated by Carole Bertol, Franklin Watts (New York, NY), 1982.

Who Works Here?, illustrated by Carole Bertol, Franklin Watts (New York, NY), 1982.

Who Keeps Us Healthy?, illustrated by Carole Bertol, Franklin Watts (New York, NY), 1982.

Who Keeps Us Safe?, illustrated by Carole Bertol, Franklin Watts (New York, NY), 1982.

Why Do We Have Rules?, illustrated by Ginger Giles, Franklin Watts (New York, NY), 1983.

What Will We Buy?, illustrated by Ginger Giles, Franklin Watts (New York, NY), 1983.

How Do We Have Fun?, illustrated by Ginger Giles, Franklin Watts (New York, NY), 1983.

How Do We Travel?, illustrated by Ginger Giles, Franklin Watts (New York, NY), 1983.

How Do We Communicate?, illustrated by Ginger Giles, Franklin Watts (New York, NY), 1983.

(Self-illustrated) *The Biggest Living Thing*, Carolrhoda (Minneapolis, MN), 1983.

Pets without Homes, illustrated by Richard Hewett, Houghton Mifflin (Boston, MA), 1983.

Summer Olympics, Franklin Watts (New York, NY), 1983, 2nd updated edition, 1988.

Winter Olympics, Franklin Watts (New York, NY), 1983.

Measurements: Fun, Facts, and Activities, Franklin Watts (New York, NY), 1984.

Maps and Globes, Franklin Watts (New York, NY), 1984.

Charts and Graphs, Franklin Watts (New York, NY), 1984.

Too Fat? Too Thin?: Do You Have a Choice?, Morrow (New York, NY), 1984.

Land Masses, Franklin Watts (New York, NY), 1985.

Natural Resources: Fun, Facts, and Activities, Franklin Watts (New York, NY), 1985.

Saving the Peregrine Falcon, Carolrhoda (Minneapolis, MN), 1985.

Music Lessons for Alex, photographs by Richard Hewett, Houghton Mifflin (Boston, MA), 1985.

(With Herma Silverstein) *Anti-Semitism: A Modern Perspective*, Messner (New York, NY), 1985.

(With Herma Silverstein) *Hoaxes That Made Headlines*, Messner (New York, NY), 1985.

Bodies of Water: Fun, Facts, and Activities, illustrated by Lynn Sweat, Franklin Watts (New York, NY), 1985.

Pain: What Is It? How Do We Deal with It?, illustrated by Frank Schwarz, Morrow (New York, NY), 1986.

Genetics: From Mendel to Gene Splicing, Franklin Watts (New York, NY), 1986.

The Golden Gate Bridge, Franklin Watts (New York, NY), 1986.

Everybody Has a Birthday, Franklin Watts (New York, NY), 1987.

How People Get Married, Franklin Watts (New York, NY), 1987.

What We Do When Someone Dies, Franklin Watts (New York, NY), 1987.

Australia Today, Franklin Watts (New York, NY), 1987.

Coping with Natural Disasters, Walker (New York, NY), 1987.

Kangaroo, Morrow (New York, NY), 1987.

Giraffe, Morrow (New York, NY), 1987.

Zebra, Morrow (New York, NY), 1987.

A Walk on the Great Barrier Reef, Carolrhoda (Minneapolis, MN), 1987.

Trapped in Tar: Fossils from the Ice Age, Houghton Mifflin (Boston, MA), 1987.

Koala, photographs by Richard Hewett, Morrow (New York, NY), 1987.

Llama, Morrow (New York, NY), 1988.

Penguin, Morrow (New York, NY), 1988.

Saving the Tule Elk, Carolrhoda (Minneapolis, MN), 1988.

Juggler, Houghton Mifflin (Boston, MA), 1988.

Ole Swenson and the Hodag, Harcourt (New York, NY), 1988.

Dinosaur Mountain: Graveyard of the Past, Clarion (New York, NY), 1989.

Hippo, photographs by Richard Hewett, Morrow (New York, NY), 1989.

Cheetah, photographs by Richard Hewett, Morrow (New York, NY), 1989.

Dinosaurs Down Under: And Other Fossils from Australia, photographs by Richard Hewett, Clarion (New York, NY), 1990.

Ostriches and Other Flightless Birds, photographs by Richard Hewett, Carolrhoda (Minneapolis, MN), 1990.

A Walk in the Woods, illustrated by Freya Tanz, Silver Press (Parsippany, NJ), 1990.

Orangutan, photographs by Richard Hewett, Morrow (New York, NY), 1990.

Wild Goat, photographs by Richard Hewett, Morrow (New York, NY), 1990.

A Walk up the Mountain, illustrated by Freya Tanz, Silver Press (Parsippany, NJ), 1990.

A Walk by the Seashore, illustrated by Freya Tanz, Silver Press (Parsippany, NJ), 1990.

Heart Disease, Franklin Watts (New York, NY), 1990.

A Walk in the Desert, illustrated by Freya Tanz, Silver Press (Parsippany, NJ), 1990.

Watch out for Sharks!, photographs by Richard Hewett, Clarion (New York, NY), 1991.

A Guide Dog Puppy Grows Up, photographs by Richard Hewett, Harcourt (New York, NY), 1991.

Flamingo, photographs by Richard Hewett, Morrow (New York, NY), 1991.

Snake, photographs by Richard Hewett, Morrow (New York, NY), 1991.

The Olympic Summer Games, Franklin Watts (New York, NY), 1991.

The Olympic Winter Games, Franklin Watts (New York, NY), 1991.

Soccer: From Neighborhood Play to the World Cup, Franklin Watts (New York, NY), 1991.

The Ancient Cliff Dwellers of Mesa Verde, photographs by Richard Hewett, Clarion (New York, NY), 1992.

Camel, photographs by Richard Hewett, Morrow (New York, NY), 1992.

Panda, photographs by Richard Hewett, Morrow (New York, NY), 1992.

House Sparrows Everywhere, photographs by Richard Hewett, Carolrhoda (Minneapolis, MN), 1992.

Pele: The King of Soccer, Franklin Watts (New York, NY), 1992.

On the Brink of Extinction: The California Condor, photographs by Michael Wallace, Harcourt (San Diego, CA), 1993.

Dinosaurs All Around: An Artist's View of the Prehistoric World, photographs by Richard Hewett, Clarion (New York, NY), 1993.

Elephant, photographs by Richard Hewett, Morrow (New York, NY), 1993.

Monkey, photographs by Richard Hewett, Morrow (New York, NY), 1993.

Prairie Dogs, illustrations by Jean Cassels, Scholastic (New York, NY), 1993.

Reindeer, illustrated by Pamela Johnson, Scholastic (New York, NY), 1993.

Cats: In from the Wild, photographs by Richard Hewett, Carolrhoda (Minneapolis, MN), 1993.

Sea Turtles, illustrated by Marshall Peck III, Scholastic (New York, NY), 1994.

Fireflies, illustrated by Pamela Johnson, Scholastic (New York, NY), 1994.

Killer Whale, photographs by Richard Hewett, Morrow (New York, NY), 1994.

Sea Lion, photographs by Richard Hewett, Morrow (New York, NY), 1994.

Watching Desert Wildlife, photographs by Arthur Arnold, Carolrhoda (Minneapolis, MN), 1994.

City of the Gods: Mexico's Ancient City of Teotihuacan, photographs by Richard Hewett, Clarion (New York, NY), 1994.

Rhino, photographs by Richard Hewett and Arthur P. Arnold, Morrow (New York, NY), 1995.

Lion, photographs by Richard Hewett, Morrow (New York, NY), 1995.

Bat, photographs by Richard Hewett, Morrow (New York, NY), 1996.

Fox, photographs by Richard Hewett, Morrow (New York, NY), 1996.

(And photographer) *El Niño: Stormy Weather for People and Wildlife,* Clarion (New York, NY), 1996.

Stories in Stone: Rock Art Pictures by Early Americans, photographs by Richard Hewett, Clarion (New York, NY), 1996.

(And photographer) *African Animals,* Morrow (New York, NY), 1997.

Stone Age Farmers beside the Sea: Scotland's Prehistoric Village of Skara Brae, photographs by Arthur P. Arnold, Clarion (New York, NY), 1997.

Hawk Highway in the Sky: Watching Raptor Migration, photographs by Robert Kruidenier, Harcourt (San Diego, CA), 1997.

Bobcats, photographs by Richard Hewett, Lerner (Minneapolis, MN), 1997.

Children of the Settlement Houses, Carolrhoda (Minneapolis, MN), 1998.

Baby Whale Rescue: The True Story of J.J., photographs by Richard Hewett, Bridgewater, 1999.

Cats, Lerner Publications (Minneapolis, MN), 1999.

Splashtime for Zoo Animals, photographs by Richard Hewett, Carolrhoda (Minneapolis, MN), 1999.

Sleepytime for Zoo Animals, photographs by Richard Hewett, Carolrhoda (Minneapolis, MN), 1999.

Noisytime for Zoo Animals, photographs by Richard Hewett, Carolrhoda (Minneapolis, MN), 1999.

Playtime for Zoo Animals, photographs by Richard Hewett, Carolrhoda (Minneapolis, MN), 1999.

Mother and Baby Zoo Animals, photographs by Richard Hewett, Carolrhoda (Minneapolis, MN), 1999.

Mealtime for Zoo Animals, photographs by Richard Hewett, Carolrhoda (Minneapolis, MN), 1999.

(And photographer) *South American Animals,* Morrow (New York, NY), 1999.

Shockers of the Sea, and Other Electric Animals, illustrated by Crista Forest, Charlesbridge (Watertown, MA), 1999.

(And photographer) *Easter Island: Giant Stone Statues Tell of a Rich and Tragic Past,* Clarion (New York, NY), 2000.

(And photographer) *Australian Animals,* Morrow (New York, NY), 2000.

Giant Shark: Megalodon, Prehistoric Super Predator, illustrated by Laurie Caple, Clarion (New York, NY), 2000.

Ostriches, photographs by Richard Hewett, Lerner (Minneapolis, MN), 2000.

Did You Hear That?: Animals with Super Hearing, illustrations by Cathy Trachok, Charlesbridge (Watertown, MA), 2001.

Dinosaurs with Feathers: The Ancestors of Modern Birds, Clarion (New York, NY), 2001.

The Geography Book: Activities for Exploring, Mapping, and Enjoying Your World, Wiley (New York, NY), 2002.

When Mammoths Walked the Earth, Clarion (New York, NY), 2002.

Birds: Nature's Magnificent Flying Machines, Charlesbridge (Watertown, MA), 2003.

(And photographer) *Uluru, Australia's Aboriginal Heart,* Clarion (New York, NY), 2003.

Who Has More? Who Has Fewer?, Charlesbridge (Watertown, MA), 2004.

(Self-illustrated) *Who Is Bigger? Who Is Smaller?,* Charlesbridge (Watertown, MA), 2004.

Pterosaurs: Rulers of the Skies in the Dinosaur Age, illustrated by Laurie Caple, Clarion (New York, NY), 2004.

The Skeletal System, Lerner (Minneapolis, MN), 2005.

(Self-illustrated) *A Zebra's World,* Picture Window Books (Minneapolis, MN), 2006.

(Self-illusrated) *A Penguin's World,* Picture Window Books (Minneapolis, MN), 2006.

(Self-illustrated) *A Panda's World,* Picture Window Books (Minneapolis, MN), 2006.

(Self-illustrated) *A Killer Whale's World,* Picture Window Books (Minneapolis, MN), 2006.

Super Swimmers: Whales, Dolphins, and Other Mammals of the Sea, illustrated by Patricia J. Wynne, Charlesbridge (Watertown, MA), 2007.

Giant Sea Reptiles of the Dinosaur Age, illustrated by Laurie Caple, Clarion (New York, NY), 2007.

(With Madeleine Comora) *Taj Mahal,* illustrated by Rahul Bushan, Carolhoda Books (Minneapolis, MN), 2007.

Author's works have been translated into Spanish.

JUVENILE FICTION

My Friend from Outer Space (picture book), illustrated by Carol Nicklaus, Franklin Watts (New York, NY), 1981.

The Terrible Hodag, illustrated by Lambert Davis, Harcourt Brace (San Francisco, CA), 1989.

An Apple a Day, Metropolitan Museum of Art (New York, NY), 2003.

The Terrible Hodag and the Animal Catchers, illustrated by John Sandford, Boyds Mills Press (Honesdale, PA), 2006.

Wiggle and Waggle, illustrated by Mary Peterson, Charlesbridge (Wattertown, MA), 2007.

OTHER

(Illustrator) Elizabeth Bremner and John Pusey, *Children's Gardens: A Field Guide for Teachers, Parents, and Volunteers,* Cooperative Extension, University of California, Los Angeles (Los Angeles, CA), 1982.

Also author of episode "Fire for Hire," *K-I-D-S* television series, broadcast 1984. Contributor to books, including *The ABC's of Writing for Children,* by Lisa Koehler-Pentakoff, Quill Driver Books, 2003; and *Authors in the Kitchen: Recipes, Stories, and More,* Libraries Unlimited, 2005. Contributor of articles and stories to magazines, including *Highlights for Children, Friend, Humpty Dumpty,* and *Cricket.*

Adaptations

My Friend from Outer Space was adapted as a filmstrip, Westport Community Group, 1981.

Sidelights

Caroline Arnold is the author of more than one hundred nonfiction books for children, her subjects ranging from monkeys, bats, and foxes to prehistoric natural history, the giant statues of Easter Island, and weather patterns. She also writes fiction and illustrates some of her own books. As Arnold once commented to *SATA:* "Like many writers of children's books, I began when my children were small. I thought I would write lovely stories for children and that because I was trained as a fine artist I would illustrate them myself. However, nearly all my books have been nonfiction, usually about scientific subjects, and most of them have been illustrated by other people. I have found that I enjoy the challenge of writing about complicated subjects in language that even a very young child can understand. My fascination with scientific subjects is reinforced by my own and other children's eagerness to know more about the world around them."

Bat is typical of Arnold's books on animals. Reviewing both *Bat* and *Fox* for *Booklist,* Carolyn Phelan called the volumes "succinct" and "readable." Although the books are short, they cover a great deal of material, including the respective creature's anatomy, habitat, be-

Arnold shares her interest in animals with readers of A Panda's World, *which features the author's cut-paper collage illustrations.* (Picture Window Books, 2006. Reproduced by permission of the author)

havior; its food and the other animals that may prey on it; myths and history involving it; and threats to its continued survival as a species. Discussing the author's books *Lion* and *Rhino* in another review, Phelan noted that Arnold offers interesting comments on the differences in the animals' behavior based on whether the creature is living in the wild or in captivity.

Lion and *Rhino*, like many of Arnold's books, are illustrated with photographs. "The advantage of a photo is that it shows what the subject really looks like," the author explained. "In today's world, where children are exposed to amazing nature films on video and television, they want to see pictures of real animals in books. But photography isn't always the best way to illustrate a book. It doesn't work well for animals such as pandas, which have elusive life styles, or animals such as sharks and whales, which live under water, or nocturnal animals. It also doesn't work for events that do not have a photographic record or which occurred before the invention of photography."

While Arnold illustrated several of her early works, as the list of her titles grew, she passed illustration duties to others. However, as she more recently explained to *SATA*, "after nearly twenty years away from my art, I have begun doing some of my own illustrating again. I am using cut-paper collage, a technique that lends itself to books for younger children. I first used this method in the baby board books *Who Is Bigger? Who Is Smaller?* and *Who Has More? Who Has Fewer?* In 2006 I expanded the technique in four large-format books about black-and-white animals: pandas, penguins, killer whales, and zebras. I wanted to give a bright, contemporary look to the books. I also felt that the black-and-white animals, which are already rather abstract in their appearance, lent themselves to this bold treatment. The

challenge in doing a series such as this is making each book stand on its own, while making sure that all of the titles have a similar approach."

Detailing an Adelie penguin family as they build a nest and harbor their eggs, *A Penguin's World* concludes by revealing a four-month old chick moving toward independence. In her review for *Booklist,* Gillian Engberg described *A Penguin's World* as featuring a "simple, well-paced text [that] weaves basic concepts into the captivating narrative." Arnold adds to the wealth of information by including a map of Antarctica giving young readers insight to where the Adelie penguins live.

Additional animal-related titles include *A Killer Whale's World, A Panda's World,* and *A Zebra's World.* Suzanne Myers Harold, writing in *School Library Journal* about these titles, noted that "each book reads like a story with scientific details woven into the narrative" and concluded that the books "work well as read-alouds and provide enough factual information for simple reports." Each animal-based book introduces the topic animal by listing various facts about the species and includes related maps and Web sites. Text boxes are also utilized to add interesting side notes without interrupting the narrative flow of the story.

Exploring another area of interest, Arnold introduces Aztec culture and its surviving artifacts in *City of the Gods: Mexico's Ancient City of Teotihuacan.* Aerial photographs provide insight into the city that was one of the most important in the Aztec world, and Arnold's text explains Teotihuacan's importance to Aztec culture. Another mysterious ancient site is explored in *Easter Island: Giant Stone Statues Tell of a Rich and Tragic Past.* Located in the South Pacific, Easter Island is home to a number of huge stone icons. For decades, no one was able to definitely answer the many questions surrounding these figures, such as how the primitive inhabitants of the island, the Rapanui, managed to carve and erect them. As a reviewer for *Horn Book* noted, "Arnold avoids theatrical speculation in this straightforward account." She also gives a great deal of information about the Rapanui and their modern descendants, and discusses the island's decline due to overpopulation and residents' disregard for their fragile environment.

Pterosaurs: Rulers of the Skies in the Dinosaur Age provides young dinosaur fans with a factual look into the ancient Pterosaurs, detailing their daily living habits and characteristic features as well as noting fossil discoveries related to the species. As Arnold notes in her book, Pterosaurs are "the only reptiles ever capable of powered flight." In addition to including descriptions of twenty Pterosaur species. The author also incorporates a list of museums that house Pterosaur fossils. Acknowledged as a "solid overview" by *Booklist* reviewer Jennifer Mattson, *Pterosaurs* presents scientific information to children in a fun and easy-to-understand manner by making comparisons between the dinosaurs and objects

One of the most fascinating civilizations of the ancient world is brought to life in **Easter Island: Giant Stone Statues Tell of a Rich and Tragic Past.** (Clarion Books, 2000. © 2000 by Caroline Arnold. Reprinted by permission of Clarion Books, an imprint of Houghton Mifflin Company. All rights reserved)

that children can relate to. Arnold, for instance, makes a comparison between the length of a Pterosaur's wings and the length of a human child's little finger. A contributor to *Kirkus Reviews* noted that the results of *Pterosaurs* "will please dino-fans at any level of expertise."

In *The Terrible Hodag and the Animal Catchers,* one of Arnold's fiction books, the author provides a fictional account of a legendary creature known as the Hodag. Originating in a Wisconsin logging-camp myth, the Hodag is a creature that has the "head of an ox, feet of a bear, back of dinosaur, and tail of an alligator." The main character—a logger by the name of Ole Swenson—is intent on saving the gentle and friendly creature from a group of city slickers who hope to capture the creature and place it in a zoo. *The Terrible Hodag and the Animal Catchers* follows Ole and his friends as they attempt to save the beast. In *Kirkus Reviews* a critic regarded Arnold's tale of the Hodag as "a bit stiff," but also noted that the Hodag, "unlike the older yarns and doctored photographs, seems more friendly than fearsome, and tales about it are rare enough that it may be new to young readers." Carolyn Janssen, reviewing the book for *School Library Journal*, predicted that *The Terrible Hodag and the Animal Catchers* "will be en-

joyed both as a read-aloud and a read-alone." The book is a sequel to Arnold's earlier book, *The Terrible Hodag,* in which the Hodag befriends the loggers and helps them get rid of a mean bossman.

Arnold once told *SATA:* "I grew up in Minneapolis, Minnesota, and when I was in elementary school I had many favorite authors, including Beverly Cleary, Laura Ingalls Wilder, and Maude Hart Lovelace. The books I loved the most were usually set in other times or far off places. One of my favorites was *Family Sabbatical* by Carol Ryie Brink. Like the children in that story, I dreamed that one day I might travel to Paris, learn to speak French, and climb the Eiffel Tower. Although I've never been to France, I do often travel to do research for my books, and that's one of the things I like best about being a writer.

"My love of reading came from my mother, who read to me from the time I was very small. But even though I loved books, I never imagined that I would be a writer when I grew up. I studied art in school and planned to be an artist and art teacher. After I got married and had my own children, I read stories to them. I realized that perhaps I could use my training in art to be a children's book illustrator. I started to write stories so that I could illustrate them and soon discovered that I liked writing very much. I've been writing ever since.

"I've always loved animals. I got my first kitten when I was three—I named her Snoozy after a character in one of my books—and have always had pets. During the summers our family spent in northern Wisconsin, I learned the thrill of spotting birds, deer, porcupines, and other wild animals in the forest. In 1971, I spent four months in East Africa with my husband and young daughter. We lived in a national park, side by side with lions, giraffes, zebras, and all sorts of other animals whose home is the African plain. A few of the photos we took on that trip are in my book *African Animals.*

"Birds have always been a favorite topic in my books. When I was a child, I went on early morning bird walks with my father, who was an amateur birdwatcher, and now my husband, Art, studies birds in his research at the University of California—Los Angeles. For my book *Hawk Highway in the Sky: Watching Raptor Migration,* I spent a week in the Goshutes watching and helping HawkWatch volunteers trap and band migrating hawks, eagles, and falcons. Nothing is more exciting than getting close to these magnificent birds, and my close involvement with the process helped me learn the details that I needed to write my book. My book *Birds: Nature's Magnificent Flying Machines* also focuses on birds and their amazing ability to fly.

"There are so many different kinds of animals in the world that I could spend the rest of my life writing about animals and never run out of ideas. When I choose an animal for a book, I often pick endangered species such as pandas or cheetahs. The more we all know about these animals, the more we will care about saving them from extinction. Sometimes, as in my book about snakes, I pick an idea suggested to me by kids. I usually spend up to a year doing background reading on the subject of a book. Then I make trips to the zoo to make my own observations of animals and also to help the photographer decide what pictures to take. After I have all the information I need, I sit down to write the book. It takes me about two months to finish the manuscript for one of my animal books.

"Truth is often stranger than fiction and certainly just as much fun to write. With every book I've written, I have learned something that I never knew before. If the children who read my books are as excited about reading them as I am about writing them, then I feel that I have accomplished a great deal.

"Children often ask me advice about becoming a writer. I tell them that the best writers, whether they write fiction or nonfiction, are those who have developed a keen sense of observation. They notice details about they way things look, feel, sound, and smell. They learn how to use words to paint a picture of a scene or action. You can develop your powers of observation by pretending you are a spy and making notes about what you see around you. Your 'spy reports' might make the beginning of a great story.

"The other secret of becoming a good writer is practice. Writing letters or keeping a journal are two ways of practicing writing. Writing is something like baseball—you are not likely to hit a home run the first time you step up to the plate. Your first stories will not be perfect either, but they will get better and better and soon you will be hitting the ball out of the park."

Biographical and Critical Sources

BOOKS

Arnold, Caroline, *The Terrible Hodag and the Animal Catchers,* illustrated by John Sandford, Boyds Mills Press (Honesdale, PA), 2006.

Arnold, Caroline, *Pterosaurs: Rulers of the Skies in the Dinosaur Age,* illustrated by Laurie Caple, Clarion (New York, NY), 2004.

Roginski, Jim, *Behind the Covers: Interviews with Authors and Illustrators of Children's Books,* Libraries Unlimited, 1989, pp. 28-40.

Something about the Author Autobiography Series, Volume 23, Thomson Gale (Detroit, MI), 1996.

PERIODICALS

Booklist, October 15, 1992, Stephanie Zvirin, review of *Camel,* p. 419; April 15, 1993, Stephanie Zvirin, review of *Dinosaurs All Around: An Artist's View of the Prehistoric World,* p. 1507, Chris Sherman, review of *On the Brink of Extinction: The California Condor,* p. 1512; August, 1993, Stephanie Zvirin, review of *Cats: In from the Wild,* p. 2051; November 1, 1993, Kay Weisman, review of *Elephant* and *Monkey,* p. 516; September 15, 1994, Carolyn Phelan, review of *Sea Lion* and *Killer Whale,* p. 128; December 1, 1994, Mary Harris Veeder, review of *Watching Desert Wildlife,* p. 670; December 15, 1994, Ilene Cooper, review of *City of the Gods: Mexico's Ancient City of Teotihuacan,* p. 747; September 15, 1995, Carolyn Phelan, review of *Rhino* and *Lion,* p. 154; December 15, 1996, Sally Estes, review of *Stories in Stone: Rock Art Pictures by Early Americans,* p. 722; October 15, 1999, Shelley Townsend-Hudson, review of *Shockers of the Sea, and Other Electric Animals,* p. 448; August, 1996, Carolyn Phelan, review of *Fox* and *Bat,* p. 1897; March 15, 1997, Julie Corsaro, review of *African Animals,* p. 1236; April 15, 1997, Ilene Cooper, review of *Stone Age Farmers beside the Sea: Scotland's Prehistoric Village of Skara Brae,* p. 1424; June 1, 1997, Candace Smith, review of *Hawk Highway in the Sky: Watching Raptor Migration,* p. 1687; September 15, 1998, Shelle Rosenfeld, review of *Children of the Settlement Houses,* p. 221; October 1, 1998, Chris Sherman, review of *El Niño: Stormy Weather for People and Wildlife,* p. 326; March 1, 1999, Lauren Peterson, review of *Baby Whale Rescue: The True Story of J.J.,* p. 1204; June 1, 1999, Susan Dove Lempke, review of *Noisytime for Zoo Animals* and *Mealtime for Zoo Animals,* p. 1832; July, 1999, Lauren Peterson, review of *South American Animals,* p. 1939; March 15, 2000, Ilene Cooper, review of *Easter Island: Giant Stone Statues Tell of a Rich and Tragic Past,* p. 1371; November 1, 2000, Todd Morning, review of *Giant Shark: Megalodon, Prehistoric Super Predator,* p. 528; December 1, 2001, Carolyn Phelan, review of *Did You Hear That? Animals with Super Hearing,* p. 654; February 15, 2002, Carolyn Phelan, review of *The Geography Book: Activities for Exploring, Mapping, and Enjoying Your World,* p. 1001; August, 2002, Julie Cummins, review of *When Mammoths Walked the Earth,* p. 1952; June 1, 2003, John Peters, review of *Birds: Nature's Magnificent Flying Machines,* p. 1762; December 15, 2003, Carolyn Phelan, review of *Uluru: Australia's Aboriginal Heart,* p. 1220; December 1, 2004, Jennifer Mattson, review of *Pterosaurs,* p. 665l; April 1, 2006, Gillian Engberg, review of *A Penguin's World,* p. 65.

Freso Bee December 15, 2002, Lisa Liberman, "Author Taps Children's Interest to Teach Writing."

Horn Book, November-December, 1992, Margaret A. Bush, review of *Camel* and *Panda,* p. 735; June-May, 1993, Margaret A. Bush, review of *On the Brink of Extinction,* p. 343; July-August, 1993, Elizabeth S. Watson, review of *Dinosaurs All Around,* p. 474; November-December, 1994, Margaret A. Bush, review of *Sea Lion* and *Killer Whale,* p. 742; March-April, 1995, Elizabeth S. Watson, review of *City of the Gods,* p. 218; May, 2000, review of *Easter Island,* p. 329; October 1, 2001, John Peters, review of *Dinosaurs with Feathers: The Ancestors of the Modern Birds,* p. 313; November-December, 2002, Danielle J. Ford, review of *When Mammoths Walked the Earth,* p. 772; November-December, 2003, Barbara Bader, review of *Uluru,* p. 760.

Kirkus Reviews, June 15, 2003, review of *Birds,* p. 855; October 1, 2003, review of *Uluru,* p. 1220; November 15, 2004, review of *Pterosaurs,* p. 1087; December 15, 2005, review of *The Terrible Hodag and the Animal Catchers,* p. 1317.

Los Angeles Times, November 8, 1996, "Author Gets a Read on What Students Want," p. 2.

Reading Teacher, September, 1998, review of *African Animals,* p. 58.

School Library Journal, November, 1992, Myra R. Oleynik, review of *Camel,* p. 100; January, 1993, Barbara B. Murphy, review of *Panda,* p. 106; May, 1993, Cathryn A. Campter, review of *Dinosaurs All Around,* p. 112; June, 1993, Amy Nunley, review of *On the Brink of Extinction,* p. 113; December, 1993, Barbara B. Murphy, review of *Monkey* and *Elephant,* p. 118; October, 1994, Frances E. Millhouser, review of *Killer Whale,* p. 130; December, 1994, Cynthia M. Sturgis, review of *City of the Gods,* p. 117; January, 1995, George Gleason, review of *Watching Desert Wildlife,* p. 110; December, 1995, Barbara B. Murphy, review of *Lion* and *Rhino,* p. 111; September, 1996, Lisa Wu Stowe, review of *Fox* and *Bat,* p. 210; December, 1996, Pam Gosner, review of *Stories in Stone,* p. 126; March, 1997, Susan Oliver, review of *African Animals,* p. 170; June, 1997, Susan Scheps, review of *Hawk Highway in the Sky,* p. 130; July, 1997, Pam Gosner, review of *Stone Age Farmers beside the Sea,* p. 99; March, 1998, Susan Oliver, review of *Bobcats,* p. 191; December, 1998, Patricia Manning, review of *El Niño,* p. 132; January, 1999, Anne Chapman Callaghan, review of *Children of the Settlement Houses,* p. 109; March, 1999, Patricia Manning, review of *Baby Whale Rescue,* p. 216; August, 1999, Dawn Amsberry, review of *Splashtime for Zoo Animals* and *Sleepytime for Zoo Animals,* p. 143; September, 1999, Frances E. Millhouser, review of *South American Animals,* p. 210; January, 2000, Patricia Manning, review of *Shockers of the Sea, and Other Electric Animals,* p. 115; April, 2000, Jeanette Larson, review of *Easter Island,* p. 144; October, 2000, Krista Grosick, review of *Australian Animals,* p. 144; November, 2000, Patricia Manning, review of *Giant Shark,* p. 167; August, 2001, Margaret Bush, review of *Did You Hear That?,* p. 166; November, 2001, Steven Engelfried, review of *Dinosaurs with Feathers,* p. 140; March, 2002, Robyn Ryan Vandenbroek, review of *The Geography Book,* p. 206; October, 2002, Ellen Heath, review of *When Mammoths Walked the Earth,* p. 136; March, 2006, Carolyn Janssen, review of *The Terrible Hodag and the Animal Catchers,* p. 174; June, 2006, Suzanne Meyers Harold, review of *A Zebra's World,* p. 132.

Wilson Library Bulletin, February, 1994, Frances Bradburn, review of *Elephant,* p. A89.

B

BANERJEE, Anjali

Personal
Born in Calcutta, West Bengal, India; married. *Education:* University of California, Berkeley, degrees (anthropology and psychology).

Addresses
Home—Pacific Northwest. *Agent*—Winifred Golden, Castiglia Literary Agency, 1155 Camino Del Mar, Ste. 510, Del Mar, CA 92014. *E-mail*—anjali@anjalibanerjee.com.

Career
Writer.

Member
Authors Guild, Society of Children's Book Writers and Illustrators, Children's Booksellers Association, Romance Writers of America, National Council of Teachers of English (member of Assembly on Literature for Adolescents), Pacific Northwest Writers Association, Pacific Northwest Booksellers' Association, Whidbey Island Writers Association.

Awards, Honors
Book of the Year Award, *ThaBiz.com*, 2005, for *Imaginary Men.*

Writings

NOVELS

Imaginary Men, Downtown Press (New York, NY), 2005.
Maya Running (for young adults), Wendy Lamb Books (New York, NY), 2005.
Rani and the Fashion Divas, Wizards of the Coast (Renton, WA), 2005.
The Silver Spell, Wizards of the Coast (Renton, WA), 2005.
Invisible Lives, Downtown Press (New York, NY), 2006.
Looking for Bapu, Wendy Lamb Books (New York, NY), 2006.

OTHER

Contributor to periodicals, including *Nerve, Green Hills Literary Lantern,* and *Lynx Eye.* Contributor to anthology *New to North America: Writing by Immigrants, Their Children, and Grandchildren,* and to three regional history books.

Sidelights
Anjali Banerjee was born in India but raised in Canada and the United States. Her upbringing in rural Manitoba informs her young-adult novel *Maya Running,* which focuses on a thirteen-year-old girl growing up in rural Canada during the late 1970s. As the only ethnically Asian student in her small Canadian middle school, Maya feels out of place: she is not Canadian enough to fit in with her classmates, and not East Indian enough to feel completely comfortable with her Hindi family. Things become more stressful when cousin Priyanka (Pinky) arrives from Asia. Wearing saris and appearing authentically Indian, Pinky wins the attention of everyone in Maya's school, including the boy Maya has a crush on. Borrowing Pinky's statue of the Hindu elephant god Ganesh, Maya pleads that the god remove all obstacles standing between her and her desires. When Ganesh grants her request, Maya finds that she is graceful, popular, has a closet full of stylish clothing, and no longer has braces on her teeth. However, the middle-grader also learns that having everything one thinks one wants does not necessarily guarantee happiness; her task now is to get Ganesh to reverse his powerful spell.

Reviewing *Maya Running* for *Publishers Weekly,* a reviewer called the book "an often touching debut novel that should appeal to readers who have ever felt torn between two cultures." Praising Banerjee's ability to weave elements of Indian culture "seamlessly" into her story, Maria B. Salvadore added in her *School Library Journal* review that "readers will see themselves in the [novel's] realistic characters." *Kliatt* reviewer Claire Rosser also praised Banerjee's novel, dubbing it "delightful." While noting that the book's second half veers into fantasy, a *Kirkus Reviews* writer had praise for the author's "engaging" story, citing "Maya's humorous voice and her familiar situation of being different."

While *Maya Running* is geared for teen readers, Banerjee also writes for an older audience. Her adult novel *Imaginary Men* opens with a wedding scene in India. Lina, the matchmaker responsible for introducing the newlyweds to each other, is unmarried herself, and her relatives are determined to find her a groom. Uncomfortable with the pressure to wed, Lina falsely claims that she is already engaged, and dreams up a perfect fiancée for herself. Complications ensue, however, when she finds herself in a real romance with a wealthy member of Indian royalty who is already promised in marriage to someone else. Now Lina and her new love must decide whether they will follow their hearts or do what is expected of them in order to please their re-

spective families. "The insights into Bengali culture are interesting," remarked a *Kirkus Reviews* writer of *Imaginary Men,* while a reviewer for *Publishers Weekly* deemed the novel "a quick, enjoyable read." *Imaginary Men* was recommended by Rebecca Vnuk, who in *Library Journal* called the novel "a light, romantic tale with an authentic ethnic twist." In *Booklist* Aleksandra Kostovski predicted that "chick-lit enthusiasts will snap it up right away."

Biographical and Critical Sources

PERIODICALS

Booklist, November 15, 2004, Ilene Cooper, review of *Maya Running,* p. 601; October 1, 2005, Aleksandra Kostovski, review of *Imaginary Men,* p. 33.

Kirkus Reviews, January 15, 2005, review of *Maya Running,* p. 116; August 15, 2005, review of *Imaginary Men,* p. 865.

Kliatt, January, 2005, Claire Rosser, review of *Maya Running,* p. 6.

Library Journal, August 1, 2005, Rebecca Vnuk, review of *Imaginary Men,* p. 64.

Publishers Weekly, March 21, 2005, review of *Maya Running,* p. 52; August 15, 2005, review of *Imaginary Men,* p. 31.

Resource Links, October, 2005, Wendy L. Hogan, review of *Maya Running,* p. 30.

School Library Journal, January, 2005, Maria B. Salvadore, review of *Maya Running,* p. 122.

ONLINE

Anjali Banerjee Home Page, http://www.anjalibanerjee. com (November 11, 2005).

Best Reviews, http://thebestreviews.com/ (September 15, 2005), review of *Imaginary Men.*

BookLoons, http://www.bookloons.com/ (November 11, 2006), Marie Hashima Lofton, review of *Imaginary Men.*

BookPage, http://www.bookpage.com/ (November 11, 2006), Belinda Anderson, review of *Imaginary Men.*

Curled Up with a Good Book, http://www.curledup.com/ (November 11, 2006), review of *Imaginary Men.*

Fresh Fiction, http://www.freshfiction.com/ (November 11, 2006), Meghan Fryett, review of *Imaginary Men.*

Olympian Online, http://www.theolympian.com/ (November 11, 2006), Barbara McMichael, review of *Imaginary Men.*

Cover of Maya Running, *by Anjali Banerjee, featuring artwork by Trisha Krauss.* (Wendy Lamb Books, 2005. Jacket illustration copyright © 2005 by Trisha Krauss. Used by permission of Random House Children's Books, a division of Random House, Inc)

*   *   *

BANKS, Paul 1952-

Personal

Born 1952, in Denver, CO; son of coffee-house owners; immigrated to Denmark, 1961.

Addresses

Home—Denmark. *Agent*—c/o Author Mail, Minedition/ Penguin Putnam, 375 Hudson St., New York, NY 10014.

Career

Author and musician. Worked as a jazz and country singer; founder and member of band Paul Banks and MusikOrkestret, 1975-85; musician with Steen Vig, 1985-95, and as solo performer. Performer on recordings with musical groups, including AnTerrach.

Awards, Honors

Folk Musician of the Year award, 1985; DJBFA honorary award, Composers Society, 1992; Best Songwriter award, Danish Music Awards Folk, 2001.

Writings

It's a Dog's Life (picture book), illustrated by Jakob Kirchmayr, Minedition/Penguin (New York, NY), 2005.

Contributor of essays and short fiction to periodicals. Translator, from English, of books, including Michael Ondaatje's *Coming through Slaughter.*

Lyricist on recordings, including *Paul Banks & Jorgen Lang,* 1979; *Desperados in Disguise,* 1981; *Twostep,* 1984; *Paul Banks & Steen Vig,* 1987; *Time Problem,* 1998; *White Noise & Diamond Nights,* 2000; *Paul Banks, Kristian Jorgensen, Thor Backhausen,* 2002; *Bones and LoveBombs,* 2003; and *One Man Band Live,* 2005.

Biographical and Critical Sources

PERIODICALS

Kirkus Reviews, March 1, 2005, review of *It's a Dog's Life,* p. 283.
Publishers Weekly, March 28, 2005, review of *It's a Dog's Life,* p. 79.
School Library Journal, March 2005, Sally R. Dow, review of *It's a Dog's Life,* p. 166.

ONLINE

Paul Banks Home Page, http://www.paulbanks.dk (October 9, 2006).*

*   *   *

BASEMAN, Gary 1960-

Personal

Born 1960; son of Ben (an electrician) and Naomi (a head bakery salesperson) Baseman; married Mel Williges, (an illustrator), 1983. *Education:* University of California, Los Angeles, graduate.

Addresses

Home—Hancock Park, CA. *Agent*—c/o Author Mail, Chronicle Books, 85 2nd St., 6th Fl., San Francisco, CA 94105. *E-mail*—basemanart@earthlink.net.

Career

Artist, film producer, toy designer, and humorist. Executive producer of Disney television program and film *Teacher's Pet;* freelance designer for such clients as Nike, Chili's, Gatorade, Mercedes-Benz, Labatt, and Thomas Cook. *Exhibitions:* Work included in permanent collections at National Portrait Gallery, Washington, DC; and Museum of Modern Art, Rome, Italy. Baseman's art has been displayed in New York, Los Angeles, Rome, and Tokyo.

Member

Phi Beta Kappa.

Awards, Honors

Three-time Emmy Award winner for *Teacher's Pet;* named among 100 Most Creative People in Entertainment by *Entertainment Weekly.*

Writings

SELF-ILLUSTRATED

Dumb Luck (collected works), Chronicle (San Francisco, CA), 2004.

ILLUSTRATOR

William H. Hooks, *A Dozen Dizzy Dogs,* Bantam (New York, NY), 1990.
John Harris, *Strong Stuff: Herakles and His Labors,* J. Paul Getty Museum (Los Angeles, CA), 2005.

Contributor of illustrations to periodicals, including *New Yorker, Time, New York Times,* and *Rolling Stone.*

Sidelights

Gary Baseman is the award-winning creator and executive producer of *Teacher's Pet,* a Disney television show featuring a dog who decides to disguise himself as a boy so he can go to school. He is also a designer and an illustrator of children's books, as well as of board games such as Cranium. Baseman "has the magical ability to look into the minds of cute little cartoon animals and masterfully paint their feverish, unsettled dreams," cartoonist Matt Groening told Anne Burke in *UCLA Magazine.* As an artist, Baseman defines himself as an advocate of "pervasive art," which he explains as "art that has a cohesive style and message but which crosses traditional boundaries between the worlds of fine art and commerce," according to Burke. This focus has led Baseman to create images and ideas that have

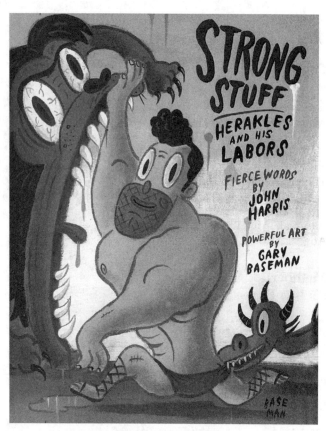

Cover of John Harris's Strong Stuff: Herakles and His Labors, *featuring artwork by Gary Baseman.* (The J. Paul Getty Museum, 2005. Illustrations © Gary Baseman. Courtesy of The J. Paul Getty Museum, Los Angeles)

qualities of fine art yet have a commercial-oriented, mass appeal. A large-format collection showcasing many examples of Baseman's independent artwork was published in 2004 under the title *Dumb Luck;* it was praised by *Booklist* contributor Gordon Flagg as a "dazzling volume [that] attests to Baseman's success."

Although Baseman illustrated his first children's book in 1990, it took some time for him to get into the children's entertainment market. As he explained to Steven Heller in *Print,* it was seven years after he completed his first pilot that he finally saw *Teacher's Pet* reach the airwaves. "In creating a TV series, storytelling is everything," the artist told Heller. "I love funny drawings. [But] With interesting visuals alone, you can capture someone's attention only for a moment." Baseman's unique approach ultimately caught the attention of viewers and critics alike; he went on to win three Emmy awards for his work on the cartoon series, and *Teacher's Pet* went on to become a full-length animated movie featuring the voice of Tony award-winning actor Nathan Lane as Spot, the dog.

After *Teacher's Pet* ended its broadcast, Baseman continued in a variety of creative endeavors, including producing illustrations for John Harris's retelling of Greek myths, *Strong Stuff: Herakles and His Labors.* A *Kirkus Reviews* contributor wrote of the book that "Baseman matches Harris's breezy tone with big, cartoony scenes." *School Library Journal* critic Judith Constantinides felt that, although the illustrations are cartoonish, they

"faithfully reproduce the salient points of each incident," while *Booklist* critic Gillian Engberg deemed Baseman's "wildly colored, energetic" cartoons "hilarious and instantly accessible."

Biographical and Critical Sources

PERIODICALS

Booklist, May 15, 2004, Gordon Flagg, review of *Dumb Luck,* p. 1587; November 15, 2005, Gillian Engberg, review of *Strong Stuff: Herakles and His Labors,* p. 39.

Choice, October, 2004, R.M. Labuz, review of *Dumb Luck,* p. 179.

Fast Company, April, 2004, Lucas Conley, "60 Seconds with Gary Baseman," p. 41.

Kirkus Reviews, August 15, 2005, review of *Strong Stuff,* p. 915.

Library Journal, May 1, 2004, David A. Beronia, review of *Dumb Luck,* p. 104.

Los Angeles Magazine, August, 1999, R.J. Smith, "Graphic Artist," p. 32; January, 2004, Robert Ito, "Zoo Revue," p. 22.

Print, January, 2001, Steven Heller, "Back Talk," p. 36.

Publishers Weekly, September 5, 2005, review of *Strong Stuff,* p. 62.

School Library Journal, May, 1991, April L. Judge, review of *A Dozen Dizzy Dogs,* p. 74; November, 2005, Judith Constantinides, review of *Strong Stuff,* p. 116.

Seventeen, February, 2004, Anne Telford, review of *Dumb Luck,* p. 197.

Time, February 2, 2004, Richard Corliss, "Best in Show," p. 73.

UCLA Magazine, winter, 2004, Anne Burke, "Off the Wall."

ONLINE

Cranium Web site, http://www.cranium.com/ (November 6, 2006), profile of Baseman.

Gary Baseman Home Page, http://www.garybaseman.com (November 6, 2006).*

* * *

BASSIL, Andrea
See NILSEN, Anna

* * *

BECKER, Shari

Personal

Born in Montreal, Quebec, Canada; married; husband's name John; children: three children. *Education:* Concordia University, graduate; New York University, M.A., 1998.

Addresses

Home—Brookline, MA. *Agent*—c/o Author Mail, Charlesbridge Publishing, 85 Main St., Ste. No. 3, Watertown, MA 02472. *E-mail*—shari@sharibecker.com.

Career

Author and illustrator. Worked for a television production company; Nickelodeon, associate producer and member of Nick's Creative Lab; Shadow Projects, consultant.

Writings

Maxwell's Mountain, illustrated by Nicole Wong, Charlesbridge (Watertown, MA), 2006.
Horris Grows Down, illustrated by Valeria Petrone, G.P. Putnam's Sons (New York, NY), 2007.

Work in Progress

A novel for middle-grade readers.

Sidelights

Canadian-born author Shari Becker wrote and illustrated her first book manuscript when she was in the third grade. Continuing her creative efforts as an adult, Becker established a career in television, working as an associate producer for Nickelodeon and working in the Nickelodeon Creative Lab, a group charged with developing innovative new strategies for the popular cable network. She also kept working at her writing, and in 2006 made her debut as a children's book author with *Maxwell's Mountain.*

Featuring illustrations by Nicole Wong, *Maxwell's Mountain* introduces readers to a small boy with large ambitions. In Becker's story, Maxwell wants to climb the large hill behind his house, despite his parents' worries that he is too little to make the ascent. To prepare for the hike, the boy practices by climbing the stairs, and he also gathers together the supplies he will need for mountain climbing. As Wong's illustrations show, seemingly insurmountable, adult-sized obstacles confront the small boy when the time comes to hike up the neighborhood hill, but his determination carries the day, and Maxwell ultimately is rewarded with a view of his entire neighborhood. Maryann H. Owen, writing in *School Library Journal,* called *Maxwell's Mountain* "a good, solid story about making the necessary preparations for attempting to reach a goal and then achieving success," and a *Kirkus Reviews* contributor deemed it "an absorbing story of determination and a boy's growing independence." As John Peters noted in *Booklist,* Becker's picture book presents an effective tale about the rewards of perseverance and "quiet determination."

On her home page, Becker explained that the inspiration for her children's books comes from many sources, most significantly her own family. In addition to telling

In Maxwell's Mountain, *featuring illustrations by Nicole Wong, Shari Becker tells a story that describes a small child's view of the wide world.* (Charlesbridge, 2006. Illustrations copyright © 2006 by Nicole Wong. Text copyright © 2006 Shari Becker. Used with permission by Charlesbridge Publishing, Inc. All rights reserved)

a good story, she hopes that her books will inspire young readers; as Becker stated of *Maxwell's Mountain,* "I want kids to understand that you can do or be anything you want if you're willing to learn and practice."

Biographical and Critical Sources

PERIODICALS

Booklist, February 1, 2006, John Peters, review of *Maxwell's Mountain,* p. 53.
Kirkus Reviews, December 15, 2005, review of *Maxwell's Mountain,* p. 1318.
School Library Journal, February, 2006, Maryann H. Owen, review of *Maxwell's Mountain,* p. 92.

ONLINE

Charlesbridge Publishing Web site, http://www.charlesbridge.com/ (October 10, 2006), "Shari Becker."
Shari Becker Home Page, http://sharibecker.com (October 10, 2006).*

C

CARY, Kate 1967(?)-
(Erin Hunter, a joint pseudonym)

Personal

Born c. 1967, in England; partner's name Geoff; children: Joshua. *Education:* University graduate.

Addresses

Home—United Kingdom. *Agent*—c/o Author Mail, HarperCollins, 10 E. 53rd St., 7th Fl., New York, NY 10022.

Career

Novelist.

Writings

FOR CHILDREN

Detective Fun File, illustrated by Barry Green, Henderson (Woodbridge, England), 1995.
French Skipping, illustrated by Dave Mostyn, Henderson (Woodbridge, England), 1996.
Gemma James' Egyptian Adventure, Henderson (Woodbridge, England), 1997.
Gemma James' Pirate Adventure, Dorling Kindersley (New York, NY), 1997.
Gemma James' Amazon Adventure, Henderson (Woodbridge, England), 1997.
Gemma James' Atlantis Adventure, Dorling Kindersley (New York, NY), 1997.
Bloodline (novel), Razorbill (New York, NY), 2005.

"WARRIORS" SERIES; WITH CHERITH BALDRY UNDER JOINT PSEUDONYM ERIN HUNTER

Into the Wild, HarperCollins (New York, NY), 2003.
Fire and Ice, HarperCollins (New York, NY), 2003.
Forest of Secrets, HarperCollins (New York, NY), 2003.

Rising Storm, HarperCollins (New York, NY), 2004.
A Dangerous Path, HarperCollins (New York, NY), 2004.
The Darkest Hour, HarperCollins (New York, NY), 2004.

"WARRIORS: THE NEW PROPHECY" SERIES; WITH CHERITH BALDRY UNDER JOINT PSEUDONYM ERIN HUNTER

Midnight, HarperCollins (New York, NY), 2005.
Moonrise, HarperCollins (New York, NY), 2005.
Dawn, HarperCollins (New York, NY), 2006.
Starlight, HarperCollins (New York, NY), 2006.
Twilight, HarperCollins (New York, NY), 2006.
Sunset, HarperCollins (New York, NY), 2007.

Work in Progress

Bloodline: Reckoning, a sequel to *Bloodline.*

Sidelights

British writer Kate Cary has published several books for children and young adults, but she also has a separate career as one half of the pseudonymous Erin Hunter. Collaborating with noted fantasy writer Cherith Baldry, Cary alternates volumes in the Hunter-penned "Warriors" series. Including the novels *Into the Wild, Fire and Ice,* and *A Dangerous Path,* the six-volume "Warriors" series has expanded to include the "Warriors: The New Prophecy" fantasy novel sequence. Cary, an avid cat lover, shares her passion for felines with readers in the "Warriors" novels, which bring to life a world in which four clans of wild forest cats compete for supremacy and undertake numerous exciting adventures. In "Fire and Ice," Fireheart becomes part of the Thunderclan after leaving his life as a house pet. Joined by friend Graystripe, he works to support his clanfellows while navigating intrigue both inside and outside the clan. In *Booklist,* Sally Estes noted that the book's protagonists "add . . . to the plausibility of events in this tension-filled story."

In addition to her collaborations with Baldry, Cary takes solo credit for the young-adult novel *Bloodline.* An engaging vampire tale that stems from the classic Dracula story, *Bloodline* introduces Mary Seward, a young woman working at the Purfleet sanatorium during World War I. Among the shell-shocked and traumatized soldiers that are sent to her ward from the front, Mary recognizes John Shaw, a young man who lived near her before becoming a lieutenant. Shaw now suffers from psychological horrors, and as a way to understand him Mary reads the diary he kept while at the front. Slowly falling in love with her recovering patient, Mary also stumbles upon the lieutenant's dark secret. Meanwhile, Shaw's sister Lily has fallen in love with her brother's commanding officer, the dashing Captain Quincy Harker. Unaware that the Romanian-born Harker is directly related to the legendary Count Dracula, Lily accompanies Harker back to his home, where the pair are destined to be married. Prior to the wedding, Lily is confronted with a grave decision: to either lose her love or live forever as a vampire. As loyal Mary vainly attempts to dissuade her friend from following her heart, other secrets are revealed that threaten her own relationship with her beloved John.

Reviewing *Bloodline* for *Booklist,* Holly Koelling praised Cary's novel, commenting that as "a solid vampire story," the "compelling . . . and . . . eminently readable book will find fans." "Each character is fully realized, as are the environs that surround them," noted Jana R. Fine in *School Library Journal,* the critic adding that Cary "maintains suspense until the end." In *Kirkus Reviews* a critic wrote that "unexpected plot twists enliven this intriguing reinterpretation of a classic."

Biographical and Critical Sources

PERIODICALS

Booklist, February 15, 2003, Sally Estes, review of *Into the Wild,* p. 1064; September 1, 2003, Sally Estes, review of *Fire and Ice,* p. 114; September 15, 2003, Sally Estes, review of *Forest of Secrets,* p. 231; January 1, 2004, Cindy Welch, review of *Rising Storm,* p. 844; August, 2004, Sally Estes, review of *A Dangerous Path,* p. 1920; September 1, 2005, Sally Estes, review of *Moonrise,* p. 102, and Holly Koelling, review of *Bloodline,* p. 110; December 1, 2005, Sally Estes, review of *Dawn,* p. 47.

Kirkus Reviews, January 1, 2003, review of *Into the Wild,* p. 61; May 15, 2003, review of *Fire and Ice,* p. 752; July, 2005, review of *Moonrise,* p. 73; July 1, 2005, review of *Bloodline,* p. 732; December 1, 2005, review of *Dawn,* p. 1275.

Publishers Weekly, December 23, 2002, review of *Into the Wild,* p. 72; November 24, 2003, "Return of the Time Travelers."

School Library Journal, May, 2003, Mara Alpert, review of *Into the Wild,* p. 154; September, 2003, Lisa Prolman, review of *Fire and Ice,* p. 49; October, 2003, Sharon Rawlins, review of *Forest of Secrets,* p. 49;

September, 2005, Jana R. Fine, review of *Bloodline,* p. 198; September, 2006, Robin Levin, review of *Starlight* (audiobook), p. 74.

ONLINE

Star Clan Graphics Web site, http://www.freeewebs.com/starclangraphics/ (October 10, 2006), "Kate Cary."*

*   *   *

COLLIER, Bryan

Personal

Born in MD. *Education:* Pratt Institute, B.F.A. (with honors), 1989. *Hobbies and other interests:* Basketball, fishing, collecting cartoon animation cells, live gospel and jazz music.

Addresses

Home—298 W. 147th St., Ste. 1E, New York, NY 10039. *E-mail*—BryCollier@aol.com.

Career

Illustrator and author of children's books. Harlem Horizon Art Studio, Harlem Hospital Center, New York, NY, assistant director, 1989—; Unity Through Murals, Harlem Hospital Center, New York, NY, art director, 1991—; Simone Nissan Films, Inc., art director, 1994—. *Exhibitions:* Collier's work has been displayed at Apercu Gallery, Brooklyn, NY, 1989; Pratt Institute, Brooklyn, NY, 1989; Art Institute and Gallery, Salsbury, MD, 1989; Manhattan Community College, New York, NY, 1990, University of Maryland Eastern Shore, Princess Ann, 1990; Gallery Sixty-nine, Bronx, NY, 1991; Tar Studio, New York, NY, 1992; Arsenal Gallery, New York, NY, 1992; Afriworks, New York, NY, 1993; Emmanuel Baptist Church, Brooklyn, NY, 1993, 1996, 1997; Zoom Gallery, 1995, Essence Music Festival, New Orleans, LA, 1996; Gallerie 500, Washington, DC, 1996; LiaZan Gallery, New York, NY, 1996; Lewis Gallery, Brooklyn, NY, 1996; City College, New York, NY, 1997; Grace Baptist Church, Mt. Vernon, NY, 1997; and Exhibition 1A, New York, NY, 1998.

Awards, Honors

First-place award in Congressional Competition, U.S. Congress, 1985; first place in Wicomico Art Council Show (MD), 1987; Brio Award, Bronx Council of the Arts, 1994, 1995; National Black Arts Festival Poster selection, National Black Arts Festival of Atlanta, 1994; Coretta Scott King Award for Illustration, American Library Association (ALA), and Ezra Jack Keats New Illustrator Award, New York Public Library/Ezra Jack Keats Foundation, both 2001, both for *Uptown;* White Ravens Award, and Coretta Scott King Honor for Illus-

Bryan Collier (Reproduced by permission of Bryan Collier)

tration, both 2001, both for *Freedom River* by Doreen Rappaport; *New York Times* Best Illustrated Children's Books of the Year citation, 2001, and Jane Addams Children's Book Award, Coretta Scott King Award Honor Book, Caldecott Medal Honor Book, Orbis Pictus Award for Outstanding Nonfiction for Children Honor book, all 2002, all for *Martin's Big Words,* by Doreen Rappaport; Coretta Scott King Award Honor Book, 2003, for *Visiting Langston,* by Willie Perdomo; Best Children's Book of the Year, Bank Street College of Education, New York Public Library One Hundred Titles for Reading and Sharing selection, and Notable Children's Books citation, ALA, all 2005, and Caldecott Medal Honor Book, and Coretta Scott King Illustrator Award, both 2006, all for *Rosa* by Nikki Giovanni.

Writings

SELF-ILLUSTRATED

Uptown, Henry Holt (New York, NY), 2000.
To All My Sisters, Henry Holt (New York, NY), 2001.

ILLUSTRATOR

Hope Lynne Price, *These Hands,* Hyperion (New York, NY), 1999.

Doreen Rappaport, *Freedom River,* Jump at the Sun (New York, NY), 2000.
Doreen Rappaport, *Martin's Big Words,* Jump at the Sun (New York, NY), 2001.
Nadine Mozon, *Kiss It up to God,* Fly by Night Press, 2001.
Willie Perdomo, *Visiting Langston,* Henry Holt (New York, NY), 2002.
Marian Wright Edelman, *I'm Your Child, God: Prayers for Our Children,* Henry Holt (New York, NY), 2002.
Joyce Carol Thomas, adapter, *What's the Hurry, Fox?; and Other Animal Stories* (based on stories by Zora Neale Hurston), HarperCollins (New York, NY), 2004.
Doreen Rappaport, *John's Secret Dreams: The Life of John Lennon,* Hyperion (New York, NY), 2004.
Nikki Giovanni, *Rosa,* Henry Holt (New York, NY), 2005.
Nikki Grimes, *Welcome, Precious,* Orchard (New York, NY), 2006.

Sidelights

Bryan Collier is an artist who works in the combined medium of watercolor and photo collage medium. In fact, the artist's early memories of his grandmother making quilts by combining colors and textures first inspired him to pursue art as a career, according to Sheilah Egan in *ChildrensLit.com.* During college, Collier began to take notice of children's books. "I could see

Collier's Uptown, *which features a vibrant, color-filled tour of Harlem, received the Coretta Scott King Award for illustration.* (Henry Holt and Company, 2000. Copyright © 2000 by Bryan Collier. Reprinted by permission of Henry Holt and Company, LLC)

what storytelling is and how powerful it can be," he explained to an online interviewer for *Reading Is Fundamental.* That realization led him to become an illustrator.

Collier's illustrations for Hope Lynne Price's picture book *These Hands* effectively portray the happiness and confidence of the African-American girl at the center of Price's story, according to Alicia Eames in *School Library Journal.* Price's short, rhyming text celebrates the many things that this girl can do, including playing, drawing, helping, and praying at the end of the day. Throughout the story, her "confidence and joy are captured by Collier's deeply hued, evocative collages," Eames stated.

In *Uptown,* Collier provides his own text along with original illustrations. The book serves as a celebration of Harlem, the traditionally African-American enclave in New York City where the artist lives and works. A tour of the area as seen through the eyes of a young boy, *Uptown* provides readers with a glimpse of some typical activities, such as shopping on 125th Street, eating chicken and waffles, listening to jazz music, and playing basketball. Some special sights are also revealed, such as the Apollo Theater, the brownstone buildings (which Collier depicts using photos of chocolate bars for the bricks), and an exhibit of James Van Der Zee's photographs. *Booklist* contributor Gillian Engberg praised the "gorgeous, textured collages" Collier paris with his story. *Uptown* garnered the prestigious Coretta Scott King Award and the first Ezra Jack Keats New Illustrator Award, both in 2001.

Several books illustrated by Collier introduce readers to notable African Americans. *Martin's Big Words,* by Doreen Rappaport, reveals fallen civil rights leader Dr. Martin Luther King, Jr.'s life and his vision of a nation where all races are equal. Because so many books for children focus on King's life, Collier did first-hand research, traveling to churches where King preached during his lifetime. "When I got into the research and tried understanding King as a person, it was really magical and inspiring," the author/illustrator told the *Reading Is Fundamental* interviewer. Susan Hepler, writing in *ChildrensLit.com,* noted of the book that "Collier's stunning collage and bold watercolor illustrations are layered with meanings, textures, light, and shadow." Susie Wilde, writing for the same Web site, added that Collier's "illustrations continue to compel readers through the book."

In *Visiting Langston* Collier joins author Willie Perdomo in paying tribute to Harlem jazz poet Langston Hughes. The book's illustrations were characterized as "rife with emotion rather than realism," by Kathleen Karr in *ChildrensLit.com.* Another civil-rights activist, Rosa Parks, is brought to life by Collier's art in Nikki Giovanni's picture-book biography *Rosa.* "Collier's large watercolor-and-collage illustrations depict Parks as an inspiring force that radiates golden light," wrote

Hazel Rochman in *Booklist,* and a *Kirkus Reviews* contributor cited the book's "dramatic foldout mural," a feature that "will make this important work even more memorable."

Along with biographies, Collier has illustrated a number of picture books that touch on children's lives. For Marian Wright-Edelman's *I'm Your Child, God: Prayers for Our Children* he uses "photo-realistic water-and-collage style to great effect," according to a *Publishers Weekly* contributor. The book's "beautiful portraits will probably attract young browsers more than the words," Engberg wrote in *Booklist.* Collier's watercolors for another project depict a family that "seems very real," as Cooper noted of Nikki Grimes' *Welcome, Precious.* As Cooper added in her *Booklist* review, the book's illustrations have "a shimmer of stardust or the glow of rainbows."

Collier has also illustrated a collection of animal stories adapted by Joyce Carol Thomas from the writings of Zora Neale Hurston and published as *What's the Hurry, Fox?; and Other Animal Stories.* The "wonderful" illustrations created by Collier "invite closer inspection," according to Mary N. Oluonye in her review of the work for *School Library Journal.*

Along with his illustration work, Collier visits schools to talk about creativity, and he works with students interested in developing their creative ability. In an interview for *School Library Journal,* he talked about visiting one specific classroom and how an embarrassing story related by one student sparked a wealth of per-

The life of civil rights activist Rosa Parks is the focus of Nikki Giovanni's Rosa, *featuring Collier's illustrations.* (Henry Holt and Company, 2005. Illustrations copyright © 2005 by Bryan Collier. Reprinted by permission of Henry Holt and Company, LLC)

Other books featuring Collier's unique art include Freedom River, *Doreen Rappaport's story about African-American life under slavery.* (Hyperion Books for Children, 2000. Illustrations copyright © 2000 by Bryan Collier. Reprinted by permission of Hyperion Books For Children)

sonal stories from other classmates. "Then we talked about creativity and how creative we can be, even with the clothes that we pick every morning to put on," Collier explained. "They're the same decisions that artists make; so we've got to drop the label of artist and find the common thread that we all have."

Biographical and Critical Sources

PERIODICALS

Black Issues Book Review, November, 2000, Khafre K. Abif and Kelly Ellis, review of *Uptown,* p. 82; June 1, 2005, Hazel Rochman, review of *Rosa,* p. 1797.

Booklist, June 1, 2000, Gillian Engberg, review of *Uptown,* p. 1906; August, 2002, Nancy McCray, review of *Martin's Big Words,* p. 1981; October 1, 2002, Gillian Engberg, review of *I'm Your Child, God: Prayers for Our Children,* p. 340; September 1, 2006, Ilene Cooper, review of *Welcome, Precious,* p. 136.

Ebony, September, 2006, review of *Welcome Precious,* p. 31.

Kirkus Reviews, October 1, 2002, review of *I'm Your Child, God,* p. 1467; July 15, 2005, review of *Rosa,* p. 789; August 15, 2006, review of *Welcome, Precious,* p. 841.

Publishers Weekly, June 19, 2000, review of *Uptown,* p. 78; October 28, 2002, review of *I'm Your Child, God,* p. 69; August 29, 2005, review of *Rosa,* p. 56.

School Library Journal, December, 1999, Alicia Eames, review of *These Hands,* p. 111; July, 2000, Alicia Eames, review of *Uptown,* p. 70; October, 2000, Cynde Marcengill, review of *Freedom River,* p. 152; May, 2001, interview with Collier, p. 21; August, 2002, Marilyn Hersh, review of *Martin's Big Words,*

p. 69; December, 2002, Marge Loch-Wouters, review of *I'm Your Child, God,* p. 158; April, 2004, Mary N. Oluonye, review of *What's the Hurry, Fox?, and Other Animal Stories,* p. 144; September, 2005, Margaret Bush, review of *Rosa,* p. 192.

ONLINE

Bryan Collier Home Page, http://www.bryancollier.com (November 5, 2006).
ChildrensLit.com, http://www.childrenslit.com/ (November 5, 2006), "Bryan Collier."
Reading Is Fundamental Web site, http://www.rif.org/ (November 5, 2006), interview with Collier.*

*   *   *

CORBETT, Sue

Personal

Born in NY; married Tom Davidson (a newspaper manager); children: Conor, Liam, Brigit. *Education:* Fairfield University, graduate; attended University of Missouri Graduate School of Journalism. *Hobbies and other interests:* Tennis.

Addresses

Home—Newport News, VA. *E-mail*—scorbett1@aol.com.

Career

Journalist and author. Television reporter in Missouri, South Carolina, and Florida; *Miami Herald,* journalist, then children's book reviewer, beginning 1996.

Awards, Honors

International Reading Association Honor Book, and California Young Readers Medal, both 2006, both for *12 Again.*

Writings

12 Again, Dutton (New York, NY), 2002.
Free Baseball, Dutton (New York, NY), 2006.

Contributor of reviews to *Publishers Weekly.*

Sidelights

According to journalist Sue Corbett, it was inevitable that she become a writer. "I put writing in the same category of essentials as food, air, and water," she told Cynthia Leitich Smith in an online interview for *Cynsations.* "I write every day. Sometimes all day, with breaks for snacks, reading, laundry, baseball games,

reading, piano lessons, homework, and reading. And tennis. Tennis is my drug." Despite her busy schedule, which revolves around three active children, Corbett found the time to write two novels for young readers, as well as maintaining her journalism career as a book reviewer for the *Miami Herald.*

Corbett's first novel, *12 Again,* is the story of a grown woman who drinks a magic potion and is stuck in a twelve-year-old body. As "Detta," the woman attends school with her twelve-year-old son; eventually, she is forced to tell all and ask the boy to help her change back to her normal self. Drawing on her own Irish-American heritage, Corbett laces the novel with concepts drawn from Irish fairy tales. "This many-layered tale of magic across generations gives the term coming-of-age fascinating new meaning," wrote *Booklist* contributor Diane Foote, and Janet Gillen noted in *School Library Journal* that "an extraordinary alchemy of elements . . . makes for an engaging read." Although some reviewers commented that Corbett's story will appeal more to adults than to young readers, as the author told Smith, "It's hard for me to believe how many kids have told me they love this book [despite] . . . the professional criticism." "Maybe every kid knows—or hopes—that's the way their sometimes difficult mother feels about them. Plus, there's a magical bunny."

In Corbett's second novel, *Free Baseball,* twelve-year-old Cuban-American Felix Piloto wants to be reunited with his father, who stayed behind in Cuba. His father is a professional baseball player, and to fill the shoes of his father's son Felix practices hard; while loving the sport, it is also a way for him to connect with his dad. When the frustrated pre-teen has the opportunity to run away from home and become a batboy for a minor-league baseball team, Felix takes the chance. On his own, he ultimately learns unexpected things about his father, and also begins to appreciate his mother's sacrifices. "Corbett remains carefully true to Felix's view and interpretation of events," noted a *Kirkus Reviews* contributor, while Kara Schaff Dean, in her *School Library Journal* review, called *Free Baseball* "an engaging, well-written story with a satisfying ending." According to a *Publishers Weekly* critic, "readers, especially those who share Felix's passion for baseball, will likely want to stick with the tale until the last pitch is thrown."

Free Baseball was inspired by Corbett's experience watching her son during a family ballpark event. All of the children in the audience were given the same colored shirt by the home team managers to wear as they ran around the bases. When Corbett commented worriedly to another mother sitting in the stands that it was difficult to identify individual children on the field, the other mother responded: "Boy, if a kid wanted to run away, this would be a good time to do it!," as the writer recalled to Smith. "I swear, it was like being struck by lightning," she added. "Felix Piloto . . . whispered in my ear that very moment."

Biographical and Critical Sources

PERIODICALS

Booklist, September 1, 2002, Diane Foote, review of *12 Again,* p. 122.

Kirkus Reviews, June 15, 2002, review of *12 Again,* p. 878; December 15, 2005, review of *Free Baseball,* p. 1320.

Kliatt, July, 2002, Claire Rosser, review of *12 Again,* p. 8.

Publishers Weekly, January 9, 2006, review of *Free Baseball,* p. 54.

School Library Journal, July, 2002, Janet Gillen, review of *12 Again,* p. 118; February, 2006, Kara Schaff Dean, review of *Free Baseball,* p. 128; May, 2006, Marilyn Taniguchi, review of *Free Baseball,* p. 61.

Voice of Youth Advocates, April, 2006, Kevin Beach, review of *Free Baseball,* p. 40.

ONLINE

Cynsations, http://cynthialeitichsmith.blogspot.com/ (February 6, 2006), Cynthia Leitich Smith, interview with Corbett.

Lee and Low Books Web site, http://www.leeandlow.com/ (November 6, 2006), Sue Corbett, "The Virtually-Do-It-Yourself Book Tour."

Sue Corbett Home Page, http://www.suecorbett.com (November 6, 2006).

*   *   *

COSTELLO, David
(David Hyde Costello)

Personal

Male. *Education:* Attended Hartford Academy of Performing Arts; Bard College, graduated.

Addresses

Home—Belchertown, MA. *Agent*—c/o Author Mail, Farrar, Straus & Giroux, 19 Union Square W., New York, NY 10003.

Career

Author and illustrator. Formerly worked in set design for films and stage plays, including Broadway productions.

Writings

SELF-ILLUSTRATED

Here They Come!, Farrar, Straus & Giroux (New York, NY), 2004.

(As David Hyde Costello) *I Can Help,* Farrar, Straus & Giroux (New York, NY), 2006.

Sidelights

Coming to his career as a children's book author/illustrator after spending several years creating set designs for movies and the theatre, David Costello brings a quirky humor to the picture books he creates. Recognizing the enjoyment young children have in seeing their favorite storybook characters come alive, Costello punctuates his author visits with specially made puppets and songs that relate to his books, which include *Here They Come!* and *I Can Help.*

In his first book, *Here They Come!,* Costello presents a playful Halloween story of goblins and ghouls in which all the green goblins gather together in the forest for their annual Halloween party. The ghouls enjoy telling each other frightening stories, each hoping to outdo the others by ending his or her story with a bigger scare than the others. However, the goblins get the biggest scare yet when a group of human trick-or-treaters stumble upon the ghoul gathering, startling those at the gathering and sending them fleeing into the night. In her review for *School Library Journal* Mary Hazelton praised the book's "delightful cover" as well as Costello's "charming rhyming text and enchanting illustrations," concluding that young "readers will be grabbed, teased, and tickled by this appealing tale." As a *Publishers Weekly* critic commented, in *Here They Come!* "Costello demonstrates good comic timing and his sympathetic main character exudes holiday excitement." "The rhyming text and too-cute-to-be-scary monsters make this worth a look" for those seeking "nonthreatening Halloween tales," commented a reviewer for *Kirkus Reviews.*

Biographical and Critical Sources

PERIODICALS

Kirkus Reviews, October 1, 2004, review of *Here They Come!,* p. 958.

Publishers Weekly, October 11, 2004, review of *Here They Come!,* p. 78.

School Library Journal, November, 2004, Mary Hazelton, review of *Here They Come!,* p. 94.

ONLINE

Reading Teacher Web site, http://www.reading.org/ (October 10, 2006), "David Costello."*

*   *   *

COSTELLO, David Hyde
See COSTELLO, David

CRANE, Jordan 1973-

Personal

Born September 8, 1973, in Los Angeles, CA.

Addresses

Home—Somerville, MA. *Agent*—c/o Author Mail, Red Ink Press, 1668 West Blvd., Los Angeles, CA, 90019. *E-mail*—blogger@reddingk.com.

Career

Graphic artist, publisher, and writer. Publisher and editor of *NON* anthologies; designer of *MOME* quarterly anthologies for Fantagraphics, Seattle, WA.

Awards, Honors

Eisner and Ignatz award nominations, both for *The Last Lonely Saturday.*

Writings

GRAPHIC NOVELS; SELF-ILLUSTRATED

The Last Lonely Saturday: A Quiet Love Story, Red Ink (Somerville, MA), 2000.
Col-dee, Red Ink (Los Angeles, CA), 2001.
The Clouds Above, Fantagraphics (Seattle, WA), 2005.
Uptight: Number 1, Red Ink (Los Angeles, CA), 2006.

Also author of *The Life Unlucky, The Hand of Gold, Keeping Two Part 1, Keeping Two Part 2, Only a Movie, The Shortcut,* and the e-book *Reproguide.*

Sidelights

Jordan Crane is a publisher and artist, as well as the creator of graphic novels for both adults and children. His stories of grade-schooler Simon and Simon's cat, Jack—both introduced in *The Shortcut*—appeal to a wide audience. *The Clouds Above,* Crane's first book-length work geared specifically for a younger audience, follows Simon and Jack as they try to sneak into Simon's classroom after the school bell has rung, but end up traveling on a stairway that leads up into the heavens. The small-format book features one full-color panel per page, and utilizes a minimal text in favor of detailed illustrations. While Crane did not originally intend *The Clouds Above* for children, he identifies with the young readers who have discovered the book. "As a child I read a lot of fantasy books," he told Patrick Giles in *Interview.* "I loved those weird worlds where people would go and have adventures."

Simon and Jack have their share of adventures in *The Clouds Above,* from battling bad weather and outsmarting violent geese to befriending a lonely cloud named Perch. Their goal is to get back to school before they

Cover illustration of Jordan Crane's child-sized graphic novel **The Clouds Above,** *in which readers join a boy and his cat on a magical journey.* (Fantagraphics Books, 2005. Courtesy of Fantagraphics Books)

are missed, but as the pair travel through the heavens, they end up asking big questions about how the world works. According to a *New Yorker* critic, Crane's "writing is playful and sharp. The artistry is in the detail." As *Booklist* contributor Stephanie Zvirin noted, Crane's book is "an enjoyable all-ages fantasy adventure, whimsical without being saccharine." Tina Coleman, also writing in *Booklist,* called *The Clouds Above* "great for any comics fan, with the added bonus of being very accessible to kids."

As a self-publisher for years and the founder of Red Ink Publishing, Crane has produced several of his own titles, and has also contributed to anthologies and providing graphic-design services to publishers such as Seattle-based Fantagraphics Books. Crane's other projects include graphic novels, anthologies, and a non-fiction guide to silk-screening and offset printing. He first gained critical attention with the publication of his *NON* anthologies, and he has also designed the *MOME* literary comics anthologies published by Fantagraphics. His *The Last Lonely Saturday: A Quiet Love Story,* which was republished in 2006 after going out of print, is a tale of loss and grief that was nominated for both Eisner and Ignatz awards. An e-book titled *Reproguide,* which Crane cowrote with three other silk-screen artists, is available for free download at the Red Ink Web site. Though Red Ink Publishing is based out of Los Angeles, where Crane grew up, he lives and works in Somerville, Massachusetts.

Biographical and Critical Sources

PERIODICALS

Booklist, October 1, 2005, Tina Coleman, review of *The Clouds Above,* p. 61; March 15, 2006, Stephanie Zvirin, review of *The Clouds Above,* p. 60.

Interview, August, 2005, Patrick Giles, "Jordan Crane: The New Poet of the Grit 'n' Graphic Genre," p. 62

Kirkus Reviews, September 1, 2005, review of *The Clouds Above,* p. 13.

Library Journal, January 1, 2006, Steve Raiteri, "Graphic Novels," p. 86.

New Yorker, December 12, 2005, review of *The Clouds Above,* p. 109.

ONLINE

Comics Interpreter Online, http://tci.homestead.com/ (October 20, 2006), interview with Crane.

Lambiek, http://www.lambiek.net/ (November 6, 2006), profile of Crane.

Red Ink Press Web site, http://www.reddingk.com/ (November 6, 2006).*

*   *   *

CUTLER, Ivor 1923-2006
(Knifesmith)

OBITUARY NOTICE— See index for *SATA* sketch: Born January 15, 1923, in Glasgow, Scotland; died March 3, 2006. Musician, cartoonist, educator, and author. Cutler was a poet, musician, and writer of a very unconventional sort, much of his work finding popularity among children due to Cutler's anti-intellectual approach to art. During World War II, he worked as an apprentice fitter for Rolls Royce. Joining the Royal Air Force Volunteer Reserve, Cutler was rejected from regular service because his mind was always in the clouds. Returning home, he began to pursue drawing and was hired as a teacher, instructing children in music and art for thirty years before retiring in 1980. Meanwhile, Cutler began writing plays, poetry, and songs, appearing on radio and television, in live concerts, and on recordings, including twelve albums. His quirky poems and stories were often directed at children and include *Cock-a-doodle Don't* (1966), *Balooky Klujypop* (1975), and *Grape Zoo* (1990). He also drew cartoons, which he contributed to such publications as *Private Eye, Observer,* and the London *Sunday Times.* Among his records are *Velvet Donkey* (1975), *Prince Ivor* (1986), and *Ludo* (1997). Awarded the Pye Radio Award for Humour in 1980, Cutler continued to perform live until 2004, when he gave his last concert at Queen Elizabeth Hall in London, England.

OBITUARIES AND OTHER SOURCES:

PERIODICALS

Times (London, England), March 7, 2006, p. 66.

D

DABBA SMITH, Frank

Personal

Born in CA; married; wife's name Cathy; children: Miriam, Lewis, Sarah. *Education:* University of California Berkeley, graduate; Baeck College, ordained as rabbi, 1994.

Addresses

Home—Harrow, Middlesex, England. *Office*—Harrow and Wembly Progressive Synagogue, Preston Rd., Harrow, Middlesex HA3, England. *E-mail*—frank_dabbasmith@hotmail.com.

Career

Rabbi and writer. Freelance photographer, with works published in the *Economist*.

Writings

My Secret Camera: Life in the Lodz Ghetto, photography by Mendel Grossman, Gulliver Books (San Diego, CA), 2000.

Elsie's War: A Story of Courage in Nazi Germany, introduction by Henri Cartier Bresson, Frances Lincoln (London, England), 2003, Frances Lincoln (New York, NY), 2005.

Sidelights

Frank Dabba Smith, a British rabbi, has long had an interest in photography and the Holocaust. Mining information learned while completing his rabbinical thesis on the subject, Dabba Smith has written two books for young readers that tell the tragic story of the Holocaust through photographs from the World War II period. Although he grew up in California, after completing his rabbinical training Dabba Smith moved to England,

where he now lives with his wife and three children. In addition to serving as a rabbi at Harrow and Wembley Progressive Synagogue, he continues to follow his interests in writing and photography.

My Secret Camera: Life in the Lodz Ghetto presents a collection of seventeen photographs taken by Mendel Grossman in Poland's Lodz Ghetto during wartime. Grossman was a photographer for the ghetto administration, and in that position he shot thousands of photographs documenting the way people were forced to live in the ghetto. Though the tragic situation faced by those confined in Lodz has been described by historians, Grossman's pictures reveal iconic scenes from real life. Dabba Smith provides a text that links each of the pictures featured in the book and includes an afterword discussing Grossman's life. A critic for the *Journal of Adolescent and Adult Literacy* recommended that

Cover of Frank Dabba Smith's Elsie's War, *the biography of Elsie Kühn-Letz and her efforts to save hundreds of Jews in Nazi Germany.* (Frances Lincoln Children's Books, 2006. Cover photograph copyright © Dr. Knut Kühn-Letz, 2003. Reproduced by permission)

"teachers might want to begin with the afterword" when sharing the book with their classes. A *Kirkus Reviews* contributor, appraising Dabba Smith's first work for children, deemed *My Secret Camera* "stunningly powerful."

Grounded in the same historical epoch, *Elsie's War: A Story of Courage in Nazi Germany* presents the biography of Elsie Kühn-Letz, an upper-class young German woman who was ultimately arrested for her efforts aiding Jews escaping from Nazi Germany. Elsie was imprisoned as a result of her resistance efforts, but was saved from imprisonment in a concentration camp due to her family's wealth (her father was a factory owner). Dabba Smith "never sentimentalizes or minimizes the facts . . . as he tells the story," wrote Hazel Rochman in *Booklist*. Though noting that the book may best be understood by readers with a basic knowledge of the Holocaust, *School Library Journal* critic Susan Scheps complimented Dabba Smith's "spare text." In contrast, Diane Samuels, writing in the London *Guardian,* found the book somewhat lacking in the human details that appeal to older readers, but nonetheless dubbed *Elsie's War* "a strangely detached, if also austerely beautiful, account." Noting that the author's text is accompanied by full-page black-and-white photographs, a *Publishers Weekly* contributor commented that Dabba Smith's "use of simple terms makes a horribly dark era comprehensible to a young audience."

Biographical and Critical Sources

PERIODICALS

Booklist, December 1, 2004, Hazel Rochman, review of *Elsie's War: A Story of Courage in Nazi Germany*, p. 650.
Faces: People, Places, and Cultures, March, 2003, "Books about Poland," p. 46.
Guardian (London, England), March 22, 2003, Diane Samuels, "Long Day's Journey."
Horn Book, May, 2000, Roger Sutton, review of *My Secret Camera: Life in the Lodz Ghetto*, p. 338.
Journal of Adolescent and Adult Literacy, May, 2002, review of *My Secret Camera*, p. 795.
Kirkus Reviews, January 15, 2005, review of *Elsie's War,* p. 119.
Publishers Weekly, May 22, 2000, review of *My Secret Camera*, p. 94; March 21, 2005, review of *Elsie's War,* p. 51.
School Library Journal, April, 2005, Susan Scheps, review of *Elsie's War,* p. 157.
Times Educational Supplement, January 24, 2003, review of *Elsie's War,* p. 29.

ONLINE

Harrow and Wembly Progressive Synagogue Web site, http://www.hwps.org/ (November 6, 2006), profile of Dabba Smith.*

D'ATH, Justin 1953-

Personal

Surname is pronounced "Darth;" born October 4, 1953, in Otaki, New Zealand; son of Ossian William (a farmer) and Noellie Claire (Caldwell) D'Ath; children: Fiona Piminni, Timothy Christopher. *Education:* Attended St. Columbans College, 1971-73. *Hobbies and other interests:* "Mountain bike riding, movies, reading, watching television sports, walking my dog."

Addresses

Home—23 Shakespeare St., Spring Gully, Victoria 3550, Australia. *Agent*—Fiona Inglis, Curtis Brown Ltd., P.O. Box 19, Paddington, New South Wales 2021, Australia. *E-mail*—jd@justindath.com.

Career

Writer. Bendigo Regional Institute, Bendigo, Victoria, Australia, TAFE teacher of professional writing. Worked as club manager at an Aborigine mission; former forklift driver, car builder, ranch worker, fruit picker, iron miner, sugar mill worker, store clerk, laboratory technician, and electrical worker.

Member

Australian Society of Authors, Fellowship of Australian Writers, Children's Book Council of Australia.

Awards, Honors

More than fifty prizes for short stories; Alan Marshall Award, Fellowship of Australia Writers, Jessie Litchfield Award, and Caltex-Bendigo Advertiser Award, all for *The Initiate;* Notable Book designation in young-adult fiction category, Children's Book Council of Australia, 2002, for *Hunters and Warriors,* and 2004, for *Shaedow Master.*

Writings

FOR CHILDREN

Infamous, Holy Angels (North Fitzroy, Melbourne, Australia), 1996.
Humungous, Holy Angels (North Fitzroy, Melbourne, Australia), 1997.
Fantabulous, Holy Angels (North Fitzroy, Melbourne, Australia), 1998.
Why Did the Chykkan Cross the Galaxy?, illustrated by Geoff Kelly, Allen & Unwin (Sydney, New South Wales, Australia), 1998.
Sniwt, illustrated by Geoff Kelly, Allen & Unwin (Sydney, New South Wales, Australia), 1999.
The Upside-Down Girl, illustrated by Terry Denton, Allen & Unwin (Sydney, New South Wales, Australia), 2000.

Justin D'Ath (Photograph reproduced by permission)

Koala Fever, illustrated by Terry Denton, Allen & Unwin (Sydney, New South Wales, Australia), 2000.

Topsy and Turvy, illustrated by Emma Quay, Penguin Australia (Camberwell, Victoria, Australia), 2001.

Goldfever, illustrated by Rachel Tonkin, Penguin Australia (Camberwell, Victoria, Australia), 2001.

Hunters and Warriors, Allen & Unwin (Sydney, New South Wales, Australia), 2001.

Echidna Mania, Allen & Unwin (Sydney, New South Wales, Australia), 2001.

(With others) *Teacher Free Day* (includes computer disk), illustrated by Liz Andrews, Burren Publications (Axedale, Victoria, Australia), 2001.

Snowman Magic, Allen & Unwin (Sydney, New South Wales, Australia), 2002.

Astrid Spark, Fixologist, illustrated by Terry Denton, Allen & Unwin (Sydney, New South Wales, Australia), 2003.

Shaedow Master (fantasy novel), Allen & Unwin (Sydney, New South Wales, Australia), 2004.

The Skyflower ("Quentaris Chronicles" series), Lothian Books (South Melbourne, Victoria, Australia), 2006.

Robbie and the Dolphins, illustrated by Jessica Johnson, National Museum of Australia Press (Canberra, Australia Capital Territory, Australia), 2006.

Author's books have been translated into several languages, including German and Italian.

"EXTREME ADVENTURES" SERIES

Crocodile Attack, Penguin Australia (Camberwell, Victoria, Australia), 2005, Penguin USA (New York, NY), 2006.

Bushfire Rescue, Penguin Australia (Camberwell, Victoria, Australia), 2005.

Shark Bait, Penguin Australia (Camberwell, Victoria, Australia), 2006

Scorpion Sting, Penguin Australia (Camberwell, Victoria, Australia), 2006.

Spider Bite, Penguin Australia (Camberwell, Victoria, Australia), 2007.

OTHER

The Initiate (novel), Collins Australia (Sydney, New South Wales, Australia), 1989.

Stories included in anthology *Terrors of Nature,* edited by Paul Collins and Meredith Costain, Addison Wesley Longman Australia, 1999, Sundance, 2000. Contributor of short stories and articles to magazines, including *Meanjin* and *Prairie Schooner.*

Sidelights

New Zealand writer Justin D'Ath creates humorous books for middle-grade readers. In addition to *Koala Fever* and *Astrid Spark, Fixologist*—the latter a quirky story about a girl with magnetic fingers that is illustrated by Terry Denton—'D'Ath has also penned several titles in the "Extreme Adventure" series. His stories, which feature subtle environmental and social themes in addition to engaging characters and humorous storylines, have gained him a large fan following among young Australasians as well as his more recent North American fans. As Neville Barnard wrote of D'Ath's sci-fi adventure *Why Did the Chykkan Cross the Galaxy?* in a *Magpies* review: While "it is tempting to describe this text as a modern fable dealing with the importance of humour and enjoying life," the book's middle-grade readers will enjoy "a funny story with masses of child appeal." Reviewing *Infamous,* D'Ath's popular novel about a boy who transforms the family dog into a Tasmanian tiger in order to attract tourists to his economically depressed home town, *Booklist* contributor Kay Weisman praised the author's "brisk writing style" and added that the "novel fairly brims with local color and colloquialisms."

D'Ath once noted: "I've always loved stories. When I was eight years old, I shared a room with two of my older brothers. The eldest, Billy, used to tell Philip and me a story every night after lights-out. Mostly they were stories he had read or the plots from movies, but when these ran out, we began inventing stories, each contributing characters and story lines. Ever since, I have been making up stories. I began my first novel when I was nine. My first published works were travel stories in magazines, but soon I was embellishing them so creatively that they became mostly fiction.

"For twenty years I wrote only for adults. It was only as my children grew up that I began thinking about children's stories. For several years I would tell bedtime stories almost every night, making them up as I went along. My daughter Fiona introduced me to contemporary children's writing, and I was hooked. Mind you, it took me another ten years to try my hand at it.

"I find writing for children is great fun. It's an escape. I laugh a lot at the unexpected things my characters say and do. I don't plan. I simply invent a character, usually ten or twelve years old, put her in an unusual situation, and start speaking in her voice. For me it's a natural process—part of me doesn't seem to have grown up.

"I've always been interested in nature and now, more than ever before, it is important to pass along a message [about nature]. Most of my books have a message,

though it is buried way underneath the plot. Children pick it up, but mostly they have fun. My main message is: enjoy reading."

D'Ath more recently commmented of his career: "I like playing games with my readers. My novel *Sniwt* (read that backwards) has the shortest chapter ever published. The books which have most influenced my early work are the Coles Funny Picture Books and the works of Roald Dahl. Lately my writing has tended more toward outdoor action adventure, and for this I owe a debt to the 'Adventure' series by Willard Price, which I still remember vividly from my childhood, and the more contemporary novel *Hatchet* by Gary Paulsen."

"Children are the most rewarding audience any writer can have," D'Ath concluded. "Read your work to an adult audience, and they will clap politely at the end. Read to children, and they will stick up their hands right in the middle of a passage and say, 'We've got a dog and his name is Robbie.' That's who I'm writing for when I sit down each morning at eight o'clock in front of my computer. All children should have books and dogs."

Biographical and Critical Sources

PERIODICALS

Australian Book Review, August, 1997, review of *Infamous,* p. 61; July, 2001, review of *Hunters and Warriors,* p. 62; May, 2004, Elizabeth Braithwaite, review of *Shaedow Master,* p. 59.
Booklist, September 1, 2004, Kay Weisman, review of *Infamous,* p. 120.
Magpies, July, 1998, Neville Barnard, review of *Why Did the Chykkan Cross the Galaxy?,* p. 33; May, 1999, review of *Sniwt,* p. 33; March, 2000, review of *The Upside-Down Girl,* p. 33; November, 2000, review of *Koala Fever,* p. 33; July, 2001, review of *Goldfever,* p. 29; July, 2001, review of *Hunters and Warriors,* p. 39; November, 2001, review of *Echidna Mania,* p. 33; September, 2002, review of *Astrid Spark, Fixologist,* p. 34; July, 2003, review of *Infamous,* p. 33; November, 2003, review of *Shaedow Master,* p. 40.
Reading Time, May, 1998.
School Librarian, spring, 2002, review of *Hunters and Warriors,* p. 43.

ONLINE

Justin D'Ath Home Page, http://www.justindath.com (October 26, 2006).*

Cover of D'Ath's Astrid Spark, Fixologist, *featuring Terry Denton's humorous watercolor-and-ink illustrations.* (Allen & Unwin, 2002. Copyright © illustrations, Terry Denton 2002. Reproduced by permission)

*   *   *

DIAKITÉ, Baba Wagué 1961-

Personal

Born 1961, in Kassoro, Mali; immigrated to United States, 1984; married Ronna Neuenschwander (a sculptor); children: Penda, Amina.

Addresses

Home—1424 SE Oak St., Portland, OR 97214; Bamako, Mali.

Career

Ceramic artist, craftsperson, and author. Participant in Oregon Art-in-Education program; founder of cultural center near Bamako, Mali. *Exhibitions:* Work exhibited in group and solo shows in New York, NY; San Diego, CA; San Francisco, CA; Houston, TX, and Portland, OR. Commissions installed at Disney World, Orlando, FL; Oregon Zoo, Oregon State University, and elsewhere.

Awards, Honors

Coretta Scott King Honor Book designation, 1997, for *The Hunterman and the Crocodile;* Aesop Prize (co-recipient), American Folklore Society Children's Folklore Section, 2004, for *The Magic Gourd.*

Writings

FOR CHILDREN; SELF-ILLUSTRATED

(Reteller) *The Hunterman and the Crocodile: A West African Folktale,* Scholastic (New York, NY), 1997.
(Reteller) *The Hatseller and the Monkeys: A West African Folktale,* Scholastic (New York, NY), 1999.
The Magic Gourd, Scholastic (New York, NY), 2003.

ILLUSTRATOR

Adwoa Badoe, *The Pot of Wisdom: Ananse Stories,* Douglas & McIntyre (Toronto, Ontario, Canada), 2001.
Penda Diakité (daughter), *I Lost My Tooth in Africa,* Scholastic (New York, NY), 2006.

Adaptations

The Hunterman and the Crocodile was adapted for video, Nutmeg Media, 2005.

Sidelights

Born and raised in a small village in the West African country of Mali, Baba Wagué Diakité shares his heritage through both his art and his writings. Appraising Diakité's fine-art paintings and sculpture as well as his crafts—he produces earthenware vessels, ceramic plates, tiles, and textiles—critics have consistently commented on the artist's talent for incorporating a story within his decorative images. Indeed, storytelling is considered a highly valued tradition within his family, and making the jump from artist to picture-book author/illustrator was, for Diakité, a natural one. Beginning with *The Hunterman and the Crocodile: A West African Folktale,* the artist has created several picture books that have been praised for featuring enriching multicultural stories enhanced by notes regarding Malian culture and the author's vividly colored ceramic-tile illustrations.

Born in 1961, Diakité was given the middle name "Wagué" (which means "man of trust") from his mother's father. Growing up in a close-knit family living in the village of Kassoro, he worked in the rice and peanut fields farmed by his grandmother, learned to tend sheep from his uncle, and spent his free time hunting and roaming the countryside with friends, or creating puppets for puppet shows. When he reached school age, Diakité moved to the capital city of Bamako to join his parents, and there he was enrolled in a French school. He remained in Mali until his early twenties; in 1985 the future artist moved to the United States and over the next few years began to learn the traditional painting techniques for which he has become known.

In his paintings, murals, and ceramic art, Diakité attempts to meld Malian tradition with his own unique aesthetic. As he explained to Victoria Rovine in *African Arts,* "Traditional artists work in one straight line of thought: to do things the way they have been done in the past. Putting too much creativity into it can cause a problem. Being in the United States, I realize that it is great to respect the past, but also having freedom in art is one of the best things you can have." Diakité has seen his work included in group shows as well as solo exhibitions in several major U.S. cities, including his home town of Portland, Oregon. He and his family—Diakité is married to sculptor Ronna Neuenschwander, with whom he has two daughters—now divide their time between their Oregon home and his family home in Bamako.

The recipient of a Coretta Scott King Honor Book designation, *The Hunterman and the Crocodile* is based on a story Diakité was told by his grandmother. In the traditional folktale, a hunter named Donso is talked into carrying a crocodile and its family to the river where they live; in exchange, the sharp-toothed crocs agree not to bite the man. However, once the hunter fulfills his part of the bargain, the crocs reconsider, arguing that hunters like Donso do not live in harmony with nature's other creatures. While many animals agree with the crocs, Donso's life is ultimately saved by a trickster rabbit. The story is illustrated with painted ceramic tiles that feature what *Booklist* contributor Julie Corsaro dubbed "striking paintings surrounded by borders with enthnic motifs." Praising the work as a "memorable debut," a *Publishers Weekly* contributor cited Diakité's "stunning primitivist" earth-toned illustrations and noted that the text's "occasional onomatopoeia and clearly delivered message about the importance of respecting nature" make *The Hunterman and the Crocodile* a perfect choice for story hours.

Other books written and illustrated by Diakité include *The Hatseller and the Monkeys: A West African Folktale* and *The Magic Gourd.* In *The Hatseller and the*

African artist and writer Baba Wagué Diakité illustrates his picture book **The Magic Gourd** *with hand-painted ceramic art.* (Scholastic Press, 2003. Copyright © 2003 by Baba Wagué Diakite. Reprinted by permission of Scholastic Inc)

Monkeys an enthusiastic artisan named BaMusa is proud of his heritage as one of a long line of hatmakers and his ability to make both dibiri hats with their wide brims and brimless fugulan caps. Heading to town to sell his colorful wares, BaMusa tires from hunger and stops to nap beneath a mango tree; he awakes to find that some mischievous monkeys, which had been feasting off the tree's delicious fruit, have made off with his hats. "Diakité's use of language is as colorful and unusual as his artwork," noted a *Publishers Weekly* writer, praising the author's use of brightly colored glazes and strong contrasts on his earthenware tiles. Noting the simple lesson woven into the story, Nancy Hurxthal wrote in *Horn Book* that *The Hatseller and the Monkeys* "will add distinction to any repertory of tales of delight and gentle instruction."

Featuring the "exquisitely painted ceramics that have become Diakité's . . . illustrative trademark," according to a *Publishers Weekly* writer, *The Magic Gourd* is also based on a traditional Malian tale. After Rabbit helps Chameleon untangle himself from a prickly bush, the reptile repays the kindness with the gift of a hollow gourd that will fill up with whatever its owner wishes. While the good-hearted Rabbit uses the gift to feed his entire village, when a greedy king steals the bowl Chameleon comes to Rabbits aid with another magic gift. Noting that Diakité resolves his story with "more kindness than . . . trickery," *Booklist* contributor John Peters wrote that the book's illustrations—including earthenware plates and bowls as well as tiles featuring traditional Malian border designs—reflect the artist's "characteristic energy and spirit." "An intense artistic experience awaits the reader of this highly moral, Ma-

lian version of a 'magic pot' folktale," a *Kirkus Reviews* contributor noted, adding that "Diakité educates, entertains, and visually enchants from beginning to end."

As an illustrator, Diakité has created artwork for books by other writers. *The Pot of Wisdom: Ananse Stories,* Adwoa Badoe's collection of folktales featuring the world's most well-known spider, benefits from the illustrator's "stunning, glazed earthenware tiles in rich, vibrant tones," according to *School Library Journal* contributor Grace Oliff. A traditional folk-tale character that appears in tales from many lands, Ananse often gets into trouble due to failings in his own character. In the story "Why Ananse Lives on the Ceiling," for example, the greedy spider is humiliated after he is discovered stealing food from his own family, and for ever more hides in shadowy corners.

In a more interesting collaboration, Diakité joins with oldest daughter Penda Diakité in the picture book *I Lost My Tooth in Africa.* A true story written by Penda at age eight, the tale focuses on little sister Amina, whose concern over a loose tooth overshadows her visit to the home of her African relatives. As her father has promised, when the tooth falls out and Amina places it under a gourd, she gets an unusual gift from the African tooth fairy in return. According to Hazel Rochman, writing in *Booklist,* the story and art in *I Lost My Tooth in Africa* combine to illustrate "the rich daily life" of Diakité's loving family, and a *Publishers Weekly* reviewer noted the "whimsical touches" that appear in the tiles' patterned borders. As Alexa L. Sandman concluded in her *School Library Review* of the picture book, the elder Diakité's "artistry supports his daughter's storytelling beautifully."

Biographical and Critical Sources

PERIODICALS

African Arts, summer, 2001, Victoria Rovine, "Baba Wagué Diakité: 'Respect Yourself as Well as Your Tradition,'" p. 64.
Booklist, March 15, 1997, Julie Corsaro, review of *The Hunterman and the Crocodile: A West African Folktale,* p. 1245; February 15, 2001, Henrietta M. Smith, review of *The Hatseller and the Monkeys: A West African Folktale,* p. 1160; December 1, 2001, GraceAnne A. DeCandido, review of *The Pot of Wisdom: Ananse Stories,* p. 641; February 15, 2003, John Peters, review of *The Magic Gourd,* p. 1088; February 1, 2006, Hazel Rochman, review of *I Lost My Tooth in Africa,* p. 68.
Bulletin of the Center for Children's Books, February, 1997, review of *The Hunterman and the Crocodile,* p. 202.
Christian Century, December 13, 2003, review of *The Magic Gourd,* p. 25.

Horn Book, May, 1999, Nancy Hurxthal, review of *The Hatseller and the Monkeys,* p. 342; January-February, 2002, Margaret A. Bush, review of *The Pot of Wisdom,* p. 87; January-February, 2006, Barbara Bader, review of *I Lost My Tooth in Africa,* p. 67.

Kirkus Reviews, August 15, 2001, review of *The Pot of Wisdom,* p. 1206; January 15, 2003, review of *The Magic Gourd,* p. 141; December 15, 2005, review of *I Lost My Tooth in Africa,* p. 1321.

New Yorker, October 6, 1997, review of *The Hunterman and the Crocodile,* p. 115.

New York Times Book Review, October 12, 1997, Robin Tzannes, review of *The Hunterman and the Crocodile,* p. 102; April 16, 2000, "Monkey Business," p. 31.

Publishers Weekly, December 9, 1996, review of *The Hunterman and the Crocodile,* p. 67; January 11, 1999, review of *The Hatseller and the Monkeys,* p. 71; December 16, 2002, review of *The Magic Gourd,* p. 67; January 2, 2006, review of *I Lost My Tooth in Africa,* p. 61.

School Library Journal, March, 1997, Beth Tegart, review of *The Hunterman and the Crocodile,* p. 173; October, 2001, Grace Oliff, review of *The Pot of Wisdom,* p. 134; February, 2003, Miriam Lang Budin, review of *The Magic Gourd,* p. 128; January, 2006, Alexa L. Sandman, review of *I Lost My Tooth in Africa,* p. 96.

ONLINE

Scholastic Web site, http://www.scholastic.com/ (November 12, 2006), "Baba Wagué Diakité."*

*   *   *

DIAKITÉ, Penda 1993(?)-

Personal

Born c. 1993; daughter of Baba Wagué Diakité (an artist) and Ronna Neuenschwander (a sculptor).

Addresses

Home—1424 SE Oak St., Portland, OR 97214; Bamako, Mali.

Career

Student, writer, and filmmaker.

Writings

Welcome to Mali (documentary film), produced 2005.

I Lost My Tooth in Africa (picture book), illustrated by father, Baba Wagué Diakité, Scholastic (New York, NY), 2006.

Sidelights

At age twelve, Penda Diakité saw her film *Welcome to Mali* headlining the Family Film Day at Portland, Oregon's 2006 Cascade Festival of African Films. A docu-

mentary of the middle-school student's trip to Bamako, Mali, where her father was born and raised, *Welcome to Mali* is designed to introduce American children to the way life in a West African village, and features Penda's younger sister Amina as well as friend Fiona.

The precocious Diakité's creative efforts have been aided and inspired by her father, noted artist and writer Baba Wagué Diakité. Working together, father and daughter have combined their talents to produce another multicultural offering, the picture book *I Lost My Tooth in Africa.* In a true story written when she was eight years old, Penda Diakité tells of a young American girl—in fact, little sister Amina—who loses a tooth while visiting her father's family in Mali. Despite her distance from home, the girl places the lost tooth under a gourd and gets an unusual gift from the African tooth fairy in exchange: a rooster and a speckled hen! In *Booklist,* Hazel Rochman noted that the book brings to life "the rich daily life" of a small African community, while a *Publishers Weekly* contributor remarked on Diakité's ability to share with readers the daily routine of her "warm and welcoming West African family." Alexa L. Sandman credited the author's inclusion of "thoughtful detail" for illuminating "the strength and enduring warmth of her African extended family," and a *Kirkus Reviews* writer deemed *I Lost My Tooth in Africa* "an excellent way to encourage children to start writing their own family stories." Critics also offered praise for Baba Wagué Diakité's ceramic-tile illustrations, the *Publishers Weekly* reviewer noting the "whimsical touches" that appear in the tiles' patterned borders. As Sandman concluded, "his artistry supports his daughter's storytelling beautifully."

Biographical and Critical Sources

PERIODICALS

Booklist, February 1, 2006, Hazel Rochman, review of *I Lost My Tooth in Africa,* p. 68.

Horn Book, January-February, 2006, Barbara Bader, review of *I Lost My Tooth in Africa,* p. 67.

Kirkus Reviews, December 15, 2005, review of *I Lost My Tooth in Africa,* p. 1321.

Publishers Weekly, January 2, 2006, review of *I Lost My Tooth in Africa,* p. 61.

School Library Journal, January, 2006, Alexa L. Sandman, review of *I Lost My Tooth in Africa,* p. 96.

ONLINE

Cascade Festival of African Films Web site, http://www.africanfilmfestival.org/ (January 1, 2006), "Local Father-Daughter Films Connect Portland and Mali."*

DOUGHTY, Rebecca 1955-

Personal

Born 1955. *Education:* Attended Sir John Cass School of Art, 1977; University of Massachusetts, Amherst, B.F.A, 1979; Vermont College, M.F.A., 1994.

Addresses

Home—MA. *Agent*—c/o Author Mail, G.P. Putnam, 375 Hudson St., New York, NY 10014.

Career

Author, artist, sculptor, and illustrator. *Exhibitions:* Paintings, drawings, and sculpture exhibited at galleries, including Bernard Toale Gallery, Boston, MA; Rose Art Museum; Mills Gallery at Boston Center for the Arts; Fuller Museum of Art, Brockton, MA; Owen Patrick Gallery, Philadelphia, PA; East West Contemporary Art, Chicago, IL; Allston Skirt Gallery, Boston; Drawing Center, New York, NY; Courthouse Gallery, County Mayo, Ireland; William-Scott Gallery, Provincetown, MA; and other galleries in North American and internationally. Works included in private collections at Simmons College, DeCordova Museum, and Ballinglen Arts Foundation, among others.

Awards, Honors

Grumbacher Award, Artists Foundation, 1984; Massachusetts artists fellowship, Artists Foundation, finalist in drawing, 1984, finalist in painting, 1990; Massachusetts Arts Lottery grant, 1987, 1990, 1992; Blanche E. Colman Foundation Award, 1992, 1996, 2000; Artists Resource Trust grant, Berkshire Taconic Community Foundation, 1998, 2003; Best Show Award, International Association of Art Critics, 2003; Ballinglen Arts Foundation fellowship (Ireland), 2004; Ucross Foundation fellowship, 2006.

Writings

SELF-ILLUSTRATED

Friends Stick Together, Scholastic (New York, NY), 2000.
You Are to Me, Putnam (New York, NY), 2004.
Lost and Found, Putnam (New York, NY), 2005.

ILLUSTRATOR

Harriet Ziefert, *39 Uses for a Friend,* Putnam (New York, NY), 2001.
Harriet Ziefert, *Toes Have Wiggles, Kids Have Giggles,* Putnam (New York, NY), 2002.
Coupons for Kids, Handprint Books (Brooklyn, NY), 2002.
Coupons for Friends, Handprint Books (Brooklyn, NY), 2002.
Coupons for Grown-ups, Handprint Books (Brooklyn, NY), 2002.
Christmas Has Merry, Handprint Books (Brooklyn, NY), 2002.
Halloween Has Boo, Handprint Books (Brooklyn, NY), 2002.
Harriet, Ziefert, *31 Uses for a Mom,* Putnam (New York, NY), 2003.
Amy Krouse Rosenthal, *One of Those Days,* Putnam (New York, NY), 2006.

Sidelights

Award-winning artist, sculptor, and illustrator Rebecca Doughty has exhibited her paintings and drawings around the world, as well as in the pages of several children's books. Frequently collaborating with writer Harriet Ziefert on such books as *39 Uses for a Friend* and *Toes Have Wiggles, Kids Have Giggles,* Doughty has also illustrated two original stories: *You Are to Me* and *Lost and Found.* Praising her work for *Toes Have Wiggles, Kids Have Giggles* in *Booklist,* Ilene Cooper noted that Doughty's pen-and-ink and watercolor illustrations, while "minimalist," also contain a "simplicity [that] is deceptive and clever," while *School Library Journal* reviewer Rosalyn Pierini deemed the collaboration between author and illustrator "winsome." Her work for Amy Krouse Rosenthal's *One of Those Days* was described by *Horn Book* contributor Kitty Flynn as featuring "idiosyncratic, scragglyline" drawings that "emanate good-humored glumness," in keeping with Rosenthal's tale.

You Are to Me stands as Doughty's authorial debut. Using a variety of unique metaphors and a rhyming text, as well as her characteristic opaque watercolor and ink, she brings to life the fondness a pig has for his friend, a bunny rabbit. Combining hand lettering and Doughty's trademark childlike art, the book's illustrations feature the story's animal characters outlined with black ink in a manner that gives them a delightfully "childlike quality," according to *School Library Journal* reviewer Maryann H. Owes. Owes went on to compliment Doughty's debut, calling *You Are to Me* "a charming exploration of the joys of sharing." Jennifer Mattson, writing in *Booklist,* commented that the book is "an ego-boosting bagatelle for children, and also fun for grown-ups, who may hear echoes of Cole Porter's 'You're the Tops.'"

In *Lost and Found* Doughty portrays the escapades of young Lucy, who is often found in a rush and always misplaces things. Finding herself late leaving for school one day, Lucy somehow manages to lose her shoes, books, and even her homework. Overwhelmed, the girl has an emotional meltdown, then regains her composure and sets about hunting down her missing belongings. Doughty sends a clear message to young readers: there are benefits to slowing down in life, and her "short, rhyming text and her characteristic uncluttered cartoon drawings will appeal to many children," in the opinion of *School Library Journal* reviewer Robin l. Gibson. Cooper wrote in *Booklist* that Doughty's "loose-lined ink drawings, highlighted in pure pastels, have an offbeat charm," while a *Kirkus Reviews* critic stated that the author's "signature childlike cartoonish mixed-media drawings" are "guileless and appeal . . . [to] the disorganized youngster in us all."

Biographical and Critical Sources

PERIODICALS

Art New England, April-May, 1995, Paul Parcellin, "Rebecca Doughty: Markers."
Booklist, June 1, 2002, Ilene Cooper, review of *Toes Have Wiggles, Kids Have Giggles,* p. 1744; January 1, 2003, Ellen Mandel, review of *31 Uses for a Mom,* p. 911; January 1, 2004, Jennifer Mattson, review of *You Are to Me,* p. 874; August, 2005, Ilene Cooper, review of *Lost and Found,* p. 2034; October, 2006, Carolyn Phelan, review of *One of Those Days.*
Boston Globe, March 12, 1998, Cate McQuaid, "Rebecca Doughty: Simple Things."
Horn Book, May-June, 2006, Kitty Flynn, review of *One of Those Days.*
Kirkus Reviews, November 15, 2003, review of *You Are to Me,* p. 1358; May 15, 2005, review of *Lost and Found,* p. 587.
Publishers Weekly, June 17, 2002, *True Companions,* p. 67; February 24, 2003, *True Companions,* p. 74; December 15, 2003, review of *You Are to Me,* p. 47.
School Library Journal, December, 2001, Alison Kastner, review of *39 Uses for a Friend,* p. 116; June, 2002, Rosalyn Pierini, review of *Toes Have Wiggles, Kids Have Giggles,* p. 116; March, 2003, Rosalyn Pierini, review of *31 Uses for a Mom,* p. 211; January, 2004, Maryann H. Owen, review of *You Are to Me,* p. 96; August, 2005, Robin L. Gibson, review of *Lost and Found,* p. 93; May, 2006, Gloria Koster, review of *One of Those Days.*

ONLINE

Allston Skirt Gallery Web site, http://www.allstonskirt. com/ (October 10, 2006), "Rebecca Doughty."
BookPage, http://www.bookpage.com/ (October 10, 2006), "Meet Rebecca Doughty."
Penguin Group USA Web site, http://us.penguingroup.com/ (October 10, 2006), "Rebecca Doughty."
William Scott Gallery Web site, http://www. williamscottgallery.com/ (October 10, 2006), "Rebecca Doughty."*

* * *

DURBIN, William 1951-

Personal

Born February 17, 1951, in Minneapolis, MN; son of Charles (a barber) and Dona (a bookkeeper) Durbin;

William Durbin (Photograph reproduced by permission)

married October 14, 1971; wife's name Barbara (a teacher); children: Jessica, Reid. *Education:* St. Cloud State University, B.S., 1973; Middlebury College, M.A. 1987. *Hobbies and other interests:* Golf, canoeing.

Addresses

Home and office—2287 Birch Pt. Rd., Tower, MN 55790. *Agent*—Barbara Markowitz, 1505 Hill Dr., Los Angeles, CA 90041. *E-mail*—Bill@williamdurbin.com.

Career

Writer and educator. Teacher of English in Minnesota public schools, grades four through college, including at Cook High School. Speaker at writing conferences and at schools and libraries; supervisor for writing research projects for National Council of Teachers of English, Middlebury College, and Bingham Trust for Charity.

Member

National Education Association, Society of Children's Book Writers and Illustrators, Children's Literature Network.

Awards, Honors

Great Lakes Booksellers Association Book Award; Minnesota Book Award, 1998, 2005; Bank Street College Children's Book-of-the-Year designation; New York

Public Library Books for the Teen-Age selection, 1998, 2005; New River Press Poetry Competition finalist; Lake Superior Contemporary Writer's Series winner; Jefferson Cup Series of Note Award; Oppenheim Toy Portfolio award; Northeast Minnesota Book Award finalist; Boosense Summer Pick, 2006.

Writings

The Broken Blade, Delacorte (New York, NY), 1997.

Tiger Woods (biography; "Golf Legends" and "Black Americans of Achievement" series), Chelsea House (Philadelphia, PA), 1998.

Arnold Palmer (biography; "Golf Legends" series), Chelsea House (Philadelphia, PA), 1998.

Wintering (sequel to *The Broken Blade*), Delacorte (New York, NY), 1999.

Song of Sampo Lake, Wendy Lamb Books (New York, NY), 2002.

Blackwater Ben, Wendy Lamb Books (New York, NY), 2003.

The Darkest Evening, Orchard (New York, NY), 2004.

El Lector, Wendy Lamb (New York, NY), 2006.

"MY NAME IS AMERICA" SERIES

The Journal of Sean Sullivan, a Transcontinental Railroad Worker: Nebraska and Points West, 1867, Scholastic (New York, NY), 1999.

The Journal of Otto Peltonen, a Finnish Immigrant: Hibbing, Minnesota, 1905, Scholastic (New York, NY), 2000.

The Journal of C.J. Jackson, a Dust Bowl Migrant: Oklahoma to California, 1935, Scholastic (New York, NY), 2002.

Contributor of poems, essays, and short stories to periodicals, including *English Journal, Great River Review, Milkweed Chronicle, Confrontation, North American Mentor, Canadian Author and Bookman, Boys Life, Loonfeather, Modern Haiku, Nebraska Language Arts Bulletin, Breadloaf News,* and *NCTE.*

Durbin's books have been translated into several languages, including Italian, and have been produced in Braille editions.

Adaptations

The Broken Blade was adapted as a cartoon serial published in *Boys' Life* magazine.

Sidelights

Making his home on the shores of Minnesota's Lake Vermilion, author and teacher William Durbin shares his enthusiasm and interests in history, golf, and canoeing in the pages of his books for young readers. In addition to biographies of golfing greats Tiger Woods and

Arnold Palmer, he has penned a number of works of historical fiction that have been praised by reviewers. Durbin's home in Minnesota provides inspiration for many of his titles.

Born in Minneapolis, Minnesota in 1951, Durbin attended St. Cloud University before earning his master's degree at Middlebury College and spending a year at Lincoln College, Oxford on a scholarship from the school's Bread Loaf School of English. Trained as a teacher, he worked for decades as a teacher and mentor to writers at Bread Loaf as well as for those students participating in writing projects sponsored by the National Council of Teachers of English. Durbin was inspired to begin writing for young adults after speaking to author Gary Paulson during the award-winning young-adult writer's workshop appearance at Durbin's wife's school.

Durbin's first book, *The Broken Blade,* was inspired by his interest in the French *voyageur* fur traders, men who canoed the waters of the northern Midwest and Canada during the eighteenth and early nineteenth centuries. In the book, which takes place in 1800, Pierre

Cover of William Durbin's Song of Sampo Lake, *about a Finnish family's efforts to establish a new home in the American heartland at the turn of the twentieth century.* (Dell Yearling, 2004. Used by permission of Random House Children's Books, a division of Random House, Inc)

Cover of Durbin's 2004 novel The Darkest Evening, *featuring artwork by Bagram Ibatoulline.* (Orchard Books, 2004. Jacket illustration copyright © 2004 by Bagram Ibatoulline. Reprinted by permission of Orchard Books, an imprint of Scholastic Inc)

LaPage's father supports his family as an oarsman for the North West Fur Company on the long, heavy voyageur canoes used by fur traders to transport pelts out of the wilderness of northern Canada. When his father is unable to make the trip after severing his thumb in an accident, thirteen-year-old Pierre leaves school, determined to take his father's place. The 1,200-mile trip from Montreal to Grand Portage requires incredible physical strength and fortitude, and ultimately tests the character of Durbin's young protagonist. Noting that the writer fills his novel with action and describes in vivid detail the events that "transform . . . Pierre from classroom-softened boy to hard-muscled man," *Bulletin of the Center for Children's Books* contributor Elizabeth Bush added that *The Broken Blade* "should appeal to reluctant readers as well as adventure buffs." Dubbing the book "an impressive coming-of-age tale," a *Kirkus Reviews* critic added that "readers will embrace . . . [Pierre's] path to true bravery, strength of character, and self-reliance."

In *Wintering,* Pierre once again leaves his home in Montreal, this time heading north into the Canadian wilds to work at the fur company's winter camp. There he learns how to survive the region's brutal conditions with help

from the native Ojibwa people. A confrontation with the death of two close friends, as well as with the hardships of daily life in the wilderness, allow for a continuation of the coming-of-age theme established in *The Broken Blade,* according to critic Susan Dove Lempke. Lempke also noted in her *Booklist* review that Durbin's use of period journals and diaries "gives the novel an authentic feel but doesn't overshadow the unfolding story of Pierre's growth and maturation." Dubbing *Wintering* an "engaging sequel," a *Kirkus Reviews* contributor praised the novel as "well-written and atmospheric" and packed with "plenty of facts" about how the Native Americans of the Great Lakes region lived.

Durbin's stand-alone historical novel *Song of Sampo Lake* takes place at the turn of the twentieth century, as a Finnish farming family makes their new home in the author's home state of Minnesota. Matti, whose achievements are constantly overshadowed in the eyes of his father by those of his older brother, works as a store clerk and teaches English at the local one-room schoolhouse in addition to working on the family farm. Writing about the novel on his home page, Durbin commented that while he did much of his research for all three of his early novels, "the 1900 setting of the book also allowed me to interview many people who had vivid memories of their family homesteads." Michael Cart, writing in *Booklist,* considered the novel "a rich introduction to both an important aspect of the American experience and a memorable and immensely likable family." As *School Library Journal* critic Carol A. Edwards noted, "Durbin keeps the pace moving, and the events unfold in a compelling fashion," while Paula Rohrlick wrote in *Kliatt* that Durbin's inclusion of "the many details . . . of what it takes to survive in a harsh land and climate make homesteading and history come alive."

Taking place in the same era as *Song of Sampo Lake, Blackwater Ben* follows Ben's effort to learn more about his dead mother from his still-grieving father. He follows his father to a logging camp in northern Minnesota, and there meets others who can help him with his quest for understanding. As Ben learns more about his family, he begins to appreciate his reserved father. "Vivid and often quite funny, the book is a lively read," noted Carol A. Edwards in *School Library Journal,* while Rohrlick wrote that "the colorful characters, practical jokes, and well-researched details . . . provide entertaining reading."

Drawing readers back to the mid-twentieth century, *The Darkest Evening* follows a Minnesota family who move from their Finnish mining community and travel to an advertised utopia in the Soviet Union. Teen narrator Jake is suspicious about the situation from the very beginning, and when they arrive in the communist country and find anything but a utopia waiting for them, Jake's suspicions only grow. When his older brother and father are both taken into custody by the KGB (the Soviet secret police), Jake leads the rest of his family

Durbin brings to light the experiences of a young European living in Minnesota during the early twentieth century in **The Journal of Otto Peltonen, a Finnish Immigrant.** (Scholastic, 2000. Photograph courtesy of University of Minnesota, Immigration Research Center. Reproduced by permission)

on a mad ski run across the Soviet border into Finland. "Durbin's historical fiction is every bit as exciting as the best adventure tale," wrote a *Kirkus Reviews* contributor. Jennifer Mattson, reviewing the novel for *Booklist,* maintained that "readers who enjoy tales of courage under fire . . . will find this exciting stuff."

El Lector takes place far from the chilly reaches of Minnesota; it is set in the Cuban-American community of Ybor City, Florida during the Great Depression. Durbin's novel tells the story of thirteen-year-old Bella, who wants nothing more than to become a reader for the men who work in the cigar factories, the same job held by her grandfather. However, because their family is poor, Bella has to take a job rather than finishing school. When her grandfather is replaced by a radio because the factory owners want to stop their workers from unionizing, Bella struggles to find a way to fulfill her dream. "It is Bella's integrity that will appeal to most readers," Mattson wrote in *Booklist.* A *Kirkus Reviews* contributor considered the novel an "engaging story," and *School Library Journal* critic Caitlin Augusta commented that in *El Lector* "Durbin succeeds admirably in creating an accessible world rich in detail."

Durbin has contributed several works of historical fiction for Scholastic's "My Name Is America" series. In

The Journal of Sean Sullivan, Transcontinental Railroad Worker: Nebraska and Points West, 1867, he recounts the experiences of a fifteen-year-old Irish immigrant who works alongside his father constricting the Transcontinental Railroad in 1867. Traveling from state to state across the western territory, Sean records the conflicts he witnesses between the railroad and the Plains Indians and cowboys, and the discrimination suffered by Chinese laborers, as well as his impressions of the region's extensive financial corruption. Noting that the book's first-person narrative "focuses on historic details to bring the Old West vibrantly alive," *Booklist* reviewer Roger Leslie dubbed *The Journal of Sean Sullivan, a Transcontinental Railroad Worker* "a rollicking, atmospheric journey" into the past.

The Journal of Otto Peltonen, a Finnish Immigrant: Hibbing, Minnesota, 1905 begins as fifteen-year-old Otto sails from Finland to America, traveling with his mother and sisters to join his father in the iron-rich lands of Minnesota. Soon working as a miner, Otto finds himself caught up in the early labor union movement. He joins with other workers in a fight for safe working and living conditions in the company-owned shantytowns of Minnesota's Mesabi Iron range. "Historical notes and authentic photos round out this captivating, dramatic view of the past," maintained Leslie in his *Booklist* review.

Durbin's third contribution to the "My Name Is America" series, *The Journal of C.J. Jackson, a Dust Bowl Migrant: Oklahoma to California, 1935,* focuses on a thirteen year old whose family is forced to abandon their farm during the devastating drought of the late 1920s. The Jacksons join many other Midwest farming families by falling into poverty while working as migrant workers. Noting that the novel will provide young readers with a good introduction to John Steinbeck's *The Grapes of Wrath, School Library Journal* contributor Ronni Krasnow added that *The Journal of C.J. Jackson, a Dust Bowl Migrant* features a "likeable protagonist" and "effectively conveys the plight of Dust Bowl families."

In addition to writing and teaching, Durbin lectures to school and library groups as well as at writing conferences. In his talks, he focuses on topics such as how to begin a narrative, how to get published, writing and researching historical fiction, generating ideas through wordplay, and overcoming writers' block.

Biographical and Critical Sources

PERIODICALS

Booklist, February 15, 1999, Susan Dove Lempke, review of *Wintering,* p. 1061; October 15, 1999, Roger Leslie, review of *The Journal of Sean Sullivan, a Transcontinental Railroad Worker: Nebraska and Points West, 1867,* p. 428; October 1, 2000, Roger Leslie, review of *The Journal of Otto Peltonen, a Finnish Immigrant: Hibbing, Minnesota, 1905,* p. 332; October 15, 2002, Michael Cart, review of *Song of Sampo Lake,* p. 401; November 15, 2004, Jennifer Mattson, review of *The Darkest Evening,* p. 582; February 1, 2006, Jennifer Mattson, review of *El Lector,* p. 47.

Bulletin of the Center for Children's Books, February, 1997, Elizabeth A. Bush, review of *The Broken Blade,* pp. 203-204; April, 1999, Elaine. A. Bearden, review of *Wintering,* p. 276.

Faces, January 2002, review of *The Journal of Otto Peltonen,* p. 46.

Kirkus Reviews, November 15, 1996, review of *The Broken Blade,* p. 1688; December 1, 1998, review of *Wintering,* pp. 1732-1733; October 1, 2000, review of *The Journal of Otto Peltonen,* pp. 1421-1422; November 1, 2003, review of *Blackwater Ben,* p. 1301; November 15, 2004, review of *The Darkest Evening,* p. 1088; December 15, 2005, review of *El Lector,* p. 1321.

Kliatt, May, 2001, Deane A. Beverly, review of *Wintering,* p. 18; May, 2002, Claire Rosser, review of *The Journal of C.J. Jackson, a Dust Bowl Migrant: Oklahoma to California, 1935,* p. 9; November, 2002, Paula Rohrlick, review of *Song of Sampo Lake,* p. 8; January, 2004, Paula Rohrlick, review of *Blackwater Ben,* p. 8; November, 2004, Paula Rohrlick, review of *The Darkest Evening,* p. 7.

Publishers Weekly, November 11, 2002, review of *Song of Sampo Lake,* p. 65; December 22, 2003, review of *Blackwater Ben,* p. 61.

St. Paul Pioneer Press, November 2, 2000, Mary Ann Grossman, "Fictional Diary Mines the Tumultuous History of the Iron Range."

School Library Journal, September, 2000, Ronni Krasnow, review of *The Journal of C.J. Jackson, a Dust Bowl Migrant,* p. 220; November, 2002, Carol A. Edwards, review of *Song of Sampo Lake,* p. 162; December, 2003, Carol A. Edwards, review of *Blackwater Ben,* p. 149; January, 2005, Ginny Gustin, review of *The Darkest Evening,* p. 126; February, 2006, Caitlin Augusta, review of *El Lector,* p. 130.

Voice of Youth Advocates, August, 2000, Nancy Zachary, review of *Tiger Woods,* pp. 202-203; December, 2000, Cindy Lombardo, review of *The Journal of Otto Peltonen,* p. 348.

ONLINE

Metronet Web site, http://www.metronet.lib.nm.us/ (November 3, 2006).

William Durbin Home Page, http://www.williamdurbin.com (November 3, 2006).

E

EMSHWILLER, Carol 1921-
(Carol Fries Emshwiller)

Personal

Born April 12, 1921, in Ann Arbor, MI; daughter of Charles Carpenter (a professor) and Agnes (Carswell) Fries; married Edmund Emshwiller (a film maker and video artist), August 30, 1949; children: Eve, Susan, Peter. *Education:* University of Michigan, B.A., 1945, B. Design, 1949; attended Ecole nationale superieure des Beaux-Arts, Paris, France, 1949-50.

Addresses

Home—210 East 15th St., Apt. 12E, New York, NY 10003. *Agent*—Wendy Weil, 232 Madison Ave., Ste. 1300, New York, NY 10016.

Career

Clarion Science-Fiction-Writing Workshop, East Lansing, MI, teacher, 1972-73; New York University, New York, NY, adjunct associate professor in continuing education, 1974-2004. Organized workshops for Science Fiction Bookstore, New York, NY, 1975-76, and Clarion Science-Fiction-Writing workshop, 1978-79. Guest member of faculty, Sarah Lawrence College, Bronxville, NY, 1982.

Member

Science Fiction Writers of America, Authors Guild of Authors League of America, PEN.

Awards, Honors

MacDowell Colony fellowship, 1973; New York State Creative Artist Public Service grant, 1975; National Endowment for the Arts grant, 1979; New York State Foundation for the Arts grant, 1988; New York University Award for Teaching Excellence, 1989; World Fan-

Carol Emshwiller (Photograph courtesy of Carol Emshwiller)

tasy Award, 1991, for *The Start of the End of It All*; Gallun Award, 1999; Icon Award, 1999; Philip K. Dick Award, Philadelphia Science Fiction Society, 2002, for *The Mount,* and nominee for *Report to the Men's Club and Other Stories;* Nebula Award in short-story category, Science Fiction Writers of America, 2002, for "Creature"; Nebula nominations, Science Fiction Writers of America, 2003, for *The Mount* and "Grandma."; Nebula Award, 2005, for short story "I Live with You."

Writings

Joy in Our Cause (short stories), Harper (New York, NY), 1974.

Pilobolus and Joan (television play), WNET, New York, NY, 1974.

Family Focus (television play), 1977.

Verging on the Pertinent (short stories), Coffee House Press (Minneapolis, MN), 1989.

The Start of the End of It All (short stories), Women's Press (London, England), 1990, revised edition, Mercury House (San Francisco, CA), 1991.

Carmen Dog (novel), Mercury House (St. Paul, MN), 1990, Peapod Classics (Northampton, MA), 2004.

Venus Rising (novella), Edgewood Press (Cambridge, MA), 1992.

Ledoyt (novel), Mercury House (San Francisco, CA), 1995.

Leaping Man Hill (novel), Mercury House (San Francisco, CA), 1999.

The Mount, Small Beer Press (Brooklyn, NY), 2002, Firebird (New York, NY), 2005.

Report to the Men's Club and Other Stories, Small Beer Press (Brooklyn, NY), 2002.

Mr. Boots (young adult), Viking (New York, NY), 2005.

I Live with You, Tachyon (San Francisco, CA), 2005.

Contributor to books, including *Pushcart Prize XXI*, Pushcart Press, 1989; *Love Stories for the Rest of Us*, Pushcart Press, 1995; *The Penguin Book of Erotic Stories by Women*, edited by Richard Glyn Jones and A. Susan Williams, Viking, 1996; *Wild Women; Women of Wonder;* and *Nebula Awards Showcase 2005*, edited by Jack Dann, ROC (New York, NY), 2005. Contributor of short stories to literary and science-fiction magazines, including *Alchemy, Polyphony, Magazine of Fantasy & Science Fiction, TriQuarterly, Croton Review, Omni,* and *Epoch*. Author of short story "Creature."

Sidelights

Carol Emshwiller's feminist science-fiction and fantasy stories began appearing in science-fiction magazines in the 1950s, but it was not until 1974, with her story collection *Joy in Our Cause*, that Emshwiller gained critical acclaim. Influenced by the New Wave science fiction of the 1960s, her often Kafkaesque short stories explore the female psyche and male-female relationships through their experimental use of language and character. In *Feminist Writers*, Denise Wiloch described Emshwiller's style as "fantastical, quirky and individualistic . . . granting insights that might have been less obvious in a story following a traditional narrative form. In all her fiction, Emshwiller's biting wit and ability to turn a phrase have drawn critical acclaim from both genre and mainstream critics alike." In a review of her collection *Report to the Men's Club, and Other Stories*, James Sallis of *Magazine of Science Fiction & Fantasy* proclaimed Emshwiller "one of the finest and most original writers in the United States. . . . Her work is undefinable. She's a feminist writer who adores men, a literary artist who often prefers to work in or springboard off fantastic literature, an experimentalist anchored firmly to plot and character interaction."

According to a critic for *Publishers Weekly,* Emshwiller's short stories are "like carnival mirrors that distort our perceptions, letting us see ourselves in new, wise ways." In her stories, which borrow elements from the science fiction and fantasy genres and are told from a feminist perspective, Emshwiller creates allegorical lessons about the condition of women in society. Writing in the *New York Times Book Review,* Deborah Stead explained that Emshwiller gets "at the truth of things by rendering them strange," while Kimberly G. Allen in *Library Journal* found that "Emshwiller explores the feminine psyche in an otherworldly way."

Emshwiller's stories often make use of characters and situations found in science fiction and fantasy. In the story "The Start of the End of It All," for example, aliens bent on conquering Earth collaborate with divorced women against the ruling male establishment. Another story tells of a highly evolved alien woman who, upon her arrival among contemporary Americans, becomes relegated to the inglorious role of housewife. In "Yukon," a woman leaves her husband in favor of living with a bear in the forest. Emshwiller's fiction, wrote Peter Bricklebank in *Library Journal,* "is inventive, whimsical, outrageous, and wise." Critics also pointed to Emshwiller's prose style. According to a *Los Angeles Times Book Review* critic, Emshwiller's stories are told in "a nervous, edgy, witty style all her own." "It would not be misleading," claimed Edward Bryant in *Locus,* "to think of Carol Emshwiller as a cleverer, frequently more subtle, John Irving."

The stories featured in *Report to the Men's Club, and Other Stories* include tales of true love (in "Nose"), faith (in "Modillion"), and abandoned children ("Mother" and the Nebula Award-winning "Creature"). The title story is structured as a speech given by a new member of a men's club who has been initiated even though, by genetic mistake, she was born female. As a critic for *Kirkus Reviews* noted, "a daring, eccentric, and welcome observer of darkly human ways emerges" from the stories in the collection. "What makes them satisfying," wrote Regina Schroeder in *Booklist,* "is the personalities of their characters." Susanna J. Sturgis, in her review for *Women's Review of Books,* called the characters in the stories complex, and mused: "Given time and necessity, most of us are capable of accepting the unusual, the outrageous, and even the appalling as downright normal. So these characters and situations insinuate themselves into our lives, questioning, enhancing, and contradicting everything we thought we knew."

In her published novels, Emshwiller has taken two different approaches. Her first novel, *Carmen Dog,* utilizes the same fantastical approach found in her short stories, presenting a world in which human women have become animals, and animals have evolved into human women. Although a critic for *Publishers Weekly* believed Emshwiller "stretches a conceit past the breaking point in this uneven allegory," Charlotte Innes, writing in the *New York Times Book Review,* dubbed *Carmen Dog* "a gentle exposition of human folly that nevertheless makes some tough points about the inequalities between the sexes." Katherine Dieckmann, writing in the *Voice Literary Supplement,* celebrated "Emshwiller's hilariously dead-on radical vision."

Although Emshwiller writes from a feminist point of view, some critics have problems with her portrayals. In the *St. James Guide to Fantasy Writers,* essayist Liz Holliday observed that the author's "fiction tends to assert that some traits—such as loyalty and nurturing—are intrinsically female, and therefore immutable. . . . Animals that are turning into humans retain the qualities traditionally associated with them; meanwhile, women turn into the animals that best embody their personalities. The underlying assumption seems to be that personalities and talents are inborn—that they cannot be changed simply by breaking social condition." Pointing out Emshwiller's efforts to deal fairly with both sexes, Wiloch observed that "despite some uneven moments, Emshwiller's allegory succeeds in whimsically scoring points about sexual inequalities and commenting on the destructive behavioral tendencies of both women and men. Women who seek to be pampered and men who try to dominate others are both satirized in Emshwiller's animal tale."

Marking a major shift from her usual fantastic fiction, Emshwiller's second novel, *Ledoyt,* employs a more conventional narrative style. A realistic story set in the American west of the early twentieth century, *Ledoyt* concerns Oriana Cochran and Beal Ledoyt, two wildly different characters who nonetheless fall in love and marry. The story focuses on the couple's stubborn and jealous daughter, Lotti, who tries to destroy her parents' marriage. A *Publishers Weekly* critic praised Emshwiller's "verbal portrait of Lotti . . . and of adolescent resentment and angst." Emshwiller tells the story in a "spare but lyrical prose and [with] a fine attention to detail," wrote Walter Satterthwait in the *New York Times Book Review.* Oriana and Beal "are endearing and admirable characters," Satterthwait concluded, and the novel contains moments "that are remarkably moving; there are scenes of great power." According to Wiloch, *Ledoyt,* "although far different from the kind of fiction for which Emshwiller is best known, is perhaps her most successful work in terms of examining the fundamental relationship between the sexes she has always explored in her writing."

Commenting about her novels to *Feminist Writers,* Emshwiller stated: "I've always hoped my stories and books (such as *Carmen Dog*) make fun of women's ways as much as of men's. With the novel *Ledoyt* my writing changed completely—no longer satire and humor. After my husband's death I felt I'd lost my material for the battle between the sexes. Also writing served a different purpose for me. I needed a family to live with since my children were grown and scattered all over. . . . And mostly I wanted to write from the omniscient point of view for a change. I did get some omnicient in, but mostly I lapsed into one person's point of view, sequentially."

In the novel *Leaping Man Hill* Emshwiller continues the drama of the Ledoyt family portrayed in *Ledoyt.* She tells the story of the healing power of love through the protagonist, Mary Catherine, who comes to the farm to teach Abel, mute son of Oriana and Ledoyt. A romance develops between Mary and Henny, Abel's angry, bitter cousin, who has lost an arm in World War I. Faye A. Chadwell, writing in *Library Journal,* praised Emshwiller's descriptions as "keen and vivid" and the dialogue as "robust yet sensitive," while a *Publishers Weekly* critic cited *Leaping Man Hill* as "mark[ing] Emshwiller as a writer of distinctive talent."

In *The Mount* Emshwiller returns to fantastic fiction, but without the focus on the battle of the sexes contained in *Carmen Dog,* and many of he earlier short stories. Instead, her focus is on the psychology of slavery or servitude. The story takes place in a future where, for several generations, humans have been enslaved by an alien race referred to as the Hoots. Humans are bred to be the mounts for Hoot riders; some are bred for their strength, others for their speed. Charley, who is called Smiley by his Hoot masters, wants to be the best racer among the Mounts, and he trains with his Hoot rider, Little Master (who will one day be the ruler of the Hoots), to win them both prestige. When Charley is "rescued" by humans living in the wilds after rebelling from their Hoot masters, Charley must decide if he wants a freedom that means the hard labor of forming and supporting a new society, or a slavery with the comforts he has always known.

"Emshwiller's peculiar, touching tale becomes a meditation on the virtues of civilization . . . versus freedom and democracy," noted a critic for *Kirkus Reviews.* Robert K.J. Killheffer commented in the *Magazine of Science Fiction and Fantasy* that, though the scenario may seem almost absurd, in *The Mount* "Emshwiller balances delicately on the beam, carrying the tale straight-faced with a combination of precise language, gentle humor, a near-perfectly pitched voice, and a tenderness toward her characters that draws us in and beguiles us." Regina Schroeder, writing in *Booklist,* called the novel "a memorable alien-invasion scenario, a wild adventure, and a reflection on the dynamics of freedom and slavery." In *Publishers Weekly,* a reviewer noted that Emshwiller's "poetic, funny, and above all humane novel deserves to be read and cherished as a fundamental fable for our material-minded times." Susanna J. Sturgis, reviewing the novel in the *Women's Review of Books,* proclaimed: "There's no doubt in my mind: *The Mount* is a brillian book."

On her home page, Emshwiller wrote: "About my writing, a lot of people don't seem to understand how planned and plotted even the most experimental of my stories are. I'm not interested in stories where anything can happen at any time. I set up clues to foreshadow what will happen and what is foreshadowed does happen." In the *St. James Guide to Science-Fiction Writers,* the essayist concluded of the author's work that Emshwiller's "stories are delightful for their artistry on all levels and [as] examples of the best that the short story as an art form has to offer. You owe it to yourself to read and reread this author."

Biographical and Critical Sources

BOOKS

Feminist Writers, St. James Press (Detroit, MI), 1996.
St. James Guide to Fantasy Writers, St. James Press (Detroit, MI), 1996.
St. James Guide to Science-Fiction Writers, St. James Press (Detroit, MI), 1996.

PERIODICALS

American Book Review, August, 1991, p. 12.
Booklist, November 15, 1989, p. 639; February 1, 1990, p. 1070; May 15, 1991, p. 1779; August, 2002, Regina Schroeder, reviews of *The Mount* and *Report to the Men's Club, and Other Stories* p. 1936.
Extrapolation, spring, 2004, "Guest of Honor Speech, WisCon 2003," pp. 9-15.
Kirkus Reviews, October 1, 1989, pp. 1421-1422; August 15, 1995, p. 1128; July 1, 2002, review of *Report to the Men's Club, and Other Stories,* p. 901; July 15, 2002, review of *The Mount,* p. 976.
Library Journal, December, 1989, p. 168; April 15, 1990, p. 122; June 1, 1991, p. 188; November 15, 1991, p. 152; October 1, 1995, p. 119; September 15, 1999, Faye A. Chadwell, review of *Leaping Man Hill,* p. 111.
Locus, May, 1992, p. 51.
Los Angeles Times Book Review, June 9, 1991, p. 6.
Magazine of Fantasy and Science Fiction, February, 2003, Robert K.J. Killheffer, review of *The Mount,* pp. 33-39; May, 2003, review of *Report to the Men's Club, and Other Stories,* pp. 36-41.
New York Times Book Review, March 18, 1990, Deborah Stead, review of *Verging on the Pertinent,* p. 20; April 29, 1990, Charlotte Innes, review of *Carmen Dog,* p. 38; October 29, 1995, Walter Satterthwait, "Suspicious of Joy," p. 28.
Publishers Weekly, November 17, 1989, p. 46; January 26, 1990, Penny Kaganoff, review of *Carmen Dog,* p. 412; April 26, 1991, p. 54; August 28, 1995, review of *Ledoyt,* p. 110; August 30, 1999, review of *Leaping Man Hill,* p. 50; July 8, 2002, review of *The Mount,* pp. 34-35.
Review of Contemporary Fiction, fall, 1991, p. 284; spring, 2003, Michael Hemmingson, review of *The Mount,* p. 158.
Science Fiction Chronicle, June, 1992, p. 35.
Small Press, June, 1990, p. 31; fall, 1991, p. 55.
Voice Literary Supplement, June, 1990, p. 19.
Women's Review of Books, January, 1997, p. 5; May, 2003, Susanna J. Sturgis, "Horse Play," pp. 11-14.

ONLINE

Carol Emshwiller Home Page, http://www.sfwa.org/members/emshwiller/ (February 9, 2005).

Autobiography Feature

Carol Emshwiller

Carol Emshwiller contributed the following autobiographical essay to *SATA:*

I was born in Ann Arbor, Michigan in 1921. The name on my birth certificate is Agnes Carolyn Fries, but so as not to be confused with my mother, I was never called Agnes. (When I started college I changed my name from Carolyn to Carol so as to be more like a boy . . . more like my brothers. I don't feel that way anymore but it's too late to change back and I'm used to being Carol now.) My father was a professor at the University of Michigan. I was the oldest of my mother's children

The author as a child (Photograph courtesy of Carol Emshwiller)

but I had an older half sister. Though she lived with us, I was hardly aware of her until I was two or three. But I was aware of my two-years-younger brother. I was jealous from the first. My two younger brothers were born much later. One is seven years younger than I and the other is twelve years younger.

In my family my older half sister was one of those old-fashioned Victorian secrets. I didn't find out she was my half sister until I was thirteen. I was sitting in front of her and overheard a friend say that, for sisters, we didn't look anything alike. My sister replied that we'd had different mothers but she didn't know if I was supposed to know. I never dared mention that I knew. My father, whose first wife died when my half sister was seven years old, had told her never to mention her mother's name again, and she didn't—except to me much later. My brothers found out our father had been married before from looking up his biography in *Who's Who*. Even after we had all found out, we never spoke of it among ourselves until we were grown up.

Mother was young, twenty-one, when I was born, and she didn't know anything about kids. Both my parents believed that if you praised children they would get swelled heads. My mother kept telling me how cute my little brother was. She thought that would make me love him. I kept wondering: Why wasn't I cute, too? Still, I've always been close to that brother, partly because later, as small children, we were thrown together

alone several times in France when my parents went to England. Also we were close enough in age to be playmates.

My maiden name, Fries, was Frisian Dutch from northern Holland. Somewhere way back, here in America, a Dutch Reform Protestant married a French Huguenot. Later there was English mixed in, too. Both sides of my father's people came to America in the 1700s, but my mother's family came from Scotland more recently.

My mother's father was a country fiddler, first in Scotland and then over here. His day job in America was as a carpenter. In Scotland he was a shepherd. I've heard that he bought his violin from a door-to-door peddler and learned to play it out on the moors as he looked after the sheep. He came over to America all by himself at age twenty-six with nothing but one small round-top trunk about the size of a medium suitcase. He drowned when my mother was seven years old. She watched from the bank as he tried to rescue her niece. Mother watched them both go down and never come up. He was a Mason and they had a large Masonic funeral for him.

There was no insurance in those days so Mother and Grandma were shunted off from relative to relative where Grandma had different jobs. In one place Grandma worked at a boarding house. One of the boarders taught Mother piano for nothing. When she was about fourteen or fifteen that teacher wanted to take her to New York as a prodigy, but Grandma didn't want her to go. I don't think Mother wanted to go either.

Mother never performed for anybody, but she played for us and herself all the time. All kinds of music. And she was into folk music before anybody else that I know of. Wherever she lived as my dad traveled, a year here and there, in England, France, Germany, or Mexico, she picked up more folk songs. (Dad played the mandolin and fife and one piece on the piano: "All through the Night." Sort of the same way he had one single dish he could cook: oyster stew.)

Mother would put us to bed and then play the piano. We went to sleep to Chopin, old fashioned "gallops," the Moonlight Sonata, etc. It would never have occurred to her to give a recital. Most women of her generation didn't, and Mother wouldn't have ventured such a thing. But she accompanied me as I learned to play the violin and later my brother as he played the French horn. And we were one of those old-fashioned families who stand around the piano and sing songs, with everybody playing some instrument or other.

Dad never was interested in money. Neither of my parents was. (And I'm not either.) During the depression we were poor—poorer than those around us. I could tell because I had fewer clothes and phonograph records and such than the other kids at school. When my kids were growing up, we lived in Levittown, Long Island.

Many of the people there were less well off than we were. I'm glad that my kids didn't have the problem of having less than their neighbors even though I don't regret that experience myself.

Linguistics was Dad's passion . . . the science of how languages are put together. (Also, while it has nothing to do with what linguistics is about—though people seem to think so—he could read several languages, but it was my mother who was good at speaking them and learning them quickly.) He was known for setting up schools and devising methods for teaching English as a foreign language. During the war he worked on ways of teaching Japanese, and at about the same time he founded the English house where Latin Americans could come and be completely immersed in English. (These were in Ann Arbor.) All kinds of people came there. I remember dancing with Baby Doc and thinking what an impressive man he was.

I did a similar language immersion myself for the one summer I spent in Freiberg, Germany, when my dad was studying there. I was fifteen at the time. I talked nothing but German all day, sang German songs in the evening. It didn't do much good. I've forgotten most of it. I might be able to ask for a cup of coffee but not much more.

In linguistics, my father was especially known as one of the professors who described English in its own terms, not using Latin as a basis for his description. I barely know the meaning of subject and predicate (well, I do), but I know "word order," "function words," and, "two-word verbs" (as: Come and come to. Run and run out. Call and call up. Fed and fed up. Give and give up. I've seen linguists get into trouble when they didn't have that two-word verb concept.) I know his terms much better than I know our Latin terms for languages.

Mine was an arguing family. Dad always used the Socratic method when trying to convince us of anything. I remember wanting to take dance so badly. He sat me down and must have talked with me for an hour, asking questions. At the end he finally asked, "So do you still want to take dance?" I said, "No," but even as I said it, I still wanted to (and I still wish I had). Then I read I.F. Stone's book *The Trial of Socrates*. In it he says Socrates was a bully. When I read that, I shouted, YES!

Mother said she never won an argument with Dad, but she couldn't believe she was *always* wrong. Mother said, "A man convinced against his will is of the same opinion still." She didn't take part in the family arguments. I don't think she liked them. Now I feel as she did, though I know it was Dad's way of telling us he loved us . . . taking all that time with us, arguing deep into the night, but did he always have to win?

My father was originally going to be a Baptist minister but he lost his religion at the Chicago Divinity School and went into linguistics instead. (Which doesn't mean he lost his morality at the same time. That, he kept.)

Carol in November 1923 (Photograph courtesy of Carol Emshwiller)

He was also very much into sports. He made sure even I, a mere girl, knew the rules of football and baseball. Later he was into swimming in particular. Mother never protested—not a single time, all through my brother's SCUBA diving and such, even though she'd watched her father drown.

My youngest brother learned to swim before he could walk. (It's easier to balance in the water than on land.) This was a slow process. Breath control came first and easily. Dad did this "scientifically," keeping notes, photographs and movies as he went along. He wrote a book on swimming with the Michigan swimming coach. The chapter on teaching babies to swim was all his own.

Dad quoted old poems constantly. I especially remember the first section of Chaucer's "Than langen folk to gang on pilgrimages." Lots of Latin, too, as, "De gustabus non disputandum est." But Mother was the one who played with words. She always noticed the rhythms of what you said as, "Bob'll be back." (Say these fast.) "Ed edited it," "Look at the catalpa tree," (I'm too old to say that fast now) and, "I need something to 'hitch it to.'" She said that was an old Indian name and we should name our island "Hitch-it-to island." (Dad had bought a small island in Georgian Bay in Canada. This sounds as if we were rich, but it cost ten thousand dollars a long time ago, and included a house and two cabins, all furnished and with Hudson bay blankets for every bed, a boat house and several boats. Dad thought this would be a place for all of us to gather every summer long after he had died. I never go there. I'm in love with mountains.)

Mother was funny all the time. She could make a joke out of anything. I guess in spite of your baby brother dying of diphtheria, your father drowning right before your eyes, growing up in poverty, and being shunted around from relative to relative, you can still have a sense of humor and enjoy life.

Besides being into music and argument, mine was a swimming and boating family and all my brothers still are. But I had to be about sixty or so before I realized I don't like swimming (I was always too cold and my sinuses always hurt) and I don't like the beach (sitting on a beach or riding around in boats bores me though I do like paddling a canoe). I was late in discovering my love of mountains and hiking up them but that's why I bought my little mobile home in the mountains of California. What I like about hiking and paddling is moving your body. Anything to do with sitting I can't stand. But most of all I love the beauty of the mountains. Since I've spent my summers there, fourteen years now, they've played a big part in my writing.

*

On my sixteenth birthday my father told me no woman had ever done anything significant. A woman could be the inspiration for deeds by men, she could be the woman behind the throne, but women weren't capable of doing anything original themselves. I'm sure he thought he was doing me a favor telling me this so I wouldn't waste my time trying to be something.

But, on the other hand, I was freer than my brothers because I didn't matter. The boys had three choices. They could become lawyers, doctors, or professors. (So my musician brother is the black sheep of the family.) But it didn't matter what *I* did.

We traveled quite a bit because Dad took year-long sabbaticals at various places. I guess they couldn't have all been sabbaticals because we traveled more often than every seven years.

He took a year off to study in Freiberg, Germany. Before that there were a couple of years he worked at the Bodleian Library in Oxford, but he wanted us two older children to learn French. At the age of eight I was dumped into a two-room country school where nobody talked English except me and my brother. I was not aware of learning French. I was not aware of not being understood. I think I just talked and gradually it must have become French. (My daughter saw the same thing when she took my ten-year-old grandchild to Peru. There was a boy his age next door and they played together, one speaking Spanish and the other English. They didn't seem to be aware that they weren't speaking the same language or not understanding each other.)

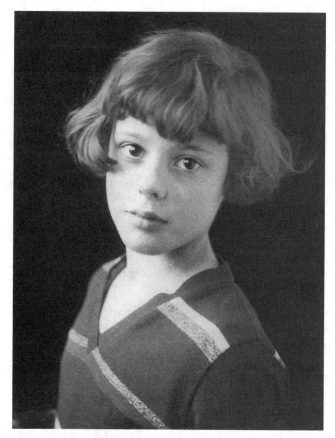

The author at age ten (Photograph courtesy of Carol Emshwiller)

So, going back and forth to and from France—I was eight years old in France, nine and ten here, then eleven in France, twelve back here, etc.—I was hopelessly confused. Somehow I missed fractions altogether (when I try to do them I have to draw pies), and I still can't spell much of anything. I remember the exact words that made me decide I couldn't learn and give up: address/adresse, and syrup/sirop. I thought, well, if that's how you spell "address" then obviously I can't learn anything so why try. I quit. I think I was eleven. It was as if a curtain came down and I didn't bother anymore. I did manage to squeak through with Cs and a few Ds. At the University of Michigan I failed freshman English and had to take it over and almost failed again. I wonder if I'd have gotten into the University without being the daughter of a professor there.

Once, in France, I found out I really was an American with American attitudes. It was the time I was fourteen and Liline, the French lady who looked after me and my brother, had a girl not much older than I was who helped with the cleaning now and then. Once I heard Liline talking about how intelligent and clever that girl was and how she should . . . , and my mind went right away to "get a good education—go to college," but Liline said, "She'll make a good little maid for somebody one of these days."

In France my brother and I stayed a year each time, usually in different places, but always with the same

Frenchwoman. My parents and little brothers stayed in Oxford, England, and later in Freiberg, Germany, so I and my brother were alone, but that Frenchwoman was a much better mother than my mother was. My mother visited now and then and watched her in action and learned how to be a good mother from imitating her. Liline made life a game. Even chores were fun. I had wet my bed when living with my mother and even when I went to camp, which I loved, but I never did when living with Liline.

One year my brother and I lived in a chateau that had an indoor outhouse, a two-holer, the only bathroom for a house with several bedrooms. It was downstairs next to the front door. That didn't matter because the Brittany maid emptied the chamber pots every morning. There was a large living room full of marble statues but they couldn't use it through the winter because they couldn't heat it. The only heated parts of the house were the small dining room (as opposed to the large one), a small playroom for my brother and me, and the kitchen. They had little stoves that the maid carried from room to room.

At a different place (a small house this time) you went up a bank outside and peed into a hole that went down into a vat. When it was full they hauled the vat out to spray on the fields.

Being alone with my brother those years made us very close. He's the only one with all those same experiences. And, though the Frenchwoman was a terrific mother, he was family. He was my main playmate each time we were in France. People lived behind walls there. Kids didn't visit from house to house. There was one school for boys and one for girls. In one place the boys called my brother, "Americain, tête de chien," and threw stones at him. Luckily they didn't play baseball and were terrible throwers. My brother did play baseball and when he threw back he usually hit. Neither of us had any good friends from our schools. When I was eight, I had a girl I walked home with everyday, but we never visited each other's houses. Cousins were the French thing then. We knew our French mother Liline's nieces and nephews. They were the only visitors we had.

We left France and Germany in 1939, just as the war was starting. We were on the last civilian ship to sail to the United States. It was so crowded they had the swimming pool full of cots. There was a blackout so, on the way to Le Havre, Dad drove all night with no lights and several cans of gas in the trunk of the car. Every town along the way was completely dark. I wasn't at all worried. I thought: Dad will take care of everything. That was the attitude he had about himself, too.

*

All my life I was a bad student and I hated writing most of all. It was too hard. But I always drew. Even in first grade, the teacher hung my drawings all along the wall above the blackboards. Nobody else's, just mine. I'm not sure I'd go along with that idea now even if I was the featured one. There must have been other kids' drawings teachers should have put up, too.

But now studying and researching are my favorite things to do . . . after writing. Now writing is my favorite *because* it's the hardest thing I know. That's why I love plots and structured stories. I love the skill it takes to get everything together. Also I love how you dredge things up from inside yourself and find out things about yourself you never knew. Also bring up memories you'd never think of without writing fiction. And it's a secret, but I think short-story writing is harder than poetry. Even harder than sonnets.

Though I didn't pay any attention in school, I did read a lot. *Tarzan* and *John Carter of Mars,* but especially books by Zane Gray and Will James. Will James was my absolute favorite. I can still read him and Zane Gray, but I can't get through more than a page or two of Edgar Rice Burroughs. My parents and brothers would go off for a Saturday or Sunday trip but I'd stay home and read. I didn't read any "girl" books. I always wanted to be a boy. (There was no doubt in my family which sex was the important one.) And I wasn't brought up as a girl, I was brought up as a defective boy.

I wouldn't have stooped to reading a book like *Little Women.* (All that was just as I was growing up. Not now. I've changed.) But I haven't changed my mind about preferring to be a cowboy instead of a princess. I hate the idea of being a princess, always have and still do.

I was a daydreamer, but what kid isn't? My parents let me alone. They didn't worry about my bad grades or whether my homework was done. They let me be. That wasn't just because I was a mere girl. They didn't worry about the boys either. They always thought we'd wise up one of these days all by ourselves and everybody did, but with me, it took a long, long time.

Dad never thought the purpose of going to college was to get a better job, or earn more money, or get a degree, or even get good grades; he just believed in getting an education and in learning and keeping on learning all your life. Except for my youngest brother, he couldn't control what classes the boys took. One was taking pre-med and the other went away to the Curtis Institute for Music. But he could control me. He had me take political science, aesthetics, Aristotelian logic, the Bible as literature, a couple of pre-med courses, behaviorist psychology, (he hated anything Freudian. It was only later that I got into that on my own) . . . his own class in linguistics. . . . I had to take all the things he was interested in or had taken himself.

Right out of high school, I went to the University of Michigan Music School. I was a typical music-school student in that I practiced violin about four hours a day,

Carol's parents, Agnes and Charles Fries, about 1950 (Photograph courtesy of Carol Emshwiller)

played three hours in orchestra Monday, Wednesday, and Friday, and in a quartet class Tuesdays and Thursdays. I played in another quartet once a week in the evenings for fun. I sang in the huge (I think it was 200 voices, maybe more) Ann Arbor Choral Union chorus. (I did *The Messiah* four times and Beethoven's Ninth Symphony twice. For the Ninth, we were conducted by Eugene Ormandy and accompanied by the Philadelphia Orchestra. Ormandy had tears rolling down his face through almost all of the performance.) But I was not a good violinist, mainly because I have slow fingers. I could play everything up to Paganini. Paganini changed everything. I couldn't play anything fast or virtuosic after he came along.

I also went to Interlochen Music Camp back when it was only a summer camp, not an all-year school as it is now. I worked on the dishwashing machine there and on the cafeteria line. (As a kid I had worked in record shops, music stores, book stores, and as a soda jerk, also in an ice-cream factory unfolding boxes to put the ice cream in.)

I think I was dyslexic before anybody knew about it. I'm such a slow reader, in reading both music and prose. I had proof of that when I tried to read when a group of us were seated in a row passing pages. I began to realize I had to skip whole paragraphs to keep up with the others. Even so I was holding things up. They finally made me go to the end of the line. Sometimes I wonder how I got myself into a teaching and writing job. I'm so unsuited for it.

After music school, I went to war. Just as I started at Michigan, the men had started being drafted for World War II. We'd look in the newspaper every day to see which of our professors had been called up. Pretty soon most of the men were gone. (They were either in Canada, or 4F, or in jail for conscientious objecting, or in the war. My future husband and my brothers went, though later my husband marched against the Vietnam War.) Though I was and am, more or less, a pacifist, I wanted to see what was going on. I wanted to experience what my generation was experiencing, so I joined the Red Cross.

I spoke French so they sent me to Italy. I handed out coffee and doughnuts, ran a club, recruited girls for dances, and supervised a little library of paperbacks—this was when paperbacks first came out. (We weren't supposed to worry if they were stolen.)

By the time I sailed into Naples on a troop ship, the war had just ended so I saw a lot of devastation (the whole waterfront was completely bombed out) but I didn't see any actual war. First I was stationed on the Isle of Capri at an R & R (rest and relaxation) place. I can't remember doing a single lick of work. I played pinochle with the guys and took groups hiking on the cliffs. My love of mountains and cliffs was there before the Sierras. Later I was stationed in Tarcento near the Yugoslavian border. In neither of these places did I wear my Red Cross uniform. I learned a lot about how gross *some* (not many) American soldiers could be with the Italians. I was cursed at and spit on by some of our guys when they thought I was Italian. They called me words I'd never heard until then and have never heard since. On Capri four or five men would get together and push down the thick mud walls surrounding the houses just for the fun of it. In Tarcento I do remember working. I drove a truck into Udine to pick up donuts. I loved doing that.

*

When I returned from Italy I went to art school. I was a good artist. I was dexterous in a different way than is required by music.

It was in art school that I met Ed Emshwiller. Actually we met in front of a naked lady—in life class. I overheard him talking about having been stationed in Tarvesio, Italy, during the war, so, shy as I was in those days, I spoke up anyway and said I'd been stationed just south of that.

Right after finishing art school and marrying, we went to France for a year and studied art at the Beaux Arts. I had a Fulbright. We went to England to buy a motorcycle, a BSA, one of the first springers. During the summer, we camped and rode all over Europe.

When I finally decided writing was what I wanted to do I was thirty and had had my first child. (I have three, so I had to struggle to get any writing time at all. Most of

The author's late husband, Ed Emshwiller (Photograph courtesy of Carol Emshwiller)

writing science fiction and then went into more experimental writing and became more literary and also part of what others called the new wave in science fiction. That was a long time ago. Now I call it the Old Wave and I'm no longer interested in that kind of experimental writing.

I hated anything to do with writing until I met science-fiction people through my husband. Freshman English—and spelling—had scared me off. The science-fiction writers talked about writing as if it could be learned and as if a normal human being could do it. You didn't have to be Shakespeare to try it. I began to sell stories right away—first to the pulpiest of the pulps. My first story appeared in 1955. Later on I took classes at the New School in New York with Anatole Broyard and Kay Boyle, but I learned the most from the class with poet Kenneth Koch.

I've only been blocked when I've learned a lot. After my class with Kenneth Koch, I couldn't write for six months. I had learned so much I had to take time to absorb it. And yet I couldn't tell anybody what I'd learned. I tried to, even right after the class, but what you learn is a secret. It's an experience you have to go through.

I also learned a lot from the various science-fiction workshops I attended off and on soon after I sold my first stories. (As I said, science fiction is a small world. You get noticed right away.) I especially learned from

the time I went around feeling as if I couldn't breathe.) I never really had writing time until my children were grown and my husband had moved to California to teach at Cal Arts. Both of us got a lot more work done that way.

I don't think I ever would have written if I hadn't gotten married and gotten lonely. You have to have quiet in order to write. I came from a big bouncy noisy family. As I said, always laughing and talking and arguing. I remember getting up, throwing on clothes, not combing my hair or brushing my teeth and rushing downstairs because I heard people laughing in the kitchen. I still have that feeling when I first get up—that I must rush to see what's happening in the world. It might be something funny. I was so lonely when I first got married with just the two of us, I didn't know what to do with myself. I kept on with art work for a while, and played in the Hofstra University orchestra, but after meeting science-fiction writers through my husband, I wanted to join them. Science-fiction people are a small cozy group who all know each other through conferences and workshops.

Ed started out as an science-fiction illustrator (using the name Emsh), but then went into abstract expressionist painting and experimental film making, and then experimental video. We influenced each other. I started

Portrait of Carol, by her husband (Courtesy of Carol Emshwiller)

the science-fiction writer Damon Knight, who co-ran the first several workshops I went to. Also it's from those workshops that I learned to teach.

But soon after those New School classes, I didn't want to have anything to do with science fiction. For several years I wanted to be only a "literary" writer and I only wanted to sell to literary magazines. I went out for grants. I was successful in both of these. I received a National Endowment and two New York State Arts Council grants. But much later I decided I wanted to carve out a niche for myself and decided to go back to science fiction. I was never interested in sciency stories, I wanted to do people stories and stories that showed our life as it is in a new light.

*

After we had three kids, I didn't travel much. Ed still did, and when the kids were grown I usually went with him. We went to avant-garde film festivals and art installations all around the world. Japan was the most amazing. I found it more science fictionish than science fiction. We went three times, twice for one week and once for two weeks. I studied up on the country and took a course in Japanese, thinking we'd go again and often, but my husband died soon after so I never had the opportunity to use the little Japanese I'd learned.

Once the kids were grown, Ed took a job at the California Institute of the Arts, teaching video art and as the dean of the video and film department. He said he'd just go try it out. He hated California and would be right back. Meanwhile I got my first real job at the New York University School of Continuing Education. That's not the real part of the university, that's adult ed. (I'd only given short workshops up till then.) So Ed and I started a bicoastal relationship that lasted ten or so years. He found he loved California. I went to stay with him that summer and I fell in love with it, too, but I also loved my new job at NYU. Luckily our vacations didn't come at the same times. He'd come to New York for his spring break and I'd go to California for mine. Then I always spent the summer out there. We learned to love the mountains and the desert. We roamed all over the Sierra Nevada, mostly camping. We also went north beyond Banff, in Canada, and south to Mexico. Our favorite town was Bishop, California, on the eastern, high side of the Sierras. Less touristy than some. Everybody there describes it as a town of cowboys and Indians and retired intellectuals. Of course mostly retired geologists, but I met some retired linguists there who knew my father.

My husband had always wanted to learn to fly but didn't because he had a family with young children. Now that all the kids were grown he did learn to fly . . . at the age of sixty-two. The scariest thing I ever did in my life (!) was to go up with him in a tiny little plane. I knew how klutzy he was and how often he forgot things, but

I did it anyway, several times. None of our kids would go up with him. They always managed to have a previous engagement.

After Ed died my writing changed completely for a while, as well as my reasons for doing it. My children were scattered all over the place, my husband gone. . . . I needed a family. I created kids, teenagers, and a husband to live with. I lived in my two westerns, *Ledoyt* and *Leaping Man Hill,* in a way I never had lived in my writing before. At that time those characters were much more real to me than my friends. I didn't go anywhere. I just stayed home and wrote.

Another big change in my life back then pertains to my novels *Ledoyt, Leaping Man Hill,* and also *The Mount.* One of my daughters said something important right after my husband died. She said go and do something you never did before. She couldn't come with me but she sent me to a dude ranch.

She also sent me on a walking tour of the Lake Country in England, but that didn't have the same effect on my life and writing as the ranch did. I've not been the same after my several visits to that ranch. It influenced not only my western novels but several short stories.

At first I kept telling my daughter: "But I don't like horses anymore. That was back when I was twelve." After I'd been at the ranch I kept saying: "It's the lore I like. All the stuff those ranchers know. How they go out as if ships, with everything to repair *anything* tied on their saddles." And I had never lived on a farm/ranch before. I had *no idea.* I guess by now I finally should say I *do* like horses.

But at first, I couldn't write at all after Ed died. (It's a good thing I had to teach or I'd not have done anything.) It took about a year before I could write. Right after I came back from the ranch and back to New York, I sat in front of the TV set watching westerns because I wanted to see the desert and the mountains. I thought I'd not only lost a person, but the mountains, too. After a while I thought, these movies are all wrong. My grandma dressed and undressed under her nightgown, and the folks at the dude ranch I went to were just regular people. They'd been on that ranch for seven generations. (Without us guests, it would have died long ago.)

I had been saving the names of my great, great, great—I don't know how many greats (besides there were two or three with the same name)—grandfathers for something special. There was Abiel Ledoyt and Biel Ledoyt. So then, when I started writing *Ledoyt* and began to fall in love with my made-up character, I decided to use that old Huguenot family name.

I'm sorry now that in the first book I used the first name Beal instead of Biel. I got worried since I couldn't find the name anywhere but in my family tree. Then, just when the novel was about to come out and it was too late to change anything, I heard of a Cajun fiddler called Abiel so in the second book I went back to Biel and Abiel.

The author and her husband, about 1960 (Photograph courtesy of Carol Emshwiller)

I was enjoying writing my Western novels in several ways. I could go back to being the cowboy I'd always wanted to be when I was twelve, and I could be a man. (As Flaubert said of *Madame Bovary,* I can say of *Ledoyt,* "Ledroit, c'est moi." But also I was madly in love with him, too. He keeps reappearing in various short stories I wrote later on as a different person, but similar. He's in *Water Master* and in *My General.*) The teenage girl in that book draws. I drew the drawings for her. They're not illustrations, they're an integral part of the book. And I could do drawings for the book exactly as I drew when I was in high school. All those side views!

The whole purpose in writing it was to get over my homesickness for my family. I was much more into characterization than I'd ever been before. (For satire, humor and adventure, you don't need to go *quite* that deeply into characters.) I used much from my own life. All the characters are made up, but many of the things they do I used from my own relatives, such as my grandma never being naked and always undressing and dressing under her nightgown. Also, as I had Ledoyt do, my father broke his toes and jammed his shoe on right away before they swelled up and didn't take his shoe off until his toes were healed.

With *Ledoyt* I loved the research so much I couldn't leave it out . . . so the recipes, and medical advice of the times, etc. are in it.

That was my first *real* novel. My earlier novel *Carmen Dog* is like a series of short stories except, like the *Perils of Pauline,* each short story gets her in more trouble. I was so confused about writing a real novel when writing *Ledoyt,* I remember lining up all the scenes and sections in a long row across the floor trying to decide the order. But after *Ledoyt, Leaping Man Hill* just went zipping along. (Some people like the mess of *Ledoyt* better.)

*

My three kids—one scientist and two who write and paint (the scientist could spell better than I could when she was eleven and the two artists don't spell much better than I do)—were born in 1955, 1957, and 1959. We didn't mean to have them so close together. I was frequently left alone with them. My husband took long trips in order to make films. He felt he could make money much more easily than I could and so why did I need him to give me time for my writing? And he was right. When I sold a story I only made a penny a word (at the beginning) if it was science fiction, and two copies if a literary magazine. Actually, I still make very little. Twice my husband was away making movies for over a month. It's the money from those two movies that, much later, put my kids through college. I guess my trouble at the time (alone with little children and with an old car that didn't work well) was worth it.

I wondered what my kids felt like with a mother struggling to write all the time, so I asked them.

One daughter wrote back: "Having a Mom and Dad who were doing their art in the house [when Ed was painting his covers, he worked in the attic. It was his movies that took him away] made making art normal and casual and an integral part of life. It made us kids do art also."

Another daughter wrote: "Getting put to bed and hearing the sound of the typewriter and knowing your mom was right there was reassuring." (She said, "We didn't know till later Mom was putting us to bed earlier than other kids our age.")

My son wrote: "I remember being proud and inspired by my mother. I would never have tried to write if it hadn't been for her." His note was full of how unfair it was that my husband got to do his art with no hassle and that I had to struggle for every minute. But, of course, it was Ed's work that made the money that kept us going, so I guess it was fair.

There's a story about how I wrote in a playpen with the children outside it. People write about this, but nobody seems to understand it. What you do is, you put your desk in the corner of a room. You take apart one corner of a playpen and open it out. Remove the floor. Attach the corners to the walls on each side of the desk. The area will be three times as big as a playpen. The kids are fenced out and can't reach your papers. Mostly my kids were hanging over the fence talking to me. My kids did *not* yell and rage outside it, as has been written recently. After all, I had learned to mother from that Frenchwoman who looked after us. I wasn't quite as good as she was, but almost. The kids came first. They were happy. I was the one who wasn't. But now I have all the time to write I want.

I should mention that I went for psychoanalysis for over twenty years. I wish I had done that first, before I went to college. I'd have done everything better and smarter and as a happier person.

One of the things my shrink told me has been important to me. He said, anybody can behave themselves when things go well, it's when things go badly that you see who a person really is. That's important to me as I think about myself and as I watch other people in action.

*

Kafka is my favorite writer. I love his short stories better than his novels. My favorites are *The Hunger Artist, Josephine the Mouse Singer,* and *Report to an Academy,* which I imitated in my story "Report to the Men's Club."I like Kafka because his stories resonate beyond the story. And I like that you can't quite put your finger on the meanings. It's merely a feeling that it's telling you more than is on the page. I recently heard a writer on the radio say that stories should be like icebergs, most of them underwater.

I've done many a story without resonance. (All my early work, in fact.) But I don't care for those stories of mine as much as my later ones.

Now I've discovered Coetzee. A different kind of strange. Also Saramago. I have three favorites now.

Actually, though I'm mostly a science-fiction writer, I read very little science fiction. Right now I'm reading Faulkner's short stories. And finding a whole new appreciation for him.

People are always asking me, isn't all this knowledge I've learned from writing and teaching getting in the way of appreciating reading? It's just the opposite. I get so excited seeing something new or great technical prowess that I can hardly contain myself. I can't think of anything more thrilling than seeing new things or old things well done. I'm much more ready to yell out loud, jump up and down, for that than for any football goal my alma mater might make.

The nicest thing that was ever said about my science-fiction writing was in a review by Jim Gunn, a science-fiction critic and writer. He wrote that my science-fiction stories "Estranged the everyday." That's what I like best

The author's children: (clockwise, from top) Eve, age six; Susan, age four; and Peter, age two; 1961 (Photograph courtesy of Carol Emshwiller)

about science fiction. Or magic realism. You can make the everyday seem strange. You can see ordinary things with new eyes. You can write about the here and now and have the reader see us as odd. Which we are. That's what I like the best to do though I don't manage it with everything I write.

As I watch myself write I see that "estranging the everyday" is often why I work on a story in the first place. (I have several beginnings hanging around that I never went on with because they were simply "telling the story," so why bother?) Also I think it's science fiction's best reason for being. I like the other stuff, too. Some of it I like a lot, just not quite as much.

I'm finding, in my new war stories, that I can make anti-war comments through science fiction in a way I wouldn't be able to if I couldn't place the stories in a sort of limbo. My story "Repository" (in the July 2003 issue of *Fantasy & Science Fiction*) would have been impossible without a science fiction premise that had wiped out the soldiers' memories so they weren't sure anymore which side they were on.

Also I don't like to write about a specific war or place or time. I prefer to universalize it. Put it in a limbo and make it stand for all wars. Science fiction is the only place I know where that can be done.

A lot of people like science fiction because they're fascinated with gadgets and inventions and odd doodads and all different kinds of aliens, and that's fun (I guess—though not to me) and takes a lot of imagination (I suppose), but I prefer stories with few science-fiction elements. I may have been brainwashed in this— that is in having as few elements and doo-dads as possible—by Damon Knight. I obey that rule of his but not his other rule, which was that if a story can be told in a non-science-fiction way, then do it that way. He forgot that if you want to be a science-fiction/fantasy writer then everything goes into that mold. I always break Damon's second rule. But I do try to keep any science-fiction or fantasy elements to a minimum.

I also have a problem with those stories where strange things, not foreshadowed, keep popping up. If anything can happen at any time, where's the suspense? (That's the main reason I don't care much for magic or for "dragons and dungeons" kinds of fantasy.) As Damon Knight wrote, it's like that old joke about waiting for the second shoe to drop. (Somebody living above somebody else is going to bed and takes of his shoe and drops it on the floor. Then he realizes he's made a big thump for the guy below him so he very carefully puts down the second shoe. Pretty soon the guy below him knocks on the door and says, "For God's sake drop the other shoe.") In my classes I always say: Be sure to drop the *first* shoe so the reader can be waiting for the second. First shoes are as important as second shoes. I consider writing to be dropping a lot of first shoes and following through with the seconds.

The Emshwiller family in 1976: (from left) Sue, Ed, Carol, Eve, and Peter (Photograph courtesy of Carol Emshwiller)

First I learned to plot and sold to science-fiction magazines. Then for a long time my writing was a search for ways of structuring that wasn't a plot. Plot pulls the reader along and when it's not there something else must pull the reader. A sort of illusion of plot. But then I went back to plot. I find it more difficult and therefore much more fun.

Though I love plots and plotting, I never know where my stories are going when I start to write, but I always end up with something plotted. Partly I think it depends on when you do your thinking: as you go along or before you start. If I knew my story before I wrote it, I wouldn't bother writing it. Also I have plotted so many stories now that plot just comes naturally. When I come to a fork in the story I usually take the path that will be the worst for the protagonist. I try to foreshadow possible bad things as I go along, though if I don't use those, I have to go back and take them out. I like people stories. I think time limits (that's not a plot) and evil people are too easy, but good people in conflict innocently are what I like best to write about.

At my summer place in California, I took several classes in prey-animal psychology, which actually were classes on the psychology of everything. About how we, being predators and having predators such as cats and dogs around us all the time, understand predators, but know very little about prey animals.

I used what I learned in this class for writing *Ledoyt,* but also in my novel *The Mount.* Especially the differences between prey and predator. I thought it would be fun to write about a prey animal riding on a predator instead of the other way around. We, who can't smell very well and can't hear very well and can only see straight out in front, being ridden by a creature who can see almost in a circle and hear and smell better than we can.

Another fun thing about those classes was that only the ranchers came to them. People with lots of horses and lots of cows and big hats that they never took off. (There was even a lot of cow psychology.)

*

When I was a literary writer I used to write very slowly, but now I write fast. (I like to call what I do magic realism though I know a lot of it actually is just plain fantasy.) I decided to do this a few years ago when I sent out five short stories, multiple submissions, each to five different literary magazines. I sent them in September when the literary magazines read. A year later the rejections started to trickle in. They were all rejected and it took over a year and a half for all of them to come back. If I were twenty years younger—as I was back when I placed most of my stories in literary magazines—I'd go on sending to those mags, but I'm too old now. I decided to stick where I was known, so now everything I write has, if sometimes only slightly, a science-fiction/fantasy slant. After I decided this, I sold everything I wrote quite quickly and my reputation in the field took off. I write the first idea that comes to mind. I can't say that those first ideas come out any worse than ideas I slave and puzzle over a long time.

About my story "Bountiful City" (in my short-story collection *I Live with You*): I was recently at a meeting that had a few writers and a poet, but was mostly a group of painters. They got to talking about all the things they'd never tell anybody and never did and still wouldn't, all the things that embarrassed them. I said that's what we write with. All the other writers and the poet agreed with me. I said I considered myself nothing but material and that it was an occupational hazard not to know what *not* to talk about. I said that a frequent exercise writing teachers assign is to write about your most embarrassing moment or to write about the thing you'd never tell anybody. As I walked home from that meeting, I started wondering if that was really true about myself. And what could I write that would embarrass me? So I wrote "Bountiful City." It begins: "I'm walking around New York saying, I love you, I love you, I love you, and I'm not in love with anybody. . . ." That's how I *do* walk around New York every day and, until then, never thought to ever tell it. I've used myself so mercilessly in my fiction that I still don't know what one shouldn't reveal about oneself. I'll tell anybody anything.

Though I use them as sparingly as possible, I do know what adjectives and adverbs are. (With my kind of a father you had to find this out for yourself even though he knew all that.) Also I avoid similes, though sometimes one of my characters will resort to one. I tell my students to use adjectives and adverbs and similes sparingly . . . if at all! And I tell my students to just use "said." Not to use a lot of fancy ways of saying "said" such as, reiterated, admonished, confirmed, and such.

Many people seem to think it's poetic writing to have a lot of similes and such, but I often find those people don't pay attention to the rhythms of their paragraphs and sentences. I pay a lot of attention to the rhythms and lengths of my sentences. Every now and then, especially in the last paragraph or the first paragraph, I try to write a long, long . . . *much* too long sentence. When I was teaching, I made a list of other authors who did this, too, and lots do. They always seem to me to be the particularly beautiful parts of a story.

I just read one by Louise Erdrich, "Disaster Stamps of Pluto," in the *New Yorker* (December 13, 2004): "So why, when I stroke my sister's valentine against the side of my face, and why, when I touch the folded linen of her vest, and when I reach for my brothers' overalls and the apron my mother died in that day, and bundle these things to my stomach together with my father's ancient, laundered, hay-smelling clothes, why, when I gather my family into my arms, do I catch my breath at the wild upsurge, as if a wind had lifted me, a black wing of air?"

I think that's gorgeous and that's what I mean by poetry in fiction.

There's one of mine at the end of my short science-fiction story "Acceptance Speech" in my short-story collection *Report to the Men's Club, and Other Stories*: "And that is how I came to be here before you, making accepting gestures, being the six hundred and twelfth poet to become president and here, my friend and servant, still alive—though in his own mind only half so, having lost all but one way of greeting you, and all but one way of showing pleasure—yet, to me alive and singing, the even humbler master, the poet, Uncertainties, and, as I am also, sure of only a few small things."

I think of writing as play, as trying things, as having fun, as taking risks. Language itself seems to me to be odd and funny.

I like to tell my class what musicians say: "Practice doesn't make perfect, practice makes permanent, only perfect practice makes perfect." I tell them, don't just go off, as Hemingway said, and write and write and write. That's one of the first things I tell them. I don't believe in "Just keep writing." I've seen too many worthless novels four hundred pages long from people who did this. I think people should learn their craft on short stories. I've taught long enough to know this is absolutely necessary. There's a lot more to learning to write fiction than most people realize and one should learn it on the shorter forms.

I generally put myself inside a first-person character and my character is almost always an unreliable narrator. I don't want people to believe that I think what they think. Their attitudes are part of their characterization. I never know more than they know. People ask about my stories, did such and such really happen? I always say I only know what the first-person character knows.

The author's mother, Agnes, "laughing as usual" (Photograph courtesy of Carol Emshwiller)

I find, now, that the worst, most anxious times for me are when I'm between stories. (Another reason why I hurry up and start something. Anything!) I always think I'll never have another story idea. I'm anxious in the middle of stories, too, when I get stuck (and I *always* do get stuck) and can't seem to get on with it, but that's not as bad as when I have nothing to work on, nothing to stew over or think about except whether I'll ever write again. Which, those times, I'm sure I won't.

I never considered myself a feminist though I'm always called one. How can I be one when I adore my three brothers and my son? (My son is more of a feminist than I am.) I was frustrated in my marriage but mostly because I was trying to find time to write. Good I've lived this long so as to get something done with everybody gone. But I miss them all.

I'm old, my hearing's not so good, and I've lost one eye to macular degeneration, but I'm still writing almost every day. I'll go on as long as I can still see. I may have to give up my mobile home in California. It's outside of town and I have to be able to drive to live there, and every year I hike less and less and more and more slowly. I'll miss hiking, I'll miss driving, but I'll miss writing most of all.

*   *   *

EMSHWILLER, Carol Fries
See EMSHWILLER, Carol

ESBAUM, Jill

Personal

Born in IA; married; children: two sons, one daughter. *Hobbies and other interests:* Reading, travel, gardening, quilting.

Addresses

Home—Eastern IA. *Agent*—Rosemary Stimola, Stimola Literary Studio, 306 Chase Court, Edgewater, NJ 07020. *E-mail*—jillsbooks@netins.net.

Career

Writer and writing consultant. Has worked as a substitute teacher's aid, 4-H leader, and girls' softball coach; writing instructor and picture-book consultant.

Member

Society of Children's Book Authors and Illustrators.

Awards, Honors

International Reading Association (IRA) Children's Choice selection, 2003, for *I Invited a Dragon to Dinner;* Bank Street College Best Children's Book of the Year designation, Friends of American Writers First-Place Juvenile Book Award, IRA Notable Children's Book selection, and Kansas State Reading Circle recommended title, all 2006, all for *Ste-e-e-eamboat A-Comin'!*

Writings

I Invited a Dragon to Dinner, and Other Poems to Make You Laugh out Loud, Philomel (New York, NY), 2002.
Stink Soup, illustrated by Roger Roth, Farrar, Straus & Giroux (New York, NY), 2004.
Ste-e-e-eamboat A-Comin'!, illustrated by Adam Rex, Farrar, Straus & Giroux (New York, NY), 2005.
Estelle Takes a Bath, illustrated by Mary Newell DePalma, Henry Holt (New York, NY), 2006.

Contributor to periodicals, including *Babybug, Boy's Quest, Cicada, Cricket, Goldfinch, Guideposts for Kids, Highlights for Children, Hopscotch, Humpty Dumpty's, Jack and Jill, Ladybug, Pockets, Spider, Teen,* and *Turtle.*

Sidelights

Still making her home in the rural area of eastern Iowa where she spent her childhood, Jill Esbaum also retains the love of books and reading she enjoyed as a young girl. Recalling the point at which she started including writing in her adult life, Esbaum noted on her home page that the writing impulse "jerked me awake one morning . . . with a funny idea for a kids' book that had me stumbling through the dark house for paper and a pen. . . . Once I blew the dust off my imagination and began making up stories, I felt strangely happy, as though I'd been gone a long time and had finally come home." Esbaum's books for children include *Stink Soup,* the critically praised *Ste-e-e-eamboat A-Comin'!,* and *Estelle Takes a Bath.*

Esbaum's debut children's book, *Stink Soup,* kicks off with brother and sister Willie and Annabelle on their way to spend the week with their grandmother. Annabelle, the oldest, has been asked to keep an eye on the rambunctious Willie, but this proves to be an impossible task; while the girl helps her grandmother throughout the day, Willie spends his time terrorizing the local farm animals and engaging in typical little-boy mischief. The boy meets his match, however, when he tangles with a skunk and suffers the unpleasant consequences. "Whether fond of tomatoes or not, kids will find this a flavorsome romp," commented a *Publishers Weekly* critic. Carolyn Janssen, writing in *School Library Journal,* cited Roger Roth's "breezy cartoon style" illustrations and added that "independent readers will enjoy this humorous story on their own." In *Kirkus Reviews* a critic exclaimed that the book's "realistic illustrations salt-and-pepper" Esbaum's "saucy tale with wry humor, comeuppance, and down-home flavor."

Ste-e-e-eamboat A-Comin'! takes its setting and inspiration from the childhood of nineteenth-century humorist Mark Twain, and brings to life the excitement generated by the arrival of a paddlewheel steamboat in a small town. Featuring a rhyming text, the book serves as "a rhythmic, emphatic evocation of a scene from days gone by," according to a *Kirkus Reviews* critic, while in *School Library Journal* Nancy Menaldi-Scanlan predicted that Esbaum's "salute to a bygone transportation era is sure to engage children." In *Estelle Takes a Bath* Estelle has been looking forward to a long, relaxing bath, but a when curious mouse suddenly appears tub-side, attracted by the girl's peppermint-scented bubble bath, pandemonium follows. "Prepare for a bunch of rowdy story-timers as they giggle over the never-quite-totally nude Estelle," warned a *Kirkus Reviews* writer.

Biographical and Critical Sources

PERIODICALS

Kirkus Reviews, February 1, 2004, review of *Stink Soup,* p. 132; March 15, 2005, review of *Ste-e-e-eamboat A-Comin'!,* p. 350; September 15, 2006, review of *Estelle Takes a Bath,* p. 952.
Publishers Weekly, March 8, 2004, review of *Stink Soup,* p. 72.
School Library Journal, March, 2004, Carolyn Janssen, review of *Stink Soup,* p. 157; March, 2005, Nancy Menaldi-Scanlan, review of *Ste-e-e-eamboat A-Comin'!,* p. 170.

ONLINE

Cynsations, http://cynthialeitichsmith.blogspot.com/ (October 10, 2006), Cynthia Leitich Smith, interview with Esbaum.
Jill Esbaum Home Page, http://www.jillesbaum.com (October 10, 2006).
Society of Children's Book Writers and Illustrators-Iowa Web site, http://www.kimn.net/scbwi/ (October 10, 2006), "Jill Esbaum."

F-G

FLEISCHER, Jane
    See OPPENHEIM, Joanne

*   *   *

FUNKE, Cornelia 1958-
    (Cornelia Caroline Funke)

Personal

Born December 10, 1958, in Dorsten, Westphalia, Germany; married, 1980; husband's name Rolfe (died, 2006); children: Anna, Ben. *Education:* University of Hamburg, degree (education theory); Hamburg State College of Design (book illustration) *Politics:* German Green Party.

Addresses

Home—Los Angeles, CA. *Agent*—c/o Author Mail, Scholastic, Inc., 557 Broadway, New York, NY 10012.

Career

Children's book author and illustrator. Social worker for three years; freelance illustrator and board game designer; writer, beginning 1994. Has worked for German state television channel ZDF.

Member

Amnesty International.

Awards, Honors

Kalbacher Klapperschlange, 2000, for *Drachenreiter;* Wildweibchenpreis, 2000, for collected works; Vache qui Lit (Venice), and Kalbacher Klapperschlange, both 2001, Preis der Jury der Jungen Leser, 2002, and Corine award, and Evangelischer Buchpreis, both 2003, all for *Herr der Diebe;* Mildred L. Batchelder Award for best translated children's book, and Torchlight Prize,

Cornelia Funke (Photograph courtesy of Ulrich Perrey/Landov)

Askews Library Services, both 2003, both for *The Thief Lord;* Nordstemmer Zuckerrübe, 2004, for *Kleiner Werwolf;* Preis der Jury der Jungen Leser, Phantastik-Preis der Stadt Wetzlar, and Kalbacher Klapperschlange, all 2004, all for *Tintenherz;* Booksense Award, and Children's Literature Book of the Year award, American Booksellers Association, 2004, for *Inkheart;* Booksense Award, 2006, for *Inkspell.*

Writings

CHILDREN'S FICTION

(Self-illustrated) *Monstergeschichten,* Loewe Verlag, 1993.
(Self-illustrated) *Rittergeschichten,* Loewe Verlag, 1994.
(Self-illustrated) *Zwei wilde kleine Hexen,* Cecilie Dressler Verlag (Hamburg, Germany), 1994.

(Self-illustrated) *Kein Keks für Kobolde,* Fischer Verlag (Frankfurt, Germany), 1994.

(Self-illustrated) *Hinter verzauberten Fenstern: eine geheimnisvolle Adventsgeschichte,* Fischer (Frankfurt, Germany), 1995.

(Self-illustrated) *Greta und Eule, Hundesitter,* Cecilie Dressler Verlag (Hamburg, Germany), 1995.

(Self-illustrated) *Der Mondscheindrache,* Loewe Verlag, 1996.

(Self-illustrated) *Hände weg von Mississippi,* Cecilie Dressler Verlag (Hamburg, Germany), 1997.

Prinzessin Isabella, illustrated by Kerstin Meyer, Friedrich Oetinger, 1997.

(Self-illustrated) *Das verzauberte Klassenzimmer,* Loewe Verlag, 1997.

(Self-illustrated) *Tiergeschichten,* Loewe Verlag, 1997.

(Self-illustrated) *Drachenreiter,* Cecelie Dressler Verlag (Hamburg, Germany), 1997, translated by Anthea Bell as *Dragon Rider,* Scholastic (New York, NY), 2004.

Dachbodengeschichten, illustrated by Wilfried Gebhard, Loewe Verlag, 1998.

(Self-illustrated) *Igraine Ohnefurcht,* Cecilie Dressler Verlag (Hamburg, Germany), 1998.

Dicke Freundinnen, illustrated by Daniela Kulot, Friedrich Oetinger, 1998, translated by Oliver G. Latsch as *Best Girl Friends,* 2003.

Kleiner Werwolf, Fischer (Frankfurt, Germany), 1999.

Das Piratenschwein, illustrated by Kerstin Meyer, Cecelie Dressler Verlag (Hamburg, Germany), 1999.

Strandgeschichten, illustrated by Karin Schliehe and Bernhard Mark, Loewe Verlag 1999.

(Self-illustrated) *Herr der Diebe,* Cecelie Dressler Verlag (Hamburg, Germany), 2000, translated by Oliver G. Latsch as *The Thief Lord,* Chicken House/Scholastic (New York, NY), 2002.

Der verlorene Wackelzahn, illustrated by Julia Kaergel, Friedrich Oetinger, 2000.

(Self-illustrated) *Mick und Mo im Wilden Westen,* Friedrich Oetinger, 2000, translated by Oliver G. Lasche as *Mick and Mo in the Wild West,* 2002.

Der geheimnisvolle Ritter Namenlos, illustrated by Kerstin Meyer, Fischer (Frankfurt, Germany), 2001, translated as *Princess Knight,* Chicken House/Scholastic (New York, NY), 2004.

Dicke Freundinnen und der Pferdedieb, illustrated by Daniela Kulot, Friedrich Oetinger, 2001, translated by Oliver G. Latsch as *Best Girl Friends and the Horse Thief,* 2005.

Als der Weihnachtsmann vom Himmel fiel, illustrated by Regina Kehn, Cecilie Dressler Verlag (Hamburg, Germany), 2001, translated by Oliver G. Latsch as *When Santa Fell to Earth,* illustrated by Paul Howard, Chicken House (New York, NY), 2006.

Emma und der Blaue Dschinn, illustrated by Kerstin Meyer, Cecilie Dressler (Hamburg, Germany), 2002.

(Self-illustrated) *Die schönsten Erstlesegeschichten,* Fischer (Frankfurt, Germany), 2002.

(Self-illustrated) *Tintenherz,* Cecelie Dressler Verlag (Hamburg, Germany), 2003, translated by Anthea Bell as *Inkheart,* Chicken House/Scholastic (New York, NY), 2003.

Die Glücksfee, illustrated by Sybille Hein, Fischer (Frankfurt, Germany), 2003.

Kápten Knitterbart und seine Bande, illustrated by Kerstin Meyer, Friedrich Oetinger, 2003.

(Self-illustrated) *Kribbel Krabbel Käferwetter,* Fischer (Frankfurt, Germany), 2003.

(Self-illustrated) *Vorlesegeschichten von Anna,* Heinrich Ellermann, 2003.

(Self-illustrated) *Lilli und Flosse,* Cecilie Dressler Verlag (Hamburg, Germany), 2004.

(Self-illustrated) *Potilla,* Cecilie Dressler Verlag (Hamburg, Germany), 2004.

Mick und Mo im Weltraum, illustrated by Tina Schulte, Friedrich Oetinger 2004.

Der wildeste Bruder der Welt, illustrated by Kerstin Meyer, Friedrich Oetinger, 2004, translated by Chantal Wright as *The Wildest Brother,* Scholastic (New York, NY), 2006.

Pirate Girl, illustrated by Kerstin Meyer, Scholastic (New York, NY), 2005.

Rosannas großer Bruder, illustrated by Jacky Gleich, Friedrich Oetinger, 2005.

(Self-illustrated) *Zottelkralle,* Cecilie Dressler Verlag (Hamburg, Germany), 2005.

(Self-illustrated) *Tintenblut,* Cecelie Dressler Verlag (Hamburg, Germany), 2005, translated by Anthea Bell as *Inkspell,* Chicken House/Scholastic (New York, NY), 2006.

Kápten Knitterbart auf der Schatzinsel, Friedrich Oetinger, 2006.

Princess Pigsty, illustrated by Kerstin Meyer, translated by Chantal Wright, Chicken House (New York, NY), 2007.

"GHOSTHUNTERS" SERIES; SELF-ILLUSTRATED FICTION

Gespernsterjäger auf eisiger spur, Loewe Verlag, 2001, translated by Helena Ragg as *Ghosthuters and the Incredibly Revolting Ghost,* Scholastic (New York, NY), 2006.

Gespernsterjäger im Feuerspuk, Loewe Verlag, 2001, translated by Helena Ragg as *Ghosthuters and the Gruesome, Invincible Lightning Ghost,* Scholastic (New York, NY), 2006.

Gespernsterjäger in der Gruselburg, Loewe Verlag, 2001, translated by Helena Ragg as *Ghosthunters and the Totally Mouldy Baroness,* Scholastic (New York, NY), 2007.

Gespernsterjäger in großer Gefahr, Loewe Verlag, 2001, translated by Helena Ragg as *Ghosthunters and the Muddy Monster of Doom,* Scholastic (New York, NY), 2007.

"WILDEN HÜHNER" SERIES; SELF-ILLUSTRATED FICTION

Die wilden Hühner, Cecilie Dressler Verlag (Hamburg, Germany), 1993.

Die wilden Hühner auf Klassenfahrt, Cecilie Dressler Verlag (Hamburg, Germany), 1996.

Die wilden Hühner: Fuchsalarm, Cecilie Dressler Verlag (Hamburg, Germany), 1998.

Die wilden Hühner un das Glück der Erde, Cecilie Dressler Verlag (Hamburg, Germany), 2000.

Die wilden Hühner: das Bandenbuch zum Mitmachen, Cecilie Dressler Verlag (Hamburg, Germany), 2001.

Die wilden Hühner und die Liebe, Cecilie Dressler Verlag (Hamburg, Germany), 2003.

Adaptations

The Thief Lord was adapted for audio (five cassettes), read by Simon Jones, Listening Library, 2002, and was adapted and directed by Richard Claus as a feature film, Warner Bros., 2006. *Tintenherz* was adapted as a musical play produced in Bonn, Germany, 2006; *Tintenblut* was adapted as a play produced in Hannover, Germany, 2006. The "Wilden Hüner in Liebe" series (translation means "Wild Chicks in Love") was adapted as a German-language film, directed by Vivian Naefe, 2006, and as audio books. *Inkheart* was adapted for a film starring Brendan Fraser, Helen Mirren, and Jim Broadbent, and produced by New Line Cinema, forthcoming, 2008. *Inkheart* and *Inkspell* were adapted as audio books read by Fraser, Listening Library, 2005. *Dragon Rider* was adapted as an audiobook, read by Fraser, and has been optioned for film.

Work in Progress

Inkdawn, 2007.

Sidelights

English-speaking readers would never have discovered the fantasy fiction of Cornelia Funke if it had not been for one particularly devoted reader. A young fan in Funke's native Germany was prompted to write to English-based publisher Chicken House when she discovered that she could not read her favorite books in English as well as in German. This letter inspired curiosity in the publisher, and a little research revealed Funke to be one of the most popular children's book writers in all of Germany. Orchestrating the translation of Funke's then-current children's book, *Herr der Diebe,* into English (by the author's cousin, because no one else would undertake it), Chicken House had a bestseller on its hands with 2002's *The Thief Lord.* The book won Funke even more English-language fans when it was released in the United States by Scholastic. In the years since, the author's popularity among English-language readers has been further enhanced by the films that have been made from her books *The Thief Lord* and *Inkheart,* and in 2005 she and her family left her native Hamburg, Germany, to make the United States her new home.

When *The Thief Lord* was first published in England, it sold out in ten days, and in the United States it reached number two on the *New York Times* children's bestseller list. The book was edited by Barry Cunningham, the man who recognized British author J.K. Rowling's talent and published Rowling's "Harry Potter" series in England. *Inkheart,* Funke's 2002 novel, was also suc-

cessful in translation, and other books that have made the move into English include *Inkheart*'s sequel, *Inkspell,* and several of Funke's books for younger readers: *Dragon Rider, The Wildest Brother,* and *The Princess Knight.* By 2005 Funke had published over three dozen books, which were published in twenty-eight countries. Appraising her work in *Time,* Clive Barker wrote that, refreshingly free of "mawkishness or attendant melodrama," Funke's books gain added depth due to "her moody, unpredictable characters and the distinctive feel of her plots."

Although Funke was educated as a social worker, after graduating from the University of Hamburg she put herself through a program in book illustration while working with underprivileged children during the day. She began an illustration career designing board games and book art, but at first had no plans to become a children's author. Exposed to the books being written for children while working as an illustrator, Funke grew frustrated with the lack of imaginative storytelling, and in the mid-1990s she saw her first book published in her native Germany. Funke's books—which are based on meticulous research and feature children stepping into magical worlds, paired with her engaging illustrations—quickly became popular.

The Thief Lord is about orphan brothers Prosper, aged twelve, and five-year-old Boniface (Bo), who run away when their childless aunt and uncle decide that they only want Bo to live with them in their house in Hamburg. Before she died, the boys' mother had told the siblings about the wonders of Venice, Italy, and that is where the fugitives now flee. Unfortunately, the boys' relatives are angered at Bo's departure and hire relentless private investigator Victor Getz to follow the children's trail. Hiding in an abandoned movie theater, they live among other street children, their hideout fitted with blankets and mattresses, and full of kittens to be petted and comic books and paperbacks to be read. Among their urchin comrades is twelve-year-old Scipio—the Thief Lord of the title—who steals from the rich to support this band of pickpockets and petty thieves. Other friends include a girl named Hornet, who *New York Times Book Review* contributor Rebecca Pepper Sinkler described as "a Wendy for the twenty-first century" because "she rides herd on the lost boys but doesn't do their laundry." While Scipio usually deals in jewels, when he accepts a job to steal a broken wooden wing from a carved lion, the children realize that the heist involves more than it at first appears. In fact, the lion is part of a magic carousel that has the power to change children into adults and adults into children. Photographer Ida Spavento, who owns the wing, agrees to give it up as long as Scipio and his band keep her posted on their search for the merry-go-round. Meanwhile, P.I. Getz finds himself drawn to the plight of Prosper and Bo and their new friends.

Praising *The Thief Lord* as a "spellbinding story," a *Kirkus Reviews* contributor wrote that "the magical city

Cover of Funke's **Inkheart,** *featuring artwork by Carol Lawson.* (Scholastic, 2005. Cover illustration copyright © 2003 by Carol Lawson. Reprinted by permission of Scholastic Inc)

of Venice, with its moonlit waters, maze of canals, and magnificent palaces, is an excellent setting." Anita L. Burkam wrote in *Horn Book* that *The Thief Lord* has a "sweet and comforting conclusion that will satisfy readers whose hearts have been touched" by the characters. *School Library Journal* critic John Peters called the book "a compelling tale, rich in ingenious twists, with a setting and cast that will linger in readers' memories," while Sinkler maintained that "what lifts this radiant novel beyond run-of-the-mill fantasy is its palpable respect for both the struggle to grow up and the mixed blessings of growing old."

In London's *Guardian Unlimited,* online contributor Diana Wynne Jones called Funke's next English-language translation, *Inkheart,* "a book about books, a celebration of and a warning about books" that "conveys so well the joys, terrors, and pitfalls of reading." The first part of a trilogy, *Inkheart* revolves around twelve-year-old Meggie, whose bookbinder father, Mo, has a special gift that has almost become a curse. Whenever Mo reads aloud, the characters from the book he is reading are pulled into the real world, while real-world people are pulled into the characters' fictional world. Almost a decade earlier problems arose when Mo read Fenoglio's

Inkheart; the characters that were released included the evil Capricorn, while Meggie's mother disappeared into the book. Now, nine years have past and a much older Meggie learns Mo's secret, which explains why her father never read to her while she was growing up. Mo's secret also explains the complexity of the chain of events that begin to unwind after Meggie meets a scarred stranger named Dustfinger. Calling Mo Silvertongue, Dustfinger warns the bookseller that Capricorn's evil henchmen are on his trail. They hope to force Mo to read a monster out of the troublemaking book, then direct the creature to kill Capricorn's enemies. Together with Dustfinger, Meggie, Mo, and Meggie's great-aunt Elinor set off to find Fenoglio, hoping that he can write a new ending to the story that now threatens their lives.

Each chapter of *Inkheart* begins with a quotation from a classic children's book, such as Kenneth Grahame's *The Wind in the Willows,* J.M. Barrie's *Peter Pan,* and J.R.R. Tolkien's *The Hobbit.* and as Jones noted, these quotes suggest the "rich sample of the books that lie behind" the novel. *School Library Journal* reviewer Sharon Rawlins wrote that Funke's "'story within a story' will delight not just fantasy fans, but all readers who like an exciting plot with larger-than-life characters," while in *Kirkus Reviews* a contributor praised *Inkheart* as "a true feast for anyone who has ever been lost in a book."

As *Inkspell,* the sequel to *Inkheart,* opens, Meggie is serving as Dustfinger's apprentice, joined in that capacity by a boy named Farid. With the aid of a stranger named Orpheus, the three are allowed to travel into the Inkworld, home of Fenoglio and the only place where the evil caused by Capricorn can be written out of *Inkheart.* Orpheus, possessing the same talent as Meggie's father, also reads several other characters back into the book, allowing Meggie and Mo to rejoin Meggie's long-lost mother. As events unfold, wars, intrigues, and other threats mask Funke's underlying question: "what might happen if authors try to change the world they have created," as Beth L. Meister phrased it in a *School Library Journal* review. In further explanation of Funke's complex premise, *Horn Book* Claire E. Gross dubbed the book a "bibliophilic fantasy" that "pits the power of words against the power of death." Noting the long list of "clearly drawn" characters that people the epic fantasy, Meister praised *Inkspell* as an "involving" novel that will leave fans eager for the sequel, *Inkdawn,* while in *Booklist* Carolyn Phelan called *Inkspell* "a stronger book than its predecessor.

In *Dragon Rider,* which Funke published in the original German in 1997, she transports readers to the wilds of Scotland, where Earth's last silver dragons live. When their secluded home is finally threatened by humans, a young dragon named Firedrake and a taciturn brownie named Sorrel set out to locate the ancient home of the silver dragons, a place located in the Himalayan mountains. On their journey to the Rim of Heaven, Firedrake and Sorrel are joined by an orphaned boy

Cover of Funke's **Dragon Rider,** *featuring artwork by Don Seegmiller.*
(Scholastic, 2004. Cover illustration copyright © 2004 by Don Seegmiller. Reprinted by permission of Scholastic Inc)

named Ben and Twigleg, a golem-like creature who is under the sway of the silver dragon's arch enemy, Nettlebrand. The journey, overshadowed by Nettlebrand's sinister machinations, involves encounters with a host of mythic creatures, including djinni, elves, basilisks, roc, sea serpents, and dwarves, and reveals the laws that underlie dragon magic. "Readers will delight in the creatures that turn up in this extended quest," wrote a *Publishers Weekly* contributor in a review of *Dragon Rider,* the critic going on to praise Funke's "lively" protagonists "and their often hilarious banter." Noting that the novel is extremely popular among the author's German fans, *Booklist* writer Jennifer Mattson compared the book to the novels of Lloyd Alexander and praised its "good, old-fashioned ensemble-cast quest." While a *Kirkus Reviews* writer praised the story's "breakneck pace," Mattson maintained that, in relation to *The Thief Lord,* the book's "gentler, lighter, and more straightforward" plot will make *Dragon Rider* a "winner" among middle-grade readers.

In addition to epic fantasies, Funke has authored a number of illustrated books for younger readers, many featuring Funke's own artwork and several a collaboration between the writer and German illustrator Kerstin Meyer. In *Pirate Girl* Funke and Meyer pair up to tell the story of an imaginative little girl named Molly, who

is sailing to the home of her grandmother. Forced to engage in such horrid activities as peeling potatoes and swabbing decks after being abducted by Captain Firebeard and his band of bloodthirsty pirates, Molly attempts to escape but gets caught. A walk on the plank is only avoided by one of the most feared pirates of all—a swashbuckler who coincidently looks a great deal like Molly's real mom! Another collaboration, *The Wildest Brother,* introduces Ben, a loving younger brother whose vivid imagination transforms the playful torments he visits on annoyed older sister Anna into battles against a terrible monster.

Meyer's "bright, droll mixed-media pen-and-ink" illustrations add to the humor of *Pirate Girl,* according to a *Kirkus Reviews* writer, while her "color-soaked cartoons" in *The Wildest Brother* "are bursting with a zany energy," according to *School Library Journal* contributor Susan Weitz. The story of "personal cleverness and parental heroism" Funke tells in *Pirate Girl* is one with "universal appeal," in the opinion of *Booklist* contributor Mattson, and a *Publishers Weekly* critic wrote that the "exploration of the relationship between a real-world sister and brother" in *The Wildest Brother* yields "rip-roaring results."

Biographical and Critical Sources

PERIODICALS

Booklist, October 15, 2002, GraceAnne A. DeCandido, review of *The Thief Lord,* p. 401; September 1, 2003, Carolyn Phelan, review of *Inkheart,* p. 114; August, 2004, Jennifer Mattson, review of *Dragon Rider,* p. 1924; June 1, 2005, Jennifer Mattson, review of *Pirate Girl,* p. 1821; October 1, 2005, Carolyn Phelan, review of *Inkspell,* p. 52.

Bookseller, June 20, 2003, review of *Inkheart,* p. 32.

Horn Book, November-December, 2002, Anita L. Burkam, review of *The Thief Lord,* pp. 754-755; September-October, 2004, Anita L. Burkam, review of *Dragon Rider,* p. 583; July-August, 2005, Kitty Flynn, review of *Pirate Girl,* p. 449; January-February, 2006, Claire E. Gross, review of *Inkspell,* p. 78.

Journal of Adolescent and Adult Literacy, September, 2003, Jean Boreen, review of *The Thief Lord,* pp. 91-93.

Kirkus Reviews, August 1, 2002, review of *The Thief Lord,* pp. 1128-1129; September 15, 2003, review of *Inkheart,* p. 1174; July 15, 2004, review of *Dragon Rider,* p. 685; June 1, 2005, review of *Pirate Girl,* p. 636; September 1, 2005, review of *Inkspell,* p. 973; April 15, 2006, review of *The Wildest Brother,* p. 406.

Language Arts, January, 2003, Junko Yokota, review of *The Thief Lord,* p. 236.

New York Times Book Review, November 17, 2002, Rebecca Pepper Sinkler, review of *The Thief Lord,* p. 1.

Publishers Weekly, June 24, 2002, review of *The Thief Lord,* pp. 57-58; July 21, 2003, review of *Inkheart,* p. 196; July 19, 2004, review of *Dragon Rider,* p. 162; May 1, 2006, review of *The Wildest Brother,* p. 63.

School Library Journal, October, 2002, John Peters, review of *The Thief Lord,* pp. 163-164; October, 2003, Sharon Rawlins, review of *Inkheart,* p. 164; October, 2004, Beth Wright, review of *Dragon Rider,* p. 164; August, 2005, Grace Oliff, review of *Pirate Girl,* p. 94; October, 2005, Beth L. Meister, review of *Inkspell,* p. 161; June, 2006, Susan Weitz, review of *The Wildest Brother,* p. 112.

Time, April 18, 2005, Clive Barker, "The Next J.K. Rowling?," p. 120.

ONLINE

Cornelia Funke Official Web site, http://www.corneliafunkefans.com (October 10, 2006).

Guardian Unlimited, http://www.guardian.co.uk/ (June 22, 2002), Jan Mark, review of *The Thief Lord;* (November 22, 2003) Diana Wynne Jones, review of *Inkheart.*

Scholastic Web site, http://www.scholastic.com/ (November 4, 2006), "Cornelia Funke."*

*   *   *

FUNKE, Cornelia Caroline
See FUNKE, Cornelia

*   *   *

GARDINER, John Reynolds 1944-2006

OBITUARY NOTICE— See index for *SATA* sketch: Born December 6, 1944, in Los Angeles, CA; died of complications from necrotizing pancreatitis, March 4, 2006, in Anaheim, CA. Engineer and author. An engineer by trade, Gardiner was the author of *Stone Fox,* a children's novel now considered to be a modern classic. Interestingly, as a child and young man he possessed poor writing and reading skills, and although he was creative, his teachers did not encourage his writing desires because of his bad spelling and grammar. Consequently, he disdained literature and did not even read a novel until age nineteen. Instead, he studied engineering at the University of California at Los Angeles, where he earned a B.S. in 1966 and an M.S. in 1968. After college, he worked as a contract engineer for aerospace companies in Los Angeles and specialized in thermal engineering. His writing career began after his brother suggested he take a script-writing class. He did so, and though his scripts were never produced, on the suggestion of his teacher he turned one of them into a book. This became *Stone Fox* (1980), a critically acclaimed novel that sold over three million copies and, ironically, was turned back into a script as a 1987 television movie. Gardiner, who wrote in his spare time when he was not doing his engineering work, published only two more juvenile titles: *Top Secret* (1985) and *General Butterfingers* (1986). These were well received by reviewers, but were not nearly as popular as his debut. He was also the author of the nonfiction titles *How to Write a Story That's Not Boring* and the self-published *How to Live a Life That's Not Boring.*

OBITUARIES AND OTHER SOURCES:

PERIODICALS

Chicago Tribune, March 17, 2006, section 3, p. 7.
Los Angeles Times, March 16, 2006, p. B9.
New York Times, March 19, 2006, p. A29.
Washington Post, March 21, 2006, p. B6.

*   *   *

GIACOBBE, Beppe 1953-

Personal

Born 1953, in Italy; married; children: one son. *Education:* Academy of Fine Arts (Milan, Italy), graduate (classical studies); School of Visual Arts (New York, NY), graduate.

Addresses

Home—Milan, Italy. *Agent*—c/o Author Mail, Hyperion Books, 77 W. 66th St., 11th Fl., New York, NY 10023. *E-mail*—b.giacobbe@beppegiacobbe.com.

Career

Illustrator. Artist and illustrator for publishers, including Rizzoli, and corporations, including United Airlines. European Institute of Design, teacher. *Exhibitions:* Work exhibited at galleries, including Galleria Affiche, Milan, Italy, 1998-89; Galleria Viago di Budapest, 1996; Galleria Hyperion, Turin, Italy, 1999; Castle Belgioioso, 2001, and others.

Awards, Honors

Prize of the Art Director, Italian Club, 1989; 3-D Illustration Award (Southampton), 1994; American Illustration Award shortlist, Society of Illustrators, 2003; Original Art Show Award shortlist, 2003.

Illustrator

Paul Fleischman, *Big Talk: Poems for Four Voices,* Candlewick Press (Cambridge, MA), 2000.
Susan Campbell Bartoletti, *Nobody's Nosier than a Cat,* Hyperion Books for Children (New York, NY), 2003.
Susan Campbell Bartoletti, *Nobody's Diggier than a Dog,* Hyperion Books for Children (New York, NY), 2005.

Illustrator of books published by Rizolli and other Italian publishers.

Biographical and Critical Sources

PERIODICALS

Booklist, November 1, 2003, Abby Nolan, review of *Nobody's Nosier than a Cat,* p. 499; January 1, 2005, Jennifer Mattson, review of *Nobody's Diggier than a Dog,* p. 86.

Horn Book, May, 2000, review of *Big Talk: Poems for Four Voices,* p. 326.

Kirkus Reviews, September 15, 2003, review of *Nobody's Nosier than a Cat,* p. 1171; January 15, 2005, review of *Nobody's Diggier than a Dog,* p. 116.

Publishers Weekly, February 28, 2000, review of *Big Talk,* p. 81; February 7, 2, 2005, review of *Nobody's Diggier than a Dog,* p. 58.

School Library Journal, December, 2003, Grace Oliff, review of *Nobody's Nosier than a Cat,* p. 103; February, 2005, Sally R. Dow, review of *Nobody's Diggier than a Dog,* p. 94.

ONLINE

Beppe Giacobbe Home Page, http://www.beppegiacobbe.com (October 10, 2006).

San Pellegrino Web site, http://www.sanpellegrino.it/ (October 10, 2006), profile of Giacobbe.*

*　　*　　*

GILLEY, Jeremy 1969-

Personal

Born 1969, in Southampton, England.

Addresses

Home—England. *Office*—Peace One Day, Block D, The Old Truman Brewery, 91 Brick Lane, London E1 6QL, England. *E-mail*—web@peaceoneday.org.

Career

Actor, documentary filmmaker, and peace campaigner. Royal Shakespeare Company, Stratford-on-Avon, England, former stage actor; actor for television, including *Alias Smith and Jones* (series), 1985, *Feasting with Panthers* (series), 1989, *The Storyteller: Greek Myths* (miniseries), 1990, *My Name's Sergeant Bergerac* (miniseries), 1990, and *Ultraviolet* (miniseries), 1998. Director and producer of documentary films, including *Where the Red Wind Blows,* 1999, and *Peace One Day,* 2004.

Writings

(And director) *Peace One Day* (documentary film), BBC Films, 2004.

Peace One Day: How September 21 Became World Peace Day (picture book), illustrated by Karen Lessen, Putnam (New York, NY), 2005.

Sidelights

Jeremy Gilley, a British actor whose credits included roles with the Royal Shakespeare Company, changed the course of his life while trying to help change the course of the world. Leaving acting behind in 1999, he dedicated the next few years to establishing one day out of each year where no warring would take place on Earth. As Gilley explained in an interview for *BBB Storyville* online: "The millennium was coming, this big moment that everyone was talking about, so I wanted to record something about the world and why we're not living peacefully. I was thinking about whether the United Nations could really unite the world and the more I thought about it the more I realized that there was no international day of peace." With this inspiration, Gilley spent three years working with international leaders, and in 2001 his efforts resulted in a U.N. resolution fixing September 21 of each year as World Peace Day.

Born in Southampton, England, in 1969, Gilley spent his early years struggling with dyslexia, and left school with one low-grade exam pass in pottery. Determined to make his mark, he enrolled in acting class and joined the Royal Shakespeare Company at age seventeen. After a decade working in theatre, film, and television, in 1994 Gilley began making his own films. Focusing his lens on a world in turmoil, Gilley launched the film project Peace One Day in 1999, hoping to document his efforts to establish an annual day of global ceasefire and non-violence.

Gilley expected that his ambitions to establish a day of world peace would fail; in actuality, he expected to make an interesting film about the world's unwillingness to unite. He traveled the world for two years, building the case on film for an annual Peace Day. As an outgrowth of these efforts, he produced both a documentary film and a picture book that recount his successful quest: On September 7, 2001, the member states of the United Nations unanimously adopted an annual day of global ceasefire and nonviolence on the U.N. International Day of Peace. The award-winning film *Peace One Day* has been screened in dozens of international film festivals, inspiring individuals around the world.

Illustrated with Karen Blessen's collage art, *Peace One Day: How September 21 Became World Peace Day* chronicles Gilley's journey and includes the remarks of world leaders such as the Dalai Lama, South African leader Nelson Mandela, and then-U.N. Secretary General Kofi Annan. Featuring images of children during wartime, along with penciled portraits of world peace leaders, the book also contains Gilley's account of his quest. "The combination of text and illustrations demonstrates the message that 'everyone can make a difference,'" commented Margaret R. Tassia in *School Library Journal, Booklist* critic Hazel Rochman called *Peace One Day* a "handsome picture book" in which "the passionate prose and stirring images how and tell that each person can make a difference."

Ironically, the date that the bell was successfully rung at the United Nations, cementing Gilley's hard-fought resolution, was September 11, 2001, the same day radical Islamic terrorists attacked the United States and provoked a lengthy war. "I think it makes it all the more poignant," Gilley remarked in his *BBC Storyville* interview. "This is why we've got to come together. We've got to stand together as one."

Biographical and Critical Sources

PERIODICALS

Booklist, October 1, 2005, Hazel Rochman, review of *Peace One Day: How September 21 Became World Peace Day,* p. 51.
Bulletin of the Center for Children's Books, November 2005, Karen Bush, review of *Peace One Day,* p. 1361.
Kirkus Reviews, July 1, 2005, review of *Peace One Day,* p. 735.
School Library Journal, September, 2005, Margaret R. Tassia, review of *Peace One Day: The Making of World Peace Day,* p. 222.
Time for Kids, September 16, 2005, "Spotlight: Jeremy Gilley," p. 8.
Vanity Fair, October, 2003, David Friend, "Vanity Fair Nominates Jeremy Gilley."

ONLINE

Adelaide Film Festival Web site, http://2005. adelaidefilmfestival.org/ (October 10, 2006), "Peace One Day."
BBC Storyville, http://www.bbc.co.uk/ (October 10, 2006), Nick Fraser, "Peace One Day."
Peace One Day Web site, http://www.peaceoneday.org/ (October 10, 2006).
Times Online, http://www.timesonline.co.uk/ (September 7, 2006), Mary Ann Sieghart, "You May Say He's a Dreamer."

*   *   *

GONZALEZ, Julie 1958-

Personal

Born 1958.

Addresses

Home—Pensacola, FL. *Agent*—c/o Author Mail, Random House Trade, 1745 Broadway, New York, NY 10019.

Career

Novelist.

Writings

Wings, Delacorte Press (New York, NY), 2005.
Ricochet, Delacorte Press (New York, NY), 2007.

Sidelights

Florida resident Julie Gonzalez made her publishing debut with the young-adult novel *Wings,* a myth-based tale that focuses on a teen's search for identity. Ever since his birth, teenager Ben Delaney—who prefers to be called Icarus—has been convinced that he is destined, at some point in his life, to grow wings and gain the ability to fly. Ben's story is told from alternating perspectives: both Ben and his older brother, Ian, deal with both opportunities and setbacks as they occur. Ben's personal determination to fulfill his dream grows strong with every year that passes, and his will drives him to jump off increasingly tall platforms as a way of challenging his limitations.

Gonzalez's "writing is clean and crisp, the chapters short," commented a *Kirkus Reviews* critic, who noted the mounting "sense of foreboding and danger" in

Cover of Julie Gonzalez's 2005 young-adult novel Wings, *featuring artwork by Michael Morgenstern.* (Delacorte Press, 2005. Jacket illustration copyright © by Michael Morgenstern. Used by permission of Random House Children's Books, a division of Random House, Inc)

Wings. Reviewer Cindy Welch commented in *Booklist* on the plot's many levels, writing that "Ben's fight against gravity and his study of natural history add a nice subtext, and the evolving relationship between the brothers is as absorbing as the wait for wings." Jeffrey Hastings, writing in *School Library Journal* enjoyed Gonzalez's debut novel, commenting that *Wings* "is a book that seems to improve slightly with each chapter; the dialogue becomes more natural, the characters more palpable." Dubbing the book a "promising first effort," Hastings added that "Gonzalez is ready to take off as a fine YA author."

Biographical and Critical Sources

PERIODICALS

Booklist, March 15, 2005, Cindy Welch, review of *Wings,* p. 1284.

Kliatt, March, 2005, Myrna Marler, review of *Wings,* p. 10.

Kirkus Reviews, March 1, 2005, review of *Wings,* p. 286.

School Library Journal, August, 2005, Jeffrey Hastings, review of *Wings,* p. 126.

Voice of Youth Advocates, April, 2005, Jan Chapman, review of *Wings,* p. 55.

ONLINE

Random House Web site, http://www.randomhouse.com/ (October 10, 2006).*

*   *   *

GRIMES, Nikki 1950-
(Naomi McMillan)

Personal

Born October 20, 1950, in New York, NY; daughter of James (a violinist) and Bernice (a keypunch operator; maiden name, McMillan) Grimes; children: Tawfiqa (daughter; deceased). *Education:* Rutgers University, B.A., 1974. *Religion:* Christian. *Hobbies and other interests:* Knitting, reading, long walks, talking with friends, cooking, playing word games.

Addresses

Home—Corona, CA. *Agent*—Elizabeth Harding, Curtis Brown, Ltd., 10 Astor Pl., New York, NY 10013. *E-mail*—nikkiwords@nikkigrimes.com.

Career

Writer. Blackafrica Promotions, Inc., New York, NY, talent coordinator, 1970-71; Rutgers University, New Brunswick, NJ, instructor in writing and applied sociol-

Nikki Grimes (Photograph by Joelle P. Adkins. Reproduced by permission)

inguistics at Livingston College, 1972-74; Harlem Teams for Self-Help, New York, NY, documentary photographer, 1975-76; WBAI-FM Radio, New York, NY, scriptwriter and producer of *The Kid Show,* 1977-78; Riksradio, Sweden, scriptwriter and producer, 1979-80; AB Exportsprak Translators, Sweden, proofreader and translator, 1980-84; freelance writer and editor, 1984-89; Walt Disney Co., Burbank, CA, writer and editor, 1989-91; freelance writer, 1991—. University of California, Los Angeles, library assistant, 1986-88; Swedish/English translator of computer systems manuals. Lecturer at colleges, universities, and workshops, including Pratt Institute, City University of New York, Studio Museum of Harlem, University of Massachusetts, and New York University; consultant to Swedish Educational Radio and New York's Cultural Council Foundation.

Member

Society of Children's Book Writers and Illustrators, PEN Center U.S.A. West, Authors Guild, Children's Literature Council.

Awards, Honors

Ford Foundation grant for research in Tanzania, 1974-75; Best Books of the Year selection, Child Study Association, and Children's Book of the Year Award, Bank Street College of Education, both for *Growin';* Books for Free Children citation, *Ms.* magazine, Children's

Book citation, Library of Congress, Best Books of the Year designation, *Philadelphia Inquirer,* and Best Books of the Season designation, *Saturday Review,* all 1978, and Notable Books citation, American Library Association (ALA), 1978-79, all for *Something on My Mind;* NAACP Image Award finalist, 1992, for *Malcolm X: A Force for Change;* Benjamin Franklin Picture Book Award, 1993, for *From a Child's Heart;* Coretta Scott King Honor Book Award, ALA, Tennessee Volunteer State Book Award nominee, Notable Books citation, ALA, and 100 Titles for Reading and Sharing includee, New York Public Library, all 1994, all for *Meet Danitra Brown;* Notable Books citation, ALA, 1997, for *Come Sunday;* Coretta Scott King Honor Book Award, Bank Street College of Education Book of the Year designation, New York Public Library Book for the Teen Age designation, and South Carolina Young-Adult Book Award, all 1998, all for *Jazmin's Notebook;* Bank Street College Children's Book of the Year, 1998, for *A Dime a Dozen;* Bank Street College Children's Book of the Year designation, Marion Vannett Ridgway Award, *Booklist* Editors' Choice, and *Riverbank Review* Children's Books of Distinction finalist, all 1999, all for *My Man Blue;* Parents Choice Award, 1999, for *Aneesa Lee and the Weaver's Gift,* and 2000, for *Is It Far to Zanzibar?;* Bank Street College Best Book of the Year designation, 2000, for *Shoe Magic* Bank Street College Best Book of the Year designation, and CCBC Choice, 2002, both for *A Pocketful of Poems;* Bank Street College Best Book of the Year designation, and Notable Social Studies Trade Book designation, both 2001, both for *Stepping out with Grandma Mac;* ATB Best Children's Book honor, 2002, for *When Daddy Prays;* Society of Illustrators Silver Medal, 2002, for *Under the Christmas Tree,* illustrated by Kadir Nelson; New York Public Library Book for the Teen Age designation, and Charlotte Young Adult Award nomination, both 2002, and Coretta Scott King Author Award, 2003, all for *Bronx Masquerade;* Coretta Scott King Honor Book, ALA Notable Book designation, and *Horn Book* Fanfare title, all 2003, all for *Talkin' about Bessie;* Award for Excellence in Poetry for Children, National Council of Teachers of English (NCTE), 2006; NCTE Notable Book in the Language Arts designation, and New York Public Library Book for the Teen Age designation, both 2005, and Coretta Scott King Honor Book, 2006, all for *Dark Sons; Booklist* Editors' Choice, 2006, for *The Road to Paris.*

Writings

FOR YOUNG PEOPLE

Growin' (novel), illustrated by Charles Lilly, Dial (New York, NY), 1977.

Something on My Mind (poems), illustrated by Tom Feelings, Dial (New York, NY), 1978.

Oh, Bother! Someone's Baby-Sitting!, illustrated by Sue DiCicco, Western Publishing (Racine, WI), 1991.

Oh, Bother! Someone's Fighting, illustrated by Darrell Baker, Western Publishing (Racine, WI), 1991.

Malcolm X: A Force for Change, Fawcett Columbine (New York, NY), 1992.

Minnie's New Friend, illustrated by Peter Emslie and Darren Hunt, Western Publishing (Racine, WI), 1992.

(Adapter) *Walt Disney's Pinocchio,* illustrated by Phil Ortiz and Diana Wakeman, Western Publishing (Racine, WI), 1992.

From a Child's Heart (poems), illustrated by Brenda Joysmith, Just Us Books (East Orange, NJ), 1993.

(Reteller) *Cinderella,* illustrated by Don Williams and Jim Story, Western Publishing (Racine, WI), 1993.

C Is for City, illustrated by Pat Cummings, Lothrop, Lee & Shepard (New York, NY), 1995.

Come Sunday, illustrated by Michael Bryant, Eerdmans (Grand Rapids, MI), 1996.

Wild, Wild Hair, illustrated by George Ford, Scholastic (New York, NY), 1996.

It's Raining Laughter (poems), photographs by Myles Pinkney, Dial (New York, NY), 1997.

Someone's Fighting, Golden Books (New York, NY), 1997.

Jazmin's Notebook, Dial (New York, NY), 1998.

A Dime a Dozen, Dial (New York, NY), 1998.

Hopscotch Love: A Family Treasury of Love Poems, Lothrop, Lee & Shepard (New York, NY), 1999.

At Break of Day, illustrated by Jan Spivey Gilchrist, Eerdmans (Grand Rapids, MI), 1999.

My Man Blue (poems), illustrated by Jerome Lagarrigue, Dial (New York, NY), 1999.

Aneesa Lee and the Weaver's Gift, illustrated by Ashley Bryan, Lothrop, Lee & Shepard (New York, NY), 1999.

When Daddy Prays, Eerdmans (Grand Rapids, MI), 2000.

Stepping out with Grandma Mac, Simon & Schuster (New York, NY), 2000.

Shoe Magic, illustrated by Terry Widener, Orchard Books (New York, NY), 2000.

A Pocketful of Poems, illustrated by Javaka Steptoe, Clarion Books (New York, NY), 2000.

Is It Far to Zanzibar? (poems), illustrated by Betsy Lewin, Lothrop, Lee & Shepard (New York, NY), 2000.

Bronx Masquerade, Dial (New York, NY), 2002.

Under the Tree: Poems of Christmas, illustrated by Kadir Nelson, HarperCollins (New York, NY), 2002.

Talkin' about Bessie: The Story of Aviator Elizabeth Coleman, Orchard Books (New York, NY), 2002.

What Is Goodbye?, Jump at the Sun (New York, NY), 2004.

Tai Chi Morning: Snapshots of China, illustrated by Ed Young, Cricket (Chicago, IL), 2004.

A Day with Daddy, illustrated by Nicole Tadgell, Scholastic (New York, NY), 2004.

Dark Sons, Jump at the Sun (New York, NY), 2005.

At Jerusalem's Gate: Poems of Easter, illustrated by David Frampton, Eerdmans (Grand Rapids, MI), 2005.

Thanks a Million, illustrated by Cozbi A. Cabrera, Greenwillow (New York, NY), 2006.

Welcome, Precious, illustrated by Bryan Collier, Orchard (New York, NY), 2006.

The Road to Paris, Putnam (New York, NY), 2006.

Voices of Christmas, Zonderkidz (Grand Rapids, MI), 2007.

When Gorilla Goes Walking, Orchard Books (New York, NY), 2007.

Oh, Brother!, illustrated by Mike Benny, Greenwillow (New York, NY), 2008.

Also author of books based on Walt Disney characters, including *Mickey Mouse Tales* and *The Little Mermaid*, published by Running Press (Philadelphia, PA); *Disney Babies Bedtime Stories; The Viking's Eye* and *Sky Island*, both in the "Mickey Mouse Adventures" series; *My Favorite Book* and *The Great Castle Contest*, in the "Minnie 'n' Me" series; *Fast Friends, Eeyore's Tail Tale*, and *Rabbit Marks the Spot*, in the "Winnie the Pooh Twin" series; *Her Chance to Dream*, in the "Tale Spin" series; and *Fake Me to Your Leader* and *Catteries Not Included*, in the "Rescue Rangers" series.

"DANITRA BROWN" SERIES; FOR YOUNG PEOPLE

Meet Danitra Brown (poems), illustrated by Floyd Cooper, Lothrop, Lee & Shepard (New York, NY), 1994.

Danitra Brown Leaves Town (poems), illustrated by Floyd Cooper, HarperCollins (New York, NY), 2002.

Danitra Brown, Class Clown, illustrated by E.B. Lewis, HarperCollins (New York, NY) 2005.

UNDER PSEUDONYM NAOMI McMILLAN

Wish You Were Here, illustrated by Vaccaro Associates, Disney Press (New York, NY), 1991.

(Reteller) *Cinderella*, McClanahan (New York, NY), 1995.

(Reteller) *Jack and the Beanstalk*, McClanahan (New York, NY), 1995.

"GOLDEN BOOKS" BOARD BOOKS; UNDER PSEUDONYM NAOMI McMILLAN

Baby's Colors, illustrated by Keaf Holliday, Western Publishing (Racine, WI), 1995.

Baby's Bedtime, illustrated by Sylvia Walker, Western Publishing (Racine, WI), 1995.

Busy Baby, illustrated by Anna Rich, Western Publishing (Racine, WI), 1996.

FOR ADULTS

Poems By, CB Broadside Publications, 1970.

Portrait of Mary (historical novel), Harcourt (San Diego, CA), 1994.

Work represented in anthologies, including *Night Comes Softly*, edited by Nikki Giovanni; *Necessary Noise, Hold Christmas in Your Heart, Daddy Poems, Stone Bench in an Empty Park, On the Wings of Peace, Pass it On, In Praise of Our Mothers and Fathers*, and *The Twentieth-Century Children's Poetry Treasury*. Theater and arts critic, *New York Amsterdam News*, 1975-76. Contributor to periodicals, including *Essence, Today's Christian Woman, National Forum, Calalloo, Greenfield Review, Obsidian, Vision, Black World, Time Capsule*, and *Sunday Woman*. Contributing editor, *Unique NY*, 1977-78.

Work in Progress

Mary, Mary, a novel.

Sidelights

A poet, novelist, and the author of picture books, Nikki Grimes manages to reach a range of audiences with her works—from very young children, to middle-grade readers, to older teens and adults. The recipient of numerous honors, including two Coretta Scott King Honor Book citations, Grimes once noted: "The word, both written and spoken, has always held a special fascination for me. It seemed uncanny that words, spread across a page just so, had the power to transport me to another time or place. But they could. I spent many hours ensconced in the local library, reading—nay, devouring—book after book after book. Books were my soul's delight. Even so, in one sense, the stories I read betrayed me. Too few gave me back my mirror image. Fewer still spoke to, or acknowledged, the existence of the problems I faced as a black foster child from a dysfunctional and badly broken home. I couldn't articulate it then, but I sensed a need for validation which the books I read did not supply. 'When I grow up,' I thought, 'I'll write books about children who look and feel like me.'"

Whether writing poetry or fiction, Grimes has succeeded in creating works featuring young African-American characters with whom children and young adults can identify. Drawing upon scenes from her own experiences growing up in Harlem, she is noted for successfully conveying the black experience as well as universal themes such as friendship, tolerance, family and community relationships, and children surviving adolescence. Despite a difficult childhood, her stories are characterized by optimism and warmth, a fact that has made volumes such as her multi-award-winning novel *Bronx Masquerade* required reading in middle-grade and high-school classrooms throughout the United States. "A fantastic choice for readers' theater," according to *Booklist* critic Gillian Engberg," *Bronx Masquerade* focuses on Tyrone Bittings, an inner city teen who discovers his writers' voice and inspires his high-school classmates to express themselves through poetry. As *Horn Book* contributor Susan P. Bloom wrote: "In shared pain and need," each of the book's teen protagonists "become poets; as readers, we want to believe their individual poetic gifts, even as we hear Grimes's considerable talent behind theirs."

"I was moved around a lot as a child," Grimes once explained, "always having to adjust to new neighborhoods, new schools, new faces. The most difficult aspect of my constant uprooting was struggling to make new friends, leaving them behind, moving to a new neighborhood, and starting the whole process over again. Yet I had no choice, but I both needed and wanted friends. The fact that each friendship was bound to be short-lived only made it the more precious to me. It is little wonder that friendship is a theme to which I return again and again. *Growin',* my first book for children, had friendship as its primary focus."

Featuring a poetry-writing African-American fifth grader named Yolanda who is nicknamed Pump (for Pumpkin), *Growin'* recounts the child's troubles as she tries to adjust to her father's death, the resultant move to a strange neighborhood, and ongoing friction with her mother. Pump, however, makes friends with the bully at her new school after they discover mutual artistic interests and find themselves aligned against their peers and school authorities. A *Kirkus Reviews* critic commended the book's "black ghetto setting and conspicuously non-sexist relationship," while Zena Sutherland, in the *Bulletin of the Center for Children's Books,* praised Grimes for her competent writing style and warm story. Although reviewers concurred that characters could have been more fully developed, they cited the story's heartening tale, ample adventure, and believable resolution to conflict.

The subject of friendship is revisited in the poetry collections *Something on My Mind* and *From a Child's Heart.* About the first book, Jeanne McLain Harms and Lucille J. Lettow, writing in *School Library Journal,* described the pairing of illustrator Tom Feelings' black-and-white sketches and Grimes' free-verse responses to black children's urban experiences as "simple, eloquent, and in tune." A *Publishers Weekly* reviewer observed that "the artist and lyricist couldn't reveal the thoughts of the boys and girls portrayed here more acutely if they were inside their subjects' skins." *School Library Journal* contributor Ruth M. McConnell further noted that reflections are not only of the African-American experience but "the universal marking-time, growing pains, and perplexities of youth in poignant, funny, and sad ways." *From a Child's Heart,* described by a *Kirkus Reviews* contributor as comprised of "thirteen subtly cadenced, accessible poems [written] in an authentically childlike voice," contains "a modicum of rhyme, a conscious if informal sense of innocence, and more than a little sentimentality," according to Betsy Hearne in the *Bulletin of the Center for Children's Books.*

"The subject [of friendship] is most squarely dealt with in *Meet Danitra Brown,* an ode to friendship if ever there was one!" Grimes continued. In this collection of thirteen poems, narrator Zuri talks about herself and her admiration for her good friend Danitra Brown. Cyrisse Jaffee, writing in the *Women's Review of Books,* summarized the collection as an "affectionate portrait of friendship and individuality" and lauded Grimes' language as "filled with energy and rhythm" which lent it-

self to reading aloud. In *School Library Journal,* Barbara Osborne Williams concluded that the book provides a glimpse of "touching moments of friendship with universal appeal." Although Hearne, writing in the *Bulletin of the Center for Children's Books,* expressed concern that readers might be put off by such an effusive display of admiration, she pointed out that for those uncomfortable with more formal poetry, "this book will prove a satisfying introduction and sturdy friend." In addition, a reviewer for *Publishers Weekly* noted that "issues of race, feminism and family structure are delicately incorporated" in Grimes' work.

A popular and likeable character, Danitra Brown also stars in two follow-up stories told in verse. In *Danitra Brown, Class Clown* Zuri is having trouble dealing with a new teacher after the woman separates her from friend Danitra in class. Despite this, Danitra does her best to help Zuri study, distract the class when Zuri makes a mistake, and an all-around good friend. "Danitra is as feisty, loyal, and adventurous as always," wrote a contributor to *Kirkus Reviews,* while Mary Elam noted in *School Library Journal* that "Grimes's text . . . neatly voices the critical self-examination of preadolescent girls."

Grimes' *Come Sunday* is a collection of fourteen poems about LaTasha, a vivacious little girl who loves to attend the community church, Paradise Baptist. As Elizabeth Bush pointed out in the *Bulletin of the Center for Children's Books,* included are "just the details children find fascinating about Sunday rituals," as well as a "sensitive look at a child's spirituality." A *Kirkus Reviews* critic lauded the "suite of pitch-perfect poems" and concluded: "Whatever their religious background, readers will smile at the jubilation." Similarly, a *Publishers Weekly* commentator summarized *Come Sunday* as "reverent, funny and wildly energetic all at the same time."

Grimes comes by her urban insights quite naturally. "Born in Harlem, I have since lived in every borough of New York City save Staten Island. Consequently, cityscapes form the backdrop of most of my writing." This is most evident in her *C Is for City,* where the delights of city life are described in alliteration, rhythm, and rhyme from A to Z. *Booklist* reviewer Julie Yates Walton called the book a "hustling, bustling, urban ABC book" that city children will surely "identify with."

Jazmin's Notebook is the story of an African-American teenager living with her sister in a small Harlem apartment. Set during the late 1960s, Grimes' middle-grade novel describes the difficult life of young Jazmin and the way in which the girl is able to find strength and meaning by writing poetry and keeping a journal of her life. *Booklist* critic Hazel Rochman called Jazmin's journal entries and occasional poems "funny, tender, angry, and tough." Through the course of these writings, the reader comes to know a teen who has spunk and is

It's Raining Laughter

❖ by Nikki Grimes ❖
Photographs by Myles C. Pinkney

Cover of Grimes' poetry collection It's Raining Laughter, ***featuring photographs by Myles C. Pinkney.*** (Boyds Mills Press, 1997. Photographs copyright © 1997 by Myles C. Pinkney. Reproduced by permission)

resourceful. Bounced around from one foster home and relative to the next, Jazmin finally finds a home with her older sister. Picked on at school for her thick glasses, she nonetheless maintains her A average and

discounts the bad advice of her counselor, who tries to talk her out of pursuing academics. "Many teens will relate to Jazmin, whether she is talking about the power of religion, friendship, or laughter, or about her attraction to a luscious guy," Rochman wrote. "Readers will be drawn into Jazmin's neighborhood," observed a reviewer for *Publishers Weekly,* the critic going on to call the teen an "articulate, admirable heroine . . . [who] leaps over life's hurdles with agility and integrity."

Much of Grimes' middle-grade fiction is told through poetry. In *What Is Goodbye?* she presents multiple viewpoints by featuring the voices of two siblings mourning their older brother. Jesse expresses anger at being abandoned by his older brother, while his sister Jerilyn handles her grief on her own. "Insightfully and concisely, Grimes . . . traces the stages of grief and healing," wrote a *Publishers Weekly* critic of the book. A *Kirkus Reviews* contributor also noted how effectively Grimes handled the feeling of loss in her poetry, writing that the author "addresses many areas of the grief process, often in a poignant fashion." Gillian Engberg commented in *Booklist* that, "moving and wise, these are poems that beautifully capture a family's heartache." *School Library Journal* contributor Nina Lindsay deemed *What Is Goodbye?* "a prime example of how poetry and story can be combined to extend one another."

Dark Sons shares the same dual-narrator poetry technique to tell a story, but the two narrators in this case are separated by thousands of years. Modern-day Samuel is angry at his father for remarrying and having a new son, while Ishmael of the Bible rails at his father Abraham for not loving him as much as Isaac. Both narrators rely on their faith to move them through their troubles; Samuel eventually learns to love his father's new family, while Ishmael is sent into the wilderness with his mother, trusting that God will provide where Abraham could not. A *Kirkus Reviews* contributor felt that the "strength of the poetry" combined with the dominance of the faith theme "distinguishes and illuminates" the book. As Hazel Rochman wrote in *Booklist,* "the elemental connections of hope . . . will speak to a wide audience." The faith element does not detract readers without a religious background, according to *School Library Journal* contributor Patricia D. Lothrop. "Even faith-challenged readers can admire and learn from these stories of struggle in vernacular verse."

Other titles by Grimes are told in straight prose, including her middle-grade novel *The Road to Paris.* Paris, a nine-year-old biracial girl, lives in a white community

One of Grimes' most popular characters stars in **Danitra Brown, Class Clown,** *featuring illustrations by award-winning artist E.B. Lewis.* (HarperCollins Publishers, Amistad, 2005. Illustrations copyright © 2005 by E.B. Lewis. Used by permission of HarperCollins Publishers)

In Dark Sons *Grimes weaves together the parallel lives of two very different sons confronting similar feelings of betrayal.* (© Steve Kaufman/ Corbis; © Nicholas DeVore/Getty Images; © Richard Berenholtz/Corbis; © Rick Gomez/ Corbis)

and struggles against the racism that is dominant in her neighborhood. Her closest friend is her brother Malcolm, with whom she runs away from an abusive foster home. Between Malcolm and her strong faith in God, Paris struggles to form a family, despite the odds against her. Rochman considered the novel to be "a beautiful story of family, friendship, and faith."

Grimes has also written biographies for young readers, introducing them to notable African Americans in history. *Talkin' about Bessie: The Story of Aviator Elizabeth Coleman* takes readers to 1920s Chicago and celebrates the life of the first African-American woman aviator. Set at the scene of her funeral, Bessie Coleman's history is told through memories of the people in her life: friends, family, and those who she inspired. "Teller by teller, the story moves chronologically and builds emotionally to the last entry," wrote *Booklist* contributor Carolyn Phelan. Lynda Jones, writing in *Black Issues Book Review,* praised the biography as "a rich and loving account of one young woman's desire to follow her dream."

Along with biographies, Grimes has written picture books with an international focus. "I inherited my fa-

ther's passion for travel," Grimes once told *SATA,* "and have been to such places as China, Russia, Austria, Trinidad, and Tanzania, where I spent one year. My longest sojourn was in Sweden, where I lived for six years. In fact, I have Sweden to thank for my favorite hobby: knitting." *Tai Chi Morning: Snapshots of China,* for example, focuses on Grimes' voyage to China, where she was part of an artists' tour that performed, read, and taught while traveling through that vast Asian nation. The text, a collection of poems, forms a travelogue of Grimes' experiences abroad and "opens up possibilities for history, culture, and poetry classes for middle graders," as a *Kirkus Reviews* contributor explained. In *Booklist,* Rochman wrote that the book portrays "the truth of the tourist experience, engaged but outside," while Allison Follos noted in *School Library Journal* that Grimes' "evocative poetry" serves a "a perfect choice to demonstrate journal writing."

Grimes ventures to the exotic world of Tanzania in creating *Is It Far to Zanzibar?,* a collection of "rhyming, sing-song verse" at once both "light and playful," as Rochman commented in *Booklist.* Here Grimes tells of children picking coffee or being chased by a lion, presenting, as Rochman further noted, "an outsider's view of a Tanzania where everyone's having fun." Writing in the *New York Times Book Review,* Julie Yates Walton commented that during Grimes' long career in prose and poetry, she has demonstrated a "breathtaking range in tone and style," and in her introduction to Tanzania she "offers a lively peek at the great big world."

It is in poetry that Grimes most writes, telling autobiographical verse stories as well as tales of the city, families, and relationships. She mines her own past in the verse collection *A Dime a Dozen* by presenting scenes from her childhood: playing hopscotch with her big-footed father, and detailing the prickly relations between her father and mother that ultimately ended in divorce. "Free-flowing and very accessible, the poetry may inspire readers to distill their own life experiences into precise, imaginative words and phrases," suggested Susan Dove Lempke in a *Booklist* review of the collection. The twenty-two poems included in *Hopscotch Love: A Family Treasury of Love Poems* are short and "upbeat," according to Rochman, while *My Man Blue* tells a more-poignant story in fourteen "knowing, heartfelt poems," as a *Publishers Weekly* contributor described. Here the reader learns of the friendship between a fatherless African-American boy named Damon and Blue, a rough-looking character who lost his own son to the streets. Together, the two shoot hoops and make outings to the park, and slowly learn to trust one another. Rochman, reviewing *My Man Blue* for *Booklist,* deemed it a "great picture book for older readers."

More poetry is served up in *Aneesa Lee and the Weaver's Gift,* a collection of thirteen short, interlocking poems that "skillfully uses the metaphor of weaving to explore the world of a talented girl," according to a contributor for *Publishers Weekly.* These poems describe the art of weaving, from gathering the materials to making dyes to spinning yarn, preparing the loom, and patterning a tapestry. Aneesa Lee, the weaver, is herself a woman of black, white, and Japanese heritages, and her weaving is, for her, a way of connecting with her larger community. "For adult weavers, the book will be a treasure," wrote the *Publishers Weekly* reviewer, "and for children, it serves as a glimpse into the intricacies not only of weaving, but the patterns of daily life."

With *Shoe Magic* Grimes again employs metaphor to look at life, this time using children's shoes as a window to their wearer's lives. "This collection clearly celebrates its child readers," wrote Kathleen Whalin in a *School Library Journal* review, while *Booklist* critic Engberg predicted that young poets "will find inspiration" in the verse collection. Similarly, in *A Pocketful of Poems* "Grimes boils poetry down to its essence," creating a "picture book homage to words," according to a reviewer for *Publishers Weekly.* "There is so much vibrant energy and freshness in this collaboration," exclaimed *Booklist* critic GraceAnne A. DeCandido, the critic adding that *A Pocketful of Poems* "will dance into the hearts of children right away." Lauralyn Persson, reviewing the same title in *School Library Journal,* found it to be a "playful and thoroughly successful pairing of words and pictures."

Although Grimes writes for children first and foremost, she has not limited herself to juvenile literature, but also writes books for older readers and magazine articles for a general audience. In the young-adult biography *Malcolm X: A Force for Change,* for example, Grimes examines the contributions and dreams of the renowned Black Muslim leader, while the novel *Portrait of Mary* presents a fictionalized version of the life of the mother of Jesus. "Passages from the Gospels punctuate the text and serve to give it a homogenized storyline," stated a critic for *Kirkus Reviews* of the latter work, while in the *Los Angeles Times Book Review* Susan Salter Reynolds cited the details Grimes interjects into her prose as injecting "life into the story" and allowing readers to "picture Mary's daily life and her hopes and fears for her son." "Grimes' Mary is a fully realized character," observed Ilene Cooper in *Booklist,* calling the novel "a compelling narrative."

Of her passions and hobbies, Grimes once told *SATA:* "I like to read, of course, go on long walks, talk with friends, cook, and play word games. But most of all," added the prolific author, "I love to write!"

Biographical and Critical Sources

BOOKS

Children's Literature Review, Volume 42, Thomson Gale (Detroit, MI), 1997, pp. 88-95.

St. James Guide to Children's Writers, 5th edition, St. James Press (Detroit, MI), 1999.

PERIODICALS

Black Issues Book Review, January-February, 2003, Lynda Jones, review of *Talkin' about Bessie: The Story of Aviator Elizabeth Coleman,* p. 65; September-October, 2004, Elise Virginia Ward, review of *What Is Goodbye?,* p. 59.

Booklist, July 15, 1978, pp. 1732-1733; February 15, 1994, p. 1085; September 15, 1994, Ilene Cooper, review of *Portrait of Mary,* p. 114; October 1, 1995, Julie Yates Walton, review of *C Is for City,* p. 322; October 1, 1997, p. 334; September 15, 1998, Hazel Rochman, review of *Jazmin's Notebook,* p. 228; December 1, 1998, Susan Dove Lempke, review of *A Dime a Dozen,* p. 664; January 1, 1999, p. 782; February 15, 1999, Hazel Rochman, review of *Hopscotch Love: A Family Treasury of Love Poems,* p. 1064; October 1, 1999, p. 374; October 15, 1999, Hazel Rochman, review of *My Man Blue,* p. 42; January 1, 2000, p. 821; March 15, 2000, Hazel Rochman, review of *Is It Far to Zanzibar?,* p. 1381; September 15, 2000, Gillian Engberg, review of *Shoe Magic,* p. 234; February 15, 2001, GraceAnne A. DeCandido, review of *A Pocketful of Poems,* p. 1154; April 1, 2001, p. 1473; May 15, 2001, p. 1750; February 15, 2002, Gillian Engberg, review of *Bronx Masquerade,* p. 1024, and Hazel Rochman, review of *Danitra Brown Leaves Town,* p. 1033; November 15, 2002, Carolyn Phelan, review of *Talkin' about Bessie,* p. 602; January 1, 2003, review of *Talkin' about Bessie,* p. 796; March 1, 2004, Hazel Rochman, review of *Tai Chi Morning: Snapshots of China,* p. 1186; May 1, 2004, Gillian Engberg, review of *What Is Goodbye?,* p. 1558; February 15, 2005, John Green, review of *At Jerusalem's Gate: Poems of Easter,* p. 1076; August, 2005, Hazel Rochman, review of *Dark Sons,* p. 2022, and *Danitra Brown, Class Clown,* p. 2038; March 15, 2006, Jennifer Mattson, review of *Thanks a Million,* p. 48; August 1, 2006, Hazel Rochman, review of *The Road to Paris;* September 1, 2006, review of *Welcome, Precious,* p. 136.

Bulletin of the Center for Children's Books, April, 1978, Zena Sutherland, review of *Growin',* p. 127; October, 1978, p. 30; February, 1994, Betsy Hearne, review of *Something on My Mind,* p. 188; July-August, 1994, Betsy Hearne, review of *Meet Danitra Brown,* p. 357; March, 1997, Elizabeth Bush, review of *Come Sunday,* pp. 248-249; January, 1998, p. 161.

Childhood Education, winter, 2002, Jonnette Zsolnay, review of *C Is for City,* p. 108.

Ebony, September, 2006, review of *Welcome Precious,* p. 31.

Five Owls, September-October, 1994, p. 14.

Horn Book, July-August, 1994, p. 467; November-December, Jennifer M. Brabander, review of *Dark Sons,* p. 730; March-April, 2006, "Coretta Scott King Author Award," p. 235.

Kirkus Reviews, December, 1977, review of *Growin',* p. 1266; July 15, 1978, p. 747; October 15, 1993, review of *From a Child's Heart,* p. 1329; July 15, 1994, review of *Portrait of Mary,* p. 935; July 1, 1996, review of *Come Sunday,* p. 822; October 15, 1998, p. 1532; October 1, 1999, p. 1580; November 15, 1999, p. 1809; March-April, 2002, Susan P. Bloom, review of *Bronx Masquerade,* p. 231; January 1, 2004, review of *Tai Chi Morning,* p. 36; April 1, 2004, review of *What Is Goodbye?,* p. 330; January 1, 2005, review of *At Jerusalem's Gate,* p. 52; June 15, 2005, review of *Danitra Brown, Class Clown,* p. 683; August 1, 2005, review of *Dark Sons,* p. 848; February 15, 2006, review of *Thanks a Million,* p. 183; August 15, 2006, review of *Welcome, Precious,* p. 84; September 1, 2006, review of *The Road to Paris,* p. 904.

Language Arts, September, 2003, Lester L. Laminack, review of *Talkin' about Bessie,* p. 78.

Los Angeles Times Book Review, September 11, 1994, Susan Salter Reynolds, review of *Portrait of Mary,* p. 6; April 8, 2001, p. 6.

New York Times Book Review, June 4, 2000, Julie Yates Walton, review of *Is It Far to Zanzibar?,* p. 449; November 19, 2000, p. 32.

Publishers Weekly, November 14, 1977, p. 67; May 29, 1978, review of *Something on My Mind,* p. 51; January 4, 1993, p. 74; October 18, 1993, p. 73; April 11, 1994, review of *Meet Danitra Brown,* p. 65; April 8, 1996, review of *Come Sunday,* p. 63; June 29, 1998, review of *Jazmin's Notebook,* p. 60; May 17, 1999, review of *My Man Blue,* p. 79; November 8, 1999, review of *Aneesa Lee and the Weaver's Gift,* p. 67; November 29, 1999, p. 69; January 17, 2000, p. 58; January 15, 2001, review of *A Pocketful of Poems,* p. 76; May 21, 2001, p. 109; December 17, 2001, review of *Bronx Masquerade,* p. 92; March 8, 2004, review of *What Is Goodbye?,* p. 74; October 31, 2005, review of *Dark Sons,* p. 58.

School Library Journal, December, 1977, p. 49; September, 1978, Ruth M. McConnell, review of *Something on My Mind,* p. 137; January, 1987, Jeanne McLain Harms and Lucille J. Lettow, "The Cupboard Is Bare: The Need to Expand Poetry Collections"; August, 1993, p. 196; December, 1993, p. 104; May, 1994, Barbara Osborne Williams, review of *Meet Danitra Brown,* p. 322; November, 1995, p. 71; June, 1997, p. 107; December, 1997, p. 90; July, 1998, p. 95; January, 1999, p. 142; May, 1999, p. 107; December, 1999, p. 119; January, 2000, p. 121; May, 2000, p. 161; October, 2000, Kathleen Whalin, review of *Shoe Magic,* p. 148; May, 2001, Lauralyn Persson, review of *A Pocketful of Poems,* p. 141; July, 2001, p. 124; January, 2002, Lynn Evarts, review of *Bronx Masquerade,* p. 132; February, 2002, Catherine Threadgill, review of *Danitra Brown Leaves Town,* p. 101; May, 2004, Alison Follos, review of *Tai Chi Morning,* p. 168; June, 2004, Nina Lindsay, review of *What Is Goodbye?,* p. 166; November, 2004, Alison Follos, review of *Bronx Masquerade,* p. 67; February, 2005, Catherine Callegari, review of *A Day with Daddy,* p. 97; March, 2005, Sally R. Dow, review of *At Jerusalem's Gate,* p. 228; April, 2005, review of *What Is Goodbye?,* p. S56; September, 2005, Mary Elam, review of *Danitra Brown, Class Clown,* p. 171; November, 2005, Patricia D. Lothrop, review of *Dark Sons,* p. 135; March, 2006, Mary N. Oluonye, review of *Thanks a Million,* p. 208.

Teacher Librarian, November, 1998, p. 45.

Voice of Youth Advocates, October, 1998, p. 274.

Women's Review of Books, November, 1994, Cyrisse Jaffee, "A World of Words," pp. 31-32.

ONLINE

Library of Congress Bookfest, http://www.loc.gov/bookfest/2003/ (November 3, 2006), "Nikki Grimes."

Nikki Grimes Home Page, http://www.nikkigrimes.com (November 3, 2006).

H

HARPER, Jamie

Personal

Married; children: Grace, Lucy, Georgia Rose. *Education:* Attended Massachusetts College of Art.

Addresses

Home—Weston, MA. *Agent*—c/o Candlewick Press, 2067 Massachusetts Ave., Cambridge, MA 02140. *E-mail*—jharper109@gmail.com.

Career

Illustrator. Formerly worked as a pastry chef and in business.

Writings

SELF-ILLUSTRATED PICTURE BOOKS

Don't Grown-ups Ever Have Fun?, Little, Brown (New York, NY), 2003.
Me Too!, Little, Brown (New York, NY), 2005.
Miss Mingo and the First Day of School, Candlewick (Cambridge, MA), 2006.

ILLUSTRATOR

Sally Warner, *Not-so-Weird Emma,* Viking (New York, NY), 2005.
Sally Warner, *Only Emma,* Viking (New York, NY), 2005.
Sally Warner, *Super Emma,* Viking (New York, NY), 2006.

Contributor of illustrations to periodicals, including *Click* and *American Girl.*

Sidelights

Jamie Harper got her first illustration job working for *Click* magazine in 2001. Two years later, her first picture book, *Don't Grown-ups Ever Have Fun?,* was published. Drawing heavily on the experiences of her own children, Harper writes and illustrates picture books about sibling rivalry, parents, and other topics that concern very young readers. Along with her self-illustrated titles, Harper has also illustrated three chapter books written by Sally Warner. The stories star Emma, an eight-year-old science-lover, and follow the girl's adventures at school.

In *Don't Grown-ups Ever Have Fun?* three siblings try to bring a little fun into their parents' lives. Through their efforts they help their dad avoid "boring" television programs like the news and give their mom a home-made spa holiday that features beautification ingredients such as "diaper goo." Despite the chaotic efforts of the children, the patient parents in *Don't Grown-ups Ever Have Fun?* ultimately have fun with their children. "This high-spirited romp will elicit both giggles and groans of recognition," wrote Kathleen Kelly MacMillan in *School Library Journal.* A *Publishers Weekly* critic cited the book for containing "laughs for everyone," and *Booklist* contributor Diane Foote noted that Harper's "scratchy, hyperactive art puts a cheerful face on chaos." According to a *Kirkus Reviews* contributor, the author/illustrator "lets the pictures tell the story here, with text kept at a comfortable minimum."

Based on the relationship of Harper's own daughters, *Me Too!* focuses on Grace, whose little sister Lucy tries to copy everything Grace does. It is not until Grace realizes that she also has someone she admires and tries to imitate that she begins to understand Lucy's perspective. "With its compassionate ending," *Me Too!* "is a must for any multi-child home," wrote a *Kirkus Reviews* contributor. Judith Constantinides noted in *School Library Journal* that Harper's "humorous ink-and-watercolor cartoons mirror Grace's frustration and Lucy's determination." *Booklist* critic Jennifer Mattson wrote that, "as children giggle, they'll feel reassured by the honest portrayal of . . . [a] sibling relationship,"

Jamie Harper introduces readers to a new feathered friend in her self-illustrated picture book Miss Mingo and the First Day of School. (Candlewick Press, 2006. Copyright © 2006 by Jamie Harper. Reproduced by permission of the publisher Candlewick Press, Inc., Cambridge, MA)

and a *Publishers Weekly* critic concluded that "readers of all ages will find plenty to chuckle about in this tale that touches on both the highs and lows of having a sibling."

Harper's third picture book, *Miss Mingo and the First Day of School,* features animal characters as they begin kindergarten with their flamingo teacher. Miss Mingo asks each student to tell one interesting thing about him-or herself, and the animals in the classroom not only share their own interesting features, but comment on each other. The book combines animal facts with comfort for readers just beginning school, and "young animal enthusiasts won't soon forget these unique students or Miss Mingo's enthusiastic celebration of their diversity," according to a *Publishers Weekly* contributor. A *Kirkus Reviews* critic called the work "a cute combination of animal fact book and a lesson in kindergarten preparedness."

As Harper admitted on her home page, she eats a giant malted milk ball every morning. The reason? "I tell myself it makes me more creative."

Biographical and Critical Sources

PERIODICALS

Booklist, July, 2003, Diane Foote, review of *Don't Grown-ups Ever Have Fun?,* p. 1896; April 1, 2005, Jennifer Mattson, review of *Me Too!,* p. 1366.

Kirkus Reviews, April 1, 2003, review of *Don't Grown-ups Ever Have Fun?,* p. 534; January 15, 2005, review of *Me Too!,* p. 120; June 15, 2006, review of *Miss Mingo and the First Day of School,* p. 634.

Publishers Weekly, February 3, 2003, review of *Don't Grown-ups Ever Have Fun?,* p. 74; April 18, 2005, review of *Me Too!,* p. 61; June 12, 2006, review of *Miss Mingo and the First Day of School,* p. 50.

School Library Journal, April, 2003, Kathleen Kelly Mac-Millan, review of *Don't Grown-ups Ever Have Fun?,* p. 122; February, 2005, Judith Constantinides, review of *Me Too!,* p. 97.

ONLINE

Jamie Harper Home Page, http://www.jamieharper.com (October 5, 2006).

Time Warner Bookmark, http://www.twbookmark.com/ (October 5, 2006), "Jamie Harper."

* * *

HARTINGER, Brent 1964-

Personal

Born 1964, in WA; son of Harold (an attorney) and Mary Anne (a homemaker) Hartinger; partner of Michael Jensen (a writer). *Ethnicity:* "Caucasian." *Education:* Gonzaga University, B.S., 1986. *Politics:* Democrat. *Hobbies and other interests:* Reading, playing computer games, traveling, attending movies and plays.

Addresses

Home—Tacoma, WA. *Agent*—Jennifer DeChiara Literary Agency, 254 Park Ave. S., Ste. 2L, New York, NY 10010. *E-mail*—brentsbrain@harbornet.com.

Career

Freelance writer. Guest columnist, *News Tribune,* Tacoma, WA. Vermont College, Montpelier, writing instructor in M.F.A. Program in Creative Writing for Children and Young Adults. Cofounder of Oasis (support group for gay and lesbian young people).

Member

Society of Children's Book Writers and Illustrators, Dramatists' Guild, Authors Supporting Intellectual Freedom (co-founder).

Awards, Honors

Audience Award, Dayton Playhouse Futurefest Festival of New Plays, and runner-up, Festival of Emerging American Theatre Award, both for *The Starfish Scream;* Popular Paperback selection, American Library Association (ALA), and Books for the Teen Age selection, New York Public Library, both for *Geography Club;* Popular Paperback selection and Quick Pick for Reluctant Readers selection, both ALA, both for *The Last Chance Texaco;* Fort Lauderdale Film Festival Screenwriting-in-the-Sun Award; Judy Blume grant for best young-adult novel, Society of Children's Book Writers and Illustrators; Seattle Arts Commission Tacoma artists initiative grant and Development of a New Work grant; University of Southwestern Louisiana Young-Adult Fiction Prize.

Writings

Geography Club, HarperTempest (New York, NY), 2003.
The Last Chance Texaco, HarperTempest (New York, NY), 2004.

Brent Hartinger (Photograph by Tim Cathersal. Reproduced by permission)

The Order of the Poison Oak, HarperTempest (New York, NY), 2005.
Grand & Humble, HarperTempest (New York, NY), 2006.
Split Screen: Attack of the Soul-Sucking Brain Zombies [and] *Bride of the Soul-Sucking Brain Zombies,* HarperTempest (New York, NY), 2007.

Contributor of over four hundred essays, articles, cartoons, and stories to periodicals, including *Omni, Boys' Life, Plays, Emmy, Seattle Weekly, Genre, San Francisco Bay Guardian, Noise,* and *Advocate.* Also author of plays, including *The Starfish Scream* (for young adults), produced at Dayton Playhouse Futurefest Festival of New Plays; a stage adaptation of *Geography Club,* produced in Seattle, WA; a stage adaptation of *Grand & Humble;* and others.

Work in Progress

"Tales of Slumberia," a series of middle-grade fantasy novels: *Dreamquest,* book 1, forthcoming 2007, and *Brainstorm,* book 2, forthcoming 2008.

Sidelights

Although for over a decade Brent Hartinger had been successfully writing articles, plays, and screenplays, it was not until he had racked up eight unpublished novels, thousands of query letters, and seventeen rejections of his then-current manuscript that his young-adult novel *Geography Club* found a home at HarperCollins in 2001. In this novel, Hartinger tells the story of high school student Russel Middlebrook, who is convinced that he is the only homosexual person in his high school. When Russel discovers differently, he and his new friends form the Geography Club, a secret support group. Unlike other publishers, HarperCollins decided to take a gamble on a book with possibly limited appeal, and the gamble paid off. "At the time, everyone claimed there was no market for a gay teen novel," Hartinger recalled on his home page. "Of course, now that the book has gotten all these great reviews and is selling strongly, all these editors are coming to my agent and [complaining that] . . . she didn't send the manuscript to them!"

Hartinger based his first-person novel on many of his own experiences growing up, and many of the characters also reflect his friends and acquaintances. *Geography Club* "gave me a chance to rewrite my teenage years but give it a little more of a happy ending," he wrote at his home page. Another influence was ancient mythology. "I always saw Russel's journey as epic," he continued. "I think of him as a classic hero who, like Odysseus and so many other Greek and Norse champions, must experience being both prince and outcast before he can claim his rightful 'crown' of true belonging." Despite the serious subject matter—acceptance—Hartinger wanted to employ a light touch, as he told Amanda Laughtland for the Tacoma, Washington *News Tribune.* "I wanted my book to be fun and funny—a fast read. Not broccoli, but dessert."

When it appeared in 2003, *Geography Club* attracted a readership among teens and adults alike, earning good reviews from a number of critics, despite sparking objections from others. For his part, Hartinger told *Publishers Weekly Online* interviewer Kevin Howell that the novel's publisher, "Tempest is known for edgier teen fiction. I was never encouraged to tone anything down. It's not for younger readers but there's not anything that teenagers today would find too threatening."

Several critics commented on the verisimilitude in *Geography Club,* among them *Horn Book* reviewer Roger Sutton, who ranked the work highly among books portraying gay characters and noted that Russel's "agonies of ostracism (and first love) are truly conveyed." A *Publishers Weekly* contributor also commented that the novel "does a fine job of presenting many of the complex realities of gay teen life." Writing in *School Library Journal,* Robert Gray praised Hartinger's characterizations, calling them "excellent" and predicting that teens of all sexual preferences would "find this novel intriguing." Several critics were a little less generous in their appraisals, among them *Booklist* reviewer Hazel Rochman and a *Kirkus Reviews* contributor. Both reviewers cited the novel's plot as flawed, Rochman writing that the plot strands are "settled a little too neatly in the end." Even so, the critic considered Hartinger's first-person narrative voice, dialogue, and portrayal of prejudice accurate. Despite imperfections in the plot,

the *Kirkus Reviews* writer deemed the book "provocative, insightful, and . . . comforting." As Hartinger noted on his home page, "many gay men like to read these books to relive their teenage years."

Hoping to escape his image as the "gay kid," Russel Middlebrook takes a job at a summer camp for childhood burn survivors in *The Order of the Poison Oak,* a sequel to *Geography Club.* Along with friends Gunnar and Min, Russel heads to Camp Serenity, where he takes charge of a group of restless ten year olds. To bond with his charges, he forms the Order of the Poison Oak, a secret group for outsiders of all types. Working past "his initial sense of discomfort around the burn survivors, with their visible scars and disabilities," as *Kliatt* reviewer Kathryn Kulpa noted, "Russel, with his less-obvious scars, gains an understanding of the common ground they occupy." He also finds himself involved in an awkward love triangle with Min and another counselor and comes to rely on the steadying influence of Otto, a burn survivor who now works at the camp. In her review for *Booklist,* Rochman praised Hartinger for spinning an "honest, tender, funny, first-person narrative that brings close what it's like to have a crush and hate a friend," while a *Kirkus Reviews* critic stated that Hartinger "creates a . . . touching and realistic portrait of gay teens."

Hartinger's novel *The Last Chance Texaco* is based on his experiences working as a counselor in a group home for troubled adolescents. The work concerns fifteen-year-old Lucy Pitt, a foster child whose parents were killed in a car accident when Lucy was seven years old. After being shuttled from one foster family to another, Lucy arrives at Kindle Home, an aging mansion known to its residents as "The Last Chance Texaco." Lucy knows that if she fails at Kindle Home, she will be sent to a high-security facility nicknamed Eat-Their-Young Island. Though Lucy's patience is tested early and often by the other teen residents, she finds Kindle Home unlike any other place she has lived and she is determined to stay. After a series of car fires in the neighborhood cast suspicion on the residents of the foster home, Lucy decides to investigate with the help of a new friend. "Hartinger clearly knows the culture, and Lucy speaks movingly (if occasionally too therapeutically) about her anger and grief," observed Rochman. Faith Brautigan, reviewing the novel in *School Library Journal,* similarly noted that "Hartinger excels at giving readers an insider's view of the subculture, with its myriad unspoken rules created by the kids, not the system."

A pair of seventeen-year-old boys from disparate backgrounds are haunted by strange premonitions in *Grand & Humble,* Hartinger's fourth novel. Told in alternating chapters, the work focuses on Harlan, a popular athlete whose father is a U.S. senator, and Manny, a sensitive theater geek whose father works hard to make ends meet. As both teens struggle to make sense of their terrifying nightmares, frequently containing visions connected to the intersection of Grand and Humble streets

Cover of Hartinger's suspenseful novel **Grand & Humble,** *featuring artwork by Dan McCarthy.* (HarperTempest, 2006. Jacket art © 2005 by Dan McCarthy. Used by permission of HarperCollins Publishers)

in their town, they begin to question their pasts and discover that a tragic event that occurred fourteen years earlier will forever link their fates. "Parallels and double meanings abound in this tricky, but satisfying, double narrative," noted a *Kirkus Reviews* critic, while Paula Rohrlick wrote in *Kliatt,* that Hartinger's "taut and clever thriller . . . will appeal to mystery and suspense fans."

Becoming a writer means being an avid reader, Hartinger maintains on his home page. "I read constantly—hundreds of books a year, and several newspapers a day," he noted. "And when I'm not reading, I go to movies and plays, and play computer games," all activities that involve a creative activity. Along with reading widely, Hartinger recommends that writers outline their works-to-be. "I know that while character and beautiful language are important, story is what keeps readers turning the pages. But story is all about structure, and structure almost never just 'happens.'"

"Finally," Hartinger wrote, "don't get discouraged. Because good writing is personal, it's hard not to take rejections personally. But being a sane writer means hav-

ing an ego of granite with a Teflon coating. And being a successful writer means being very, very, very, very persistent."

Biographical and Critical Sources

PERIODICALS

Booklist, April 1, 2003, Hazel Rochman, review of *Geography Club,* p. 1387; January 1, 2004, Hazel Rochman, review of *The Last Chance Texaco,* p. 844; January 1, 2005, Hazel Rochman, review of *The Order of the Poison Oak,* p. 845; January 1, 2006, Hazel Rochman, review of *Grand & Humble,* pp. 83-84.

Childhood Education, winter, 2004, Ann Pohl, review of *The Last Chance Texaco,* p. 107.

Horn Book, March-April, 2003, Roger Sutton, review of *Geography Club,* pp. 209-211.

Kirkus Reviews, December 15, 2002, review of *Geography Club,* p. 1850; March 1, 2004, review of *The Last Chance Texaco,* p. 223; January 15, 2005, review of *The Order of the Poison Oak,* p. 120; December 15, 2005, review of *Grand & Humble,* p. 1322.

Kliatt, March, 2004, Claire Rosser, review of *The Last Chance Texaco,* p. 11; January, 2006, Paula Rohrlick, review of *Grand & Humble,* p. 8; March, 2006, Kathryn Kulpa, review of *The Order of the Poison Oak,* p. 22.

Public Libraries, July-August, 2006, "Geography of a Writer," p. 27.

Publishers Weekly, February 3, 2003, review of *Geography Club,* pp. 76-77; January 26, 2004, review of *The Last Chance Texaco,* p. 255; February 13, 2006, review of *Grand & Humble,* p. 90.

School Library Journal, February, 2003, Robert Gray, review of *Geography Club,* pp. 141-142; March, 2004, Faith Brautigan, review of *The Last Chance Texaco,* pp. 212-213; April, 2005, Hillias J. Martin, review of *The Order of the Poison Oak,* p. 134; February, 2006, Suzanne Gordon, review of *Grand & Humble,* p. 132; April, 2006, Brent Hartinger, Nancy Reeder, and Trev Jones, "Censorship or Information?," pp. 13-14.

Voice of Youth Advocates, February, 2006, Melissa Potter, review of *Grand & Humble,* pp. 485-486.

ONLINE

Brent's Brain: The Brent Hartinger Home Page, http://www.brenthartinger.com (October 15, 2006).

Debbi Michiko Florence Web site, http://debbimichikoflorence.com/ (October 2, 2006), interview with Hartinger.

News Tribune Online (Tacoma, WA), http://www.Tribnet.com/ (March 2, 2003), Amanda Laughtland, "Gay Teen Novel Fills a Void."

Publishers Weekly Online, http://www.publishersweekly.com/ (March 21, 2003), Kevin Howell, "Gay YA Novel, *Geography Club,* Goes to the Head of the Class."

HARTMAN, Rachel 1972-

Personal

Born July 9, 1972, in KY; daughter of an art teacher; married Scott Hartman (a physicist). *Education:* Attended Washington University. *Hobbies and other interests:* Reading, playing role play games, dancing, playing cello.

Addresses

Home—250 Wynnewood Rd., E-13, Wynnewood, PA 19096. *E-mail*—amyunbounded@yahoo.com.

Career

Cartoonist and author. Children's Book World, Haverford, PA, clerk. Pug House Press, Wynnewood, PA, founder, c. 1996.

Awards, Honors

Ignatz Award for Best Minicomic, 1998, for *Amy Unbounded;* Xeric grant, 2001.

Writings

GRAPHIC NOVELS

Amy Unbounded: Belondweg Blossoming (originally published as a minicomic), Pug House Press (Wynnewood, PA), 2002.

Author of three children's books on tree care for International Society of Aboriculture; author of minicomics and of comic strips "Ellen of Troy" and "Amy Unbounded," 1998—. Contributor to anthologies, including *Brainbomb* and *Rampage*. Contributor of articles to Web site *Strange Horizons*.

Sidelights

Rachel Hartman is a pioneer in the comics genre: she created the minicomic, a self-published, black-and-white product that the author/illustrator photocopies herself and staples while watching *Star Trek* television-show re-runs. Despite its home-made quality, Hartman's minicomic series, *Amy Unbounded,* is anything but amateurish. The story of a spirited, nine-year-old girl growing up in the fictional land of Goredd, the comic began four-times-a-year publication in 1996. Hartman won a Xeric Foundation grant in 2001 that funded a book-length work containing six interlocking issues of the minicomic. Published in graphic-novel format as *Amy Unbounded: Belondweg Blossoming,* the work was described as a "gently paced ensemble comedy of manners," by a reviewer for *Publishers Weekly.*

Although Hartman is the daughter of an artist and former art teacher, as a child growing up in Kentucky, she dreamed of becoming an author or poet. Interest-

ingly, given her adult work, Hartman was not a fan of comics as a child, although she did read comic strips such as "Calvin and Hobbes, The Far Side, Doonesbury" and "Pogo." In the seventh grade she wrote a poem about Amy, a "little girl knight," as she told Lee Atchison of *Sequential Tart,* whose "mother was a Valkyrie-style warrior, and the father had a black bear somewhere up his family tree." Titled "The First Adventure of Sir Amy," the poem would later inspire Hartman's minicomic series.

Another influence from Hartman's childhood was her sense of place. "I grew up in the Middle Ages," she explained in an article for *Strange Horizons,* adding: "Well, not the Middle Ages exactly, but in Kentucky, which is close, and with a father who believed that if you didn't have garden soil under your nails, you just weren't working hard enough. . . . We grew berries and vegetables, canned tomatoes and made jam, chopped wood and spread mulch; and when I wasn't imagining I was really a princess in exile amongst the surly serfs, I gained an appreciation for the timeliness of growing things."

Years later, in college as a literature and classics major, Hartman responded to an advertisement in her school paper and began writing a comic strip titled "Helen of Troy." Given that she had no formal training, she produced the strip with a fervor that surprised her. Although she had intended a life of scholarly pursuit, suddenly writing and drawing comic books took hold. Graduating from college, Hartman returned to the little poem she had composed as a seventh-grader with an eye to adapting it as a children's book. She sent it out with some of her own illustrations, but it was rejected. "By then I was hooked on this little girl," Hartman told Atchison in *Sequential Tart.* "I had other adventures mapped out for her, I could tell you about her family—so I couldn't just let go of her. With a few changes . . . she became the Amy of my comic."

The minicomic *Amy Unbounded* premiered in October of 1996, with the episode *Amy in the Grip of Good Weather.* This premier issue introduces young Amy and her parents, Bob, a weaver in the village of Eddybrook in the medieval kingdom of Goredd, and Nahulla, a barbarian clockmaker. The story arc follows the plucky girl as she accompanies her father on a visit to widow Sampander, a great believer in the rule that children should be seen but not heard. Amy must muster all her patience to stay silent for her father's sake.

In the five stand-alone issues that followed through the spring of 1998, readers meet the other characters in Amy's medieval universe: older friends Molly and Susa; Uncle Cuthberte, a knight of the banished Order of the Rabbit Rampant; next-door-neighbor Bran Ducanahan, a frustrating boy in Amy's life; Bran's sister Niesta the cheesemaker; and other assorted personages, including a dragon named Lalo. Amy is rambunctious; she wishes she were a knight or explorer or scholar. Her imagination often causes misadventures, and as the series progresses she goes to fairs, has tea for the first time, tells tall tales, and experiences her first romantic crush. "I have this fascination with scholars and scholarship which I think comes through in a lot of the issues," Hartman explained to Atchison, adding: "The comic . . . frequently gets framed as a scholarly treatise of some sort, usually an anthropological monograph, and of course there's the whole scholarly race of dragons at my disposal." "We all know the comic is just an excuse for me to buy lots of medieval books," the author/artist also quipped.

Hartman originally intended her minicomic as a children's book for girls from ages nine to thirteen. However, she discovered that readers of all ages and both genders were purchasing books from her improvised distribution system, which consisted of online ordering and sales at comic-book conventions. An Ignatz award for best minicomic in 1998 helped make her name known to comics readers, and her naïve drawings of people with bulbous noses and dots for eyes coupled with her gentle humor and subtle feminist tone gained her a growing following.

The "Amy" series' coming-of-age theme also attracted readers. "Amy is at an age where her cognitive skills are well developed, but there's still a lot she hasn't experienced," Hartman explained to Atchison. "Much of the world is new to her, and she struggles to figure it all out." Hartman went on to note: "I think a lot of what Amy experiences, even though the story is set in the Middle Ages, is pretty universal. She has to figure out how to live—how to treat people, who is worth respecting, how to overcome her own prejudices and assumptions, what is love . . . all those really basic questions."

Begun in the fall of 1998 as six separate comic books comprising a single story arc, *Amy Unbounded: Belondweg Blossoming* wound up as a volume on bookstore shelves with the help of a grant. The storyline follows Amy and Bran Ducanahan during the summer they both turn ten years old. Amy has begun to read the national epic poem of Goredd, *Belondweg*, about a mythical queen who saved her people from fierce invaders. Inspired by this stirring epic, Amy wishes for such adventures in her own life. Amy and Bran meet the dragon Lalo, who is disguised as scholarly Mr. Ollpheist, and she becomes an assistant to the dragon as he researches the odd bit of Goreddi life and culture. Conflict erupts when Amy's father is ejected from the local weavers' guild, and love enters the picture when Amy discovers an attraction for a boy.

"What Hartman is doing here is subtle and more difficult that it looks," wrote Shaenon Garrity in a *Strange Horizons* review of *Amy Unbounded: Belondweg Blossoming*. The critic praised Hartman for "creating a place so vibrant and real that readers ache to step" into it. The same reviewer also found the "unadorned black-and-white art" to be "rough . . . but charming." Tom Spurgeon, writing in the *Comics Journal,* was less enthusiastic. While noting that "there is a great deal to appreciate in what Hartman does," he also deemed the "writing, art, story, and character insights . . . accessible but never compelling." However, a reviewer for *ArtBomb.net* was more positive, concluding that *Amy Unbounded: Belondweg Blossoming* "is a book meant for reading and re-reading and reading once again." Similarly, Rich Watson, writing in *View from the Cheap Seats* online, praised the "endearing charm" of Hartman's writing, and further noted that she "has a fabulous eye for . . . detail, and for drawing . . . in a manner that, while cartoonish, is convincing and true." A *Publishers Weekly* critic also commended Hartman's "bold, cartoon style" and her "elegant writing," as well as the "memorable and vivid" characters.

For Hartman, self-publishing her comic books provides a certain artistic freedom she could not have if they were produced conventionally. "I like the fact that I can afford to produce them and keep them in print," she told Atchison. "I like the fact that nobody in the world can keep me from making them—they'll never be canceled, or edited beyond recognition, or be put into any other kind of publishing limbo." As she told Jen Contino on *Comicon.com,* doing the art is about the best occupation she can think of. "There is nothing in this world as wondrous as a day spent drawing, a day that just slips by and is gone without your ever noticing, leaving behind a very nice page or two."

Biographical and Critical Sources

PERIODICALS

Comics Journal, June, 2002, Tom Spurgeon, review of *Amy Unbounded: Belondweg Blossoming.*
Publishers Weekly, August 12, 2002, review of *Amy Unbounded,* p. 278.
Voice of Youth Advocates, December 2002, review of *Amy Unbounded,* p. 371.

ONLINE

Amy Unbounded Web site, http://www.amyunbounded.com/ (September 2, 2005).
ArtBomb.net, http://www.artbomb.net/ (September 2, 2005), review of *Amy Unbounded.*
Comicon.com, http://www.comicon.com/ (September 9, 2002), Jen Contino, "Getting to Know Rachel Hartman."
iComics, http://www.icomics.com/ (June 22, 2000), Greg McElhatton, review of *Amy Unbounded.*
Mindspring.com, http://www.mindspring.com/ (August 7, 2003), "Amy Unbounded."
Sequential Tart, http://www.sequentialtart.com/ (July, 1999), Lee Atchison, "Plucky, Imaginative Heroines: Rachel Hartman"; (September, 2005) Lee Atchison, "Emotional Trajectories: Rachel Hartman."

Silver Bullet Comics Web site, http://www.
silverbulletcomics.com/ (October 5, 2004), Darren
Schroeder, interview with Hartman; (September 2,
2005) review of *Amy Unbounded.*

StrangeHorizons.com, http://www.strangehorizons.com/
(February 12, 2001), Rachel Harman, "The Medieval
Agricultural Year"; (June 23, 2003) Shaenon Garrity,
"I Sing, Ye Gods, of Amy: *Amy Unbounded: Belond-
weg Blossoming.*"

View from the Cheap Seats Online, http://www.orcafresh.
net/ (September 2, 2005), Rich Watson, review of
Amy Unbounded.*

*   *   *

HENRY, April 1959-

Personal

Born 1959, in Portland, OR; daughter of Hank (a television broadcaster) and Nora (a florist; maiden name,
Meeker) Henry; married; children: one daughter. *Education:* Oregon State University, Corvallis, B.A.; attended University of Stuttgart. *Politics:* Democrat. *Religion:* "Nondenominational Christian." *Hobbies and
other interests:* Reading, cooking, running.

Addresses

Home—Portland, OR. *Agent*—Wendy Schmalz, Harold
Ober Associates, Inc., 425 Madison Ave., New York,
NY 10017. *E-mail*—April@aprilhenrymysteries.com.

Career

Novelist. Kaiser Foundation Health Plan, Inc., Portland,
OR, communication specialist; has worked as a cook,
maid, German translator, life-drawing model, and in
data entry.

Member

International Association of Business Communicators,
Healthcare Communicators of Oregon, Willamette
Writers.

Awards, Honors

Nominations for Pacific Northwest Bookseller's Association Award, Spotted Owl Mystery Award, Agatha
Award for best first mystery, and Anthony Award for
best first mystery, all for *Circles of Confusion;* Booksense 76 Choice, and Oregonian Book Club Choice,
both 2000, both for *Circles of Confusion.*

Writings

"CLAIRE MONTROSE" MYSTERY SERIES

Circles of Confusion, HarperCollins (New York, NY),
1999.
Square in the Face, HarperCollins (New York, NY), 2000.

Heart-shaped Box, HarperCollins (New York, NY), 2001.
Buried Diamonds, Thomas Dunne Books/St. Martin's Mi-
notaur (New York, NY), 2003.

MYSTERY NOVELS

Learning to Fly, Thomas Dunne Books/St. Martin's Mino-
taur (New York, NY), 2002.
Shock Point (for young adults), G.P. Putnam's Sons (New
York, NY), 2006.

Sidelights

Among the odd jobs April Henry had prior to establishing herself as a writer in the mystery genre was a brief
stint jumping out of a cake. However, her fictional protagonist tops even that as far as sheer quirkiness goes:
inspecting vanity license plates for profanities is the
day job that launches Henry's protagonist, Claire Montrose, on her stint as an amateur sleuth. Detailed in
books such as *Circles of Confusion, Heart-shaped Box,*
and *Buried Diamonds,* Claire's cases involve her in art
forgery and theft, questionable adoptions, and even
murder. Despite such grave elements, the "Clair Montrose" novels are lighthearted, and Henry sustains the
mood by ending each chapter with a "mystery" vanity
plate anagram for readers to solve.

Although Henry's writing career technically began with
her first novel, *Circles of Confusion,* she actually became a published writer as a pre-teen, when one of her
short stories won the approval of noted British writer
Roald Dahl and was printed in an international children's magazine. In her book-length debut—the first installment in the "Claire Montrose" series—Claire's aunt
has died and left the forty-something amateur sleuth an
oil painting with a provenance shrouded in mystery.
Suspecting the painting may have been smuggled from
Germany during World War II, when German Chancel-
lor Adolf Hitler and his Nazi cohorts confiscated many
works of fine art, Claire flies to New York City to have
the work appraised. Although an expert tells her the
work is a forgery, the continued attempts by thieves to
steal the painting cause Claire to suspect that there may
be more to the story. A *Publishers Weekly* reviewer
commented that Henry's amateur detective "proves
clever enough to outwit even the wiliest villain in her
offbeat, vital first outing as a sleuth," while in *Library
Journal* a reviewer noted that "the good news is that
Claire will be back in a second mystery." In addition to
earning critical approval, *Circles of Confusion* was
nominated for several writing awards.

Claire returns in *Square in the Face,* as one of her
friends asks for help in locating a child who had been
given up for adoption years before. Hoping to help the
distraught mother, Claire poses as a pregnant woman in
order to obtain access to the clinic where her friend's
daughter was born. After finding the birth mother's
records, she narrows down the list of possible adoptive
parents, but when these leads fall short of success,

Claire is forced to return to the clinic for real answers. "The book's strength is Claire, its likable protagonist," noted Jenny McLarin in a review of *Square in the Face* for *Booklist,* and in *Publishers Weekly* a reviewer commented that "Henry writes an absorbing and at times moving mystery with a lively heroine." According to *Library Journal* critic Rex E. Klett, "agreeable prose" combines with "a steadily engaging plot [to] . . . make this a recommended purchase."

Henry's third "Claire Montrose" mystery, *Heart-shaped Box,* follows Claire as she travels to her twentieth high school reunion, hoping to see how her former classmates have—and have not—changed since their graduation. When several of her female classmates receive heart-shaped boxes and one of them subsequently suffers a sudden death, Claire's detective work begins. A *Publishers Weekly* reviewer observed that Henry relegates Claire to the back seat for this adventure outing, leaving much of the actual investigating work to one of Claire's former classmates, a police officer. While noting that Henry's series is somewhat uneven in the plot department, *Booklist* reviewer Jenny McLarin cited the strength of the story line in *Heart-shaped Box,* commenting that this installment "takes a step in the right direction." In another favorable review, Klett wrote in *Library Journal* that "lively action, a tidy circle of appealing characters, and a focused, small-town location make [*Heart-shaped Box*] . . . a solid work."

In *Buried Diamonds* Claire finds a diamond engagement ring while going for her morning jog. According to elderly housemate Charlie, a Holocaust survivor, the ring belonged to a woman named Elizabeth, who committed suicide decades earlier. Hoping to return the ring to its rightful owner, Claire traces it back to Elizabeth's former fiancée, the Korean War veteran Allen, as well as the late woman's sister, best friend, and neighbors. The elderly cast is soon transformed into a list of suspects, as Claire's sleuthing reveals Elizabeth's death to have been murder. Praising *Buried Diamonds* as "a solid entry in a solid series," *Booklist* contributor Jenny McLarin commended Henry's inclusion of "historical material," and Klett dubbed the novel "a warm prize for a chilly day."

While the "Claire Montrose" novels constitute the bulk of Henry's fictional output, the author has also produced the highly praised solo mystery *Learning to Fly,* and has also won over younger fans with her first young-adult thriller, *Shock Point.* A nineteen year old takes advantage of tragedy when she finds herself seated beside several fatalities of a fifty-two-car accident in *Learning to Fly,* the novel in which Henry "really hits her stride," according to McLarin in *Booklist.* Although her shaved head, tattoo, and pierced nose say otherwise, Free Meeker wants a normal life away from her hippie parents and the loser boyfriend that has left her pregnant. When hitchhiker Lydia dies in the crash, Free trades identities with the deceased young woman; a bag containing over 700,000 dollars in cash, the property of another crash victim, allows Free to assume Lydia's identity in style. Unfortunately, the new identity and the cash both come with strings, and Free soon finds herself pursued by Lydia's abusive husband and a drug dealer intent upon retrieving his ill-gotten gains. As *Learning to Fly* winds to its conclusion, McLarin described the tension created by Henry as "deliciously unbearable," and dubbed the novel a "dynamic" and "hard-to-put-down suspense tale." "In tone, mood and structure," the novel constitutes a shift from the light-heared "Claire Montrose" novels, according to a *Publishers Weekly* writer, the contributor characterizing the novel's accident scene as "harrowing." In *Library Journal,* Klett praised Henry's style for its "easy grace, choice characterization, and mounting tension," recommending *Learning to Fly* to fans of the "Claire Montrose" mysteries.

Teen readers are Henry's focus in *Shock Point,* which focuses on sixteen-year-old Cassie Streng. Cassie's growing concern over her psychiatrist stepfather Rick's treatment of misguided teens lands her in Peaceful Cove, an ironically named juvenile detention facility. The experimental drug Socom, which Rick uses to treat his adolescent patients, has resulted in several suicides. When Cassie begins to express concern over the drug Rick has two thugs take her to the facility, which is located in a remote area of New Mexico. Assured that her daughter is now in boarding school, Cassie's mom does not suspect Rick's machinations, leaving the teen alone to escape her harsh prison and put an end to the drug's use. Describing the novel as "Dickensian," *Booklist* contributor Connie Fletcher praised *Shock Point,* noting that Cassie is a "likeable heroine who's a good match for the nefarious adults in her life." Praising the author's use of short chapters and a narrative that alternates between Cassie's current plight and the events that got her there, Beth Gallego wrote in *School Library Journal* that Henry's novel features "a nicely executed technique that keeps the plot moving and readers engaged."

Biographical and Critical Sources

PERIODICALS

Booklist, January 1, 2000, Jenny McLarin, review of *Square in the Face,* p. 884; December 15, 2000, Jenny McLarin, review of *Heart-shaped Box,* p. 791; March 15, 2002, Jenny McLarin, review of *Learning to Fly,* p. 1215; November 1, 2003, Jenny McLarin, review of *Buried Diamonds,* p. 482; February 1, 2006, Connie Fletcher, review of *Shock Point,* p. 44.

Business Journal-Portland, February 16, 2001, Kristina Brenneman, "Mystery Writer Emerges at Kaiser," p. 19.

Kirkus Reviews, March 1, 2002, review of *Learning to Fly,* p. 292; September 15, 2003, review of *Buried Diamonds,* p. 1156; December 15, 2005, review of *Shock Point,* p. 1322.

Library Journal, October 1, 1999, review of *Circles of Confusion,* p. 50; March 1, 2000, Rex E. Klett, review of *Square in the Face,* p. 127; January 1, 2001, Rex E. Klett, review of *Heart-shaped Box,* p. 162; May 1, 2002, Rex E. Klett, review of *Learning to Fly,* p. 137.

Publishers Weekly, January 18, 1999, review of *Circles of Confusion,* p. 331; January 17, 2000, review of *Square in the Face,* p. 46; January 8, 2001, review of *Heart-shaped Box,* p. 51; April 8, 2002, review of *Learning to Fly,* p. 209.

School Library Journal, June, 2006, Beth Gallego, review of *Shock Point,* p. 158.*

*   *   *

HOCE, Charley E.

Personal

Born in Hamilton, OH; married; wife's name Joanele; children: C.J. (son). *Education:* Ohio University, graduate. *Hobbies and other interests:* Fishing, reading, walking, writing, travel.

Addresses

Home—West Manchester, OH. *Agent*—c/o Author Mail, Boyds Mills Press, 815 Church St., Honesdale, PA 18431. *E-mail*—miamian@infinet.com.

Career

Educator and writer. National Trail Elementary School, New Paris, OH, teacher, beginning c. 1980.

Awards, Honors

Silver Gertie award, 2005; named Outstanding Elementary Language Arts Teacher, Ohio Council of Teachers of English Language Arts, 2005.

Writings

Daredevil Dan, illustrated by Christine Tripp, Ideals Children's Books (Nashville, TN), 2000.

Beyond Old MacDonald: Funny Poems from down on the Farm, illustrated by Eugenie Fernades, Wordsong/ Boyds Mills Press (Honesdale, PA), 2005.

Biographical and Critical Sources

PERIODICALS

Kirkus Reviews, March 1, 2005, review of *Beyond Old MacDonald: Funny Poems from down on the Farm,* p. 287.

School Library Journal, March, 2005, Shawn Brommer, review of *Beyond Old MacDonald,* p. 194.

Teaching Pre K-8, March, 2004, Becky Rodia, "Write around the Clock: A Day in the Life of Charley Hoce, Teacher and Poet on the Go."

ONLINE

Midwest Book Review Online, http://www.midwestbooksreview.com/rbw/ (October 10, 2006), review of *Beyond Old MacDonald.*

*   *   *

HOLM, Matthew 1974-

Personal

Born 1974; son of William W. (a pediatrician) and Beverly A. (a pediatric nurse) Holm. *Education:* Graduated from college.

Addresses

Home—Upstate NY. *Agent*—c/o Author Mail, Random House Trade, 1745 Broadway, New York, NY 10019.

Career

Illustrator and author. Has worked as a magazine editor.

Awards, Honors

American Library Association Notable Book designation, 2006, for *Babymouse: Queen of the World!*

Writings

"BABYMOUSE" GRAPHIC-NOVEL SERIES; WITH JENNIFER L. HOLM; AND ILLUSTRATOR

Babymouse: Our Hero, Random House (New York, NY), 2005.

Babymouse: Queen of the World!, Random House (New York, NY), 2005.

Babymouse: Beach Babe!, Random House (New York, NY), 2006.

Babymouse: Heartbreaker, Random House (New York, NY), 2006.

Babymouse: Rock Star!, Random House (New York, NY), 2006.

OTHER

(With Jonathan Follett) *Gray Highway: AN American UFO Journey,* Toadspittle Hill Productions (New York, NY), 1998.

(With Jonathan Follett) *Suburbageddon; or, How Two Middle-Class American Guys Prepare for the Apocalypse,* Toadspittle Hill Productions (New York, NY), 1999.

Contributor to periodicals, including *Country Living*.

Sidelights

Drawing on his experience as a writer as well as his work in cartooning, Matthew Holm joined sister Jennifer L. Holm to create Babymouse, an engaging character that appears in a number of pint-sized graphic novels. Geared for girls from ages six to eleven, the "Babymouse" books—which include *Babymouse: Our Hero*, *Babymouse: Queen of the World!*, and *Babymouse: Rock Star*—feature a petite, pink-loving mouse with big dreams. Described by *Horn Book* reviewer Robin Smith as "sassy" and "smart," the Holms' heroine makes her picture-book debut in *Babymouse: Our Hero*, featuring what Smith described as "familiar situations, humorous asides, and humorous plots" brought to life by Matthew Holm's engaging illustrations. The "Babymouse" books, geared for beginning readers, have been popular with boys as well as girls.

Babymouse's pink-hued adventures continue in *Babymouse: Queen of the World!*, as she covets an invitation to arch nemesis Felicia Furrypaws' slumber party. When other methods prove unsuccessful, the wily young rodent resorts to trading her homework in exchange for an invite from the cagey kitty, only to be disappointed when she finally arrives at the party. In black-and-white drawings highlighted with bright pink, Matthew Holm brings to life the high-energy mouse's optimistic vision of life. Jesse Karp, writing in *Booklist*, noted that "the Holms spruce up some well-trod ground with breathless pacing and clever flights of Babymouse's imagination," while Sadie Mattox commented in *School Library Journal* that "Babymouse has a distinct voice and is a real charmer." *Babymouse: Rock Star* and *Babymouse: Beach Babe* also pair a hand-lettered text with Holm's humorous art. Praising *Babymouse: Beach Babe*, Karp wrote that the Holms' "squiggly whiskered heroine" captivates readers in a "hyperkinetic, pink-washed adventure as frolicsome and breathlessly paced" as ever.

The Holms' collaboration continues to be successful, despite the fact that Matthew Holm lives in upstate New York while Jennifer, a successful children's-book writer in her own right, lives in Maryland. Crediting the existence of e-mail and overnight mail services, Matthew Holm also discussed the genesis of the series in an interview with a *Seattle Post-Intelligencer* contributor. After Jennifer came up with the character, she gave her younger brother a sketch and he refined the character. "She's very imaginative and she's very enthusiastic about things, even when they don't go all that well," he explained of Babymouse. "She has the usual trials and tribulations (of a young girl). She has bad whisker days."

Biographical and Critical Sources

PERIODICALS

Booklist, December 1, 2005, Jesse Karp, review of *Babymouse: Our Hero*, p. 48; March 15, 2006, Jesse Karp, review of *Babymouse: Beach Babe*, p. 56.
Bookseller, November 18, 2005, Benedicte Page, "The Mouse with Pink Daydreams," p. 32.
Bulletin of the Center for Children's Books, December, 2005, review of *Babymouse: Queen of the World!*, p. 186.
Horn Book, January-February, 2006, Robin Smith, review of *Babymouse: Our Hero*, p. 80; October, 2006, Robin Smith, review of *Babymouse: Rock Star*, p. 585.
Kirkus Reviews, April, 2006, review of *Babymouse: Beach Babe*, p. 408.
School Library Journal, March, 2006, Sadie Mattox, review of *Babymouse: Our Hero*, p. 251; September, 2006, Scott La Counte, review of *Babymouse: Rock Star*, p. 238; October, 2006, Ronnie Gordon, review of *Babymouse: Beach Babe*, p. 128.

ONLINE

BookLoons, http://www.bookloons.com/ (October 10, 2006), review of *Babymouse: Queen of the World!* and *Babymouse: Our Hero*.
Cynsations Web site, http://www.cynthialeitichsmith. blogspot.com/ (October 10, 2006), Cynthia Leitich Smith, interview with Holm.
Seattle Post-Intelligencer Online, http://seattlepi.nwsource. com/ (January 20, 2006), "A Moment with . . . Authors Jennifer L. Holm and Matthew Holm."*

*   *   *

HUNTER, Erin
See CARY, Kate

I-J

IBATOULLINE, Bagram 1965(?)-

Personal

Surname pronounced "E-bat-too-LEEN"; born c. 1965, in USSR (now Russia). *Education:* Art College of Kazan, graduate; State Academic Institute of Arts (Moscow, USSR), graduate.

Addresses

Home—282 Barrow St., Jersey City, NJ 07302. *Agent*—c/o Author Mail, Candlewick Press, 2067 Massachusetts Ave., Cambridge, MA 02140.

Career

Illustrator.

Awards, Honors

Boston Globe/Horn Book Book Award for Fiction, 2006, for *The Miraculous Journey of Edward Tulane* by Kate DiCamillo; New York Public Library 100 Best Books for Reading and Sharing designation, 2006, for *The Adventures of Marco Polo.*

Illustrator

Philip E. Booth, *Crossing,* Candlewick Press (Cambridge, MA), 2001.

Michele Benoit Slawson, *Signs for Sale,* Viking (New York, NY), 2002.

Stephen Mitchell, reteller, *The Nightingale* (based on the story by Hans Christian Andersen), Candlewick Press (Cambridge, MA), 2002.

Paul Fleischman, *The Animal Hedge,* Candlewick Press (Cambridge, MA), 2003.

Celeste Davidson Mannis, *The Queen's Progress: An Elizabethan Alphabet,* Viking (New York, NY), 2003.

James Giblin, *Secrets of the Sphinx,* Scholastic Press (New York, NY), 2004.

Deborah Noyes, *Hana in the Time of the Tulips,* Candlewick Press (Cambridge, MA), 2004.

M.T. Anderson, *The Serpent Came to Gloucester,* Candlewick Press (Cambridge, MA), 2005.

Paul Fleischman, *Graven Images: Three Stories,* Candlewick Press (Cambridge, MA), 2006.

Kate DiCamillo, *The Miraculous Journey of Edward Tulane,* Candlewick Press (Cambridge, MA), 2006.

Stephen Mitchell, adaptor, *The Tinderbox* (based on the story by Hans Christian Andersen), Candlewick Press (Cambridge, MA), 2006.

Diane Stanley, *Bella at Midnight: The Thimble, the Ring, and the Slippers of Glass,* HarperCollins (New York, NY), 2006.

Elizabeth Winthrop, *The First Christmas Stocking,* Random House Children's Books (New York, NY), 2006.

Russell Freedman, *The Adventures of Marco Polo,* Arthur Levine Books (New York, NY), 2006.

Sidelights

As far back as he can remember, Russian-born illustrator Bagram Ibatoulline has been actively exploring different artistic styles and mediums. Beginning his artistic training at a children's art school in the then-Soviet Union, he subsequently attended the Art College of Kazan, where he studied for four years. After graduation, Ibatoulline moved to Moscow to attend the State Art Institute. As an illustrator inspired by classical art and the works of the Old Masters, he is recognized for his ability to work in a variety of styles, making each of his illustration projects—which range from Celeste Davidson Mannis's Elizabethan-inspired *The Queen's Progress: An Elizabethan Alphabet* to a revised version of Paul Fleishman's 1983 picture book *The Animal Hedge*—an unexpected delight. "I enjoy any style—it is never my intention to copy a particular look or aesthetic," Ibatoulline noted in an online interview for *Bookbrowse.* "Instead I do a lot of groundwork and extensive research on the time period in order to come up with my own approach."

In *The Nightingale* the classic story by Hans Christian Andersen is retold by Stephen Mitchell in a version that incorporates contemporary elements. The book's illus-

Bagram Ibatoulline's detailed art has appeared in many picture books, among them **The Animal Hedge** *by Paul Fleischman.* (Illustrations copyright © 2003 by Bagram Ibatoulline. Text copyright © 1983, 2003 Paul Fleischman. Calligraphy by Judythe Sieek. Reproduced by permission of the publisher Candlewick Press, Inc., Cambridge, MA)

trations reflect a Chinese setting and are formatted as detailed, scroll-like panels painted in vibrant jewel tones. As Gillian Engberg wrote in *Booklist,* Ibatoulline's contributions to *The Nightingale* are "stunning," and a *Publishers Weekly* praised the illustrator's "elaborate, harmonious watercolors [that] pay homage to the flat style of Chinese brush paintings with iconic fidelity."

In his work for *The Queen's Progress,* Ibatoulline once again demonstrates his penchant for detail by capturing the stylistic nuances of the Elizabethan era in "handsome illustrations evoking the period," according to Carolyn Phelan in *Booklist.* Nancy Menaldi-Scanlan had similar praise in her *School Library Journal* review, commenting that "Ibatoulline's acrylic paintings are superb in their elegance and fascinating in their detail." The queen's "ornate gowns and her courtly accoutrements are delightfully offset by her servants' plain garb and earnest expressions," the critic added, noting the illustrator's insertion of humor into his complex images. Deeming the book "dense, erudite, and absorbing," a *Publishers Weekly* contributor cited Ibatoulline's use of "period touches, whether . . . outfitting the courtiers in brocade or depicting a maze of hedgerows."

As a *Kirkus Reviews* writer noted, Ibatoulline "exhibits chameleon-like adaptability with his chapter-introducing

illustrations" to Russell Freedman's *The Adventures of Marco Polo,* "varying style from Western to Eastern to suit the subject." An exploration of the many versions of the noted explorer's book titled *The Description of the World,* first published in the thirteenth century, Freedman's text retraces Polo's trip through the Middle and Far East, lacing the explorer's own words into a compelling original narrative. As a *Publishers Weekly* contributor noted, Ibatoulline works in a similar fashion, creating "accomplished paintings [that] reflect the artistic conventions of the cultures Marco encountered . . . and act as a visual bridge between the events of the text" and archival images. Calling the book "as beautiful as many of the sights the explorer observed," Ilene Cooper added in her *Booklist* review that *The Adventures of Marco Polo* stands as another example of Ibatoulline's versatility, as well as "a glorious piece of bookmaking [that] readers will find it a pleasure to explore."

Biographical and Critical Sources

PERIODICALS

Booklist, August, 2002, Denise Wilms, review of *Signs for Sale,* p. 1976; November 1, 2002, Gillian Engberg, review of *The Nightingale,* p. 488; April 1, 2003, Carolyn Phelan, review of *The Queen's Progress: An Elizabethan Alphabet,* p. 1394; November 1, 2004, Gillian Engberg, review of *Hana in the Time of the Tulips,* p. 498; September 15, 2004, Hazel Rochman, review of *Secrets of the Sphinx,* p. 240; June 1, 2005, Jennifer Mattson, review of *The Serpent Came to Gloucester,* p. 1805; February 1, 2006, Ilene Cooper, review of *Bella at Midnight: The Thimble, the Ring, and the Slippers of Glass,* p. 49; January 1, 2006, Ilene Cooper, review of *The Miraculous Journey of Edward Tulane,* p. 112; October 6, 2006, Ilene Cooper, review of *The Adventures of Marco Polo,* p. 46.

Horn Book, November-December, 2004, Betty Carter, review of *Secrets of the Sphinx,* p. 727; March-April, 2006, Susan Dove Lempke, review of *The Miraculous Journey of Edward Tulane,* p. 184; April, 2006, Susan Dove Lempke, review of *Bella at Midnight,* p. 194; September-October, 2006, p. 636.

Kirkus Reviews, September 15, 2001, review of *Crossing,* p. 1354; April 15, 2002, review of *Signs for Sale,* p. 579; September 15, 2004, review of *Hana in the Time of the Tulips,* p. 197; June 1, 2005, review of *The Serpent Came to Gloucester,* p. 632; January 15, 2006, review of *The Miraculous Journey of Edward Tulane,* p. 83; September 15, 2006, review of *The Adventures of Marco Polo.*

Publishers Weekly, October 8, 2001, review of *Crossing,* p. 64; April 22, 2002, review of *Signs for Sale,* p. 69; October 14, 2002, review of *The Nightingale,* p. 84; April 28, 2003, review of *The Queen's Progress,* p. 69; September 8, 2003, review of *The Animal Hedge,* p. 76; November 22, 2004, review of *Hana in the*

Time of the Tulips, p. 60; May 16, 2005, review of *The Serpent Came to Gloucester,* p. 62; December 12, 2005, Katherine Paterson, review of *The Miraculous Journey of Edward Tulane,* p. 67; October 2, 2006, review of *The Adventures of Marco Polo,* p. 65.

School Arts, January, 2005, Ken Marantz, review of *Hana in the Time of the Tulips,* p. 67.

School Library Journal, November, 2001, Wanda Meyers-Hines, review of *Crossing,* p. 140; July, 2002, Carol Schene, review of *Signs for Sale,* p. 99; November, 2002, Heide Piehler, review of *The Nightingale,* p. 110; May, 2003, Nancy Menaldi-Scanlan, review of *The Queen's Progress,* p. 138; October, 2004, Kathy Krasniewicz, review of *Hana in the Time of the Tulips,* p. 126; November, 2004, Daryl Grabarek, review of *Secrets of the Sphinx,* p. 163; June, 2005, Margaret Bush, review of *The Serpent Came to Gloucester,* p. 51; March, 2006, Kathleen Isaacs, review of *Bella at Midnight,* p. 230.

ONLINE

BookBrowse, http://www.bookbrowse.com/ (October 10, 2006), interview with Ibatoulline.

Storyopolis.com, http://www.storyopolis.com/ (October 10, 2006), "Bagram Ibatoulline."*

*   *   *

IVERSEN, Jeremy 1980(?)-
(Jeremy Watt Iversen)

Personal

Born c. 1980, in New York, NY. *Education:* Stanford University, graduate (international relations and political science; with distinction).

Addresses

Home—Los Angeles, CA. *Agent*—c/o Author Mail, Atria Books, Simon & Schuster, 1230 Avenue of the Americas, New York, NY 10020. *E-mail*—contact@ jeremyiversen.com.

Career

Writer. Formerly print model; Merrill Lynch, New York, NY, former investment banker; has been involved in scientific research into neurotheology; active in political fundraising; associate producer of documentary film.

Member

Phi Beta Kappa.

Writings

21 (young-adult novel), Simon Pulse (New York, NY), 2005.

High School Confidential: Secrets of an Undercover Student (nonfiction), Atria Books (New York, NY), 2006.

Sidelights

Manhattan born and raised with the proverbial silver spoon, Jeremy Iversen took the advantages he gained from a boarding-school education, earned a degree with distinction from Stanford University, and then went out to make his mark on the world. While his energies have been far-flung—he has tested the waters of investment banking and found them tepid, and explored the machinery underlying the American political landscape as both a political fundraiser and documentary filmmaker—Iversen's most noteworthy effort has been as a respected young writer. Cited by *Kliatt* reviewer Joseph DeMarco as "a frightening story that should make parents, school officials, and students take notice," his novel *21* explores campus drinking and the fraternity tradition through the fictional story of a college student trying to fit in, and is based in part on his experiences as vice president of the Delta Tau Delta fraternity. Iverson's second book, *High School Confidential: Secrets of an Undercover Student,* is his provocative exposé of student life in an American high school.

Viewing the lackluster existence stretching out before him as an employee at the brokerage firm Merrill Lynch, the high-achieving Iversen decided he wanted more dimension from his life than a promising corporate career could give. A graduate of the prestigious Phillips Exeter Academy, he realized that his nose-to-the-grindstone schooling had cheated him of a "normal" high-school experience. He was also curious about an educational system that appeared to churn out graduates lacking critical-thinking skills. In 2004, the then-twenty-four-year-old Iversen moved to Los Angeles and went undercover as seventeen-year-old transfer student Jeremy Hughes. Casting himself as a surfer dude at California's Claremont High School, he recorded his experiences in furtive note-taking, and he reveals his insider perspective on modern teens and the educational system in *High School Confidential.*

During his undercover experience, Iversen became immersed in the reality of social cliques, peer pressure, and the lackluster educational standards American teens must reconnoiter during their public-school experience. He witnessed his high-school "peers" engaging in risky behavior such as steroid use and unprotected sex, but to preserve his undercover status he could do little more than offer prudent advice. Instead, he tried to relate to teens on their level, mimicking the talk and behavior of his classmates while hoping to inspire his new friends to gain the self-confidence needed to make smart choices.

Several of the insights Iversen gained during his undercover experience concern the failings of the contemporary educational system. In an interview with David Kent Randall for *Salon.com,* he cited low teacher expectations as the cause of some of the system's weaknesses. "We were never assigned to write a paper longer than a page, we were never asked to find a source beyond the textbook," he explained of his experience as a high school student. "No one ever said, 'Find an opinion and defend it with proof.' The best you got was, 'Regurgitate the textbook in full sentences.' And what ends up happening is that you get people who aren't able to ask challenging questions or find independent answers, so they just repeat what they hear around them with increasing conviction." Reviewing *High School Confidential, Booklist* contributor Stephanie Zvirin appreciated Iversen's insights, writing that his "extensive use of dialogue gives the episodic, realistically raunchy narrative the patina of fiction," allowing readers to become "wrapped up in the lives of his composite kids. He catches then at their very worst and their best as they rage, dream, and struggle to move on with their lives."

Biographical and Critical Sources

PERIODICALS

Booklist, April 1, 2005, Gillian Engberg, review of *21,* p. 1352; September 1, 2006, Stephanie Zvirin, review of *High School Confidential: Secrets of an Undercover Student,* p. 27.
Kliatt, May, 2005, Joseph DeMarco, review of *21,* p. 26.
Kirkus Reviews, February 15, 2005, review of *21* p. 229.
Publishers Weekly, April 18, 2005, review of *21,* p. 64.
School Library Journal, April, 2005, Sharon Morrison, review of *21,* p. 134.

ONLINE

Jeremy Iversen Home Page, http://www.jeremyiversen. com (October 10, 2006).
Salon.com, http://www.salon.com/ (October 10, 2006), David Kent Randall, "Big Man on Campus" (interview).
U.S. News & World Report Online, http://www.usnews. com/ (October 10, 2006), Elizabeth Weiss Green, "Fast Times, Revisited."

*   *   *

IVERSEN, Jeremy Watt
See IVERSEN, Jeremy

*   *   *

JASSEM, Kate
See OPPENHEIM, Joanne

*   *   *

JEAPES, Ben 1965-
(Sebastian Rook)

Personal
Born 1965, in Belfast, Northern Ireland. *Education:* Graduated from Warwick University.

Addresses
Agent—c/o David Fickling Books, 61-63 Uxbridge Rd., London W5 5SA, England. *E-mail*—ben-jeapes@sff. net.

Career
Writer, editor, and publisher. Jessica Kingsley Publishers, London, England, editor, 1987-91; Learned Information Europe Ltd., Oxford, England, editor, 1991-97; Isis Medical Media, Oxford, editor, 1997-2000; founder and owner of Big Engine (publishing house), Abingdon, England, 2001-04; United Kingdom Education and Research Network Association, Oxfordshire, England, documentation officer, 2004—. Has also worked for Lawtext Publishing.

Writings

SCIENCE FICTION

His Majesty's Starship, Scholastic (London, England), 1998, published as *The Ark,* Scholastic (New York, NY), 2000.
Wingèd Chariot, Scholastic (London, England), 2000.
The Xenocide Mission, David Fickling Books (New York, NY), 2002.
The New World Order, David Fickling Books (New York, NY), 2005.

"VAMPIRE PLAGUES" SERIES; UNDER PSEUDONYM SEBASTIAN ROOK

Vampire Plagues: London, Scholastic (London, England), 2004.
Vampire Plagues: Paris, Scholastic (London, England), 2004.
Vampire Plagues: Mexico, Scholastic (London, England), 2004.

Contributor to *Digital Dreams,* edited by David Barrett, NEL, 1990, *DECALOG 3: Consequences,* Virgin Publishing, 1996; and *DECALOG 4: Re: Generations,* 1997. Contributor to periodicals, including *Interzone, Aboriginal SF, Altair, Fantasy and Science Fiction, Odyssey,* and *Substance.*

Sidelights
British novelist and short-story writer Ben Jeapes is the author of a number of critically acclaimed works of science fiction and fantasy, among them *His Majesty's Starship* and *The New World Order.* Jeapes was introduced to these two genres through the television shows

of his youth; as he stated on his home page, "an awareness began to creep in that *Star Trek* and *Dr. Who* contained ideas that couldn't really happen in the world as I knew it." "And it was this, I think," he continued, "that sparked in my infant mind the concept of *what if?* The ability to look at an aspect of our world and imagine it differently. This works just as well for fantasy as for science fiction: you can imagine what if magic were possible just as well as *what if* we could travel to the stars."

Jeapes made his literary debut in 1990, publishing the short story "Digital Cats Come out Tonight" in the anthology *Digital Dreams.* He contributed more than a dozen more stories to *Interzone* and other periodicals before his debut novel, *His Majesty's Starship*—published in the United States as *The Ark*—appeared in 1998. In the work, an alien race of quadrupeds, the First Breed, invites the people of Earth to share in the joint development of their home planet. Each nation will send a corps of diplomats to negotiate with the aliens, and the United Kingdom selects Captain Michael Gilmore, a self-doubting but capable leader, to carry the Prince of Wales aboard the starship *Ark Royal*. Suspicions abound, however; the humans mistrust not only the aliens but each other, and Gilmore must ultimately find a way to salvage the once-peaceful mission.

Reviewers found much to praise in *His Majesty's Starship.* Lijana Howe, writing in *SFX,* called the work "a veritable fount of plot, characterisation and intrigue, with some astoundingly original ideas," and *Times Educational Supplement* contributor Jan Mark praised Jeapes's novel as characteristic of the "all solid traditional space fiction of the kind we see far too seldom now."

The Xenocide Mission, a sequel to *His Majesty's Starship,* concerns Joel Gilmore, an officer at an interstellar observation post which monitors a fearsome alien race called the Xenocides. After an attack on the outpost, Joel and his First Breed companion Boon Round flee to a dead planet while Joel's father Michael, now retired, plans a rescue mission. "Told from the point of view of many characters and moving among the personalities, species, and power groups," a *Kirkus Reviews* critic wrote, *The Xenocide Mission* "allows details—historical, personal, and cultural—to emerge as the plot unfolds." The author's "imagination is at the service of a set of very real questions about how groups get on with each other," remarked a *School Librarian* contributor.

In *Wingèd Chariot* Jeapes introduces a future society wherein overpopulation no longer exists because of the Home Time, a system of time travel that allows humans to be redeployed throughout past eras and parallel timelines. The singularity that makes such travel possible is decaying, however, and the Home Time will end in twenty-seven years. The only hope for humanity, it appears, is to send someone to the past to deliberately

In **The Xenocide Mission** *Ben Jeapes draws readers into an adventure involving an isolated space station and a pack of murderous aliens.* (Laurel-Leaf Books, 2004. Used by permission of Random House Children's Books, a division of Random House, Inc)

alter the future. "The ideas being played with are hellishly complex, made more so by Jeapes's antic sense of humour," wrote Jan Mark in the *Times Educational Supplement.*

Set during the English Civil War of the seventeenth century, *The New World Order* is a "complex, ingeniously imagined alternate history," according to a critic in *Kirkus Reviews.* When a gateway opens to another world, allowing alien troops with modern weapons to join the conflict and seize power, the disruption creates political intrigue, divided loyalties, and a clash of cultures. "There is a terrific cast of characters, which makes the political, religious, and actual battles that much more interesting," noted *Kliatt* reviewer Claire Rosser. According to a critic in *Publishers Weekly,* "Jeapes's novel is an admirable achievement on a technical and imaginative level."

Biographical and Critical Sources

PERIODICALS

Booklist, April 15, 2002, Sally Estes, review of *The Xenocide Mission*, p. 1416; January 1, 2005, Chris Sherman, review of *The New World Order*, p. 845.

Bulletin of the Center for Children's Book, June, 2002, review of *The Xenocide Mission*, p. 369; January 15, 2005, Krista Hutley, review of *The New World Order*, p. 253.

Interzone, May, 1999, David Mathew, review of *His Majesty's Starship*; June, 2000, review of *Wingèd Chariot*; October, 2000, Molly Brown, "Memoirs of a Publisher" (interview).

Kirkus Reviews, May 1, 2002, review of *The Xenocide Mission*, p. 658; January 15, 2005, review of *The New World Order*, p. 122.

Kliatt, March, 2005, Claire Rosser, review of *The New World Order*, p. 13.

Publishers Weekly, April 25, 2005, review of *The New World Order*, p. 57.

School Librarian, summer, 1999, review of *His Majesty's Starship*, p. 101; autumn, 2002, John Peters, review of *The Xenocide Mission*, p. 156; spring, 2005, Sandra Bennett, review of *The New World Order*, p. 47.

School Library Journal, June, 2002, John Peters, review of *The Xenocide Mission*, p. 140; April, 2005, Carolyn Lehman, review of *The New World Order*, p. 134.

SF Crowsnest, June, 2004, Stephen Hunt, "Big Ben" (interview).

SFX, June, 1999, Lijana Howe, review of *His Majesty's Starship*.

Times Educational Supplement, March 12, 1999, Jan Mark, review of *His Majesty's Starship*; March 10, 2000, Jan Mark, review of *Wingèd Chariot*; December 17, 2004, review of *The New World Order*.

Vector, January-February, 2005, review of *The New World Order*.

Voice of Youth Advocates, August, 2002, review of *The Xenocide Mission*, p. 202; April, 2005, Kevin Beach, review of *The New World Order*, p. 56.

ONLINE

Ben Jeapes Home Page, http://www.sff.net/people/benjeapes (October 20, 2006).

Emerald City Web site, http://www.emcit.com/ (March 1, 2004), interview with Jeapes.

SF Site, http://www.sff.net/ (October 16, 2006), David Mathew, "Ben Jeapes and Big Engine" (interview).

*   *   *

JENKINS, A.M.
(Amanda McRaney Jenkins)

Personal

Born in TX; children: three sons.

Addresses

Home—Benbrook, TX. *Agent*—c/o HarperCollins Publishers, 10 E. 53rd St., New York, NY 10022.

Career

Writer. Has also worked as an ice-cream scooper, pizza maker, aerobics instructor, and math teacher.

Awards, Honors

Delacorte Press Prize for First Young-Adult Novel, 1996, and California Young Reader's Medal, 2000, both for *Breaking Boxes*; Best Books for Young Adults selection, American Library Association, for *Damage*; PEN/Phyllis Naylor Working Writer fellowship, 2005.

Writings

YOUNG-ADULT NOVELS

Breaking Boxes, Delacorte (New York, NY), 1997.
Damage, HarperCollins (New York, NY), 2001.
Out of Order, HarperCollins (New York, NY), 2003.
Beating Heart: A Ghost Story, HarperCollins (New York, NY), 2006.

Work in Progress

Night Road, a novel.

Sidelights

Young-adult novelist A.M. Jenkins is the author of such critically acclaimed works as *Breaking Boxes* and *Out of Order*. Despite her success in the genre, Jenkins does not see herself strictly as an author for teens. As she told Sue Reichard in an online interview for *Suite101*, "I don't really write to any particular audience; I write about characters that interest me, that I can spend days, months, weeks, years with, and yet still look forward to being with them and peeling them apart every day. I like to be free to explore any aspect of these characters, and I like to write as tightly as possible, in a straight line without many digressions. Luckily for me, all this also fits into a niche called 'YA.'"

Jenkins's debut title, *Breaking Boxes*, garnered the Delacorte Press Prize for First Young-Adult Novel. The honor did more than simply bring notice to the author's work; it also marked a sea change in her life. At the time, Jenkins was ready to give up writing and had composed an e-mail to a friend telling her of the decision. "I was at the end of my rope," the author admitted to *Publishers Weekly* contributor Emily Jenkins. "I told her I would have to quit writing. Although I had found what I loved to do, I was going to have to quit because I wasn't good enough." When Jenkins received a phone call from editor Wendy Lamb, informing her of the award, she was overwhelmed. "I just started bawling away on the phone," the author recalled. "I couldn't speak or say anything! But I never did send that e-mail."

Breaking Boxes tells the story of sixteen-year-old Charlie Calmont, a loner from the rough side of town who has lived with his older brother, Trent, since the boys' widowed father abandoned the family; their mother drank herself to death years earlier. Following a scuffle with a group of the wealthy students at school because they teased him, Charlie is sent to detention, along with Brandon Chase, one of his tormentors. As a peace offering, Brandon offers Charlie a ride home, and the pair strike up an unlikely but genuine friendship. When Brandon learns that Trent is gay, however, he is horrified and rejects Charlie's friendship. "The dialogue, both spoken and unspoken, rings true, and Jenkins delivers a devastatingly accurate portrayal of adolescent males," noted *Booklist* reviewer Debbie Carton. Several critics praised the author's realistic depiction of the brothers' relationship; *Horn Book* contributor Lauren Adams, for instance, wrote that "sensible, articulate Trent is a good foil for Charlie's sometimes callous behavior, especially toward girls." According to a reviewer in *Publishers Weekly*, "this earnest drama's message of tolerance is loud and clear."

A high school football star battles depression in *Damage,* Jenkins's second novel. Senior Austin Reid, quarterback of the Parkersville Panthers, seems to have everything going for him: he is handsome, popular, and athletic, and he even dates the prettiest girl in school. Despite all that he has, Austin still suffers from the loss of his father when he was a child. Consumed by thoughts of suicide, the popular teen simply goes through the motions of his daily life. Austin finds some solace with his best friend, Curtis, and his girlfriend, Heather, but soon Heather's own emotional issues begin to threaten the couple's already complicated relationship. "Jenkins uses an intriguing second-person point of view to depict Austin's detachment, and lets the story drift, echoing Austin's own aimlessness," remarked *Booklist* critic Roger Leslie. "Appropriately," wrote Todd Morning in *School Library Journal,* "the book's ending is somewhat ambiguous, with Austin just beginning to understand his fragile mental state." "Not only is [*Damage*] . . . a grippingly realistic novel," observed Claire Rosser in *Kliatt,* "it gets across to YA readers how devastating depression is and how hard the struggle may be to avoid suicide."

Out of Order focuses on Colt Trammel, a cocky high school sophomore who is interested in little else besides baseball and his brainy girlfriend, Grace. Colt's struggles with schoolwork, however, threaten his eligibility to play sports and cause Grace to end their relationship. He finds salvation in Corinne, a unconventional green-haired school newcomer who sees beneath his tough surface and begins tutoring him in English. "Jenkins shows admirable restraint by not defining Colt's learning disabilities (he appears to be dyslexic), focusing instead on how he uses an aggressive exterior to cover his fears of exposure," wrote *Horn Book* contributor Peter D. Sieruta. In *School Library Journal* Morning also complimented Jenkins's portrait of Colt, stating that "every part rings true, from his rough language and obsession with sex to his need to act cool at all costs." According to Paula Rohrlick, writing in *Kliatt, Out of Order* "isn't a sports story, but rather a tale about learning to know oneself and to relate to others."

Jenkins turns readers' attention to the supernatural in *Beating Heart: A Ghost Story.* After seventeen-year-old Evan moves into a Victorian fixer-upper with his newly divorced mother and younger sister, the teen realizes the house is also inhabited by a spirit of a young woman named Cora who lived there a century earlier. Cora's ghost develops a romantic interest in Evan, and as he begins having erotic dreams about her, he also loses interest in his longtime girlfriend. "The third-person narrative works as an excellent foil," a *Publishers Weekly* critic stated, adding that Jenkins "portray[s] . . . Evan's kind nature with an even tone as opposed to the growing urgency of the dead girl's obsession." "Filled with the heat of awakening sexuality," remarked *Kliatt* reviewer Michele Winship, *Beating Heart* "crosses decades and genres as memory and reality meet each other in a dance shrouded in tragedy."

Asked by Reichard how she manages to create realistic male protagonists in her fiction, Jenkins replied: "I try to be honest and nonjudgmental. I grew up among friends who were boys, and spent time tagging along after my boy cousins, so that may have something to do with feeling comfortable with their conversations." While Jenkins finds ample rewards in the career she once almost abandoned, as she told Reichard, perhaps none is greater than "giving voice to characters who wouldn't exist, if I didn't put fingers to keyboard."

Biographical and Critical Sources

PERIODICALS

Booklist, September 1, 1997, Debbie Carton, review of *Breaking Boxes,* p. 106; September 15, 2001, Roger Leslie, review of *Damage,* p. 227; September 1, 2003, Frances Bradburn, review of *Out of Order,* p. 115; February 1, 2006, Frances Bradburn, review of *Beating Heart: A Ghost Story,* p. 45.

Bulletin of the Center for Children's Books, November, 1997, review of *Breaking Boxes,* p. 88; July, 2001, review of *Damage,* p. 410.

Horn Book, September-October, 1997, Lauren Adams, review of *Breaking Boxes,* p. 573; September, 2001, Peter D. Sieruta, review of *Damage,* p. 587; November-December, 2003, Peter D. Sieruta, review of *Out of Order,* p. 749.

Kirkus Reviews, October 15, 2001, review of *Damage,* p. 1485; August 1, 2003, review of *Out of Order,* p. 1018; December 1, 2005, review of *Beating Heart,* p. 1276.

Kliatt, May, 2003, Claire Rosser, review of *Damage,* p. 18; September, 2003, Paula Rohrlick, review of *Out of Order,* p. 8; January, 2006, Michele Winship, review of *Out of Order,* p. 8.

Publishers Weekly, July 14, 1997, review of *Breaking Boxes,* p. 85; December 22, 1997, Emily Jenkins, "Flying Starts," p. 28; November 12, 2001, review of *Damage,* p. 60; September 8, 2003, review of *Out of Order,* p. 77; December 5, 2005, review of *Beating Heart,* p. 56.

School Library Journal, October, 2001, Todd Morning, review of *Damage,* p. 162; September, 2003, Todd Morning, review of *Out of Order,* p. 214; March, 2006, Hillias J. Martin, review of *Beating Heart,* p. 223.

Voice of Youth Advocates, December, 1997, review of *Breaking Boxes,* p. 318; October, 2001, review of *Damage,* p. 279; February, 2006, Kevin Beach, review of *Beating Heart,* p. 499.

ONLINE

Suite101.com, http://www.suite101.com/ (October 1, 2004), Sue Reichard, "Award Winning YA Writer: Amanda Jenkins."*

* * *

JENKINS, Amanda McRaney
See JENKINS, A.M.

* * *

JENKINS, Emily 1967-
(E. Lockhart)

Personal

Born 1967, in New York, NY; daughter of Len Jenkin (a playwright) and Johanna Jenkins (a psychotherapist; maiden name, Robertson); married; children: one daughter. *Education:* Vassar, B.A., 1989; Columbia University, Ph.D. (English literature), 1998.

Addresses

Home—Brooklyn, NY. *Agent*—Elizabeth Kaplan Literary Agency, 80 5th Ave., Ste. 1101, New York, NY 10011.

Career

Novelist, picture-book author, and critic. Magazine writer and critic, 1998-2002; *New York Times Book Review,* New York, NY, book critic. Also taught at Gallatin School, New York University.

Awards, Honors

Blue Ribbon designation, *Bulletin of the Center for Children's Books,* 2001, *Boston Globe/Horn Book* Honor Award, 2001, Notable Children's Books selection, American Library Association, 2002, Charlotte Zolotow Honor Award, Cooperative Children's Book Center, 2002, Best Children's Book Award, *Child* magazine, Parents' Guide Children's Media award, Parents' Choice Award, and Children's Books of Distinction designation, *Riverbank Review,* all for *Five Creatures; Boston Globe/Horn Book* Honor Award, Blue Ribbon designation, *Bulletin of the Center for Children's Books,* New York Public Library 100 Titles for Reading and Sharing inclusion, and Parents' Choice Award, all 2005, all for *That New Animal;* Oppenheim Toy Portfolio Platinum Book Award, and New York Public Library 100 Titles for Reading and Sharing includion, both 2006, both for *Toys Go Out.*

Writings

CHILDREN'S FICTION

(With father, Len Jenkin) *The Secret Life of Billie's Uncle Myron* (novel), Henry Holt (New York, NY), 1996.

Five Creatures, illustrated by Tomek Bogacki, Frances Foster Books (New York, NY), 2001.

Daffodil, illustrated by Tomek Bogacki, Frances Foster Books (New York, NY), 2004.

My Favorite Thing (according to Alberta), illustrated by Anna Laura Cantone, Anne Schwartz Books (New York, NY), 2004.

That New Animal, illustrated by Pierre Pratt, Frances Foster Books (New York, NY), 2005.

Toys Go Out: Being the Adventures of a Knowledgeable Stingray, a Toughy Little Buffalo, and Someone Called Plastic, illustrated by Paul O. Zelinsky, Schwartz & Wade (New York, NY), 2006.

Love You When You Whine, illustrated by Sergio Ruzzier, Frances Foster Books (New York, NY), 2007.

Daffodil, Crocodile, illustrated by Tomek Bogacki, Frances Foster Books (New York, NY), 2007.

"BEA AND HAHA" BOARD-BOOK SERIES; FOR CHILDREN

Hug, Hug, Hug!, illustrated by Tomek Bogacki, Frances Foster Books (New York, NY), 2006.

Num, Num, Num!, illustrated by Tomek Bogacki, Frances Foster Books (New York, NY), 2006.

Plonk, Plonk, Plonk!, illustrated by Tomek Bogacki, Frances Foster Books (New York, NY), 2006.

Up, Up, Up!, illustrated by Tomek Bogacki, Frances Foster Books (New York, NY), 2006.

YOUNG-ADULT NOVELS; UNDER PSEUDONYM E. LOCKHART

The Boyfriend List, Delacorte (New York, NY), 2005.

Fly on the Wall: How One Girl Saw Everything, Delacorte (New York, NY), 2006.

The Boy Book: A Study of Habits and Behaviors, plus Techniques for Taming Them, Delacorte (New York, NY), 2006.

Dramarama, Hyperion (New York, NY), 2007.

Contributor of short story "Bake Sale," to *Not Like I'm Jealous or Anything: The Jealousy Book,* edited by Marissa Walsh, Delacorte (New York, NY), 2006.

OTHER

Tongue First: Adventures in Physical Culture (essays), Henry Holt (New York, NY), 1998.
Mister Posterior and the Genius Child (adult novel), Penguin Putnam (New York, NY), 2002.

Contributor to books, including *Surface Tension: Love, Sex, and Politics between Lesbians and Straight Women,* edited by Meg Daly, Simon & Schuster (New York, NY), 1996, and *Letters of Intent: Women Cross the Generations to Talk about Family, Work, Sex, Love, and the Future of Feminism,* edited by Meg Daly and Anna Bondoc, Free Press (New York, NY), 1999. Contributor to *New York Times Book Review.*

Adaptations

Five Creatures and *That New Animal* were adapted for video by Weston Woods; *The Boyfriend List* and *Fly on the Wall* were adapted as audiobooks by Listening Library.

Work in Progress

What Happens on Wednesdays, for Farrar, Strauss, expected 2008; *Skunkdog,* for Farrar, Straus & Giroux, expected 2008; *The Little Bit Scary People,* for Hyperion, expected 2008; *Sugar Would Not Eat It,* for Schwartz & Wade, expected 2009.

Sidelights

Novelist, essayist, and picture book writer Emily Jenkins has written widely for children and adults, and received the *Boston Globe/Horn Book* Honor Award for her children's titles *Five Creatures* and *That New Animal.* Under the pseudonym E. Lockhart, Jenkins has also published a number of highly regarded novels for teens, including *The Boyfriend List.*

Jenkins took an early interest in literature. "Growing up, I spent large parts of my life in imaginary worlds: Neverland, Oz, and Narnia, in particular," she wrote on her home page. "I read in the bath, at meals, in the car, you name it. Around the age of eight, I began working on my own writing. My early enterprises began with a seminal picture book featuring an heroic orange sleeping bag, followed by novel-length imitations of *The Wolves of Willoughby Chase* by Joan Aiken and *Pippi Longstocking* by Astrid Lindgren." Her love of books continued through college; the year after graduating from Vassar, she started what she once told *SATA* was "an amusing joint project" with her father, playwright Len Jenkin. "It eventually became my first published work," the imaginative novel *The Secret Life of Billie's Uncle Myron,* which she followed with a handful of picture books, including the popular *Five Creatures.*

Jenkins cites a number of writers as influences on her children's books, including P.G. Wodehouse, James Thurber, and Roald Dahl for their imaginations, as well as James Marshall, Rosemary Wells, Maurice Sendak, and Kay Thompson for their creative use of language. These two qualities are also evident in Jenkins's works, claim critics. Her novel *The Secret Life of Billie's Uncle Myron,* for example, tells what happens when eleven-year-old Billie and her brother Bix become tired of living in hotels while their rock star parents are away on tour after tour. They hitch a ride with their mysterious Uncle Myron and find themselves in Borderland, a fantastical place full of bizarre creatures. In *Publishers Weekly,* a reviewer likened the quick pace and "plenty of fizz and pizzazz" in this novel to the ambiance of a television cartoon, dubbing it a "lushly colored crazy quilt of a fantasy."

In writing her first picture book, *Five Creatures,* Jenkins drew on her personal experience in writing this work. "*Five Creatures* came from a Venn diagram I drew of my own household—although in the book it's highly fictionalized," Jenkins once explained to *SATA.* "I wanted to convey the sense of family I had with my pets." Her family includes a husband, daughter, and two cats, all with different abilities and tastes. As many primary school students learn, a Venn diagram is made of overlapping circles in which the overlapped portion contains the elements common to the two sets under consideration. Thus, *Five Creatures* points out in an easily understandable and nonjudgmental way, the abilities and tastes of a family. Reviewers praised the work for its humor, warmth, and straightforward logic, *Booklist* reviewer Ilene Cooper predicting that "parents and teachers will finds lots of ways to use this—along with just enjoying it." Writing in *Horn Book,* Leonard S. Marcus noted that Jenkins "artfully" encourages readers to ponder categorizations, so that they are simultaneously learning and having fun, which makes *Five Creatures* a useful addition to the classroom. It is, in the words of a *Kirkus Reviews* contributor, "a great introduction to Venn diagramming."

Daffodil concerns a young girl's quest for self-expression. This story, Jenkins once revealed to *SATA,* "comes from a real problem my mother had as a child, when she was forced to wear a hateful yellow party dress while her sisters got pink and blue. *Daffodil* is about taste—how likes and dislikes are incredibly important to our sense of ourselves, both for adults and children." In the work, identical triplets Daffodil, Violet, Rose are almost impossible to tell apart, so their mother outfits them in color-coded gowns that match their names. When Daffodil refuses to wear her dress, protesting its ghastly shade of yellow, her sisters join the rebellion, with surprising results. According to *Booklist* critic Gillian Engberg, "Jenkins tells a sly story, and most children will recognize the irritating grown-ups who squelch individuality."

Likes and dislikes are also the subject of Jenkins's picture book *My Favorite Thing (according to Alberta).*

Alberta has very specific tastes: she likes cats, but not dogs, unless they are tiny and do not drool. She likes stuffed owls, but not baby dolls. She adores the color orange, and she tolerates fish, as long as they are swimming in the ocean and are not part of her meal. One-by-one, Alberta presents the items that bring her joy, ultimately revealing her absolute favorite: herself. "There's no reason a self-esteem-boosting picture book has to be deadly earnest, as this playful guessing game shows," noted *School Library Journal* contributor Christine M. Heppermann.

In *That New Animal* a pair of pooches learn to cope with a new addition to their household. Marshmallow and FudgeFudge grow jealous when their masters begin devoting more and more time to a loud, smelly intruder—a new baby—and less and less time to them. The twosome devise a number of solutions to rid themselves of "that new animal," including burying it and sleeping on it. When Grandpa stops by to visit the infant, however, Marshmallow and FudgeFudge become not only possessive but protective of the newcomer. "Jenkins's funny and well-paced text flows smoothly and sticks solidly to the dogs' point of view," observed Jennifer M. Brabander in *Horn Book,* and a *Publishers Weekly* contributor stated that the author's "gift for melding irony with empathy results in the kind of resonant and quotable text that youngsters will demand to hear again and again."

A trio of playthings discover the world outside their owner's bedroom in *Toys Go Out: Being the Adventures of a Knowledgeable Stingray, a Toughy Little Buffalo, and Someone Called Plastic,* an "utterly delightful peek into the secret lives of toys," according to *School Library Journal* critic Elizabeth Bird. In a series of six interconnected tales, StingRay the stuffed fish, Lumphy the plush buffalo, and Plastic the bouncy ball delight in new escapades, overcome their fears, and learn the true meaning of friendship. "The simple prose is clever and often hilarious, incorporating dialogue and musings that ring kid-perspective true," wrote *Booklist* critic Shelle Rosenfeld.

Love You When You Whine addresses the unwavering bond between a parent and a child. In the work, a mother cat patiently endures despite her mischievous kitten's naughty deeds, including placing crayons in the dryer, pouring cereal on the floor, and spreading paint on the walls. Jenkins's scenarios "capture the universally difficult yet amusing . . . aspects of life with a preschooler, Heppermann commented in *Horn Book,* while a *Publishers Weekly* critic predicted that "youngsters will smile at both the kitten's tolerance-testing tricks and also the knowledge that a parent's devotion will withstand a bit of a whine and other transgressions."

Using the pen name E. Lockhart, Jenkins is also the author of *The Boyfriend List* and other critically acclaimed young-adult novels. *The Boyfriend List* focuses on

(15 guys, 11 shrink appointments, 4 ceramic frogs and me, ruby oliver)

the
boyfriend
list
e. lockhart

Cover of Emily Jenkins's young-adult novel **The Boyfriend List,** *which the author published under her pen name E. Lockhart.* (Delacorte Press, 2005. Used by permission of Random House Children's Books, a division of Random House, Inc)

fifteen-year-old Ruby Oliver, whose spate of panic attacks prompt her to seek treatment from a therapist. When Ruby admits that her troubles started after her boyfriend dumped her for her best friend, the therapist suggests that Ruby compile a list of all the boyfriends—current or past, real or imagined—in her life. "It's a clever gimmick," observed a critic for *Kirkus Reviews,* and the author "uses it as a prism through which Ruby . . . can view her life and herself." A *Publishers Weekly* critic wrote that "spot-on dialogue and details make this a painfully recognizable and addictive read," and *School Library Journal* contributor Elaine Baran Black noted that Jenkins's "comedy of errors will have readers laughing out loud."

Ruby Oliver returns in *The Boy Book: A Study of Habits and Behaviors, plus Techniques for Taming Them,* a sequel to *The Boyfriend List.* Ruby, now in her junior year, is still coping with the fallout over losing both her boyfriend and her best friend. With her therapist's help, the teen begins to develop new interests and a new circle of friends. Ruby also turns for guidance to "The Boy Book," a journal she wrote with a group of ex-girlfriends that contains advice about relationships with the opposite sex. "Ruby's intimate, first-person narrative . . . is lively, descriptive, frequently humorous, and peppered with periodic footnotes," Rosenfeld stated, and *Kliatt* reviewer Joanna Solomon observed that the conflicts Ruby faces "are universal and important without being earth shattering, making this novel a pleasurable read."

A teen's wish comes true in bizarre fashion in *Fly on the Wall: How One Girl Saw Everything*. When Gretchen Yee, an artistic loner who feels unappreciated and ignored at school, longs to be a "fly on the wall" in the boy's locker room, she wakes to find herself transformed into a winged insect. "Stuck in observer mode (upon pain of squishy death)," as Claire E. Gross explained in her review for *Horn Book*, Gretchen "learns to consider others' perspectives," and the knowledge she gains helps her draw closer to her family and friends. Once she returns to human form, "Gretchen emerges to make some changes in herself and her world as a result of her new perspective," noted a contributor in *Kirkus Reviews*.

Jenkins's ability to life a writing life was earned after years of hard work. "I write full time," she noted in an online interview with Nichelle Tramble posted on Tramble's Web site. "I have books coming out every year for the next few years. After struggling for a long time, patching together a life with teaching and other jobs, I find it most rewarding to be solidly employed."

Biographical and Critical Sources

PERIODICALS

Booklist, March 15, 2001, Ilene Cooper, review of *Five Creatures*, p. 1401; March 15, 2004, Gillian Engberg, review of *Daffodil*, p. 1308; April 1, 2005, Shelle Rosenfeld, review of *The Boyfriend List*, p. 1354, and Ilene Cooper, review of *That New Animal*, p. 1367; September 1, 2006, Shelle Rosenfeld, review of *The Boy Book: A Study of Habits and Behaviors, plus Techniques for Taming Them*, p. 111; October 1, 2006, Shelle Rosenfeld, review of *Toys Go Out: Being the Adventures of a Knowledgeable Stingray, a Toughy Little Buffalo, and Someone Called Plastic*, p. 52.

Bulletin of the Center for Children's Books, February, 2001, Deborah Stevenson, review of *Five Creatures*, p. 226; March 1, 2005, Timnah Card, "True Blue: Emily Jenkins"; April, 2006, Loretta Gaffney, review of *Fly on the Wall: How One Girl Saw Everything*, p. 364.

Commonweal, June 18, 1999, Gabrielle Steinfels, review of *Tongue First: Adventures in Physical Culture*, p. 24.

Entertainment Weekly, September 18, 1998, Clarissa Cruz, review of *Tongue First*, p. 82.

Girls' Life, February-March, 2005, review of *The Boyfriend List*, p. 40.

Horn Book, March, 2001, Kitty Flynn, review of *Five Creatures*, p. 197; January-February, 2002, Leonard S. Marcus, review of *Five Creatures*, p. 24; May-June, 2004, Lauren Adams, review of *Daffodil*, p. 316; July-

August, 2004, Christine M. Heppermann, review of *My Favorite Thing (according to Alberta)*, p. 439; March-April, 2005, Jennifer M. Brabander, review of *That New Animal*, p. 189; March-April, 2006, Claire E. Gross, review of *Fly on the Wall*, p. 191; September-October, 2006, Christine M. Heppermann, *Love You When You Whine*, p. 567.

Kirkus Reviews, March 15, 2001, review of *Five Creatures*, p. 411; September 15, 2002, review of *Mister Posterior and the Genius Child*, p. 1337; May 15, 2004, review of *My Favorite Thing (according to Alberta)*, p. 493; April 15, 2004, review of *Daffodil*, p. 395; January 15, 2005, review of *That New Animal*, p. 122; February 15, 2005, review of *The Boyfriend List*, p. 232; February 15, 2006, review of *Fly on the Wall*, p. 186; August 1, 2006, review of *Love You When You Whine*, p. 788; August 15, 2006, review of *Toys Go Out*, p. 844; September 1, 2006, review of *The Boy Book*, p. 907.

Kliatt, March, 2006, Michele Winship, review of *Fly on the Wall*, p. 14; September, 2006, Joanna Solomon, review of *The Boy Book*, p. 14.

Observer (London, England), January 10, 1999, Nicci Gerrard, review of *Tongue First*, p. 13.

Publishers Weekly, October 14, 1996, review of *The Secret Life of Billie's Uncle Myron*, p. 84; June 15, 1998, review of *Tongue First*, p. 48; March 26, 2001, review of *Five Creatures*, pp. 91-92; November 4, 2002, review of *Mister Posterior and the Genius Child*, p. 60; May 3, 2004, review of *Daffodil*, p. 191; July 12, 2004, review of *My Favorite Thing (according to Alberta)*, p. 63; February 28, 2005, review of *That New Animal* p. 66, and *The Boyfriend List*, p. 68; February 27, 2006, review of *Fly on the Wall*, p. 62; August 28, 2006, review of *The Boy Book*, p. 55; July 24, 2006, review of *Love You When You Whine*, p. 56; July 31, 2006, review of *Hug, Hug, Hug!* and *Num, Num, Num!*, p. 77; October 30, 2006, review of *Toys Go Out*, p. 62.

School Library Journal, November, 1996, John Sigwald, review of *The Secret Life of Billie's Uncle Myron*, p. 107; May, 2001, Sheryl L. Shipley, review of *Five Creatures*, p. 124; May, 2004, Kathy Krasniewicz, review of *Daffodil*, p. 114; September, 2004, Roxanne Burg, review of *My Favorite Thing (according to Alberta)*, p. 169; March, 2005, Rosalyn Pierini, review of *That New Animal*, p. 174; April, 2005, Elaine Baran Black, review of *The Boyfriend List*, p. 136; March, 2006, Stephanie L. Petruso, review of *Fly on the Wall*, p. 227; June, 2006, Amelia Jenkins, review of *Hug, Hug, Hug!* and *Num, Num, Num!*, p. 120; September, 2006, Tamara E. Richman, review of *Plonk, Plonk, Plonk!* and *Up, Up, Up!*, p. 174, Elizabeth Bird, review of *Toys Go Out*, p. 174, and Sheilah Kosco, review of *The Boy Book*, p. 210; October, 2006, Joy Fleishhacker, review of *Love You When You Whine*, p. 113.

Teacher Librarian, December, 2005, review of *The Boyfriend List*, p. 10.

Teaching Children Mathematics, April, 2002, David J. Whitlin, review of *Five Creatures*, p. 488.

Voice of Youth Advocates, April, 2005, Geneva Scully Napolitano, review of *The Boyfriend List*, p. 43.

ONLINE

Beatrice, http://www.beatrice.com/ (May 27, 2005), Megan Crane, interview with Jenkins.

The Boyfriend List: The Official Web site of E. Lockhart, http://www.theboyfriendlist.com/ (October 20, 2006).

Cynsations Web site, http://cynthialeitichsmith.blogspot.com/ (November 6, 2005), Cynthia Leitich Smith, interviews with E. Lockhart.

Emily Jenkins Home Page, http://www.emilyjenkins.com (November 1, 2006).

Nichelle D. Tramble Web site, http://www.nichelletramble.com/ (April 27, 2006), Nichelle D. Tramble, interview with Lockhart.

Random House Web site, http://www.randomhouse.com/ (October 20, 2006), "E. Lockhart."

Young Adult (& Kids) Book Central Web site, http://yabookscentral.com/ (March 1, 2005), interview with Lockhart.*

K-L

KERRIN, Jessica Scott

Personal

Born in Edmonton, Alberta, Canada. Married; husband's name Peter; children: Elliott. *Education:* University of Calgary, B.A. psychology and political science); Nova Scotia College of Art and Design, B.F.A.; Dalhousie University, M.A. (public administration). *Hobbies and other interests:* Sailing.

Addresses

Home—Halifax, Nova Scotia, Canada.

Career

Writer and arts administrator. Has managed art galleries, dance schools, and museums.

Member

Canadian Society of Authors, Illustrators, and Performers, Canadian Children's Book Centre, Writers' Federation of Nova Scotia.

Awards, Honors

Top Books designation, New York City Public Library, 2005, Notable Books selection, American Library Association, and Saskatchewan Young Readers' Choice Willow Award nomination, both 2006, and Hackmatack Award nomination, 2007, all for *Martin Bridge: Ready for Takeoff!*; Gate City Book Award nomination (New Hampshire), 2007, for *Martin Bridge: On the Lookout!*

Writings

"MARTIN BRIDGE" SERIES; FOR CHILDREN

Martin Bridge: Ready for Takeoff!, illustrated by Joseph Kelly, Kids Can Press (Toronto, Ontario, Canada), 2005.

Martin Bridge: On the Lookout!, illustrated by Joseph Kelly, Kids Can Press (Toronto, Ontario, Canada), 2005.

Martin Bridge: Blazing Ahead!, illustrated by Joseph Kelly, Kids Can Press (Toronto, Ontario, Canada), 2006.

Work in Progress

More books in the "Martin Bridge" series.

Sidelights

Jessica Scott Kerrin is the author of the "Martin Bridge" series of chapter books for younger elementary-grade readers. The works follow the humorous adventures of grade-schooler Martin Bridge and his best friends Alex and Stuart. In fact, Kerrin's own family helped inspire the series; the Nova Scotian author developed the character of Martin after her husband and son returned from a boy scout troop outing with a tale about a model rocket exhibition gone horribly awry. That incident served as the basis for "Smithereens," a story in Kerrin's debut title, *Martin Bridge: Ready for Takeoff!* As the series has expanded, Kerrin's friends have supplied her with additional story ideas, many taken from their own comic misadventures.

Martin Bridge: Ready for Takeoff!, a collection of three stories, appeared in 2005. In the first tale, Martin learns that even his surly school bus driver has feelings after the boy becomes fond of the woman's temporary replacement. In "Faster Blaster," he faces a moral dilemma when a neighbor's hamster dies while under his care. The final tale, "Smithereens," concerns Martin's jealous reaction to a friend's model-rocket design. "Kerrin does quite a good job of showing the shades and intensity of Martin's feelings throughout," *Booklist* critic Carolyn Phelan stated of *Martin Bridge: Ready for Takeoff!*, and *School Library Journal* contributor Pat Leach noted that the author "relates the episodes in a straightforward way that incorporates rich language." Reviewing *Martin Bridge: Ready for Takeoff!* in *Resource Links,* Myra Junyk wrote that "young readers

Cover of Jessica Scott Kerrin's middle-grade novel Martin Bridge: On the Lookout!, *featuring artwork by Joseph Kelly.* (Kids Can Press, 2005. Illustrations © 2005 Joseph Kelly. Used by permission of Kids Can Press Ltd., Toronto)

will be able to relate to this likeable hero and to the situations which he encounters."

Martin makes the best of several awkward yet amusing situations in *Martin Bridge: On the Lookout!* In one episode, the grade-schooler is forced to entertain his least-favorite classmate when she arrives a day late for his birthday party, but his opinion of Laila changes after they spend a fun-filled afternoon together. In another story, Martin forgets his permission slip for a school field trip and remains behind with his former teacher and the younger students. He also faces his classmates' scorn when he opens a window just as the class parakeet is released from her cage, allowing the bird to escape. According to *Horn Book* critic Kitty Flynn, Martin's "earnest (though sometimes bungled) attempts at righting his wrongs are realistically portrayed and handled with a deft and light touch." *Canadian Review of Materials* critic Mary Thomas called the likeable young protagonist "a believable and appealing hero placed in recognizably understandable situations," and a contributor for *Kirkus Reviews* predicted that "young readers will identify with Martin and will celebrate his successes, while recognizing his shortcomings."

Martin survives a camping trip and helps fix a cranky lawnmower in *Martin Bridge: Blazing Ahead!* In "Relish," the boy shares a cabin with his buddy Alex, a no-

torious prankster with a jar of green slime at the ready. "Lightning Bolts" focuses on Martin's relationship with his father as they restore an old lawnmower named Laverne to working condition. A *Kirkus Reviews* critic praised the work, noting that it is "written with affection and humor."

Kerrin plans additional books in the "Martin Bridge" series. Asked if she had any advice for beginning writers, she noted on the *Kids Can Press Web site:* "Pay attention to interesting people around you who do ordinary things and ordinary people around you who do interesting things. Try to find the humor in both."

Biographical and Critical Sources

PERIODICALS

Booklist, March 15, 2005, Carolyn Phelan, review of *Martin Bridge: Ready for Takeoff!,* p. 1294.

Canadian Review of Materials, November 10, 2005, Mary Thomas, review of *Martin Bridge: On the Lookout!*

Horn Book, May-June, 2005, Robin Smith, review of *Martin Bridge: Ready for Takeoff!,* p. 329; November-December, 2005, Kitty Flynn, review of *Martin Bridge: On the Lookout!,* p. 719; January-February, 2006, review of *Martin Bridge: Ready for Takeoff!,* p. 10; September-October, 2006, Robin Smith, review of *Martin Bridge: Blazing Ahead!,* p. 589.

Kirkus Reviews, February 15, 2005, review of *Martin Bridge: Ready for Takeoff!,* p. 230; August 15, 2005, review of *Martin Bridge: On the Lookout!,* p. 917; July 15, 2006, review of *Martin Bridge: Blazing Ahead!,* p. 725.

Resource Links, June, 2005, Myra Junyk, review of *Martin Bridge: Ready for Takeoff!,* p. 20; February, 2006, Mavis Holder, review of *Martin Bridge: On the Lookout!,* p. 24.

School Library Journal, May, 2005, Pat Leach, review of *Martin Bridge: Ready for Takeoff!,* p. 86; November, 2005, Debbie Stewart Hoskins, review of *Martin Bridge: On the Lookout!,* p. 96.

ONLINE

Kids Can Press Web site, http://www.kidscanpress.com/ (October 20, 2006), "Jessica Scott Kerrin."

Writers' Federation of Nova Scotia Web site, http://www.writers.ns.ca/ (October 20, 2006), "Jessica Scott Kerrin."

*   *   *

KNIFESMITH
See CUTLER, Ivor

KOGLER, Jennifer Anne 1982(?)-

Personal

Born c. 1982, in Tustin, CA. *Education:* Princeton University, B.A. (English), 2003.

Addresses

Home—Washington, DC. *Agent*—Trident Media Group, 41 Madison Ave., 36th Fl., New York, NY 10010. *E-mail*—jenniferannekogler@gmail.com.

Career

Writer. Has worked as a waitress.

Writings

Ruby Tuesday (novel), HarperCollins (New York, NY), 2005.

Work in Progress

A second novel.

Sidelights

Being a writer was Jennifer Anne Kogler's dream beginning in childhood, and she completed her first novel while studying for her B.A. in English at Princeton University. After graduation, she took a restaurant job in her home town, and quickly realized that her dream had led her into one of the oldest stereotypes given to creative people: that of the waitress/would-be writer. Determined to throw off this stereotype, Kogler got busy and in less than a year revised her novel manuscript, sent it out for consideration, and wound up with a publisher for *Ruby Tuesday* within months.

Ruby Tuesday follows thirteen-year-old Ruby Tuesday Sweet and her eccentric, sometimes larcenous family. Ruby lives with her father, Hollis, who is involved in illegal gambling. Her mother, Darlene, is a hard-partying rock-and-roller better suited to going to concerts than raising a child. When Ruby's "Uncle Larry"—Hollis's bookie—is found murdered and Hollis is arrested on suspicion of the crime, Darlene arrives to take Ruby out of harm's way. Soon mother and daughter make their way to Las Vegas, where Ruby meets Nana Sue, her casino-loving, heavy smoking, tough-talking, hard-drinking grandmother. Nana Sue, an inveterate gambler, lives in the casino and is often accompanied by her pet iguana, Twenty-One. Complicating matters is the presence of a winning ticket from a secret bet placed by Ruby's father on the 1988 World Series—a ticket worth two million dollars that has sparked considerable interest from the mob. As Ruby and her family dodge criminals and seek to exonerate Hollis, Ruby sees how strange and chaotic the world of adults can be and starts on her own journey to adulthood.

Noting that Kogler's fiction debut "is full of amusing detail, snappy dialogue and Technicolor characters," a contributor to *Kirkus Reviews* also found the novel to be "rather less well supplied with discipline." However, the critic concluded, any flaws in *Ruby Tuesday* will be enjoyed by readers, many of whom will identify with the book's likeable protagonist. *Kliatt* reviewer Claire Rosser called *Ruby Tuesday* an "excellent first novel," and remarked that "what makes this story so much fun, along with these flamboyant characters, are the wonderful descriptions Kogler creates with her writing." Nana Sue "is possibly the most unconventional grandmother to hit the pages of middle-grade fiction," observed Connie Tyrrell Burns in her review of *Ruby Tuesday* for *School Library Journal.*

Biographical and Critical Sources

PERIODICALS

Kirkus Reviews, March 1, 2005, review of *Ruby Tuesday,* p. 289.
Kliatt, March, 2005, Claire Rosser, review of *Ruby Tuesday,* p. 13.
Publishers Weekly, May 23, 2005, review of *Ruby Tuesday,* p. 79.
School Library Journal, April, 2005, Connie Tyrrell Burns, review of *Ruby Tuesday,* p. 136.

ONLINE

Blogcritics.org, http://www.blogcritics.org/ (October 15, 2006), Vikk Simmons, review of *Ruby Tuesday.*
Jennifer Anne Kogler Home Page, http://www.jenniferannekogler.com (October 15, 2006).*

*   *   *

LACOME, Julie 1961-

Personal

Born January 20, 1961, in Fife, Scotland; daughter of Myer (principal of an art college) and Jacqueline (a homemaker) Lacome. *Education:* Edinburgh College of Art, B.A. (with honours), 1982; Central St. Martin's School of Art, post-diploma certificate (illustration), 1983. *Hobbies and other interests:* Traveling, cinema, swimming, cycling, walking, collecting.

Addresses

Home—Edinburgh, Scotland. *Agent*—c/o Author Mail, Walker Books, 87 Vauxhall Walk, London SE11 5HJ, England.

Career

Children's book author, illustrator, and muralist. Freelance greeting card and magazine illustrator, 1983-86; British Broadcasting Corporation, London, England, illustrator for children's television program *Playschool,* 1984. Part-time tutor in illustration in Edinburgh, Scotland; conducts workshops in collage and mixed media for children throughout Scotland. *Exhibitions:* Works include a mural installation at Netherbow Arts Centre, Edinburgh, Scotland.

Awards, Honors

Design Centre Label Award, 1985, for greeting-card designs; Reading Magic Award, *Parenting* magazine, and Nottinghamshire Children's Book Award shortlist, both 1993, both for *Walking through the Jungle;* Scottish Arts Council Children's Book Award, 2001, for *Ruthie's Big Old Coat.*

Writings

SELF-ILLUSTRATED; FOR CHILDREN

My First Book of Words, Platt & Munk (New York, NY), 1986, second edition, Candlewick Press (Cambridge, MA), 1996.

There Was a Crooked Man, and Little Miss Muffet, Walker Books (London, England), 1986.

Baa, Baa Black Sheep, and Jack and Jill, Walker Books (London, England), 1986.

Mary Had a Little Lamb, and Rub-a-Dub-Dub, Walker Books (London, England), 1986.

Wee Willie Winkie, and Hey Diddle Diddle, Walker Books (London, England), 1986.

Noisy Noises on the Farm, Walker Books/Mothercare (London, England), 1988.

Sing a Song of Sixpence: Book of Nursery Songs, Walker Books (London, England), 1989.

Hocus Pocus, Morrow (New York, NY), 1991.

Funny Business, Morrow (New York, NY), 1991.

Colours, Walker Books (London, England), 1991.

Walking through the Jungle, Candlewick Press (Cambridge, MA), 1993.

I'm a Jolly Farmer, Candlewick Press (Cambridge, MA), 1994.

In the Jungle, Candlewick Press (Cambridge, MA), 1995.

Garden, Candlewick Press (Cambridge, MA), 1995.

On the Farm, Candlewick Press (Cambridge, MA), 1995.

Seashore, Candlewick Press (Cambridge, MA), 1995.

Noah's Ark, Grosset & Dunlap, 1996.

Green Tractor (board book), Orchard Books (London, England), 1997.

Big Hen Little Chicks, Orchard Books (London, England), 1997.

Ruthie's Big Old Coat, Candlewick Press (Cambridge, MA), 2000.

Big Nursery Rhyme Book, Walker Books (London, England), 2002.

ILLUSTRATOR

Pam Ayers, *Guess What?,* Walker Books/Mothercare (London, England), 1987, Candlewick Press (New York, NY), 1994.

Pam Ayers, *Guess Who?,* Walker Books/Mothercare (London, England), 1987, Candlewick Press (New York, NY), 1994.

David Bennett, *Whose Ears?,* Octopus Books, 1988.

David Bennett, *Whose Dinner?,* Octopus Books, 1988.

David Bennett, *Whose Legs?,* Octopus Books, 1988.

David Bennett, *Whose Home?,* Octopus Books, 1988.

David Bennett, *The Christmas Party,* Kingfisher (London, England), 1991.

Edward Lear, *"A" Was an Apple Pie,* Candlewick Press (New York, NY), 1992.

Pam Ayers, *Guess Why?,* Candlewick Press (New York, NY), 1994.

Pam Ayers, *Guess Where,* Candlewick Press (New York, NY), 1994.

Dayle Ann Dodds, *The Shape of Things,* Candlewick Press (New York, NY), 1994.

Alison Boyle, *Where Is Little Croc?,* Walker Books (London, England), 1999.

Jane Salt, *Starting to Read: Book 3* Hamlyn Young Books, 1999.

Carole Lexa Schaefer, *Beep! Beep! It's Beeper!,* Candlewick Press (Cambridge, MA), 2001.

Carole Lexa Schaefer, *Beeper's Friends!,* Candlewick Press (Cambridge, MA), 2002.

Susan Rennie, *Sweetieraptors: A Book o' Scots Dinosaurs,* Black and White Publishing, 2002.

Vivian French, *Buck's Truck,* Walker Books (London, England), 2005.

Sidelights

Julie Lacome is a prolific illustrator and author whose books are familiar to many toddlers in both Lacome's native United Kingdom and the United States. Her brightly colored art, which incorporates simple shapes and friendly characters, had definite child appeal; in a

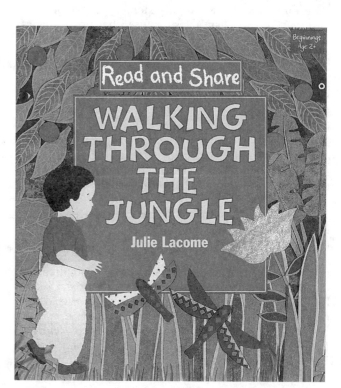

Cover of Julie Lacome's self-illustrated picture book **Walking through the Jungle,** *a rhyming beginning reader.* (Candlewick Press, 1999. Copyright © 1993 by Julie Lacome. Reproduced by permission of the publisher Candlewick Press, Inc., Cambridge, MA)

Lacome's brightly colored paper-collage illustrations are featured in **The Shape of Things,** *a picture book written by Dayle Ann Dodds.* (Candlewick Press, 1996. Illustrations copyright © 1994 by Julie Lacome. Reproduced by permission of the publisher Candlewick Press, Inc., Cambridge, MA)

review of her popular rhyming picture book *Walking through the Jungle,* a *Publishers Weekly* contributor praised Lacome's use of "clean patterns" and a "deep, dramatic palette" of opaque colors, both of which combine in a rhyming game that is "likely to keep vicarious jungle-goers on their toes." A *Horn Book* critic dubbed the book "jaunty" and a source of inspiration for "imaginative play."

Featuring what a *Horn Book* contributor dubbed "bouncy" images, *Ruthie's Big Old Coat* introduces a young bunny who inherits a big red coat from older cousin Frances. Dismayed at first with the gift, she finds a way to make the oversized garment into a fun game with help from best-friend Fiona. Even when things do not go quite right, the two bunny friends pull together to solve problems and make things come out right. Lacome's gentle story "shows all the fun two friends can have" when they let their imagination loose, according to *Booklist* contributor Marta Segal, while Roxanne Burg wrote in *School Library Journal* that the author/illustrator's "charming acrylic-and-gouache illustrations are colorful and quirky."

"From an early age, I always loved drawing and making things," Lacome once told *SATA.* "As my father taught in an art college, I visited it frequently and knew that when I left school I simply wanted to 'go to art college.' My elder sister was an art student when I was a teenager and became a freelance illustrator, so I followed on after her.

"I didn't decide specifically to illustrate purely children's books, but after working freelance for a couple of years in London doing mainly greeting-card designs and also working for a short period for children's TV, the imagery and color of my work seemed more suited to children than adults. The day before I returned to live in Scotland, an old tutor of mine suggested that I

go to see the children's book publisher Walker Books, so I took my portfolio to show them and have received a steady list of book commissions from them ever since!"

In Lacome's early work, collage was her medium of choice, "mainly because I enjoy the immediacy with which color choices can be made and the intensity of color in colored papers," as she once explained. In books such as *The Shape of Things* she "began experimenting with texture and printing methods in the same way as children do using sponge and potato prints, and different crayons and chalks." Most recently, she has moved into simple line drawings, where her humor is most clearly expressed.

"My favorite images are animals, as I enjoy the color and humor found in them," Lacome added. "My book *Walking through the Jungle* was extremely enjoyable to do as the subject matter of the animals and the vegetation of the jungle allowed me to experiment with color and textures."

Biographical and Critical Sources

PERIODICALS

Booklist, April 15, 1993, Julie Corsaro, review of *Walking through the Jungle,* p. 1519; June 1, 1994, Kay Weisman, review of *I'm a Jolly Farmer,* p. 1840; January 15, 1995, Ilene Cooper, review of *The Shape of Things,* p. 931; April 15, 1995, Carolyn Phelan, review of *Seashore* and *Garden,* p. 1506; April 1, 2000, Marta Segal, review of *Ruthie's Big Old Coat,* p. 1469.
Horn Book, September-October, 1992, Ellen Fader, review of *Walking through the Jungle,* p. 609; May, 2000, review of *Ruthie's Big Old Coat,* p. 297.

Magpies, March, 2000, review of *Ruthie's Big Old Coat,* p. 29.

Publishers Weekly, January 11, 1993, review of *Walking through the Jungle,* p. 62.

School Library Journal, March, 1992, Mary Lou Budd, review of *"A" Was Once an Apple Pie,* p. 231; August, 1994, p. 139; February, 1995, Ruth Semrau, review of *The Shape of Things,* p. 90; September, 1995, Emily Kutler, review of *Seashore,* p. 181; May, 2000, Roxanne Burg, review of *Ruthie's Big Old Coat,* p. 146; February, 2002, Anne Knickerbocker, review of *Beep! Beep! It's Beeper!,* p. 100.

* * *

LAMBERT, Stephen 1964-

Personal

Born 1964. *Education:* Trained at Reigate and Lincoln art colleges.

Addresses

Home—Cornwall, England. *Agent*—c/o Author Mail, Random House, 1745 Broadway, 3rd Fl., New York, NY 10019.

Career

Illustrator and author of children's book.

Writings

SELF-ILLUSTRATED

The Magpie and the Star, Hutchinson (London, England), 1991.

ILLUSTRATOR

June Jones, *A Happy Time at Eid-ul-Adha,* Blackie (London, England), 1986.

June Jones, *Going to Mosque School,* Blackie (London, England), 1986.

June Jones, *Kausar at Home,* Blackie (London, England), 1986.

June Jones, *Praying with Ammi,* Blackie (London, England), 1986.

June Jones, *Ramadan and Eid-ul-Fitr,* Blackie (London, England), 1986.

June Jones, *Shakoor Is Born,* Blackie (London, England), 1986.

Richard Edwards, *Phoots!,* Orchard (London, England), 1989.

James Riordan, reteller, *The Snowmaiden,* Hutchinson (London, England), 1990.

June Crebbin, *Fly by Night,* Candlewick Press (Cambridge, MA), 1993.

Reeve Lindbergh, *What Is the Sun?,* Candlewick Press (Cambridge, MA), 1994.

June Crebbin, *The Train Ride,* Candlewick Press (Cambridge, MA), 1995.

Jill Paton Walsh, *Connie Came to Play,* Viking (London, England), 1995.

Liz Rosenberg, *Moonbathing,* Harcourt (San Diego, CA), 1996.

Richard Brown, *The Moonlight Owl,* Cambridge University Press (Cambridge, England), 1996.

Jill Paton Walsh, *When I Was Little like You,* Viking (New York, NY), 1997.

Pippa Goodhart, *Row, Row, Row Your Boat,* Crown (New York, NY), 1997, published as *Row Your Boat: Rhyme,* Heinemann Young Books (Oxford, England), 1997.

Margaret Nash, *Secret in the Mist,* Levinson Books (London, England), 1998.

Joan Blos, *Bedtime!,* Simon & Schuster (New York, NY), 1998.

Pippa Goodhart, *Happy Sad,* Mammoth (London, England), 1999.

Pippa Goodhart, *Jack's Mouse,* Mammoth (London, England), 1999.

Simon Puttock, *Coral Goes Swimming,* Hodder Children's (London, England), 2000.

Adrian Mitchell, *Nobody Rides the Unicorn,* Arthur A. Levine Books (New York, NY), 2000.

Robert E. Swindells, *The Orchard Book of Egyptian Gods and Pharaohs,* Orchard (London, England), 2000, published as *The Orchard Book of Stories from Ancient Egypt,* 2003.

Geraldine McCaughrean, *My Grandmother's Clock,* Clarion Books (New York, NY), 2002.

Beverly Birch, *Shakespeare's Tales,* Hodder Children's (London, England), 2002.

Vivian French, *The Kingfisher Book of Nursery Tales,* Kingfisher (Boston, MA), 2003.

David Almond, *Kate, the Cat, and the Moon,* Random House (New York, NY), 2005.

Sidelights

English-born illustrator Stephen Lambert has created artwork for over a dozen books for children, among them Adrian Mitchell's *Nobody Rides the Unicorn* and Geraldine McCaughrean's *My Grandmother's Clock.* Using vibrantly colored pastels in the majority of his illustrations, Lambert has been praised for the ethereal effects and gentle tones he achieves in his art. Moving into illustration after attending art school in his native England, Lambert began his publishing career creating art for a series of multicultural picture books by June Jones, and has also illustrated an original story, published in 1991 as *The Magpie and the Star.*

What Is the Sun?, in which he illustrates the text by Reeve Lindbergh, captures the curiosity of children as it follows a young boy as he questions the purpose of the sun and other natural elements of Earth, including the moon, the wind, and the rain. In *Publishers Weekly* a critic commented that "Lambert's colorful pastels are rendered sweetly" and remarked that the book's illus-

Stephen Lambert's softly rendered art is a perfect match for Joan Blos's lights-out picture book **Bedtime!** (Simon & Schuster Books for Young Readers, 1998. Illustrations copyright © 1998 by Stephen Lambert. Reprinted by permission of Simon & Schuster Books for Young Readers, an imprint of Simon & Schuster Children's Publishing Division)

trations provide "a festive yet peaceful backdrop for a tender bedtime exchange." Lambert also contributed illustrations to Joan Blos's *Bedtime!*, a nighttime tale that captures a child's reluctance to go to bed. "Lambert's softly focused illustrations are just right," noted *Booklist* reviewer Stephanie Zvirin. "Lit by shimmery moonlight, they glow with cozy warmth."

Lambert's whimsical and soft-toned art also complements Adrian Mitchell's fantasy picture book, *Nobody Rides the Unicorn*. Mitchell's story follows the trials of its protagonist, Zoe, as she saves a forest unicorn from the King of Joppardy, a ruler who intends to slay the mythic creature unicorn for its horn. In illustrating *Nobody Rides the Unicorn* Lambert varies his perspective, including both panoramic views and detailed close-ups. "There is a misty quality to the soft-edged artwork," commented *School Library Journal* critic Carol Schene,

the reviewer adding that "muted colon and the almost fuzzy, cottony look of the unicorn help to create a mythical, mystical atmosphere." Likewise, a writer for *Publishers Weekly* acknowledged Lambert's fantastical images, which "lift the book to a higher level. His sophisticated use of mist-filtered light and shadow, and his seamless blend of old-world elegance and hints of modern life, make this a cautionary tale with a sense of immediacy," the critic added.

The rhythms of time are explored in Geraldine Mc-Caughrean's *My Grandmother's Clock,* a picture book augmented by Lambert's "large sculptural illustrations with rounded shapes and soft colors" according to *Book* reviewer Kathleen Odean. In her story, McCaughrean details how a grandmother keeps track of time through her daily activities, and "Lambert's hazy illustrations depict characters with gentle expressions and soft, rounded features whiling away the day," acknowledged *School Library Journal* reviewer Catherine Threadgill. "The effect," added Threadgill, "is charming."

Biographical and Critical Sources

PERIODICALS

Book, March-April, 2003, Kathleen Odean, review of *My Grandmother's Clock,* p. 36.

Booklist, May 15, 1998, Stephanie Zvirin, review of *Bedtime!,* p. 1629.

Publishers Weekly, May 9, 1994, review of *What Is the Sun?* p. 71; April 24, 2000, review of *Nobody Rides the Unicorn,* p. 90.

School Library Journal, January, 2001, Carol Schene, review of *Nobody Rides the Unicorn,* p. 104; September, 2002, Catherine Threadgill, review of *My Grandmother's Clock,* p. 200.

ONLINE

Houghton Mifflin Web site, http://www.houghton-mifflinbooks.com/ (October 6, 2006).

Walker Books Web site, http://www.walkerbooks.co.uk/ (October 6, 2006).*

*   *   *

LAMSTEIN, Sarah 1943-
(Sarah Marwil Lamstein)

Personal

Born July 28, 1943, in Boston, MA; daughter of Milton (a bookseller) and Lenore (a bookseller) Marwil; married Joel Lamstein (a management consultant), June 25, 1966; children: Josh, Emily Rynd, Abby. *Education:* University of Michigan, B.A., 1965, M.A., 1966; Simmons College, M.L.S., 1984; Vermont College, M.F.A., 2003. *Politics:* Democrat. *Religion:* Jewish. *Hobbies and other interests:* Reading, walking, gardening.

Addresses

Home—45 Pine Crest Rd., Newton, MA 02459. *E-mail*—sml@sarahlamstein.com.

Career

Children's book author. Formerly worked as an English teacher at Lynbrook Junior High School, Lynbrook, NY, and Arlington High School, Arlington, MA; school librarian at Milton Academy and Roxbury Latin School, 1982-2000; Mather School, Boston, MA, former consultant. Puppeteer; Puppet Showplace Theatre, Brookline, MA, clerk of board, 2004—.

Member

Society of Children's Book Writers and Illustrators (New England chapter), Boston Area Guild of Puppetry.

Awards, Honors

Booklist Top Ten Religious Books for Youth listee, 1998, for *Annie's Shabbat;* Bank Street College Best Books for Children designation, 2000, for *I Like Your Buttons!;* Julia Ward How Prize for Young Readers finalist, Boston Authors Club, 2005, for *Hunger Moon.*

Writings

(Under name Sarah Marwil Lamstein) *Annie's Shabbat,* illustrated by Cecily Lang, Albert Whitman (Morton Grove, IL), 1997.

(With Kavita Ram Shrestha) *From the Mango Tree, and Other Folktales from Nepal,* Libraries Unlimited (Englewood, CO), 1997.

(Under name Sarah Marwil Lamstein) *I Like Your Buttons!,* illustrated by Nancy Cote, Albert Whitman (Morton Grove, IL), 1999.

Hunger Moon (young-adult novel), Front Street Books (Asheville, NC), 2004.

Sleepy Birds, illustrated by Anna Alter, Charlesbridge (Watertown, MA), 2006.

Sidelights

"Perhaps, like most authors, it was reading that got me writing," children's book writer and former librarian Sarah Lamstein told *SATA.* "As a small child, I was captivated by everything about books—their stories, their illustrations, their feel, their smell, even their typeface—the whole package a delight. It's no surprise, then, that I wanted to create my own books. As an early teenager, I took every opportunity to do just that. For my father's birthday, I compiles a book of praise from all five of us kids; for my sister, I wrote a story with her as the heroine; for my parents' anniversary, I compiled a book of photographs, a history of their years together.

"What spurred me to make these early books was a desire to celebrate loved ones. To this day, that is what writing is to me: a celebration of what I love. My book *From the Mango Tree, and Other Folktales from Nepal* is a celebration of the magnificent country of Nepal, *Annie's Shabbat* celebrates my family's observance of the Sabbath, and *I Like Your Buttons!* celebrates the joy of being kind.

"Though my writing is primarily an expression of joy, it became an exploration of emotional pain in the writing of my young-adult novel *Hunger Moon.* When I was eleven or twelve, I scared my disabled younger brother. I'm not sure why I did it, but I do know that the memory of my tormenting him has always made me

Cover of Sarah Lamstein's **I Like Your Buttons!,** ***featuring artwork by Nancy Cote.*** (Albert Whitman & Company, 1999. Illustrations copyright © 1999 by Nancy Cote. Reproduced by permission)

feel ashamed. When I was a student in the Vermont College M.F.A. Program in Writing for Children and Young Adults, we were urged to go deep in our writing, deep into our memories and emotions. I went deep and remembered the time I frightened my brother. I began to write about it, creating a story that explored why a sister would do such a thing.

"Though the motivation for writing *Hunger Moon* was a departure for me, there is a celebratory aspect to it, as there is so strongly in my other books—a celebration of twelve-year-old Ruthie's development, of her finding her own voice. The book's form is a bit unconventional—it is not written in chapters, but in short vignettes, like poems, moments of action and emotion—and this, again, was not a departure for me. I'd written poetry before writing books for children. And my picture books depend on poetry, on compressed language to convey emotion and tell a story.

"The form of *Hunger Moon* came not only from my own poetic leanings, but was also inspired by the work of Karen Hesse in *Out of the Dust* and Virginia Euwer Woolf in *Make Lemonade*. These books so moved and impressed me that my writing may have mimicked theirs, coming out in short little pieces, like poems.

Cover of Lamstein's novel **Hunger Moon**, *which finds a middle schooler attempting to navigate adolescence while her parents' fighting creates a tumultuous home life.* (Front Street, 2004. Reproduced by permission of Boyds Mills Press)

"So you see, reading still gets me writing, sometimes influencing the form my writing takes, consciously or unconsciously. I'm grateful that my reading led me to be a maker of children's books, for this work allows me to explore what is deep within me and to celebrate what I love."

Biographical and Critical Sources

PERIODICALS

Booklist, October 1, 1997, Ilene Cooper, review of *Annie's Shabbat,* p. 324; August, 1999, Ilene Cooper, review of *I Like Your Buttons!,* p. 2064; June 1, 2004, Jennifer Mattson, review of *Hunger Moon,* p. 1726.
Kirkus Reviews, May 1, 2004, review of *Hunger Moon,* p. 444.
Publishers Weekly, August 25, 1997, review of *Annie's Shabbat,* p. 66.
School Library Journal, June, 2004, Susan Oliver, review of *Hunger Moon,* p. 145.
Voice of Youth Advocates, December, 2004, review of *Hunger Moon,* p. 384.

ONLINE

Boston Globe Online, http://www.boston.com/news/education/k_12/articles/ (June 26, 2005), Donna Goodison, "From Reader to Writer."
Sarah Lamstein Home Page, http://www.sarahlamstein.com (October 20, 2006).*

*   *   *

LAMSTEIN, Sarah Marwil
See LAMSTEIN, Sarah

*   *   *

LATTA, Sara L. 1960-

Personal

Born December 11, 1960, in Harper, KS; daughter of Norman (a farmer) and Joyce (a homemaker) Latta; married Tony Liss (a physicist); children: Alison and Caitlin (twins); Eli. *Education:* University of Kansas, B.A. (microbiology and English), 1983; University of Chicago, M.S. (immunology), 1985; Lesley University, M.F.A. (creative writing), 2006. *Hobbies and other interests:* Baking, running, reading, gardening.

Addresses

Home—Champaign, IL. *Agent*—Barbara Markowitz, P.O. Box 41709, Los Angeles, CA 90041. *E-mail*—saralatta@sbcglobal.net.

Career

Science writer and children's book author. University of Chicago Hospitals, Chicago, IL, science writer and editor, 1986-88; American Oil Chemists' Society, staff science writer, 1990-93; freelance science writer and author, 1993—.

Member

Society of Children's Books Writers and Illustrators (Illinois chapter), National Association of Science Writers, Authors Guild.

Writings

Allergies, Enslow Publishers (Springfield, NJ), 1998.
Food Poisoning and Foodborne Diseases, Enslow Publishers (Berkeley Heights, NJ), 1999.
Dealing with the Loss of a Loved One, Chelsea House (Philadelphia, PA), 2003.
The Good, the Bad, the Slimy: The Secret Life of Microbes, Enslow Publishers (Berkeley Heights, NJ), 2006.
Stella Brite and the Dark Matter Mystery, illustrated by Meredith Johnson, Charlesbridge (Watertown, MA), 2006.
What Happens in Fall?, Enslow Publishers (Berkeley Heights, NJ), 2006.
What Happens in Spring?, Enslow Publisehrs (Berkeley Heights, NJ), 2006.
What Happens in Summer?, Enslow Elementary (Berkeley Heights, NJ), 2006.
What Happens in Winter?, Enslow Publishers (Berkeley Heights, NJ), 2006.

Work in Progress

Into the Fire, a young-adult novel set in 1925; two books for Enslow's "Extreme Science Careers" series: *Antarctic Scientists* and *Volcano Scientists;* a biography of a Nobel Prize-winning scientist.

Sidelights

Sara L. Latta told *SATA:* "I grew up on a farm in Kansas, and I was very much influenced by the animals and the landscape around me. I read all the time—I was always teased for being a bookworm—but I had no idea that I might become an author. I thought I might become a veterinarian, a doctor, or a scientist. Science won out, although I continued to love reading and writing. Now, science writing allows me to combine my interest in science with my passion for worlds. In turn, I believe my fiction writing benefits from the scientist's attention to detail, as well as a love for research (whatever the topic!)."

Biographical and Critical Sources

PERIODICALS

Kirkus Reviews, December 15, 2005, review of *Stella Brite and the Dark Matter Mystery,* p. 1324.
School Library Journal, November, 1999, review of *Food Poisoning and Foodborne Diseases,* p. 172; April, 2006, Kristine M. Casper, review of *Stella Brite and the Dark Matter Mystery,* p. 110; December, 2006, Tracey Bell, review of *What Happens in Spring?*

ONLINE

Eclectica Web site, http://www.eclectica.org/ (October-November, 2006), Colleen Mondor, review of *Stella Bright and the Dark Matter Mystery.*
Greenbay Press-Gazette Online, http://www.greenbaypressgazette.com/ (October 10, 2006), Jean Peerenboom, "Science Writer Finds Niche in Children's Books."
National Science Teachers Association Web site, http://www.www2.nsta.org/ (October 20, 2006), Judy Kraus, review of *What Happens in Spring?*
Sara L. Latta Home Page, http://www.saralatta.com (October 10, 2006).

*   *   *

LOCKHART, E.
See JENKINS, Emily

M

MacCULLOUGH, Carolyn

Personal

Female. *Education:* Grinnell College, B.A.; New School University, M.F.A. (creative writing), 2002.

Addresses

Home—New York, NY. *Agent*—c/o Roaring Brook Press, 143 West St., New Milford, CT 06776.

Career

Writer. New School University, New York, NY, teacher of creative writing; Gotham Writers' Workshop, teacher of creative writing and children's book writing.

Awards, Honors

New York Public Library Best Books for the Teen Age selection, for *Falling through Darkness*.

Writings

YOUNG-ADULT NOVELS

Falling through Darkness, Roaring Brook Press (Brookfield, CT), 2003.
Stealing Henry, Roaring Brook Press (New Milford, CT), 2005.
Drawing the Ocean, Roaring Brook Press (New Milford, CT), 2006.

Sidelights

Young-adult novelist Carolyn MacCullough is the author of such critically acclaimed works as *Falling through Darkness, Stealing Henry,* and *Drawing the Ocean.* Though she did not initially plan to write for a teen audience, MacCullough finds great satisfaction in her work. "I think you can do all the things in a YA novel that you do in a novel for adults," she commented in an interview with Deborah Brodie for *Voice of Youth Advocates.* "Young adults or teenagers are going through all the same emotions and experiences that adults do. The only difference is that maybe teens are having these experiences for the first time."

MacCullough published her debut title, *Falling through Darkness,* in 2003. The work concerns seventeen-year-old Ginny, the survivor of a tragic car accident that took the life of Ginny's boyfriend, Aidan. Ginny sinks into a dark depression after the tragedy, refusing to talk about it with either her father or her best friend, neither of whom is aware of the terrible secret she keeps. When her father rents the apartment above their garage to Caleb, an older man who lost his son, Ginny finally opens up, confiding to Caleb about her relationship with Aidan, whose abuse at the hands of his father led to his final, desperate act. "No false cheer at the end, but a sliver of hopefulness as Ginny begins to gain clarity," remarked a *Kirkus Reviews* contributor. Critics praised the author's plotting and characterization. "MacCullough expertly fleshes out the scenes," noted a *Publishers Weekly* critic, "enabling readers to visualize the action and intuit the implications for the characters." According to *Booklist* critic Hazel Rochman, the author "gets the seventeen-year-old's viewpoint, haunting memories, and interminable days on the edge absolutely right." In *Horn Book,* Martha V. Parravano was apt in deeming the novel a "promising debut"; *Falling through Darkness* was honored as a New York Public Library Best Book for the Teen Age.

A teenage girl takes to the road to escape her unhappy life in *Stealing Henry,* which MacCullough released in 2005. When she can no longer endure her stepfather's violent outbursts, seventeen-year-old Savannah wallops the man with a frying pan and flees their home with Henry, her eight-year-old half brother, in tow. The pair ventures first to New York City and then north to Maine, where they reconnect with Savannah's great aunt. Interspersed with the tale of the siblings' journey is the

Cover of Carolyn MacCullough's young-adult novel Stealing Henry, *featuring photography by Orlando Corral.* (Roaring Brook Press, 2005. Reprinted by permission of Henry Holt and Company, LLC)

story of Alice, their estranged mother, who left home at age eighteen after becoming pregnant and roamed the country for years, living a nomadic life with Savannah. "MacCullough captures the panicky quality of the escape," noted *School Library Journal* critic Kathleen Isaacs, "telling the story obliquely but with intermittent flashes of minute detail." "Tiny strokes of details paint whole backstories for the characters, revealing the tenuous love between mother and daughter," observed *Booklist* reviewer Cindy Dobrez.

In *Drawing the Ocean,* published in 2006, sixteen-year-old Sadie, a talented painter, wants nothing more than to fit in at her new school. Complicating matters are Sadie's relationships with Ryan, the school outcast, and Ollie, her twin brother who died years ago but now reappears to her in a vision. "MacCullough's subtle use of present tense and visually evocative writing create an eloquent portrait," noted a critic in *Kirkus Reviews,* and in *Voice of Youth Advocates* a reviewer concluded that the novel's "pacing and dramatic tension are lovely."

In addition to her career as a novelist, MacCullough also teaches creative writing. She acknowledges that the process of completing a novel can be both exhausting and exhilarating. "Writing a book feels a lot like being in a relationship," she remarked in *Voice of Youth*

Advocates. "Sometimes it's magical, sometimes it's a lot of work. When things go really well, it doesn't even feel like writing. It feels like flying. . . ."

Biographical and Critical Sources

PERIODICALS

Booklist, November 15, 2003, Hazel Rochman, review of *Falling through Darkness,* p. 607; April 1, 2005, Cindy Dobrez, review of *Stealing Henry,* p. 1359.

Horn Book, November-December, 2003, Martha V. Parravano, review of *Falling through Darkness,* p. 750.

Kirkus Reviews, September 15, 2003, review of *Falling through Darkness,* p. 1178; March 1, 2005, review of *Stealing Henry,* p. 290; September 15, 2006, review of *Drawing the Ocean,* p. 960.

Publishers Weekly, October 13, 2003, review of *Falling through Darkness,* p. 81.

School Library Journal, November, 2003, Francisca Goldsmith, review of *Falling through Darkness,* p. 142; April, 2005, Kathleen Isaacs, review of *Stealing Henry,* p. 137.

Voice of Youth Advocates, February, 2004, Carolyn MacCullough and Deborah Brodie, "AuthorTalk: Listening In," pp. 458-460; April, 2004, Amy Alessio, review of *Falling through Darkness,* p. 49; April, 2005, Ed Goldberg and Abbe Goldberg, review of *Stealing Henry,* p. 92.

*   *   *

MADDIGAN, Beth 1967-

Personal

Born February 1, 1967, in St. John's, Newfoundland, Canada; daughter of Philip (an airline manager) and Christine (maiden name Crummey, a bank teller) Maddigan; married Robert Pound (a courier), 1998. *Education:* Memorial University of Newfoundland, B.A., 1990; University of Western Ontario, M.L.I.S., 1996.

Addresses

Home—10 Ivy Crescent, Paris, Ontario N3L 4A9, Canada. *E-mail*—bmaddigan@cambridgelibraries.ca.

Career

Librarian and writer. A.C. Hunter Children's Library, Newfoundland, Canada, library technician, 1990-95; Cambridge Libraries, Cambridge, Ontario, Canada, librarian, 1997-98, children's services coordinator, 1998—; Memorial University of Newfoundland, instructor, 1997-2003. Lecturer at University of Western Ontario, 2005; presenter at conferences and workshops.

Awards, Honors

Bernice Adams Civic Award nominee, City of Cambridge, Ontario, 2004.

Writings

(With Stefanie Drennan and Roberta Thompson) *The Big Book of Stories, Songs, and Sing-Alongs: Programs for Babies, Toddlers, and Families,* Libraries Unlimited, 2003.
(With Stefanie Drennan and Roberta Thompson) *The Big Book of Reading, Rhyming, and Resources: Programs for Children Ages 4-8,* Libraries Unlimited, 2005.

Contributor to periodicals, including *School Library Journal.*

Biographical and Critical Sources

PERIODICALS

Canadian Review of Materials, September 19, 2003, review of *The Big Book of Stories, Songs, and Sing-Alongs: Programs for Babies, Toddlers, and Families.*
School Library Journal, January, 2004, Leslie Barban, review of *The Big Book of Stories, Songs, and Sing-Alongs,* p. 167.*

* * *

MARTINO, Alfred C. 1964-

Personal

Born 1964. *Education:* Duke University, B.A., 1986; University of Southern California, M.B.A., 1993.

Addresses

Home—P.O. Box 817, Roseland, NJ 07068. *E-mail*—ACM673@msn.com.

Career

Journalist, novelist, and entrepreneur. Listen & Live Audio, founder and president. Staff writer and sports reporter for newspapers; youth wrestling coach.

Awards, Honors

Writer's Network Screenplay and Fiction Competition semi-finalist, 1995, 2004; Quills Award nomination in Teen/Young Adult category, Capitol Choices Booksworthy designation, YALSA Best Books designation, Texas Library Association Tayshas Reading List inclusion, *ForeWord* magazine Audiobook of the Year Silver Medal, and *AudioFile* magazine Earphones Award, all 2005, all for *Pinned.*

Writings

Pinned (young-adult novel), Harcourt (Orlando, FL), 2005.

Alfred C. Martino (Photograph by Alisa S. Webeman. Courtesy of Alfred Martino)

Contributor of short fiction to anthologies and periodicals, including *Rockford Review, Writers' Journal,* and *Aguilar Expression;* contributor of articles to periodicals, including *Duke, Beach Reporter,* and *El Segundo Herald.*

Adaptations

Pinned was adapted as an audiobook, narrated by Mark Shanahan, Listen & Live Audio, 2005.

Sidelights

Sports journalist Alfred C. Martino wrote *Pinned,* his first novel, as a way of sharing his passion for the sport of amateur wrestling. Martino's passion for the sport was gained during his high school years, when he began wrestling, and after participating in the sport during his college years he continued to be involved as a youth wrestling coach. Eventually establishing a career in the publishing business—Martino is the president of Listen & Live Audio, the award-winning audiobook publishing company he founded while earning his M.B.A. at the University of Southern California's Marshall School of Business—he started writing part time. Martino worked on *Pinned* for almost a decade before it was published, and the audiobook version was released by Listen & Live Audio in 2005.

In *Pinned* readers meet high school seniors Ivan Korske and Bobby Zane, two teens from different backgrounds who share one thing: the skill and desire to be the next state wrestling championship. Hailing from a small rural town, Ivan hopes that the championship will help him win the college scholarship he will need to escape the blue-collar life that will otherwise become his destiny. In contrast, Bobby has all the material advantages his upper-class family can provide; for him, wrestling is a way to escape from the emotional upheaval caused by his parents' impending divorce. Through the experiences of each teen—the training, practice, and willingness to endure hunger and thirsty in order to attain the weight required in competition—readers begin to understand the dedication and sacrifice required to be a competitive athlete, and to get inside the mind of a young man for whom winning means everything.

Pinned is narrated "with such visceral acuity that the reader can almost feel the burn of the mat," wrote a *Kirkus Reviews* writer in praise of Martino's novel. For Todd Morning in *Booklist,* the "rich portraits" of Ivan and Bobby function as a major element in the author's "compelling" story, while a *Publishers Weekly* contributor praised *Pinned* as a "gritty" coming-of-age story that features a "compelling" sports element. Explaining that the book's dual narratives reveal flaws in each of Martino's teen protagonists, Joel Shoemaker added that while the athletes' language is, at times, "raw," "many teens will identify with the boys' struggles both on and off the mat."

Cover of Martino's **Pinned,** *which finds two high-school wrestlers vying for their state's championship medal.* (Harcourt, Inc., 2005. Jacket photograph © Dimitri Iundt/Corbis)

"Sports books sometimes occupy a sort of ghetto in the world of young adult literature," Lori Witcop commented in her review of *Pinned* for *Curledupkids.com.* Noting that such books are, like Martino's novel, frequently categorizes as "reluctant-reader friendly," Witcop added that "classifying *Pinned* . . . solely as a book about wrestling does it a great disservice. This is a story of dedication, grief, love, lust, friendship, betrayal, pride, redemption and so many other universal ideals."

Biographical and Critical Sources

PERIODICALS

Booklist, March 1, 2005, Todd Morning, review of *Pinned,* p. 1184.
Kirkus Reviews, February 15, 2005, review of *Pinned,* p. 232.
Kliatt, July, 2005, Edna Boardman, review of *Pinned* (audiobook), p. 55.
Publishers Weekly, March 14, 2005, review of *Pinned* (audiobook), p. 26; March 28, 2005, review of *Pinned,* p. 80.
School Library Journal, February, 2005, Joel Shoemaker, review of *Pinned,* p. 139.

ONLINE

Alfred C. Martino Home Page, http://www.alfredmartino. com (October 10, 2006).
Curled up with a Good Kid's Book Web site, http://www. curledupkids.com/ (October 10, 2006), Lori Witkop, review of *Pinned.*

* * *

McKILLIP, Patricia A. 1948-
(Patricia Anne McKillip)

Personal

Born February 29, 1948, in Salem, OR; daughter of Wayne T. and Helen McKillip. *Education:* San Jose State University, B.A., 1971, M.A., 1973. *Hobbies and other interests:* Music.

Addresses

Home—OR. *Agent*—c/o Author Mail, Ace, Penguin Putnam, 375 Hudson St., New York, NY 10014.

Career

Writer.

Awards, Honors

World Fantasy Award for best novel, 1975, and American Library Association Notable Book selection, both for *The Forgotten Beasts of Eld;* Hugo Award nomina-

Patricia A. McKillip (Photograph by David Lunde. Reproduced by permission of Patricia Anne McKillip)

tion, World Science Fiction Convention, 1979, for *Harpist in the Wind;* Mythopoeic Fantasy Award for adult literature, 1995, for *Something Rich and Strange;* World Fantasy Award for best novel and Mythopoeic Fantasy Award for adult literature, both 2003, both for *Ombria in Shadow.*

Writings

FANTASY

The House on Parchment Street, Atheneum (New York, NY), 1973.

The Throme of the Erril of Sherill, Atheneum (New York, NY), 1973.

The Forgotten Beasts of Eld, Atheneum (New York, NY), 1974.

The Night Gift, Atheneum (New York, NY), 1976.

The Riddle-Master of Hed (first book in trilogy), Atheneum (New York, NY), 1976.

Heir of Sea and Fire (second book in trilogy), Atheneum (New York, NY), 1977.

Harpist in the Wind (third book in trilogy), Atheneum (New York, NY), 1979.

Riddle of the Stars (trilogy; contains *The Riddle-Master of Hed, Heir of Sea and Fire,* and *Harpist in the Wind*), Doubleday (Garden City, NY), 1979, published as *Chronicles of Morgan, Prince of Hed,* Future Publications (London, England), 1979, published as *Riddle-Master: The Complete Trilogy,* Ace Books (New York, NY), 1999.

The Changeling Sea, Atheneum (New York, NY), 1988.

The Sorceress and the Cygnet, Ace Books (New York, NY), 1991.

The Cygnet and the Firebird, Ace Books (New York, NY), 1993.

Something Rich and Strange ("Brian Froud's Faerielands" series), illustrated by Brian Froud, Bantam (New York, NY), 1994.

Winter Rose, Ace Books (New York, NY), 1996.

Song for the Basilisk, Ace Books (New York, NY), 1998.

The Tower at Stony Wood, Ace Books (New York, NY), 2000.

Ombria in Shadow, Ace Books (New York, NY), 2003.

In the Forests of Serre, Ace Books (New York, NY), 2003.

Alphabet of Thorn, Ace Books (New York, NY), 2004.

Od Magic, Ace Books (New York, NY), 2005.

Harrowing the Dragon: Collected Tales, Ace Books (New York, NY), 2005.

Solstice Wood, Ace Books (New York, NY), 2006.

SCIENCE FICTION

Moon-Flash, Atheneum (New York, NY), 1984, reprinted, Firebird (New York, NY), 2005.

The Moon and the Face, Atheneum (New York, NY), 1985.

Fool's Run, Warner (New York, NY), 1987.

The Book of Atrix Wolfe, Ace Books (New York, NY), 1995.

OTHER

Stepping from the Shadows (young-adult novel), Atheneum (New York, NY), 1982.

Contributor of short fiction to anthologies, including *Xanadu 2.*

Sidelights

Patricia A. McKillip is a critically acclaimed author of works in a variety of literary genres. "Ranging from fairytale to young adult realistic fiction, from high fantasy to science fiction to adult contemporary fiction," McKillip's "sweeping vision focuses on elemental themes unified by love, power, and magic," noted an essayist in the *St. James Guide to Science-Fiction Writers.* The concentration on basic human traits and themes is a characteristic common to all McKillip's works, which include such novels as *The Cygnet and the Firebird, The Forgotten Beasts of Eld,* and *Solstice Wood.* Noting that McKillip imbues her fantasy worlds with music and a "sense of history and culture," an essayist in *Children's Books and Their Creators* added that "the main attraction to [her] . . . books . . . remains the irresistible and timeless combination of adventure, magic, and romance."

McKillip was born in Salem, Oregon, in 1948. The second of six children, she developed a talent for storytelling because, as she recalled, "the baby-sitting duties were pretty constant. I don't know how old I was when I started telling stories to my younger siblings to while away the boredom of sitting in a car waiting while our

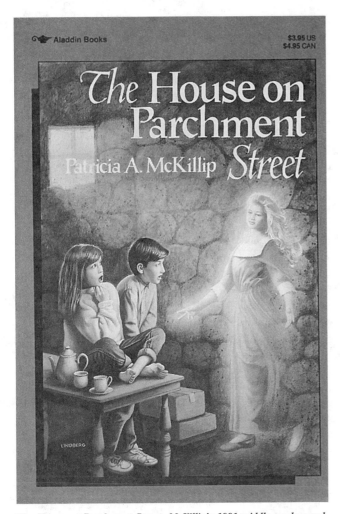

The House on Parchment Street, *McKillip's 1991 middle-grade novel, features a cover illustration by Jeffrey Lindberg.* (Aladdin Books, 1991. Cover illustration copyright © 1991 by Jeffrey Lindberg. All rights reserved. Reproduced by permission of Jeffrey Lindberg)

parents shopped." McKillip began working on her first novel, *The House on Parchment Street,* as a teenager. "I started to write when I was fourteen," she once stated, "during one of those 'moody' periods teenagers have when they know they want something, but don't quite know what it is. I was living in England at the time (my father was stationed at a local air base) in a big old house facing a graveyard: the 'house on Parchment Street.' The countryside was very peaceful, and evocative of all kinds of tales. I spent that summer, between eighth grade and high school, writing fairy tales, reading them to my younger brothers and sisters, and feeling that I had at least found one of the things I didn't know I wanted."

McKillip wrote constantly after that discovery, "all through high school and college—anything and everything—poems, plays, novels, short stories, fantasies. What I really wanted to be was a musician, a pianist, but I realized finally that I was far better at writing. Since I didn't think I was capable of holding down a full-time job, I thought I'd better get published before I left college, so I could support myself." As she recalled,

"no one discouraged me, and I rarely made writing as a career a subject for discussion. I knew the kinds of things I'd hear, so I just kept quiet about it and wrote. My parents never chased me outside when I wanted to write—which was most of the time. They let me grow at my own speed, which strikes me now as an extraordinary way for modern parents to behave."

Although she was determined to be a writer, McKillip did not initially plan to become a children's author. "I never deliberately decided to write for children," she once explained; "I just found them particularly satisfying to write about, and *The House on Parchment Street* happened to be the first thing I sold."

Many reviewers of McKillip's work have noted her ability, regardless of the genre in which she is writing, to touch on basic human traits and themes. For example, *The Forgotten Beasts of Eld,* published in 1974, is filled with the trappings of the fantasy adventure novel: dragons, talking animals, doorless towers, and glass mountains. As *New York Times Book Review* contributor Georgess McHargue wrote, the novel "works on a strictly human level. Trust, loneliness, love's responsibilities and the toxicity of fate are the themes that underlie the fantasy love story." Published separately as *The Riddle-Master of Hed, Heir of Sea and Fire,* and *Harpist in the Wind,* McKillip's well-known "Riddle of the Stars" fantasy trilogy garnered similar praise. The plot follows the fortunes of Morgan from his beginnings as ruler of Hed, a peaceful, sleepy kingdom, to his ultimate destiny as a trained "riddle-master." Referring to the first volume in the trilogy, *The Riddle-Master of Hed,* Glenn Shea stated in the *New York Times Book Review* that McKillip "understands that we spend much of our time choosing, not between good and evil, but the lesser of two ills."

McKillip's young-adult novel *Stepping from the Shadows* is an apparent departure from her usual fantasy adventure format. In terms of its concentration on universal human themes, however, this 1982 novel develops naturally from McKillip's earlier work. The book revolves around the private torments of Frances, a young girl who shares, through conversation and writing, her rich fantasy life with an imaginary sister. "McKillip has put an imaginary playmate on paper and the more sophisticated truth that we all have an outside view of ourselves as well as an inside view," noted Charles Champlin in a *Los Angeles Times* review. The novelist's "memory of the coming of age of an author is rich, particular and extremely appealing," Champlin added.

In the mid-1980s McKillip turned her attention to science fiction, publishing such works as *Moon-Flash, The Moon and the Face,* and *Fool's Run.* She returned to fantasy with the debut volume of another series, *The Sorceress and the Cygnet.* The story of Corleu, a young man who is different in appearance and interests from his Wayfolk kin, is "a richly imagined tale of enchantment, intrigue, and romance," according to *Voice of Youth Advocates* contributor Carolyn Shute.

The fantasy world of *The Sorceress and the Cygnet* also serves as the backdrop for McKillip's *The Cygnet and the Firebird.* In this 1993 novel a mage's plot to steal a magical ancient key is thwarted after a firebird appears that magically transforms things around it into gold and precious gems. The mystery surrounding the creature grows deeper still when it is discovered to be a young warrior who returns to his own shape under certain circumstances, but has no knowledge of his name or his past. Sorceresses, dragons, and the power of the dead also figure into this story, which a *Kirkus Reviews* critic dubbed "often charming and inventive." "McKillip weaves a magic spell of words almost as intoxicating as a drug," noted *School Library Journal* contributor Cathy Chauvette, the critic adding the caveat that while some will enjoy McKillip's lush style, others "will be confused and long for a breath of fresh air."

In *The Book of Atrix Wolfe* McKillip weaves shapeshifting, the lust for power, and magecraft into the mix as Prince Talis, a student of wizardry, finds a book collecting spells possessing undisclosed meanings. Returning home, he meets a queen in search of her daughter, Sorrow, and then joins with Mage Atrix Wolfe to discover Sorrow's whereabouts and dispel a dark power that threatens both the world of humans and that of faerie. Praising McKillip's "masterfully evocative" language, a *Publishers Weekly* contributor maintained that "connoisseurs of fine fantasy will delight in this expertly wrought tale." *Song for the Basilisk* follows another young man, Rook, as he survives the uprising that kills the rest of his family and then travels to another land to lead a quiet life. Haunted by violent dreams, Rook is forced to confront the evils in the land of his childhood. In doing so, he discovers his destiny as Caldrius as well as his fate: to demand justice from the prince who killed his family. While calling the novel "a trifle cerebral" for some fantasy fans, *Booklist* contributor Roland Green noted that McKillip works her usual magic in *Song for the Basilisk,* bringing her "archetypal characters and plot . . . to life with dozens of subtle touches."

In *Winter Rose,* a young woman who falls in love with a man trapped in a magical otherworld pines away for lack of him, leaving her determined sister Rois to solve the murder that caused the man to become captive in this perpetual dream world. Calling McKillip's prose a "delightful, delicate filigree," a *Kirkus Reviews* contributor noted that the "frail and undeveloped" plot seemed inadequate by comparison; in *Booklist,* however, a reviewer labeled *Winter Rose* "compelling."

In a *Booklist* review of *The Tower at Stony Wood* Green observed that McKillip's story retells the medieval fable about the Lady of Shalott. In this tale, a king marries a woman who is an imposter; meanwhile, the woman to whom he is truly engaged and is meant to be his queen is imprisoned. In order to avoid a looming curse, the king must free her. "This is McKillip at close to the height of her powers," wrote Green, "which is to say

close to the highest pinnacle in contemporary fantasy." Michelle West, writing in the *Magazine of Fantasy and Science Fiction* that each novel McKillip writes is a "cause for celebration," referred to *The Tower at Stony Wood* as a "a tapestry—a weaving of disparate threads into whole cloth that is greater than its parts, which when seen singly only hint at the finished weave if one is paying attention and dissecting as one goes."

In the award-winning *Ombria in Shadow* the kingdom of Ombria is in crisis as its prince is near death. Now a handful of treacherous stand-ins are more than willing to assume power—in particular the woman known as the Black Pearl, the prince's mysterious and power-hungry aunt. The eventual death of the prince leads to fighting between those who want the throne for themselves and those who may have it thrust upon them, including an abandoned child who has been raised by a reclusive sorceress. In her review for *Kliatt,* Deirdre B. Root stated that McKillip's "hallucinatory novel . . . is wonderful, and fans of historical fantasy will love it."

Also focusing on a prince attempting to retain power over his kingdom, *In the Forests of Serre* focuses on Prince Ronan of Serre as he struggles to withdraw from the depression that overcame him following the death of his wife and child. Unsuccessful in his attempt to sacrifice himself during battle as a way of avoiding a second marriage arranged by his father, Ronan sees a firebird flying into a forest. Paula Luedtke, writing for *Booklist,* deemed *In the Forests of Serre* a "hauntingly beautiful tale."

The fantasy novel *Alphabet of Thorn* focuses on palace intrigue in the land of Raine. On the day of the new queen's coronation, Nepenthe, a young scribe and translator who works in the royal library, discovers a book written in an unusual language composed of thornlike characters. Together, Nepenthe and the queen work to solve the book's mysteries, which they believe hold the key to Raine's future. "Those who have bemoaned the death of the true fairy tale will be delighted by this charming foray," noted a contributor in *Publishers Weekly.* Frieda Murray, reviewing the work in *Booklist,* called *Alphabet of Thorn* "a novel that won't in the least disappoint McKillip's loyal readers or their high expectations."

A wizard rebels against a king's strict laws in *Od Magic.* After saving the land of Numis from ruin, the great wizard Od was allowed to start her own school of magic in the city of Kelior. As the years passed, the school came under the control of King Galin, and wild magic was outlawed. However, when Od hires Brendan Vetch to work as the school's gardener she knows that Vetch possesses amazing powers. At the same time, a wily street magician arrives in town, drawing the king's scrutiny. In *Od Magic,* McKillip "demonstrates once again her exquisite grasp of the fantasist's craft," remarked a *Publishers Weekly* contributor, while in *Library Journal,* Jackie Cassada observed that the novelist "finds poetry in every story she tells."

McKillip's *Solstice Wood* is a "lovely tale of fairy and human worlds meeting and melding," according to *Booklist* critic Paula Luedtke. After her grandfather dies, bookstore owner Sylvia Lynn returns home to Lynn Hall, a decaying mansion surrounded by thick woods that hide a shadowy Otherworld. Sylvia's grandmother introduces her to the Fiber Guild, a coven of witches whose magical weavings protect the town from the Fay, evil spirits that inhabit the surrounding forest. When the Fay break through the barriers and kidnap Sylvia's cousin, the young woman must venture into the Otherworld to rescue him. "As always," noted a contributor in *Kirkus Reviews*, "McKillip writes sparely, with elegance and precision."

In addition to novel-length works, McKillip has also proved her ability to master the art of short fiction. *Harrowing the Dragon: Collected Tales* contains fifteen previously published fantasy stories. Among the works are "Star-Crossed," an investigation into the deaths of Romeo and Juliet; "The Lion and the Lark," about the romance between a young woman and a shapechanger; and "Voyage into the Heart," concerning the hunt for a unicorn. *School Library Journal* contributor Sandy Freund praised McKillip's "elegant prose," and a reviewer in *Publishers Weekly* stated that "each of these tales is a gem of storytelling."

"I started writing because I was too young to know better," the prolific McKillip stated in a *Locus* interview. "And I had an imagination, and I had to do something with it. It's still there—it doesn't grow less with age. In fact it seems, the more you use it, the more you have of it." Charles de Lint, writing in the *Magazine of Fantasy and Science Fiction*, cited McKillip as one of the few fantasy novelists still able to create an original story. As de Lint commented, within modern fiction there are only "a small handful of authors who do what fantasy is supposed to do: kindle our sense of wonder with novels that tell their own stories, rather than retelling something we've already been told. Patricia McKillip does this for me, and has been doing it for years."

Biographical and Critical Sources

BOOKS

Children's Books and Their Creators, Houghton (Boston, MA), 1995.

Perret, Patti, *The Faces of Fantasy,* Tor (New York, NY), 1996.

St. James Guide to Fantasy Writers, St. James Press (Detroit, MI), 1996.

St. James Guide to Science-Fiction Writers, 4th edition, St. James Press (Detroit, MI), 1996.

St. James Guide to Young-Adult Writers, 2nd edition, St. James Press (Detroit, MI), 1999.

PERIODICALS

Analog, January, 1980.

Booklist, August, 1995, Sally Estes, review of *The Book of Atrix Wolfe,* p. 1936; January, 1997, review of *Winter Rose,* p. 763; August, 1998, Roland Green, review of *Song for the Basilisk,* pp. 1978-1979; April 15, 2000, Roland Green, review of *The Tower at Stony Wood,* p. 1534; May 15, 2003, Paula Luedtke, review of *In the Forests of Serre,* p. 1652; January 1, 2004, Frieda Murray, review of *Alphabet of Thorn,* p. 840; November 1, 2005, Roland Green, review of *Harrowing the Dragon: Collected Tales,* p. 32; February 1, 2006, Paula Luedtke, review of *Solstice Wood,* p. 38.

Bulletin of the Center for Children's Books, January, 1975, p. 82; July, 1979, p. 196; September, 1984, p. 10.

Christian Science Monitor, November 2, 1977, p. B2.

Fantasy Review, November, 1985.

Kirkus Reviews, July 15, 1993, review of *The Cygnet and the Firebird,* p. 898; May 15, 1996, review of *Winter Rose,* p. 718; April 15, 2005, review of *Od Magic,* p. 456; December 15, 2005, review of *Solstice Wood,* p. 1304.

Kliatt, May, 2003, Deirdre B. Root, review of *Ombria in Shadow,* p. 26.

Library Journal, May 15, 2003, Jackie Cassada, review of *In the Forests of Serre,* p. 131; June 15, 2005, Jackie Cassada, review of *Od Magic,* p. 65; November 15, 2005, Jackie Cassada, review of *Harrowing the Dragon,* pp. 64-65; January 1, 2006, Jackie Cassada, review of *Solstice Wood,* p. 105.

Locus, January, 1990, p. 52; August, 1992, "Moving Forward" (interview); July, 1996, "Spring Surprises" (interview).

Los Angeles Times, March 26, 1982, Charles Champlin, review of *Stepping from the Shadows.*

Magazine of Fantasy and Science Fiction, October, 2000, Michelle West, review of *The Tower at Stony Wood,* p. 44; May, 2002, Charles de Lint, review of *Ombria in Shadow,* p. 27.

New York Times Book Review, October 13, 1974, Georgess McHargue, review of *The Forgotten Beasts of Eld,* p. 8; March 6, 1977, Glenn Shea, review of *The Riddle-Master of Hed,* p. 29.

Publishers Weekly, October 3, 1994, review of *Brian Froud's Faerielands,* p. 54; June 26, 1995, review of *The Book of Atrix Wolfe,* p. 90; January 19, 2004, review of *Alphabet of Thorn,* p. 58; May 2, 2005, review of *Od Magic,* pp. 181-182; September 19, 2005, review of *Harrowing the Wood,* pp. 48-49; December 12, 2005, review of *Solstice Wood,* pp. 42-43.

School Library Journal, October, 1991, p. 160; May, 1994, Cathy Chauvette, review of *The Cygnet and the Firebird,* p. 143; March, 2006, Sandy Freund, review of *Harrowing the Dragon,* p. 255.

Science Fiction and Fantasy Book Review, May, 1979, Roger C. Schlobin, review of "Riddlemaster" trilogy, pp. 37-38.

Science Fiction Chronicle, July, 1991, p. 30.

Voice of Youth Advocates, October, 1982, p. 32; June, 1991, Carolyn Shute, review of *The Sorceress and the Cygnet,* p. 112; December, 1993, Esther Sinofsky, review of *The Cygnet and the Firebird,* p. 311; April, 1999, review of *Song for the Basilisk,* p. 14.

Washington Post Book World, January 9, 1986; October 23, 1994, Gregory Feeley, review of *Something Rich and Strange,* p. 6.*

* * *

McKILLIP, Patricia Anne
See McKILLIP, Patricia A.

* * *

McMILLAN, Naomi
See GRIMES, Nikki

* * *

MILICH, Zoran

Personal

Born July 7, in Yugoslavia; children: Hannah. *Hobbies and other interests:* Digital video.

Addresses

Home—Toronto, Ontario, Canada; Rio de Janeiro, Brazil. *Agent*—c/o Kids Can Press, 29 Birch Ave., Toronto, Ontario M4V 1E2, Canada. *E-mail*—zoranmilich@mac.com.

Career

Photojournalist. *Toronto Star,* Toronto, Ontario, Canada, photojournalist, beginning 1980. *Exhibitions:* Work included in solo exhibition at King Street Station, Toronto, Ontario, Canada, 1994; and Brazilian Embassy, Belgrade, Serbia, 2006.

Awards, Honors

Alcuin Society Book Design Award, 2001, and Independent Book Publisher Award finalist, 2002, both for *The City ABC Book.*

Writings

(And photographer) *The City ABC Book,* Kids Can Press (Toronto, Ontario, Canada), 2001.
(And photographer) *City Signs,* Kids Can Press (Toronto, Ontario, Canada), 2002.
(And photographer) *City Colors,* Kids Can Press (Toronto, Ontario, Canada), 2004.
(And photographer) *City 1 2 3,* Kids Can Press (Toronto, Ontario, Canada), 2005.

Photographs have appeared in numerous periodicals, including Toronto *Globe & Mail.*

Sidelights

Zoran Milich is an acclaimed photojournalist who uses his talents to create concept books for young children, and his titles include *City Signs* and *City 1 2 3.* Born in Yugoslavia, Milich immigrated to Canada at a young age. He took an early interest in photography and eventually served apprenticeships with photographers Tony Hauser and Joy and Rudy von Tiedemann. He began working for the *Toronto Star* during the 1980s and has also published photo essays in the Toronto *Globe & Mail.* Two years before the collapse of the USSR, Milich documented the changing face of Eastern Europe with his Leica camera, and he eventually became the first Western photojournalist allowed to travel with communist Cuba's national baseball team during their playing season. Milich's career as a documentary photographer has also taken him to Haiti, Germany, and Czechoslovakia, among other nations.

Milich turned his attention to children's books after the birth of his own daughter, Hannah. Inspired by the daily walks he took with Hannah through their Toronto neighborhood when she was a toddler, he created *The City ABC Book,* a work featuring "a brilliantly simple idea executed in a simple manner," according to *Horn Book* critic Lolly Robinson. In the work, Milich presents a series of black-and-white photos that reveal letter shapes hidden in everyday objects, such as the letter "C" on a manhole cover and the letter "S" on a bridge railing. To assist young readers, Milich highlights each letter shape in bold red and reprints the uppercase and lowercase letter at the bottom of each page. *Resource Links* contributor Linda Ludke praised *The City ABC Book,* calling it "a visually striking alphabet lesson," and Kelly Milner Halls, reviewing the work in *Booklist,* stated that each letter is "a clear, playful image to consider and behold."

Milich's picture book *City Signs* presents thirty photographs featuring printed messages located in familiar urban settings. Each picture offers a clue to a specific word's meaning; one photo, for instance, shows a railroad crossing sign as a train passes in the background, and another photo shows a restaurant displaying a "pizza" sign in its window. *Booklist* contributor Lauren Peterson noted that Milich's pictures "are nicely composed, clear, and often colorful," and added that "the setting makes the words or phrase easy to understand." According to Nancy Cohen, writing in *Resource Links,* "young children will enjoy pouring over this book and discovering that they know how to read many of the signs."

Again featuring Milich's photographic images, *City Colors* contains "a veritable rainbow of photographs of objects found in cities around the world," according to Valerie Nielsen in *Canadian Review of Materials.* The work focuses on both primary and secondary colors—a yellow traffic cone, a green swing, a purple stool, and an orange curb block are among the items pictured.

Cover of Zoran Milich's City Signs, *which encourages even barely beginning readers to navigate the wide world with confidence.* (Kids Can Press, 2002. Photographs © 2002 Zoran Milich. Used by permission of Kids Can Press Ltd., Toronto)

School Library Journal reviewer Karen Land called the book "dazzling" and remarked that Milich's pictures "create a well-planned city landscape."

A counting book by Milich, *City 1 2 3* appeared in 2005. Here, children can search through color photographs of taxis, truck wheels, and skyscrapers to discover numbers from one to ten. According to a critic in *Kirkus Reviews, City 1 2 3* "offers an irresistible invitation to count, and also to look more closely at the world all around."

Though he has recently found success as a children's book author, Milich still considers himself a photojournalist first and foremost. "I shoot images that simply move me," he stated on the *Digital Railroad* Web site. "I am fortunate that my images get through the mountains of technology to art directors who use them in their vision."

Biographical and Critical Sources

PERIODICALS

Booklist, April 15, 2001, Kelly Milner Halls, review of *The City ABC Book,* p. 1562; October 15, 2002, Lauren Peterson, review of *City Signs,* p. 408; May 15, 2005, Hazel Rochman, review of *City 1 2 3,* p. 1662.

Canadian Review of Materials, December 14, 2001, Dave Jenkinson, review of *The City ABC Book*; February 14, 2003, Valerie Nielsen, review of *City Signs.*

Horn Book, July, 2001, Lolly Robinson, review of *The City ABC Book,* p. 442; January, 2003, review of *City Signs,* p. 59; July-August, 2005, Lolly Robinson, review of *City 1 2 3,* p. 456.

Kirkus Reviews, March 1, 2004, review of *City Colors,* p. 227; March 1, 2005, review of *City 1 2 3,* p. 291.

Resource Links, June, 2001, Linda Ludke, review of *The City ABC Book,* p. 4; December, 2002, Nancy Cohen, review of *City Signs,* p. 12; April, 2004, Kathryn McNaughton, review of *City Colors,* p. 7; June, 2005, Susan Miller, review of *City 1 2 3,* p. 7.

School Library Journal, June, 2001, Alicia Eames, review of *The City ABC Book,* p. 139; May, 2004, Karen Land, review of *City Colors,* p. 134; May, 2005, Melinda Piehler, review of *City 1 2 3,* p. 112.

ONLINE

Digital Railroad Web site, http://www.digitalrailroad.net/ (October 20, 2006), "Zoran Milich."

Kids Can Press Web site, http://www.kidscanpress.com/ (October 20, 2006), "Zoran Milich."

Zoran Milich Home Page, http://www.zoranmilich.com (October 20, 2006).*

* * *

MWANGI, Meja 1948-

Personal

Born David Dominic Mwangi, December 27, 1948, in Nanyuki, Kenya; son of a domestic worker. *Education:* Attended Kenyatta College; attended University of Iowa, 1975.

Addresses

Home—United States. *Agent*—c/o Author Mail, Groundwood Books, Douglas & McIntyre Publishing Group, Ste. 500, 720 Bathurst St., Toronto, Ontario M5S 2R4, Canada.

Career

Writer, film director, and casting agent. TV ORTF (French-language television station), Nairobi, Kenya, soundman, 1972-73; British Council, film librarian, 1974-75; freelance writer. Assistant director of films *Out of Africa,* 1985, and *Gorillas in the Mist,* 1985; second assistant director of *White Mischief,* 1987.

Awards, Honors

Jomo Kenyatta Prize, 1974, for *Carcase for Hounds,* 2001, for *The Last Plague;* Iowa University fellow in writing, 1975-76; Commonwealth Writers Prize nomination, 1990, for *Striving for the Wind;* Deutscher Jugendliteratur Preis, 1992, for German-language edition of *Little White Man;* Afro-Asian Writers Award; Adolf Lotus Grimme Award.

Writings

FICTION

Kill Me Quick, Heinemann Educational (London, England), 1973.

Carcase for Hounds, Heinemann Educational (London, England), 1974.

Taste of Death, East African Publishing House (Nairobi, Kenya), 1975.

Going down River Road, Heinemann Educational (London, England), 1976.

The Cockroach Dance, Longman Kenya (Nairobi, Kenya), 1979.

The Bushtrackers (adapted from a screenplay by Gary Strieker), Longman Drumbeat (Nairobi, Kenya), 1980.

Bread of Sorrow, Longman Kenya (Nairobi, Kenya), 1987.

Weapon of Hunger, Longman Kenya (Nairobi, Kenya), 1989.

The Return of Shaka, Longman Kenya (Nairobi, Kenya), 1990.

Striving for the Wind, Heinemann Kenya (Nairobi, Kenya), 1990, Heinemann (Portsmouth, NH), 1992.

The Last Plague, East African Education Publishers, 2000.

Author's works have been translated into several languages, including Basque, French, German, Japanese, and Russian.

FOR CHILDREN

Jimi the Dog, Longman Kenya (Nairobi, Kenya), 1990.

Little White Man, Longman Kenya (Nairobi, Kenya), 1990, published as *The Mzungu Boy,* Groundwood Books (Toronto, Ontario, Canada), 2005.

The Hunter's Dream, Macmillan (London, England), 1993.

The Last Plague, East African Educational Publishers (Nairobi, Kenya), 2000.

Adaptations

Kill Me Quick was adapted as a stage play; *Carcase for Hounds* was adapted for film as *Cry Freedom,* 1981.

Sidelights

A two-time winner of Kenya's Jomo Kenyatta Prize for Literature, novelist and filmmaker Meja Mwangi focuses on the changing social and political landscape of his native Kenya. While Mwangi's early works, such as *Taste of Death* and *Carcase for Hounds,* deal with the anti-colonial sentiment that led to the Mau-Mau uprising of the 1950s, he has also produced crime novels, thrillers, and novels for children, among them *Little White Man,* which also takes place during Kenya's anti-colonial era. Social themes ground many of Mwangi's early novels; for example, *Kill Me Quick, Going down River Road,* and *The Cockroach Dance* focus on the problems brought about by the rapid industrialization Kenya underwent after achieving independence in 1963. More recently, with his award-winning novel *The Last Plague,* Mwangi has refocused on social concerns. The second of his novels to win the Jomo Kenyatta Prize, *The Last Plague* focuses on the ravages of the AIDS epidemic throughout Africa.

Mwangi's first published novel, *Kill Me Quick,* is set in the days immediately following Kenyan independence, and focuses on two boys who are trying to improve their lives by attending school. The boys, lifelong friends, move to Nairobi in order to find work, only to discover that their classroom education is actually worth little in the job market. Penniless and stranded in the hostile city, the boys turn to crime and are apprehended; ironically, only after they are incarcerated does the quality of their lives improve. A *Choice* contributor called *Kill Me Quick* "an incisive look at the way crime is created by poverty rather than by innate evil," and Simon Gikandi, writing in the *Dictionary of Literary Biography,* noted that the "poignancy and immediacy" of Mwangi's novel "overshadow its limited literary achievement."

Considered one of Mwangi's greatest works, *Going down River Road* returns to the horrors of the urban jungle. According to *World Literature Today* contributor Charles R. Larson, Mwangi presents readers with a culture "composed . . . of young bar girls, urban thugs or youths." Noting that the novel features themes characteristic of its author, Gikandi called *Going down River Road* "remarkable" due to the "stark, detailed images with which Mwangi represents the vital and volatile clandestine culture of the Nairobi underworld. Nobody else has captured this subculture with as much understanding and empathy." In *The Cockroach Dance,* Mwangi balances social commentary with entertainment in his story about a water-meter reader who is driven to despair and, ultimately, violence as a result of the hopelessness and injustice he witnesses every day on his job.

The son of a maid who worked for white families in the British town of Nyeri, Kenya, Mwangi grew up during the Mau Mau massacres, as militant Kikuyu nationalists based in the country's highlands, murdered dozens of Europeans and over 11,000 black Africans—many of them Christians—who opposed nationalizing the country. Jomo Kenyatta, for whom the Kenyan literary prize is named, was a leader of the movement. While violence raged on the outskirts of Nyeri, the future writer absorbed many aspects of White European culture through his mother's contact with British settlers as well as from his reading of the European children's books that were gifts from his mother's employers. Several members of Mwangi's family were eventually sent to detention camps because of their participation in the Mau Mau uprising. According to Gikandi, Mwangi and his mother were also held in a detention camp for a short time. The boy was so affected by what he witnessed, and the stories he heard from others regarding the Mau Mau uprising that the revolution became the focus of his first novel-length work, *Taste of Death,* written when Mwangi was seventeen years old. Completed two years after Kenya had achieved independence, *Taste of Death* would not be published until 1975 due to the sensitivity of its subject matter.

In the pages of *Taste of Death* readers meet Kariuki, a young man who is swept along by the passion and excitement of the Mau Mau insurrection and Kenya's

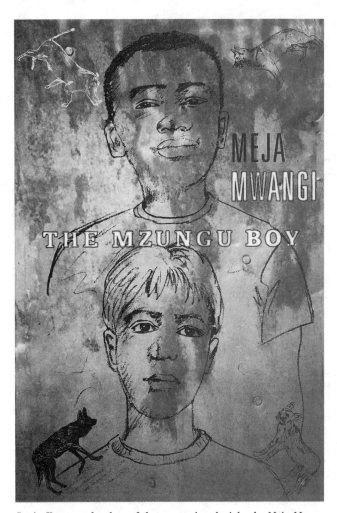

Set in Kenya at the close of that country's colonial rule, Meja Mwangi's The Mzungu Boy *features cover art by Michael Solomon.* (Groundwood Books/House of Anansi Press, 2005. Reproduced by permission of Groundwood Books, Ltd)

fight for independence. However, because he does not understand the basis of the conflict, Kariuki is not ready to join those who are sacrificing their own lives for the rebellion. In his novel Mwangi glorifies the Kenyan conflict, and describes the freedom fighters' futile attempt to avoid death at the hands of well-armed colonial forces. According to Gikandi, while the novel is obviously the work of an idealistic young man, it is significant in the author's body of work because it addresses the themes and concerns that reoccur in Mwangi's subsequent writings.

Written for children, *Jimi the Dog* and *Little White Man*—the latter also published as *The Mzungu Boy*—also focus on Kariuki, although this time the hero of *Taste of Death* is younger. Although *Jimi the Dog* can be read by children as the story of a little boy and his puppy, it also addresses the social issues prevalent during the 1950s. In contrast, *Little White Man* deals directly with the Mau Mau uprising through its focus on twelve-year-old Kariuki's friendship with Nigel, a white planter's son who is derogatorily dubbed "Mzungu Boy" or "Westerner" by the villagers. While the two boys are searching the nearby jungle for the giant warthog known to villagers as Old Moses, Nigel is captured by Mau Mau nationalists. Searching the jungle for his friend, Kariuki discovers that his own brother, Hari, is one of the rebels holding Nigel. Tragically, after Kariuki convinces Hari to negotiate with colonial soldiers for Nigel's release, Hari is killed by the British. In *School Library Journal*, Mary N. Oluonye praised Mwangi for creating a story that is "exciting, action-packed, and full of detail." Although the novel's historic backdrop is not familiar to many Western readers, as Gillian Engberg noted in her *Booklist* review of *The Mzungu Boy*, through Kariuki's first-person narration, young readers "will easily connect with the friendship, the exhilarating freedom of exploring nature, and the boys' bewilderment at the adult world." As Oluonye concluded, Mwangi's novel provides readers with a "riveting tale that introduces the landscape, history, and culture of colonial Kenya."

One of Mwangi's most well-known novels, *Carcase for Hounds* views the Mau Mau uprising from a more mature perspective, one of pessimism, futility, and hopelessness. In the novel, a Mau Mau soldier and his mortally wounded revolutionary commander are trapped in a forest and surrounded by hostile British colonial forces. Mwangi uses their plight as a metaphor for the hopelessness both sides feel in this stand-off. In *Carcase for Hounds* "Mwangi has usurped the language of the American thriller, of Raymond Chandler, Mickey Spillane, and Chester Himes," according to Gikandi, the critic calling the author's use of American slang somewhat "incongruous." Nonetheless, he praised the novel as "remarkable for the sheer amount of detail than Mwangi provides about the logistics and organization of the Mau Mau movement."

Mwangi's decision to write several books for younger readers was inspired by his belief that far too little literature featuring an African perspective has been made available to Kenyan children. According to critics, it was also his response to the negative critical reception given to the more mainstream novels he produced during the late 1980s, such as *Bread of Sorrow, Weapon of Hunger,* and *The Return of Shaka.* With *Striving for the Wind,* however, Mwangi "return[ed] to his roots," according to Gikandi, reviewing the author's story about a Kenyan father and son who ponder the future of their country. In *Striving for the Wind,* added the critic, the novelist focuses "on a static, weary, and worn-out landscape; he rejects the idiom of the movies, seeking instead to capture the language of rural despair and the tyranny of the nouveau riche" by adopting an authorial voice "that sustains the pessimism and angst of the rural poor." Although Gikandi cited portions of the novel as "as dull as the land and people [the novel] represents," Mwangi's depiction of the depleted Kenyan landscape and the exhausted humans who till its soil earned *Striving for the Wind* a nomination for the prestigious Commonwealth Writers Prize.

Biographical and Critical Sources

BOOKS

Anyidoho, Kofi, and others, editors, *Interdisciplinary Dimensions of African Literature,* Three Continents (Washington, DC), 1985, pp. 11-25.

Chakava, Henry, *Notes on Meja Mwangi's "Kill Me Quick,"* Heinemann Educational (Nairobi, Kenya), 1976.

Dictionary of Literary Biography, Volume 125: *Twentieth-Century Caribbean and Black African Writers: Second Series,* Thomson Gale (Detroit, MI), 1993.

Johansson, Lars, *In the Shadow of Neocolonialism: A Study of Meja Mwangi's Novels, 1973-1990,* Faculty of Arts, University of Umea (Stockholm, Sweden), 1992.

Killam, G.D., editor, *The Writing of East and Central Africa,* Heinemann (London, England), 1984, pp. 177-191.

Lindfors, Bernth, editor, *Mazungumzo,* Ohio University Center for International Studies (Athens, OH), 1980, pp. 74-79.

Nichols, Lee, *Conversations with African Writers,* Voice of America (Washington, DC), 1981, pp. 195-204.

Parasuram, A.N., *Guide to Meja Mwangi: Kill Me Quick,* Minerva (Madras, India), 1977.

Wanjala, Chris, *The Season of Harvest: Some Notes on East African Literature,* Kenya Literature Burwau (Nairobi, Kenya), 1978.

Zell, Hans M., and others, *A New Reader's Guide to African Literature,* Holmes & Meier, 1983.

PERIODICALS

African Literature Today, number 9, 1978; number 13, 1983, pp. 146-157.

Afriscope, April, 1976, pp. 25-28.

Association for Commonwealth Literature and Language Studies Bulletin, Volume 7, number 4, 1986, pp. 45-52.

Black Scholar, November-December, 1984, pp. 61-63.

Booklist, August, 2005, Gillian Engberg, review of *The Mzungu Boy,* p. 2029.

Choice, March, 1976, p. 78; June, 1976, p. 528.

Research in African Literatures, summer, 1985, pp. 179-209.

Resource Links, October, 2005, Gail Lennon, review of *The Mzungu Boy,* p. 20.

School Library Journal, November, 2005, Mary N. Oluonye, review of *The Mzungu Boy,* p. 144.

Times Literary Supplement, September 18, 1992, Robert Brain, review of *Striving the Wind,* p. 24.

World Literature Today, autumn, 1977, p. 565; autumn, 1978.

ONLINE

Contemporary Africa Database, http://www.people.africadatabase.org/en/ (June 1, 2003), Douglas Killam and Ruth Rowe, "Meja Mwangi."

Michigan State University Web Site, http://www.msupress.msu/edu/ (November 2, 2006), "M. Mwangi."*

N

NILSEN, Anna 1948-
(Andrea Bassil)

Personal

Born September 16, 1948, in England. *Ethnicity:* "White Caucasian." *Education:* Attended Eastbourne School of Art, 1966-67; Edinburgh College of Art, diploma in art and design, 1972; Moray House College of Education, Scottish certificate of education, 1973. *Hobbies and other interests:* Photography, travel, gardening, walking.

Addresses

Office—16 Emery St., Cambridge CB1 2AX, England; fax: 01228-364266. *E-mail*—andrea.bassil@ntlworld.com; anna.nilsen@ntlworld.com.

Career

Educator, author, and illustrator. Mussleburgh Grammar School, assistant teacher of art, 1973-74; St. Margaret's School, Newington, England, assistant teacher of art, 1974-85; Bournemouth & Poole College of Art and Design, Poole, England, course director in natural-history illustration, 1985-90; Anglia Ruskin, artist, writer, designer, and illustrator, 1995—. Lamp of Lothian Art Centre, evening class lecturer, 1973-74; Anglia Polytechnic University, head of illustration until 1995, visiting lecturer, 2002—. Pixel Magic, art director, screen designer, and games consultant, 1995-96; educational games consultant to Multimedia Corp. Has worked for LEGO, National Gallery London and Scotland, and Chicago Art Institute. *Exhibitions:* Artwork exhibited in solo shows and group shows in England and Scotland.

Member

Society of Authors, Authors Licensing and Collecting Society, Children's Book Circle, Cambridge Illustration Group.

Anna Nilsen (Photograph reproduced by permission of Anna Nilsen)

Awards, Honors

Goldsmiths' Hall scholarship for Paris, France, 1981; award in activity-book category, *Parents' Guide to Children's Media,* and shortlist for BPF Book Design and Production Award, both 2001, ABC Children's Booksellers Choice Award, 2002, Department of the Ministry of Education in Mexico award, 2003, and Blue Peter

Award shortlist, all for *Art Fraud Detective;* Sheffield Baby Book Award shortlist.

Writings

FOR CHILDREN

Jungle, illustrated by Peter Joyce, Walker Books (New York, NY), 1994.

Farm, illustrated by Annie Axworthy, Walker Books (New York, NY), 1994.

Friends, illustrated by Sue Coney, Walker Books (New York, NY), 1994.

Wheels, illustrated by Joe Wright, Walker Books (New York, NY), 1994.

Dinosaurs, illustrated by Annie Axworthy, Walker Books (New York, NY), 1994.

Terrormazia: A Hole New Kind of Maze Game, illustrated by Dom Mansell, Walker Books (New York, NY), 1995.

Flying High, illustrated by Tony Wells, Walker Books (New York, NY), 1996.

Fairy Tales, illustrated by Sue Coney, Walker Books (New York, NY), 1996.

Under the Sea, illustrated by Tania Hurt-Newton, Walker Books (New York, NY), 1996.

Drive Your Car, illustrated by Tony Wells, Walker Books (New York, NY), 1996.

Drive Your Tractor, illustrated by Tony Wells, Walker Books (New York, NY), 1996.

Where Are Percy's Friends?, illustrated by Dom Mansell, Walker Books (New York, NY), 1996.

Where Is Percy's Dinner?, illustrated by Dom Mansell, Walker Books (New York, NY), 1996.

Percy the Park Keeper Activity Book, HarperCollins (New York, NY), 1996.

Follow the Kite, HarperCollins (New York, NY), 1997.

Let's Dig and Burrow, Zero to Ten, 1998.

Let's Hang and Dangle, Zero to Ten, 1998.

Let's Leap and Jump, Zero to Ten, 1998.

Let's Swim and Dive, Zero to Ten, 1998.

Spy Catcher ("LEGO Puzzle Book" series), DK Publishing (New York, NY), 1998.

Treasure Smuggler ("LEGO Puzzle Book" series), DK Publishing (New York, NY), 1998.

Gold Robber ("LEGO Puzzle Book" series), DK Publishing (New York, NY), 1998.

I Can Spell—Words with Four Letters, Kingfisher (New York, NY), 1998.

I Can Spell—Words with Three Letters, Kingfisher (New York, NY), 1998.

Insectoids Invasion, illustrated by Philip Nicholson, DK Publishing (New York, NY), 1998.

Jewel Thief ("LEGO Puzzle Book"), DK Publishing (New York, NY), 1998.

My Favorite Fairy Tales: A Sticker Book, illustrated by Sue Cony, Candlewick Press (Cambridge, MA), 1999.

I Can Count 1 to 10, illustrated by Mandy Stanley, Kingfisher (New York, NY), 1999.

I Can Count 10 to 20, illustrated by Mandy Stanley, Kingfisher (New York, NY), 1999.

Mousemazia, illustrated by Dom Mansell, Candlewick Press (Cambridge, MA), 2000.

I Can Subtract, illustrated by Mandy Stanley, Kingfisher (New York, NY), 2000.

I Can Add, illustrated by Mandy Stanley, Kingfisher (New York, NY), 2000.

Art Fraud Detective, Kingfisher (New York, NY), 2000.

I Can Multiply, illustrated by Mandy Stanley, Kingfisher (New York, NY), 2001.

Moo Cow Moo!, illustrated by Jonathan Bentley, Little Hare Books (Sydney, New South Wales, Australia), 2003.

Swim Duck Swim!, illustrated by Jonathan Bentley, Little Hare Books (Sydney, New South Wales, Australia), 2003.

The Great Art Scandal: Solve the Crime, Save the Show!, illustrated by Mandy Stanley, Kingfisher (Boston, MA), 2003.

Art Auction Mystery: Find the Fakes, Save the Sale!, illustrated by Jason Ford, Kingfisher (Boston, MA), 2005.

Bella's Mid-Summer Secret, Chrysalis (London, England), 2005.

Peepers Jungle, Orchard (London, England), 2005.

Peepers People, Orchard (London, England), 2005.

Peepers Farm, Orchard (London, England), 2005.

Peepers Pet, Orchard (London, England), 2005.

"MY BEST FRIENDS" SERIES

My Best Friends, illustrated by Emma Dodd, Gingham Dog Press (New York, NY), 2003.

My Best Dad, illustrated by Emma Dodd, Zero to Ten (England), 2003.

My Best Mum, illustrated by Emma Dodd, Zero to Ten (England), 2003.

SELF-ILLUSTRATED

Magnificent Mazes, Mathew Price, 2001.

Let's Learn Numbers, Miles Kelly, 2001.

Let's Learn Words, Miles Kelly, 2001.

Let's Learn Colours, Miles Kelly, 2001.

Let's Learn Shapes, Miles Kelly, 2001.

The Great Race, Little Hare Books (Sydney, New South Wales, Australia), 2002.

Let's Learn Actions, Miles Kelly, 2002.

Let's Learn Noises, Miles Kelly, 2002.

Let's Learn Sizes, Miles Kelly, 2002.

Let's Learn Opposites, Miles Kelly, 2002.

The aMAZEing Journey of Marco Polo, Little Hare Books (Sydney, New South Wales, Australia), 2002.

Pirates, Little Hare Books (Sydney, New South Wales, Australia), 2003.

Magnificent Mazes: 20th Century, Mathew Price, 2003.

The aMAZEing Journey of Charles Darwin, Little Hare Books (Sydney, New South Wales, Australia), 2003.

AMAZEing Journeys, Little Hare Books (Sydney, New South Wales, Australia), 2004.

Robotics Math Games and Puzzles, Little Hare Books (Sydney, New South Wales, Australia), 2004.
Famous Journeys, Little Hare Books (Sydney, New South Wales, Australia), 2005.
The aMAZEing Journey through Time, Little Hare Books (Sydney, New South Wales, Australia), 2006.

ILLUSTRATOR

My House, Oxford University Press (Oxford, England), 2002.
Circus, Oxford University Press (Oxford, England), 2002.
Games Consultant, Oxford University Press (Oxford, England), 2003.
(And devisor) *3-D Mathematical Maze Puzzle Cube,* Zoo Book Cube (England), 2003.
(With others) *Happy Friends,* Oxford University Press (Oxford, England), 2004.

Author of several other puzzle, jigsaw, and game books.

Author's works have been translated into French, Polish, Czech, Chinese, Icelandic, Belgian, Bulgarian, Danish, Swedish, Slovakian, Japanese, Taiwanese, Latvian, German, Korean, Spanish, Dutch, and Finnish.

UNDER NAME ANDREA BASSIL

Design in Partnership, 1989.
Jaguar Expedition to Belize, Royal Geographic Society (London, England), 1989.
(Illustrator) Helen Kinnier Wilson, *Cambridge Reflections,* Silent (Cambridge, England), 1992.
Van Gogh (juvenile nonfiction), Gareth Stevens Publishing (Milwaukee, WI), 2004.

Under name Andrea Bassil, author of *Aqua Quest* game book. Contributor to books, including (as Andrea Bassil) *The Complete Guide to Illustration,* Quarto, 1989; and *Compendium of Puzzles and Brainteasers,* Reader's Digest Books (Pleasantville, NY), 2000. Contributor of illustrations to *National Association of Field Study Officers' Journal.*

Sidelights

Anna Nilsen, the pseudonym of Andrea Bassil, is the author and illustrator of over fifty books for young readers. Along with writing, she has worked to devise novelty items, puzzles and games, jigsaws, and educational CD-ROM programs. Most of her books are nonfiction or educational, and several teach about the art industry while also providing puzzles for young readers to solve. "Sometimes I simply devise the concept [for a book] but more often I write and illustrate. Sometimes when I'm busy other illustrators are employed," Nilsen explained of her work schedule on her home page.

Most of Nilsen's books are categorized as concept books. *Let's Dig and Burrow* and *Let's Hang and Dangle* encourage young readers to think about the

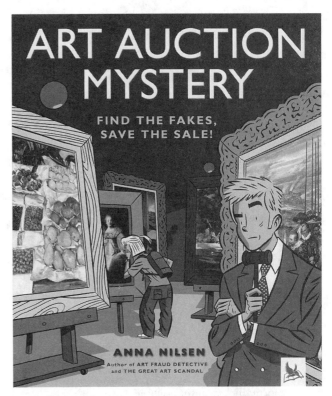

Cover of Anna Nilsen's **Art Auction Mystery,** *which hides a lesson on fine art in an entertaining, interactive story.* (Kingfisher, 2005. Illustrations © Jason Ford 2005. Reprinted by permission of Kingfisher Publications Plc, an imprint of Houghton Mifflin Company. All rights reserved)

ways various animals move. *My Best Friends* describes what having a best friend is like. Nilsen's most notable books, however, are her mystery-art books. The first, *Art Fraud Detective,* drew attention for its combination of visual mystery, comic-book format, and educational information about famous artists. *The Great Art Scandal: Solve the Crime, Save the Show!* continues the theme, presenting readers with a quest: they must identify fraudulent artwork to save an exhibition. Readers are given details about fraudulent artists, and must match which artist copied which great artist's painting. "For those who like to solve puzzles and who have a keen eye, this is a humdinger," wrote Carol Schene in *School Library Journal.*

In *Art Auction Mystery: Find the Fakes, Save the Sale!* readers must identify sixteen of thirty-four possible fakes at an art auction. "For art appreciators, a prize; for puzzle fans, a challenging set of interlocking clues," summed up a *Kirkus Reviews* contributor. *Booklist* contributor Francisca Goldsmith noted that "Nilsen combines art appreciation, decoding skills, computation, and a sense of adventure" in the book, while Linda M. Kenton wrote in *School Library Journal* that, "if your library has budding sleuths who are ready for a more complex challenge and who like art, this is the book for them."

Publishing under her real name, Nilsen has also written the juvenile biography *Van Gogh,* in which she traces the life and works of the famous artist, setting Van

Gogh's troubled personal life within the context of the era in which he lived. *Booklist* contributor Gillian Engberg considered *Van Gogh* characteristic of the other titles it joins as part of the "Lives of the Artists" series: "solid, intriguing overviews of the artists, their work, and their legacies."

Nilsen once noted: "In 1990 Walker Books invited me to develop an 'original' concept for a puzzle book. This challenge was my first encounter with children's books, and it inspired me to produce *Terrormazia: A Hole New Kind of Maze Game.* I had submitted an illustrated children's box for a competition run by Jonathan Cape, and it was selected for their exhibition of best entries. This had impressed my editor at Walker Books. She identified my potential as a 'deviser' of children's books. For the next five years I worked exclusively for Walker Books. In 1995 I retired as the head of illustration at Anglia Polytechnic University to follow a full-time career in children's books. Since then I have had books contracted with a variety of publishers.

"Since I am a deviser of children's books, my ideas usually start with a visual idea that incorporates an activity (mental and/or physical) around which the narrative is then woven. In this sense I am not a traditional author; normally an author would start with a written script, which is then illustrated. I find that even when developing a narrative concept, I start by sketching a series of visual images. This is due to my art college training, which included a wide range of specialties and a strong emphasis on drawing. Many of my ideas contain an educational element, probably due to the number of years I spent in the academic world. Often my aim is to provide children with an entertaining learning platform. I am interested in combining information with a game, a puzzle, or other activity to encourage children to be inquisitive about the real world. The *Aqua Quest* book, an information maze game book, is a good example. In the book, the Aquazone kits have been set in different oceans around the world, which introduces children to real fish on their maze journey around the world."

As Nilsen more recently noted of her writing career: "I have started to write picture-book texts prompted by *My Best Friends.* I decided to explore emotional issues which are of personal importance to me and have found this new departure very rewarding. I hope these new books will also enrich the lives of their young readers."

Biographical and Critical Sources

PERIODICALS

Booklist, June 1, 2004, Gillian Engberg, review of *Van Gogh,* p. 1751; November 1, 2005, Francisca Goldsmith, review of *Art Auction Mystery: Find the Fakes, Save the Sale!,* p. 56.

Bookseller, May 12, 1995, p. 35; June 1, 2004.

Kirkus Reviews, October 1, 2005, review of *Art Auction Mystery,* p. 1985.

Nursery World, February 22, 1996, p. 12.

Publishers Weekly, June 3, 1996, p. 85; November 21, 2005, "You Gotta Have Art," p. 50.

School Librarian, February, 1996, p. 21.

School Library Journal, March, 2002, Jody McCoy, review of *Let's Dig and Burrow* and *Let's Hang and Dangle,* p. 218; January, 2004, Shelley B. Sutherland, review of *My Best Friends,* p. 102; March, 2004, Carol Schene, review of *The Great Art Scandal: Solve the Crime, Save the Show!,* p. 240; January, 2006, Linda M. Kenton, review of *Art Auction Mystery,* p. 160.

Time out for Kids, March-April, 1995, p. 10.

ONLINE

Anna Nilsen Home Page, http://www.annanilsen.com (September 19, 2001).

Houghton Mifflin Web Site, http://www.houghtonmifflinbooks.com/ (November 3, 2006), "Anna Nilsen."

O-P

OPPENHEIM, Joanne 1934-
(Jane Fleischer, Kate Jassem)

Personal

Born May 11, 1934, in Middletown, NY; daughter of Abe P. (an electrical engineer) and Helen Fleischer; married Stephen Oppenheim (a lawyer), June 27, 1954; children: James, Anthony, Stephanie. *Education:* Attended University of Miami, 1951-52; Sarah Lawrence College, B.A., 1960; Bank Street College of Education, M.S., 1980. *Hobbies and other interests:* Community theater.

Addresses

Home—New York, NY. *Office*—Oppenheim Toy Portfolio, 40 E. 9th St., No. 14M, New York, NY 10003. *E-mail*—toyport2@aol.com.

Career

Educator, writer, and consumer advocate. Elementary school teacher in Monticello, NY, 1960-80; Bank Street College of Education, New York, NY, member of Writer's Laboratory, 1962—, senior editor in publications department, 1980-92; Oppenheim Toy Portfolio (consumer organization), New York, NY, president and co-founder, 1989—. Monthly contributor to *Today Show* (television program), 2000—. Member of board of directors, U.S.A. Toy Library, 1993—.

Awards, Honors

Outstanding Teachers of America Award, 1973; Children's Choice citation, International Reading Association, 1980, for *Mrs. Peloki's Snake,* and 1981, for *Mrs. Peloki's Class Play;* Ruth Schwartz Children's Book Award, Ontario Arts Council, 1987, Elizabeth Mrazik-Cleaver Award, 1987, and Outstanding Science Book citation, all for *Have You Seen Birds?;* Outstanding Science Book citation, 1994, for *Oceanarium;* YALSA Best Books for Young Adults award nomination, 2007, for *Dear Miss Breed.*

Writings

FOR CHILDREN

Have You Seen Trees?, illustrated by Irwin Rosenhouse, Young Scott Books (New York, NY), 1967, illustrated by Jean and Mou-sien Tseng, Scholastic (New York, NY), 1995.

Have You Seen Birds?, illustrated by Julio de Diego, Young Scott Books (New York, NY), 1968, illustrated by Barbara Reid, Scholastic (New York, NY), 1986.

Have You Seen Roads?, illustrated by G. Nook, Young Scott Books (New York, NY), 1969.

Have You Seen Boats?, Young Scott Books (New York, NY), 1971.

On the Other Side of the River, illustrated by Aliki, F. Watts (New York, NY), 1972.

Have You Seen Houses?, Young Scott Books (New York, NY), 1973.

Sequoyah, Cherokee Hero, illustrated by Bert Dodson, Troll Associates (Mahwah, NJ), 1979.

Osceola, Seminole Warrior, illustrated by Bill Ternay, Troll Associates (Mahwah, NJ), 1979.

Black Hawk, Frontier Warrior, illustrated by Hal Frenck, Troll Associates (Mahwah, NJ), 1979.

(Under pseudonym Jane Fleischer) *Tecumseh, Shawnee War Chief,* illustrated by Hal Frenck, Troll Associates (Mahwah, NJ), 1979.

(Under pseudonym Jane Fleischer) *Sitting Bull, Warrior of the Sioux,* illustrated by Bert Dodson, Troll Associates (Mahwah, NJ), 1979.

(Under pseudonym Jane Fleischer) *Pontiac, Chief of the Ottawas,* illustrated by Robert Baxter, Troll Associates (Mahwah, NJ), 1979.

(Under pseudonym Kate Jassem) *Chief Joseph, Leader of Destiny,* illustrated by Robert Baxter, Troll Associates (Mahwah, NJ), 1979.

(Under pseudonym Kate Jassem) *Pocahontas, Girl of Jamestown,* illustrated by Allan Eitzen, Troll Associates (Mahwah, NJ), 1979.

(Under pseudonym Kate Jassem) *Sacajawea, Wilderness Guide,* illustrated by Jan Palmer, Troll Associates (Mahwah, NJ), 1979.

(Under pseudonym Kate Jassem) *Squanto, the Pilgrim Adventure,* illustrated by Robert Baxter, Troll Associates (Mahwah, NJ), 1979.

Mrs. Peloki's Snake, illustrated by Joyce Audy dos Santos, Dodd (New York, NY), 1980.

James Will Never Die, illustrated by True Kelly, Dodd (New York, NY), 1982.

Mrs. Peloki's Class Play, illustrated by Joyce Audy dos Santos, Dodd (New York, NY), 1984.

Barron's Bunny Activity Books, Barron's (Hauppauge, NY), 1985.

You Can't Catch Me!, illustrated by Andrew Shachat, Houghton (Boston, MA), 1986.

(With Betty Boegehold and William H. Hooks) *Read-a-Rebus: Tales and Rhymes in Words and Pictures,* illustrated by Lynn Munsinger, Random House (New York, NY), 1986.

The Story Book Prince, illustrated by Rosanne Litzinger, Harcourt (San Diego, CA), 1987, published as *The Prince's Bedtime,* illustrated by Miriam Latimer, Barefoot Books (Cambridge, MA), 2006.

Mrs. Peloki's Substitute, illustrated by Joyce Audy Zarins, Dodd (New York, NY), 1987.

Left and Right, illustrated by Rosanne Litzinger, Harcourt (San Diego, CA), 1989.

"Not Now!" Said the Cow, illustrated by Chris Demarest, Bantam (New York, NY), 1989.

Could It Be?, illustrated by S.D. Schindler, Bantam (New York, NY), 1990.

Wake Up, Baby!, illustrated by Lynn Sweat, Bantam (New York, NY), 1990.

Follow That Fish, illustrated by Devis Grebu, Bantam (New York, NY), 1990.

Eency Weency Spider, illustrated by S.D. Schindler, Bantam (New York, NY), 1991.

The Donkey's Tale, illustrated by Chris Demarest, Bantam (New York, NY), 1991.

Rooter Remembers: A Bank Street Book about Values, illustrated by Lynn Munsinger, Viking (New York, NY), 1991.

(With Barbara Brenner and William H. Hooks) *No Way, Slippery Slick!: A Child's First Book about Drugs,* illustrated by Joan Auclair, HarperCollins (New York, NY), 1991.

Show-and-Tell Frog, illustrated by Kate Duke, Bantam (New York, NY), 1992.

(With William H. Hooks and Barbara Brenner) *How Do You Make a Bubble?,* illustrated by Doug Cushman, Bantam (New York, NY), 1992.

(Adaptor) *One Gift Deserves Another* (based on the story by the Brothers Grimm), illustrated by Bo Zaunders, Dutton (New York, NY), 1992.

Row, Row, Row Your Boat, illustrated by Kevin O'Malley, Bantam (New York, NY), 1993.

Do You Like Cats?, illustrated by Carol Newsom, Bantam (New York, NY), 1993.

(Reteller) *The Christmas Witch: An Italian Legend,* illustrated by Annie Mitra, Bantam (New York, NY), 1993.

"Uh-Oh!" Said the Crow, illustrated by Chris Demarest, Bantam (New York, NY), 1993.

Oceanarium, illustrated by Alan Gutierrez, Bantam (New York, NY), 1994.

Floratorium, illustrated by S.D. Schindler, Bantam (New York, NY), 1994.

Money, Atheneum (New York, NY), 1995.

Have You Seen Bugs?, illustrated by Ron Broda, North Winds Press (Richmond Hill, Ontario, Canada), 1996, Scholastic (New York, NY), 1997.

Painting with Air, illustrated by Stephanie Carr, Little Simon (New York, NY), 1999.

Big Bug Fun: A Book of Facts and Riddles, illustrated by Jerry Zimmerman, Scholastic (New York, NY), 2000.

Have You Seen Dogs?, illustrated by Susan Gardos, North Winds Press (Markham, Ontario, Canada), 2001.

The Miracle of the First Poinsettia: A Mexican Christmas Story, illustrated by Fabian Negrin, Barefoot Books (Cambridge, MA), 2006.

Dear Miss Breed: True Stories of the Japanese-American Incarceration during World War II and the Librarian Who Made a Difference, foreword by Elizabeth Kikuchi Yamada, afterword by Snowden Becker, Scholastic (New York, NY), 2006.

The Prince's Bedtime, illustrated by Miriam Latimer, Barefoot Books (Cambridge, MA), 2006.

The Diary of Stanley K. Hayami, Asian-American Curriculum Project (San Mateo, CA), 2007.

Also author of six activity books for children on maps, time, money, communications, and safety. Contributor to "Bank Street Readers" basal series, Macmillan (New York, NY), 1965.

FOR ADULTS

Kids and Play, Ballantine (New York, NY), 1984.

(With Betty D. Boegehold and Barbara Brenner) *Raising a Confident Child: The Bank Street Year-by-Year Guide,* Pantheon (New York, NY), 1984.

(With Betty D. Boegehold and Barbara Brenner) *Growing up Friendly: The Bank Street Guide to Raising a Sociable Child,* Pantheon (New York, NY), 1985.

KidSpeak about Computers, Ballantine (New York, NY), 1985.

(With Betty D. Boegehold and Barbara Brenner) *Choosing Books for Kids: Choosing the Right Book for the Right Child at the Right Time,* Ballantine (New York, NY), 1986.

Buy Me! Buy Me! The Bank Street Guide to Choosing Toys for Children, Pantheon (New York, NY), 1987.

The Elementary School Handbook: Making the Most of Your Child's Education, Pantheon (New York, NY), 1989.

(With daughter, Stephanie Oppenheim) *The Best Toys, Books, and Videos for Kids: The 1994 Guide to 1,000+ Kid-tested, Classic and New Products for Ages 0-10,* HarperCollins (New York, NY), 1993.

(With daughter, Stephanie Oppenheim) *Oppenheim Toy Portfolio Baby and Toddler Play Book,* illustrated by Joan Auclair, Oppenheim Toy Portfolio (New York, NY), 1999.

Read It! Play It! With Kids Three to Seven, Oppenheim Toy Portfolio (New York, NY), 2005.

(With Stephanie Oppenheim) *Read It! Play It! With Babies and Toddlers,* Oppenheim Toy Portfolio (New York, NY), 2006.

Oppenheim Toy Portfolio, Oppenheim Toy Portfolio Annual (New York, NY), 2007.

Contributor to *Pleasure of Their Company,* Chilton (Radnor, PA), 1980. Contributor of articles to magazines, including *Family Circle, Parent and Child,* and *Working Mother.*

Author's works have been translated into Spanish.

Sidelights

Joanne Oppenheim is known for works for and about children, and her fans range from preschoolers to young adults. and Her picture books appeal to children due to their pleasing rhymes and sense of humor, while her more recent works, nonfiction, center on the Japanese-American incarceration during World War II. Oppenheim's books for adult readers are directed to parents, teachers, librarians, and caregivers, and center on the importance of play, learning, and literacy. Oppenheim, who spent ten years as an elementary school teacher and another twelve as a senior editor of the Bank Street College of Education's publication department, pens books that are both entertaining and educational. Her realistic stories have also been praised for creating characters and situations with which young readers will identify.

Oppenheim's first books in the "Have You Seen?" series combine fanciful verse with illustrations that employ unusual perspectives to give children new looks at ordinary items such as roads, trees, birds, boats, and houses. In *Have You Seen Trees?* her "pleasant, read-aloud rhythms" and "touch of humor" distinguish it from other science books, according to *New York Times Book Review* writer Alice Fleming. Similarly, as George A. Woods noted in a *New York Times Book Review* appraisal, "the rhythm of Joanne Oppenheim's descriptive verse text" in *Have You Seen Roads?* will "transport" young readers, and a *Kirkus Reviews* critic wrote that the rhymes in *Have You Seen Boats?* "titillate, educate, [and] play with the mind's ear." Although the series does not provide information directly, a *Junior Bookshelf* reviewer observed that the series' aim is "to put . . . subjects in an environmental context and this is well done in an easy unforced style." "Oppenheim's poetry is magical," stated Susan Perren in a *Quill & Quire* review of *Have You Seen Birds?* Praising the author's "use of alliteration and repetition," Perren added: "Her poetry swoops and rolls, pecks and hoots, bringing the birds alive on the page."

Developing the series for over thirty years, Oppenheim has continued to add new titles to her "Have You Seen?" books. She turns to the insect world in *Have You Seen Bugs?,* a picture book illustrated by Ron Broda that features three-dimensional paper artwork to accompany Oppenheim's text. Told in rhyming verse, *Have You Seen Bugs?* shares with young readers the differing characteristics of a wide range of small creatures, in-

Joanne Oppenheim's **Have You Seen Bugs?** *features informative and entertaining verse alongside detailed paintings by artist Ron Broda.* (Scholastic Press, 1998. Illustrations © 1996 by Ron Broda. Reproduced by permission)

cluding spiders, caterpillars, and dragonflies. How bugs grow, what they eat, and how they move are all covered, as are functions that specific creatures fulfill in the environment. Calling the work "a sensational book in praise of insects," a *Publishers Weekly* critic claimed that Oppenheim and Broda "cover a lot of ground and . . . pack in a surprising amount of information." Writing in *School Library Journal,* Patricia Manning also noted the wealth of information offered in *Have You Seen Bugs?,* describing the work as "perfect for any youngster."

Canines receive the "Have You Seen?" treatment in *Have You Seen Dogs?* Here Oppenheim details the wide variety of shapes, sizes, and colors in which man's best friend can appear. While not offering information on specific breeds, the author does explain to young readers how dogs differ in their appearance and bark. Told in verse, *Have You Seen Dogs?* also shares the many different responsibilities canines can have, such as helping handicapped people, protecting livestock, and entertaining crowds. Described as a "must for dog lovers," the book is "a good read-aloud . . . and useful resource when researching certain aspects about dogs," according to *Resource Links* contributor Judy Cottrell.

Oppenheim brings her classroom experiences to bear in her stories about elementary teacher Mrs. Peloki. In *Mrs. Peloki's Snake,* the discovery of a reptile in the boys' bathroom prompts a classroom uproar. This "sprightly tale of reptilian high jinks [is] nicely tuned to the first-grade funny bone," Kristi L. Thomas commented in *School Library Journal*. The trials of staging a production of "Cinderella" are set forth in humorous fashion in *Mrs. Peloki's Class Play*, which *School Library Journal* contributor Catherine Wood called "true to life," with "class members' personalities and humor [that] emerge on almost every page." Ilene Cooper likewise praised Oppenheim in a *Booklist* review, citing the author's "real grasp of second graders and their habits." Another true-to-life episode of classroom escapades is found in *Mrs. Peloki's Substitute*, according to a *Kirkus Reviews* writer, who said the book contains "enough humor and verisimilitude to entertain children." In this story, after their cherished teacher leaves class sick, the students try to misdirect her unfortunate replacement, hoping to avoid a spelling test. While some critics faulted the book for potentially inspiring misbehavior, *Bulletin of the Center for Children's Books* writer Zena Sutherland found the tale "nicely appropriate" in length and vocabulary, adding that most young readers "will enjoy a story about a familiar situation."

Another situation familiar to many children—sibling rivalry—is portrayed in *James Will Never Die*. In this tale, young Tony can never beat his older brother in their imaginary games, for James always manages to turn everything Tony thinks of into a victory. Tony's efforts to best his brother make for a "zippy story of sibling rivalry and affection," a *Publishers Weekly* critic noted. Barbara McGinn likewise found the brothers' adventures "refreshingly imaginative," adding in a review for *School Library Journal* that, although though many of these adventures revolve around someone dying, the book is "otherwise fast-moving [and] well-written." Another book about troublesome brothers, *Left and Right*, finds two cobbler brothers learning that they make better teammates than rivals. "Invitingly told in a rhythmic rhyme," according to *Booklist* reviewer Beth Herbert, the book explains concepts of left and right as well as cooperation and "entices with its amusing insights on siblings."

A catchy refrain distinguishes *You Can't Catch Me!*, in which an annoying black fly bothers every animal on the farm without fear. Oppenheim's rhymes "are deft and simple," remarked a *Kirkus Reviews* writer, the critic adding that the story "has the rolling accumulative power of an old tale like *The Gingerbread Boy*." As Betsy Hearne similarly observed in the *Bulletin of the Center for Children's Books*, "It's rare to find contemporary verse with a true nursery rhyme ring, but this has it." Another rhyming story with an old-time air is *The Story Book Prince*, in which Oppenheim tells of the efforts of a royal household to get the prince to sleep. "The couplets frolic along," Susan Powers commented in *School Library Journal*, making this "a book for those [who] really enjoy clever word romps."

Oppenheim has also turned to familiar songs and fairy tales for material, updating them for new generations of children. Based on a story by the Brothers Grimm, for example, *One Gift Deserves Another* relates how two brothers are rewarded by their king for the gifts they bring. The poor brother, who unselfishly gives the king a giant turnip from his garden, is given wealth, while his greedy, rich brother, in exchange for a calculated gift of money and jewels, is given the king's most treasured possession: the turnip. Karen K. Radtke praised Oppenheim's retelling, noting in her *School Library Journal* review that by eliminating several adult elements from the original tale, the author "has distilled the remaining premise into an enjoyable story for children." "Oppenheim's lively retelling . . . captures its delicious ironies while lining out its tasty moral," a *Publishers Weekly* critic likewise stated. Kathryn Jennings also had warm words for Oppenheim's "upbeat version," concluding in the *Bulletin of the Center for Children's Books* that *One Gift Deserves Another* "has the humor of a 'Fractured Fairytales' episode and could become a storyhour favorite."

Oppenheim brings the legend of the holiday poinsettia to life in *The Miracle of the First Poinsettia: A Mexican Christmas Story*. Juanita, a young girl living in rural Mexico, worries that her impoverished family will not be able to follow tradition and provide a gift for the Christ child on Christmas Eve. As Juanita walks through her village, she encounters a stone angel that directs her to gather some weeds and bring them to midnight mass. When the young girl enters the church that night, the weeds are miraculously transformed into glorious red poinsettias. "Oppenheim enriches the Mexican flavor by sprinkling Spanish words throughout the text," noted a critic in *Kirkus Reviews*, and Susan Patron, reviewing the work in *School Library Journal*, observed that "the perspective is consistently and effectively that of the child."

The above-ground world of flora and undersea world of the oceans are featured in two works by Oppenheim, *Floratorium* and *Oceanarium* both use a make-believe museum to structure their information. In the first work, the author creates a floor plan for her museum that looks like a flower, with each petal branching off to a individual chapter explaining different types of plants, including deciduous, saltwater, and desert varieties. At the end of the tour, readers are encouraged to visit the museum store, which, instead of selling souvenirs, offers information about important scientists in the field of botany, as well as the beneficial role plants play in the environment. *Oceanarium* takes readers on a different type of journey, this time exploring changes in sea life as one travels ever deeper into the ocean. Oppenheim covers topics such as life in a coral reef, a shark tank, and in the tidal waters, with each chapter providing material about the types of creatures found in their respective environments. Concluding *Oceanarium* by explaining the importance of keeping the ocean free from pollutants, the author also shares with readers the dangers of exhausting the limited fish populations that may stabilize the delicate balance of the ocean's ecosystem.

Oppenheim retells a Mexican-themed Christmas tale in **The Miracle of the First Poinsettia,** *featuring illustrations by Fabian Negrin.* (Barefoot Books, 2003. Illustrations copyright © 2003 by Fabian Negrin. Reproduced by permission)

Writing in *Science Activities,* Albert C. Jensen found *Floratorium* and *Oceanarium* "ingenious and intriguing in design," going on to claim that they "represent an impressive melding of accurate text and interesting artwork that actually illustrates what it is intended to illustrate." Also commenting on both volumes, *School Library Journal* writer Carolyn Angus believed that "these appealing books offer good introductions to their topics," while *Booklist* critic Janice Del Negro deemed the books "accessible and enjoyable introductions to a wide variety of ecosystems."

Oppenheim's critically acclaimed nonfiction work, *Dear Miss Breed: True Stories of the Japanese-American Incarceration during World War II and the Librarian Who Made a Difference,* was the result of four years spent researching and writing. The book concerns Clara Breed, a librarian in San Diego who maintained contact with a number of her Japanese-American students after these children were sent with their families to an internment camp in Arizona during World War II. Oppenheim first learned of Breed's efforts while searching for an Asian-American high-school classmate; her search took her to the Web site of the Japanese-American National Museum. "When the young people were being moved out of San Diego," Oppenheim noted on her home page, "Clara [Breed] went to the train station and gave them all stamped, self addressed postcards. She urged them to write so that she could send them books and anything else they might need. It was online that I began to read some of the 250 letters that they wrote to Clara. Their letters not only chronicle the incarceration, they reflect the sense of loyalty and hope these young Americans held onto despite the treatment they were given by their own country."

After locating her classmate, Oppenheim discovered that, as a child, the woman been incarcerated at the same camp as Breed's young charges. "As a writer, I recognized from the start that this was a story that had to be told and in the words of those who lived it," the author noted on her home page. "I wanted to know what had happened to these young people? Where were they now and how had the incarceration and Clara

Breed changed their lives?" Oppenheim managed to contact the surviving correspondents and conducted interviews with them; as she stated, "finding those who could tell the story was like playing detective—an adventure with exciting leads found on microfilm, through conversations, and the letters. I have never met more generous people, who have shared the story so that it will not be forgotten!"

A work that holds a special place in Oppenheim's heart, *Dear Miss Breed* received positive reviews. The story of the children, "along with that of Miss Breed, is both remarkable and inspiring, and Oppenheim has done a fine job of assembling these poignant eyewitness accounts," remarked *School Library Journal* contributor Marilyn Taniguchi. "Although the letters (and interviews with their grown-up authors) form the narrative's bedrock, Oppenheim weaves them into a broader account, amplified by photos, archival materials and moving quotations from the later reparation hearings," observed Jennifer Mattson in *Booklist*. A critic in *Kirkus Reviews* noted that the author "creates a scathing picture of the living conditions those children and their families were forced to endure," and Margaret A. Bush stated in *Horn Book* that Oppenheim constructs "a disturbing account of the widespread racism that led rapidly to the labeling of all Japanese-American residents . . . as enemy aliens." As Oppenheim commented on her home page, *Dear Miss Breed* "is the story of how one person can make a difference in the lives of so many others. It is also a story of courage and friendship told in the voices of those who lived through one of the darkest times in our country's history."

Biographical and Critical Sources

PERIODICALS

Booklist, September 1, 1984, Ilene Cooper, review of *Mrs. Peloki's Class Play,* p. 70; November 1, 1989, Beth Herbert, review of *Left and Right,* p. 556; January 1, 1994, Janice Del Negro, reviews of *Floratorium* and *Oceanarium,* p. 823; January 15, 1995, Julie Corsaro, review of *Have You Seen Trees?,* p. 993; April, 1998, Carolyn Phelan, review of *Have You Seen Bugs?,* p. 1326; November 1, 2003, Ilene Cooper, review of *The Miracle of the First Poinsettia: A Mexican Christmas Story,* p. 499; January 1, 2006, Jennifer Mattson, *Dear Miss Breed: True Stories of the Japanese-American Incarceration during World War II and the Librarian Who Made a Difference,* p. 93.

Bulletin of the Center for Children's Books, July, 1973, p. 174; November, 1984; September, 1986, Betsy Hearne, review of *You Can't Catch Me!,* p. 15; June, 1987, Zena Sutherland, review of *Mrs. Peloki's Substitute,* p. 193; September, 1992, Kathryn Jennings, review of *One Gift Deserves Another,* p. 11.

Christian Science Monitor, May 1, 1987, p. B7.

Horn Book, March-April, 2006, Margaret A. Bush, review of *Dear Miss Breed,* pp. 207-208.

Junior Bookshelf, December, 1977, reviews of *Have You Seen Roads?* and *Have You Seen Houses?,* p. 339.

Kirkus Reviews, August 1, 1971, review of *Have You Seen Boats?,* p. 804; September 1, 1980, p. 1159; July 15, 1986, review of *You Can't Catch Me!,* p. 1121; December 15, 1986, p. 1858; January 15, 1987, review of *Mrs. Peloki's Substitute,* p. 136; November 1, 2003, review of *The Miracle of the First Poinsettia,* p. 1319; December 15, 2005, review of *Dear Miss Breed,* p. 1326.

Library Journal, March, 2006, Marilyn Taniguchi, review of *Dear Miss Breed,* p. 246.

New York Times Book Review, May 7, 1967, Alice Fleming, "First Steps in Science," p. 49; October 5, 1969, George A. Woods, review of *Have You Seen Roads?,* p. 34.

Publishers Weekly, October 22, 1982, review of *James Will Never Die,* p. 56; August 24, 1984, p. 79; October 5, 1992, review of *One Gift Deserves Another,* p. 69; April 10, 1995, review of *Have You Seen Trees?,* p. 61; May 4, 1998, review of *Have You Seen Bugs?,* p. 213; September 22, 2003, review of *The Miracle of the First Poinsettia,* p. 70; August 28, 2006, review of *The Prince's Bedtime,* p. 52.

Quill & Quire, December, 1986, Susan Perren, "Picture-Book Plums for Christmas Gift-Giving," p. 16; June, 2001, review of *Have You Seen Dogs?,* p. 50.

Resource Links, June, 2001, Judy Cottrell, review of *Have You Seen Dogs?,* p. 20.

Cover of Oppenheim's **Dear Miss Breed,** *which contains the stories of Japanese-American children incarcerated during World War II and the librarian who aided them.* (Scholastic Nonfiction, 2006. Reproduced by permission of Scholastic Inc)

School Library Journal, August, 1980, pp. 63-64; October, 1980, Kristi L. Thomas, review of *Mrs. Peloki's Snake,* p. 138; February, 1983, Barbara McGinn, review of *James Will Never Die,* p. 70; October, 1984, Catherine Wood, review of *Mrs. Peloki's Class Play,* p. 150; April, 1987, Susan Powers, review of *The Story Book Prince,* pp. 87-88; June-July, 1987, p. 88; August, 1987, p. 72; December, 1989, p. 87; June, 1991, p. 87; February, 1993, Karen K. Radtke, review of *One Gift Deserves Another,* p. 83; April, 1994, Carolyn Angus, review of *Floratorium* and *Oceanarium,* p. 142; April, 1995, Wendy Lukehart, review of *Have You Seen Trees?,* pp. 126, 128; September, 1998, Patricia Manning, review of *Have You Seen Bugs?,* p. 196; October, 2003, Susan Patron, review of *The Miracle of the First Poinsettia,* pp. 66-67.

Science Activities, spring, 1995, Albert C. Jensen, review of *Oceanarium* and *Floratorium,* p. 44.

Voice of Youth Advocates, February, 2006, Parri Sylvester Spencer, review of *Dear Miss Breed.*

ONLINE

Joanne Oppenheim Home Page, http://www.dearmissbreed.com (October 15, 2006).

*   *   *

PALATINI, Margie

Personal

Born in Edison, NJ; married; children: Jamie (son). *Education:* Moore College of Art and Design, B.F.A.

Addresses

Home—1442 Highland Ave., Plainfield, NJ 07060. *E-mail*—margiepalatini@netscape.net.

Career

Children's writer and illustrator. Co-owner of interior design business.

Awards, Honors

American Library Association (ALA) Notable Book designation, National Council of Teachers of English (NCTE) Notable Trade Book in Language Arts designation, Pennsylvania Keystone State Reading Award, Kentucky Bluegrass Children's Book Award, Vermont Red Clover Award, Kansas Reading Association's Bill Martin, Jr., Picture-Book Award, Colorado Children's Choice Book Award, Florida Reading Association Award Honor designation, Nebraska Golden Sower Award honor designation, California Young Readers' Medal nomination, Washington Children's Choice nomination, Ohio Buckeye Award nomination, and Georgia Children's Book Award nomination, all c. 1995, all for *Piggie Pie!;* Indiana Young Hoosier Award nomi-

Margie Palatini (Photograph reproduced by permission)

nation, 1995, for *Piggie Pie!,* 2002, for *Bedhead,* and 2003, for both *The Web Files* and *Earthquack!;* International Reading Association Children's Choice designation, 1997, for *Moosetache,* 1998, for *Zak's Lunch,* 2000, for *Good as Goldie,* and 2004, for both *Stinky Smelly Feet* and *The Perfect Pet;* Bank Street College Irma S. and James H. Black Award, 1998, for *Zak's Lunch;* Tennessee Volunteer State Book Award nominee and Wyoming Buckaroo Award nominee, both 1998, both for *Zoom Broom;* Pennsylvania Keystone State Reading Award, 2002, Golden Sower Award, 2003, and North Dakota Flicker Tale Award nominee and M. Jerry Weiss Book Award nominee, both 2004, all for *Bedhead;* ALA Notable Book designation, 2002, Keystone State Reading Award, Maryland Black-eyed Susan Award, Colorado Children's Book Award nominee, North Carolina Children's Book Award nominee, Pennsylvania Young Readers Award nominee, Golden Sower Award nominee, and South Dakota Prairie Bud Award nominee, all, 2003, and Michigan Great Lakes Great Books Award honor designation, 2004, all for *The Web Files;* New Hampshire Ladybug Picture Book Award nominee, 2004, for *Tub-Boo-Boo;* Georgia Picture Storybook Award nominee, Tennessee Volunteer State Book Award nominee, and Pennsylvania Young Readers Award nominee, all 2004, and Oregon Patricia Gallaher Picture Book Award nominee, 2005, all for *Earth-*

quack!; Children's Literature Choice, Missouri Show Me Book Award, Black-eyed Susan Award nominee, Kentucky Bluegrass Award nomination, all 2004, North Carolina Children's Book Award, 2005, and Pennsylvania Young Readers Award nominee and Tennessee Volunteer State Book Award, both 2006, all for *Bad Boys;* Wyoming Buckaroo Award nominee, Flicker Tale Award nominee, and New Hampshire Ladybug Picture Book Award nominee, all 2005, all for *Moo Who?;* Chicago Public Library Best of the Best designation, 2005, and Oppenheim Toy Portfolio Platinum Award and CCBC Choice designation, both 2006, all for *Three French Hens;* Florida Reading Association Award nominee and North Carolina Children's Book Award nominee, both 2006, and Bill Martin, Jr., Picture Book Award nominee, 2007, all for *The Three Silly Billies.*

Writings

Piggy Pie!, illustrated by Howard Fine, Clarion Books (New York, NY), 1995.

The Wonder Worm Wars, Hyperion Books for Children (New York, NY), 1997.

Moosetache, illustrated by Henry Cole, Hyperion Books for Children (New York, NY), 1997.

Zak's Lunch, illustrated by Howard Fine, Clarion Books (New York, NY), 1998.

Elf Help, illustrated by Mike Reed, Hyperion Books for Children (New York, NY), 1998.

Zoom Broom, illustrated by Howard Fine, Hyperion Books for Children (New York, NY), 1998.

Ding Dong Ding Dong, illustrated by Howard Fine, Hyperion Books for Children (New York, NY), 1999.

Lab Coat Girl in Cool Fuel, Hyperion Books for Children (New York, NY), 1999.

Lab Coat Girl and the Amazing Benjamin Bone, Hyperion Books for Children (New York, NY), 1999.

Mooseltoe, illustrated by Henry Cole, Hyperion Books for Children (New York, NY), 2000.

Lab Coat Girl in My Triple-Decker Hero, Hyperion Books for Children (New York, NY), 2000.

Bedhead, illustrated by Jack E. Davis, Simon & Schuster Books for Young Readers (New York, NY), 2000.

(And illustrator) *Good as Goldie,* Hyperion Books for Young Readers (New York, NY), 2000.

The Web Files, illustrated by Richard Egielski, Hyperion Books for Children (New York, NY), 2001.

Tub-Boo-Boo, illustrated by Glin Dibley, Simon & Schuster Books for Young Readers (New York, NY), 2001.

(And illustrator) *Goldie Is Mad,* Hyperion Books for Children (New York, NY), 2001.

Earthquack!, Simon & Schuster Books for Young Readers (New York, NY), 2002.

The Perfect Pet, illustrated by Bruce Whatley, HarperCollins Publishers (New York, NY), 2003.

Broom Mates, illustrated by Howard Fine, Hyperion Books for Children (New York, NY), 2003.

Bad Boys, illustrated by Henry Cole, Harpercollins Children's Books (New York, NY), 2003.

Mary Had a Little Ham, illustrated by Guy Francis, Hyperion Books for Children (New York, NY), 2003.

Moosekitos: A Moose Family Reunion, Hyperion Books for Children (New York, NY), 2004.

Stinky Smelly Feet: A Love Story, illustrated by Ethan Long, Dutton Children's Books (New York, NY), 2004.

Moo Who?, illustrated by Keith Graves, Katherine Tegen Books (New York, NY), 2004.

The Sweet Tooth, illustrated by Jack E. Davis, Simon & Schuster Books for Young Readers (New York, NY), 2004.

The Three Silly Billies, illustrated by Barry Moser, Simon & Schuster Books for Young Readers (New York, NY), 2005.

Three French Hens, illustrated by Richard Egielski, Hyperion Books for Children (New York, NY), 2005.

Oink?, illustrated by Henry Cole, Simon & Schuster Books for Young Readers (New York, NY), 2006.

Shelly, illustrated by Guy Francis, Dutton Children's Books (New York, NY), 2006.

Bad Boys Get Cookie!, illustrated by Henry Cole, Katherine Tegen Books (New York, NY), 2006.

The Cheese, illustrated by Steve Johnson and Lou Fancher, Katherine Tegen Books (New York, NY), 2007.

No Biting, Louise!, illustrated by Matthew Reinhart, Katherine Tegen Books (New York, NY), 2007.

Work in Progress

Gorgonzola, illustrated by Tim Bowers, for Katherine Tegen Books, expected 2008; *Sour Grapes,* illustrated by Barry Moser, for Simon & Schuster; *Gone with the Wand,* illustrated by Brian Ajhar, for Orchard Books.

Sidelights

Margie Palatini is a highly regarded author of picture books for young readers whose humorous titles include *Bad Boys, The Three Silly Billies, Zak's Lunch, Bedhead,* and *Oink?* In praise of her work, critics especially note Palatini's use of offbeat humor, rhyme, and allusion; her "lively wordplay—in the form of puns, allusions, and wink-wink-nudge-nudge humor—ensure that, whatever the story, the reader or listener can be assured of a giggle-inducing ride," remarked Loretta M. Gaffney in the *Bulletin of the Center for Children's Books.* "Palatini also propels sentence-level (and often, phrase-level) frolicking into satisfying arcs," Gaffney added, "giving old stories fresh twists and familiar characters new life, splicing genres together to create a whole that is more than the sum of its punny parts."

The Web Files features the characteristic trademarks of a popular book by Palatini. In this story, which is a parody of the 1960s television show *Dragnet,* two "ducktectives" try to "quack" cases that involve robberies on a farm. Fairytale characters abound; Little Boy Blue has an alibi that eliminates him as a potential suspect in a crime where the pilfered objects include,

Palatini whets the imaginative appetite of young readers in her lighthearted fantasy picture book Zak's Lunch, ***featuring illustrations by Howard Fine.*** (Clarion Books, 2004. Illustrations copyright © 1998 by Howard Fine. Reprinted by permission of Clarion Books, an imprint of Houghton Mifflin Company. All rights reserved)

among other things, a peck of pickled peppers. Beloved by readers, *The Web Files* was named a notable book by the American Library Association and earned several state book awards.

Earthquack! is a takeoff on the Henny Penny warning that "the sky is falling," except that in this case, it is the ground that is rumbling. "Palatini's text is funny, with contemporary dialogue, puns, and a fast-paced narrative rich in rhythm and alliteration (but not overwhelmingly so)," noted *School Library Journal* contributor Carol L. MacKay. In *Bad Boys*—a spin-off of "Little Red Riding Hood" and "The Three Little Pigs"—Willy and Wally Wolf have escaped from the three very angry pigs and Red and now disguise themselves as sheep by wearing "sheep's clothing." In this case, the "sheep" in question are wearing dresses, so the wily wolves rename themselves Willimina and Wallanda and infiltrate the flock in drag. All goes well until the shearer relieves them of their furry coats, leaving the two wolves knitting to cover their nakedness. According to a reviewer for *Publishers Weekly,* the author's "flair for puns and arch repartee shines through every exchange." Palatini provides a fresh take on 'The Three Billy Goats Gruff' in *The Three Silly Billies.* In the work, a surly troll demands a fee from anyone who wishes to cross the wooden bridge he guards. Billy Bob, Billy Bo, and Just Plain Billy do not have the necessary funds, so they convince other travelers, including the Three Bears,

Little Red Riding Hood, and Jack the beanstalk climber, to pool their resources. "The sounds of the words and the puns . . . are as much fun as the quarrels," remarked *Booklist* critic Hazel Rochman.

The pig in Palatini's slightly askew fairy tale *Mary Had a Little Ham* is named Stanley. A talented porker, he begins a career on Broadway with the encouragement from his friend, Mary. This is one of several Palatini tales that may induce chuckles from adults as well as from children; in sly references, Stanley appears in classic productions such as *Pork Chop on a Hot Tin Roof,* the cast of which includes a voluptuous Liz Taylor-look-alike sow. A *Kirkus Reviews* contributor wrote that Palatini "keeps the puns and jokes coming thick and fast, even as she keeps narrative tongue firmly in cheek."

A young girl tries every trick imaginable to convince her parents to buy her a furry friend in *The Perfect Pet.* Despite Elizabeth's best efforts, her parents resist the girl's suggestions to trade in her prickly cactus for something more cuddly, such as a dog, a horse, or even a rat. Then the youngster comes up with the ideal solution: adopting a bug that fits perfectly with the family on their living room couch. "Palatini is once again exercising her masterful grip on picture-book humor," noted a critic for *Kirkus Reviews.* In *Broom Mates* Gritch the witch—who also appears in Palatini's debut book *Piggie Pie!,* as well as in *Zoom Broom*—is busy throwing a "howliday" party. When her sister, Mag the Hag, shows up early, sibling rivalry ensues, sparking a witches' competition for the affection of their "mummy." *Booklist* writer Jennifer Mattson noted that Gritch and Mag favor fashion accessories that look like they may have come from country singer Dolly Parton's wardrobe and concluded that, "throughout, [the author's inclusion of] puns and witchy bons mots will carry children along on a comic tidal."

Palatini's *Stinky Smelly Feet: A Love Story* finds duck sweethearts Dolores and Douglas in love. Unfortunately, poor Dolores—as well as everyone else who comes in contact with her true love—keels over in the vicinity of Douglas and his feet. Their love survives, however, in spite of the smell. A *Kirkus Reviews* critic noted that Palatini "delivers her story with her usual sly, understated humor." The author's "characteristic exaggeration and outrageousness are in full swing in this goofy tale," wrote *School Library Journal* reviewer Marge Loch-Wouters, adding that the story will be especially enjoyed by kids "who delight in subversive humor."

In *Moosekitos: A Moose Family Reunion* the moose with the enormous moosetache—a character Palatini also features in *Moosetache* and *Mooseltoe*—summons his relatives from Moosechusetts and Moossissippi for a family reunion. Poor Moose cannot get them all to

The humorous farmyard characters in Palatini's Earthquack! *are brought to life through Barry Moser's detailed art.* (Simon and Schuster Books for Young Readers, 2002. Illustrations Copyright © 2002 by Barry Moser. Reprinted with the permission of Simon & Schuster Books for Young Readers, an imprint of Simon & Schuster Children's Publishing Division)

stay in one place long enough to take a family picture, however, because busy family members set out in all different directions from the lodge to hike, swim, and bike. "The puns are fun for confident readers, and work well when read aloud," noted Jane Barrer in *School Library Journal*. Featuring an anthropomorphosized bovine, *Moo Who?* finds Hilda Mae Heifer hit by a flying cow pie and knocked unconscious, only to wake up unable to recall what sound she is supposed to make. The other animals help her by giving Hilda hints, and it is the cat that finally returns the befuddled cow to normal, leaving the other animals running for earplugs. "Palatini maintains a simultaneously arch and familiar tone throughout, narrating like a daffy relative," wrote a contributor for *Publishers Weekly*. In *The Sweet Tooth,* Stewart has a molar with a life of its own. The tooth craves sweets at inappropriate times, and so Stewart punishes it by eating only vegetables until it gives up and falls out. *Booklist* contributor Todd Morning wrote that kids "are sure to enjoy this funny . . . look at the dangers of a sweet tooth enjoying unchecked power," while a *Publishers Weekly* critic deemed the book "a deliciously fly story that will likely satisfy a craving for lively fun."

Wily animals are the focus of many of Palatini's farmyard tales. A pair of slovenly pigs turn the tables on their barnyard neighbors in *Oink?* as, try as they might, they are unable to competently master the fine arts of house painting, harvesting, or shoveling, and end up being waited on by the other animals. *Shelly* concerns a young duckling who refuses to come out of his shell, despite the protestations of his three older sisters. Each sister attempts to coax Shelly outside by exhibiting her unique talent, but it is not until the siblings leave that the little fellow emerges, ready to engage in the quiet activities he loves. According to *School Library Journal* reviewer Robin L. Gibson, "this is a story for all children who march to a different drummer." Birds of another feather are the subject of *Three French Hens,* a "clever and original tale," in the words of a *Kirkus Reviews* writer. When Poulette, Colette, and Fifi get lost in the mail during the holidays, they wind up at the home of the bushy-tailed down-on-his-luck Phil Fox from the Bronx, who perks up with the thought that he has scored a free meal. As *Horn Book* reviewer Claire E. Gross stated, "this feel-good farce will leave readers speaking in French accents."

As her list of publications continues to grow, Palatini's works remain consistently popular with readers and critics alike. The reason is simple; as Gaffney explained: The popular author's "snort-worthy way with words puts puns, rhymes, and refrains to work in the service of narrative, using familiar hooks to snare readers in a refreshingly original whole."

Biographical and Critical Sources

PERIODICALS

Booklist, April 15, 1997, Lauren Peterson, review of *Moosetache,* p. 1436; October 1, 1998, Stephanie Zvirin, review of *Zoom Broom*, p. 336; September 1, 2000, Ilene Cooper, review of *Mooseltoe*, p. 134; May 1, 2001, Ilene Cooper, review of *The Web Files*, p. 1690; September 1, 2001, Kathy Broderick, review of *Tub-Boo-Boo*, p. 117; July, 2002, Hazel Rochman, review of *Earthquack!*, p. 1860; July, 2003, Helen Rosenberg, review of *The Perfect Pet*, p. 1898; November 1, 2003, Jennifer Mattson, review of *Broom Mates*, p. 505; November 15, 2003, GraceAnne A. DeCandido, review of *Bad Boys*, p. 602; December 15, 2003, Jennifer Mattson, review of *Mary Had a Little Ham*, p. 754; August 1, 2004, GraceAnne A. DeCandido, review of *Moosekitos: A Moose Family Reunion*, p. 1944; September 1, 2004, Terry Glover, review of *Moo Who?*, p. 135; October 1, 2004, Todd Morning, review of *The Sweet Tooth*, p. 335; March 1, 2005, Hazel Rochman, review of *The Three Silly Billies*, p. 1205; November 1, 2005, Ilene Cooper, review of *Three French Hens*, p. 41; February 1, 2006, Gillian Engberg, review of *Shelly*, p. 56; March 15, 2006, Kathleen Odean, review of *Oink?*, p. 53.

Horn Book, March-April, 1996, Ann A. Flowers, review of *Piggie Pie*, p. 189; May, 2000, review of *The Web Files*, p. 314; November-December, 2005, Claire E. Gross, review of *Three French Hens*, p. 695.

Kirkus Reviews, May 1, 2002, review of *Earthquack!*, p. 664; March 15, 2003, review of *The Perfect Pet*, p. 475; June 15, 2003, review of *Broom Mates*, p. 862; August 1, 2003, review of *Bad Boys*, p. 1021; September 15, 2003, review of *Mary Had a Little Ham*, p. 1180; May 1, 2004, review of *Stinky Smelly Feet: A Love Story*, p. 446; May 15, 2004, review of *Moo Who?*, p. 496; June 1, 2004, review of *Moosekitos*, p. 539; August 1, 2004, review of *The Sweet Tooth*, p. 748; June 1, 2005, review of *The Three Silly Billies*, p. 642; November 1, 2005, review of *Three French Hens*, p. 1195; December 15, 2005, review of *Shelly*, p. 1326; August 15, 2006, review of *Bad Boys Get Cookie*, p. 849.

Publishers Weekly, March 3, 1997, review of *Moosetache*, p. 74; April 27, 1998, review of *Zak's Lunch*, p. 66; November 9, 1998, review of *Zoom Broom*, p. 76; September 13, 1999, review of *Ding Dong Ding Dong*, p. 83; May 14, 2001, review of *The Web Files*, p. 81; July 2, 2001, review of *Goldie Is Mad*, p. 78; August 20, 2001, review of *Tub-Boo-Boo*, p. 79; March 15, 2002, review of *The Perfect Pet*, p. 475; May 6, 2002, review of *Earthquack!*, p. 57; August 4, 2003, review of *Broom Mates*, p. 77; October 6, 2003, review of *Bad Boys*, p. 83, review of *Mary Had a Little Ham*, p. 84; April 26, 2004, review of *Stinky Smelly Feet*, p. 65; June 14, 2004, review of *Moo Who?*, p. 62; November 1, 2004, review of *Sweet Tooth*, p. 60; September 26, 2005, review of *Three French Hens*, p. 86; February 13, 2006, review of *Shelly*, p. 89.

School Library Journal, May, 2000, Shawn Brommer, review of *Good as Goldie*, p. 151; October, 2000, review of *Mooseltoe*, p. 62; April, 2001, Elaine Lesh Morgan, review of *Lab Coat Girl in My Triple-Decker Hero*, p. 148; July, 2001, Laura Scott, review of *Goldie Is Mad*, p. 86; October, 2001, Linda M. Kenton, review of *Tub-Boo-Boo*, p. 128; November, 2001, John Peters, review of *The Web Files*, p. 132; June, 2002,

Carol L. MacKay, review of *Earthquack!*, p. 106; May, 2003, Marlene Gawron, review of *The Perfect Pet*, p. 128; September, 2003, Maryann H. Owen, review of *Broom Mates*, p. 186; November, 2003, Helen Foster Jones, review of *Bad Boys*, p. 112, Ellen A. Greever, review of *Mary Had a Little Ham*, p. 112; June, 2004, Marge Loch-Wouters, review of *Stinky Smelly Feet*, p. 116; July, 2004, Steven Engelfried, review of *Moo Who?*, p. 84, and Jane Barrer, review of *Moosekitos*, p. 84; November, 2004, James K. Irwin, review of *Sweet Tooth*, p. 114; June, 2005, Steven Engelfried, review of *The Web Files*, p. 56; August, 2005, Susan Hepler, review of *The Three Silly Billies*, p. 103; February, 2006, Robin L. Gibson, review of *Shelly*, p. 108; March, 2006, Maryann H. Owen, review of *Oink?*, p. 200.

ONLINE

Bulletin of the Center for Children's Books Online, http://bbcb.lis.uiuc.edu/ (July, 2006), Loretta M. Gaffney, "Rising Star—Margie Palatini."

Margie Palatini Home Page, http://www.margiepalatini.com (November 5, 2006).

*   *   *

PARKER, Kim 1963-

Personal

Born 1963; married Felipe Porto (a Web designer and publicist). *Education:* Oberlin Conservatory of Music, degree (flute performance); attended Queens College (New York, NY).

Addresses

Agent—c/o Author Mail, Scholastic, 557 Broadway, New York, NY 10012. *E-mail*—kim@kimparker.tv.

Career

Artist, lifestyle designer, musician, and artist. International School of Brussels, former flute teacher; textile designer for fashion industry; Kim Parker Designs, New York, NY, founder.

Awards, Honors

Design and Decoration Award, *Elle* magazine Decoration U.K. Award, and London *Observer* magazine award, all 2004, all for best British flooring design.

Writings

Counting in the Garden, Orchard Books (New York, NY), 2005.

Work in Progress

A fairy tale and an alphabet book for children; a sequel to *Counting in the Garden; Kim Parker: Interior Gardens*, an art and design book focusing on Parker's design career, for Stewart, Tabori & Chang, c. 2008.

Sidelights

Kim Parker is an internationally acclaimed lifestlye designer, artist, and author. The winner of several design accolades, including London's prestigious Design & Decoration award as well as the Elle Decoration U.K. Award, she has also launched her own label, Kim Parker® Home, which includes dinnerware, stationary, rugs, giftware, cookware, and home textiles featuring Parker's signature floral motifs. In addition to designing interior decor, Parker also lends her artwork to stationery and posters. In 2005 Parker's first children's picture book, *Counting in the Garden,* was published by Scholastic. The New York City-based publisher has also been involved in introducing Kim Parker® Kids, a line of plush educational toys, backpacks, and other items through its Scholastic Media division.

In *Counting in the Garden* Parker displays a luxuriant array of colors, enhancing the rich visuals of a floral garden by setting her art against a stark white background. The author/illustrator also incorporates into her book's counting theme the many animals and insects that can be found within a garden; for instance, a trio of pups play in a bed of posies and half a dozen ladybugs tiptoe up a long flower stem.

A *Publishers Weekly* contributor acknowledged *Counting in the Garden* for its "luscious colors" and added that Parker's illustrations "lend the pages a genuine vibrancy and visual depth." Linda M. Kenton, writing in *School Library Journal,* commented that the author/illustrator's "lively text" is enhanced by her use of "descriptive words and phrases," while a *Kirkus Reviews* contributor wrote that Parker "makes a promising young-audience debut" with her first self-illustrated children's title.

Biographical and Critical Sources

PERIODICALS

Kirkus Reviews, March 15, 2005, review of *Counting in the Garden,* p. 356.
New York Times, April 9, 2006, Ellen Tien, review of *Counting in the Garden,* "Sunday Times Style" section.
Publishers Weekly, April 4, 2005, review of *Counting in the Garden,* p. 59.
School Library Journal, April, 2005, Linda M. Kenton, review of *Counting in the Garden,* p. 108.

ONLINE

Kim Parker Home Page, http://www.kimparker.tv (October 6, 2006).
Kim Parker® Kids Web site, http://www.kimparkerkids. com/ (October 6, 2006).
Oberlin Alumni Online, http://www.oberlin.edu/alummag/ winter2004/ (November 2, 2006), Penne Derethik, "In Bloom."*

PERRY, Elizabeth 1959-
(Elizabeth Goodwin Perry)

Personal

Born 1959. *Education:* Degree in writing. *Hobbies and other interests:* Knitting, drawing.

Addresses

Home—Pittsburgh, PA. *Agent*—c/o Author Mail, Clarion Books, 215 Park Ave. S., New York, NY 10003. *E-mail*—mail@elizabethperry.com.

Career

Writer, poet, new-media artist, and designer of interactive art. Multimedia projects include interactive archeological sites, panoramas, and Pittsburgh Signs Project (collaborative online museum. Active in local community organizations.

Awards, Honors

Bank Street College Best Children's Books of the Year, 2006, for *Think Cool Thoughts.*

Writings

Think Cool Thoughts, illustrated by Linda Bronson, Clarion Books (New York, NY), 2005.
Selected Days: 2005: Images from www.elizabethperry. com, privately published, 2006.

Also author of nonfiction and short stories.

Sidelights

Elizabeth Perry works primarily in electronic media, creating interactive exhibitions and other projects that unite learning with creativity and the versatility provided by new computerized technology. In 2005 she also moved to a more-traditional medium, the picture book, by creating *Think Cool Thoughts.* Featuring illustrations by Linda Bronson, Perry's story takes place one hot summer evening, as a girl named Angel, together with her mother and her visiting Aunt Lucy, wonders how to escape the heat. The two older sisters decide to reenact a tradition from their own childhood: sleeping up on the roof under the stars. The three haul a mattress and linens up to top of their city apartment building, where they tell stories and Angel drifts off to sleep. Awakened by a sudden rain shower, the trio hurry to bring their bedding back down the stairs, then go back outside to dance in the rain like children.

Praising Bronson's illustrations, in which "characters are portrayed with swirling, soft circles with jazzy, stylized facial features and elongated limbs," *School Library Journal* reviewer Jane Marino dubbed *Think Cool*

Elizabeth Perry's picture book about a hot day in the city is enhanced by Linda Bronson's vibrant acrylic paintings. (Clarion Books, 2005. Illustrations copyright © 2005 by Linda Bronson. Reprinted by permission of Clarion Books, an imprint of Houghton Mifflin Company. All rights reserved)

Thoughts a "charming story" that makes "a perfect antidote to the summer's swelter." A *Kirkus Reviews* critic also enjoyed Perry's picture-book debut, writing that "readers will be counting ice cubes along with Angel, and feeling the same sense of refreshment," and in *Booklist* Ilene Cooper deemed the work "a jubilant celebration."

Biographical and Critical Sources

PERIODICALS

Booklist, July, 2005, Ilene Cooper, review of *Think Cool Thoughts,* p. 1930.
Bulletin of the Center for Children's Books, July-August, 2005, review of *Think Cool Thoughts,* p. 506.
Kirkus Reviews, June 15, 2005, review of *Think Cool Thoughts,* p. 689.
School Library Journal, August, 2005, Jane Marino, review of *Think Cool Thoughts,* p. 104.

ONLINE

Elizabeth Perry Home Page, http://www.elizabethperry. com (October 10, 2006).*

*   *   *

PERRY, Elizabeth Goodwin
See PERRY, Elizabeth

PETERSON, Cris 1952-

Personal

Born October 25, 1952, in Minneapolis, MN; daughter of Willard C. (an engineer) and Carmen (a political consultant) Hoeppner; married Gary Peterson (a dairy farmer), February 10, 1973; children: Ben, Matt, Caroline. *Ethnicity:* "Scandinavian." *Education:* University of Minnesota, B.S. (history and geography; cum laude), 1972; earned teacher certification (social studies, grades 7-12). *Politics:* Republican. *Religion:* Lutheran. *Hobbies and other interests:* Flower gardening, quilting, knitting, collecting antiques, participating in a variety of sports.

Addresses

Home—23250 South Williams Rd., Grantsburg, WI, 54840. *Agent*—c/o Karen Klockner, Transatlantic Literacy Agency, 23825 Stanford Road, Shaker Heights, OH 44122. *E-mail*—fourcubs@grantsburgtelcom.net.

Career

Children's author and workshop presenter. Dairy farmer and substitute teacher in Grantsburg, WI, 1973—; insurance agent, Grantsburg, 1986-98; Universal Press Syndicate, Kansas City, MO, nationally syndicated columnist, 1992-2000. Local historical society, president, 1974-86; 4-H Club, general leader, 1986-94; Sunday school superintendent, 1993—; new children's literature consultant for regional elementary schools.

Member

International Reading Association, Society of Children's Book Writers and Illustrators, State Historical Society of Wisconsin, Minnesota Historical Society, Count Historical Society (past president), Wisconsin Department of Commerce Dairy 2020 Council (co-chair, 1999-present), Wisconsin Dairy Business Association (member of executive board, 2001—), Professional Dairy Products of Wisconsin.

Awards, Honors

Author of the Month citation, *Highlights for Children,* October, 1989; Science Feature of the Year citation, *Highlights for Children,* 1992, for article "New Dining for Dairy Cows"; Woman's Award for Children's Literature, Ohio Farm Bureau, 1995, for *Extra Cheese, Please!: Mozzarella's Journey from Cow to Pizza,* and for *Harvest Year;* Outstanding Children's Book designation, Wisconsin Library Association, 1996; Children's Book of the Year designation, Wisconsin Farm Bureau, 1997; Children's Book of the Year designation, Ohio Farm Bureau, 1996, 1998; named Wisconsin Dairy Woman of the Year, 1999; Book of the Year Award, Wisconsin Farm Bureau, 2000, and Woman's Award for Children's Literature, Ohio Farm Bureau, both for *Century Farm: One Hundred Years on a Family Farm;* se-

Cris Peterson (Photograph courtesy of Cris Peterson)

lected as Woman of the Year, American Women in Agriculture and National Dairy, both 2002; named World Dairy Expo Dairy Woman of the Year, 2004.

Writings

FOR CHILDREN

Extra Cheese, Please!: Mozzarella's Journey from Cow to Pizza, photographs by Alvis Upitis, Boyds Mills Press (Honesdale, PA), 1994.

Harvest Year, photographs by Alvis Upitis, Boyds Mills Press (Honesdale, PA), 1996.

Horsepower: The Wonder of Draft Horses, photographs by Alvis Upitis, Boyds Mills Press (Honesdale, PA), 1997.

Century Farm: One Hundred Years on a Family Farm, photographs by Alvis Upitis, Boyds Mills Press (Honesdale, PA), 1999.

Amazing Grazing, photographs by Alvis Upitis, Boyds Mills Press (Honesdale, PA), 2002.

Wild Horses: Black Hills Sanctuary, photographs by Alvis Upitis, Boyds Mills Press (Honesdale, PA), 2003.

Fantastic Farm Machines, photographs by David R. Lundquist, Boyds Mills Press (Honesdale, PA), 2006.

Also author of "Huckleberry Bookshelf" (weekly children's book column), for Universal Press Syndicate, until 1998. Contributor of stories and articles to periodicals, including *Highlights for Children* and *Cricket.*

Work in Progress

Birch Bark Brigade: A Fur Trade History, a children's book about the history of the North American fur trade, for Boyds Mills Press.

Sidelights

Cris Peterson has expanded her multiple roles of dairy farmer, mother, 4-H leader, and teacher into another dimension as the author of picture books that both express her love of farm life and explain facets of it to suburban and urban children. She first met photographer Alvis Upitis when he visited her family's dairy farm in Wisconsin to shoot photographs for a magazine article about century farms. Working together, Peterson and Upitis have collaborated on a number of picture books about farming and ranching. Her longtime interest in children's books also led to her syndicated children's book review column, "Huckleberry Bookshelf," which appeared in newspapers across the nation until 1998. In addition to her writing, Peterson also speaks to audiences on reading, writing, history, and farming.

"My writing career began when I gave mouth-to-mouth resuscitation to a newborn calf and I knew I had a good story," Peterson recalled on the Boyds Mills Press Web site. She named the calf Breathless, and that was also be the name of Peterson's first short story about a twelve-year-old boy who saves a breech calf by administering mouth-to-mouth. The publication of "Breathless" in *Highlights for Children* magazine commenced Peterson's writing career in children's literature.

Peterson got the idea for her first children's book, *Extra Cheese, Please!: Mozzarella's Journey from Cow to Pizza,* after attending a writers' workshop in 1988. "I knew I wanted to help kids understand where their food comes from," she stated in the *Bridge.* However, self-doubts and her busy daily life on the farm prevented her from developing the story for over two years. Finally, Upitis convinced Peterson to move writing a book higher on her list of things to do. The result was *Extra Cheese, Please!,* which provides children with an inside view of every step in the cheese-production process. "Already a self-proclaimed dairy cow expert, I spent a day at our local cheese factory learning the cheese-making process," Peterson noted in the *Bridge.* "I formed the resulting information into a tightly written, somewhat boring text." Boyds Mills Press accepted the idea for publication, but it took another two years of working closely with an editor for Peterson to complete the final version.

Extra Cheese, Please! begins on the author's dairy farm—where Annabelle the cow has a calf and produces milk—and follows each step of the process, including milking the cows, pasteurizing the milk, converting milk into curds and whey, processing these byproducts at the cheese factory, packaging the resulting cheese, and selling it at a retail store for its final destination as part of a pizza. The book also includes a

Extra Cheese, Please!

MOZZARELLA'S JOURNEY FROM COW TO PIZZA

BY *Cris Peterson* ▲ PHOTOGRAPHS BY *Alvis Upitis*

Cover of Peterson's **Extra Cheese, Please!,** *featuring colored photographs by Alvis Upitis.* (Boyds Mills Press, 1994. Jacket photographs © 1994 by Alvis Upitis. Reproduced by permission)

glossary and Peterson's own pizza recipe. In order to stage Upitis's photo of kids eating pizza for the cover of the book, Peterson cooked a total of twelve pizzas and gave her family indigestion. Despite all the hard work, however, she felt the final product was worth it, and so did reviewers. *School Library Journal* reviewer Carolyn Jenks called the book "attractive and informative," and *Booklist* critic Kay Weisman commented that the "clear, simple text" makes it "an appealing addition to primary farm and nutrition units."

In the process of writing *Extra Cheese, Please!,* Peterson learned important lessons about writing children's books, and she draws on these skills in her second work. In *Harvest Year,* a "very nicely executed photographic essay," to quote Paula M. Fleming in *Catholic Library World,* Peterson tells about the wide variety of crops

that are harvested annually throughout the United States. Following a calendar format, she explains when, where, and how crops are gathered from the farm or orchard. According to Lee Bock in *School Library Journal,* Peterson's "spare and clear [text], with well-chosen details," makes the book "engaging."

Peterson takes a broader view of farming in *Century Farm: One Hundred Years on a Family Farm.* Though Peterson was born and raised in Minnesota, when she married Gary Peterson, she became part of a farming family that had worked the same land for five generations: over one hundred years. For her book, Peterson tells the farm's story from her husband's point of view, creating "a distinctly personal story," as a *Kirkus Reviews* contributor noted. The technology used on the Peterson farm has changed over the years, and these changes are reflected in the photographs, which range from sepia-toned family photos to Upitis's full-color images, chronicling both the family and how the hard work of farming has changed over the years. *Booklist* reviewer Susan Dove Lempke praised Peterson's "smooth, personal, descriptive narrative," while a *Publishers Weekly* critic cited the book for its "pleasing mixture of old and new." In a review for the *Bulletin of the Center for Children's Books,* Janice M. Del Negro praised the visual and textual presentation of *Century Farm,* remarking on Peterson's "friendly and congenial tone" and the "squeaky clean, wholesome farm setting" portrayed in the illustrations. Eldon Younce, writing in *School Library Journal,* found the photo captions "interesting" as well, remarking that they "add even more information" to a work that clearly evinces Peterson's knowledge and appreciation of farming.

Agricultural technology is the subject of *Fantastic Farm Machines,* as Peterson focuses on the mechanical tools that are essential in running a large farm, from mini-loaders to eight-wheel tractors. Narrating her book from a personal perspective, Peterson often interjects biographical information about herself; she explains, for instance, why she loves being a dairy farmer and describes the joys of running her family's Wisconsin dairy farm. The text is accompanied by color photographs ranging in size and point of view. In addition to aerial photos of the farm, Upitis provides close-range views of farm equipment. "Writing in an invitingly personal way," noted *Booklist* reviewer John Peters, the book provides readers with "an informative overview of the various farm machines, and *School Library Journal* reviewer Carolyn Janssen deemed the text "easy to understand." Elizabeth Bush, in a review of *Fantastic Farm Machines* for the *Bulletin of the Center for Children's Books,* noted that Peterson's book will make "farm kids . . . beam with pride" while "city kids [will] just eat their envious hearts out."

Peterson has also created two books about horses, one showing the breeds commonly found in a farm setting and the other focusing on the wild horses of the American West. Although draft horses no longer play the role they once did on many farms, they are raised for pleasure and are still used productively among such technology-eschewing populations as the Amish. Peterson celebrates the draft horse in her title *Horsepower: The Wonder of Draft Horses.* Introducing readers to the three main types of draft horses—Belgians, Clydesdales, and Percherons—she uses "appealing details," to quote Deborah Stevenson in the *Bulletin of the Center for Children's Books.* Peterson covers a range of topics, from the training of a young foal to horse shows and competitions, to workaday farm life. Writing in *School Library Journal,* Maura Bresnahan deemed *Horsepower* a "fine effort," noting that the "short, smoothly written text . . . nicely balances the past and present." Likewise, a *Kirkus Reviews* critic found "fascinating nuggets of draft-horse lore . . . embedded in the simple

text," illustrating for readers both the beauty and importance of these gentle giants.

In *Wild Horses: Black Hills Sanctuary* the author takes a look at the wild mustangs at the Black Hills Sanctuary in western South Dakota. Peterson explains how "cowboy-conservationist" Dayton Hyde purchased 11,000 acres of range in 1980 and created this preserve, where rescued mustangs are free to live out their lives in a natural state. According to *School Library Journal* reviewer Carol Schene, Peterson's "sparse, flowing text melds with vivid color photos to capture the beauty of these creatures." Writing in *Publishers Weekly,* a contributor claimed that author and photographer and Upitis successfully create "another eye-catching story of unusual interest."

Crucial to any grazing animal, wild or tame, is fodder, and this is the topic of Peterson's *Amazing Grazing.* In this "accessible title," to use *School Library Journal* reviewer Carolyn Janssen's description, Peterson describes the environmentally sound practices of three Montana cattle ranchers. Remarking that little has been written for children on this topic, *Booklist* critic Helen Rosenberg complimented author and illustrator, respectively, on the "cleary written text" and "beautifully formatted color photos" presented in *Amazing Grazing.*

Peterson told *SATA:* "I live on a dairy farm in northern Wisconsin where the winters are icy cold and the summers are filled with the sounds of corn growing, loons

Photographer Alvis Upitis has collaborated with Peterson on several books, including Amazing Grazing, *which focuses on America's cattle industry.* (Boyds Mills Press, 2002. Photograph © 2002 by Alvis Upitis. Reproduced by permission)

In **Horsepower** *Peterson introduces young readers to the Percherons, Clydesdales, and Belgian draft horses that have done much of mankind's heavy lifting for centuries.* (Boyds Mills Press, 1997. Photographs copyright © 1997 by Alvis Upitis. Reproduced by permission)

calling, and cows mooing. It's a great place to live and an awesome place to write about. When I'm not milking cows or feeding calves or staring at my computer screen, my favorite thing to do is speak to kids in schools and to parents and others about literacy and agriculture.

"I think it's important for kids and their families to know where their food comes from. Farming is a complicated, risky, amazing business that feeds our nation and the world and is a far cry from the Old McDonald's farm of storybook fame. My goal in writing books about farming is to create a sense of wonder: the 'wow, I didn't know that!' reaction that connects readers to new experiences and information."

Biographical and Critical Sources

PERIODICALS

Booklist, March 15, 1994, Kay Weisman, review of *Extra Cheese, Please!: Mozzarella's Journey from Cow to Pizza,* pp. 1368-1369; September 15, 1996, Susan DeRonne, review of *Harvest Year,* p. 224; March 1, 1999, Susan Dove Lempke, review of *Century Farm:*

One Hundred Years on a Family Farm, p. 1210; April 1, 2002, Helen Rosenberg, review of *Amazing Grazing,* pp. 1322-1323; February 15, 2006, John Peters, review of *Fantastic Farm Machines,* p. 100.

Bulletin of the Center for Children's Books, April, 1997, Deborah Stevenson, review of *Horsepower: The Wonder of Draft Horses,* p. 292; March, 1999, Janice M. Del Negro, review of *Century Farm,* p. 253.

Catholic Library World, March, 1997, Paula M. Fleming, review of *Harvest Year,* p. 55; December, 2001, Rosanne Steitz, review of *Horsepower,* p. 133.

Farm Journal, December, 2002, Pamela Henderson, review of *Amazing Grazing,* p. S1.

Kirkus Reviews, February 1, 1997, review of *Horsepower,* p. 226; February 1, 1999, review of *Century Farm,* p. 227.

Knight Ridder/Tribune News Service, March 9, 1994, Cathy Collison, review of *Extra Cheese, Please!*

Plays, May, 2001, review of *Horsepower,* p. 69.

Publishers Weekly, February 1, 1999, review of *Century Farm,* p. 85; December 9, 2002, review of *Wild Horses: Black Hills Sanctuary,* p. 84.

Reading Teacher, November, 1997, review of *Harvest Year,* pp. 256-257; October, 1998, review of *Horsepower,* p. 168.

School Library Journal, April, 1994, Carolyn Jenks, review of *Extra Cheese, Please!,* pp. 121-122; November, 1996, Lee Bock, review of *Harvest Year*, p. 117; April, 1997, Maura Bresnahan, review of *Horsepower*, p. 130; April, 1999, Eldon Younce, review of *Century Farm*, p. 122; April, 2002, Carolyn Janssen, review of *Amazing Grazing*, p. 180; March, 2003, Carol Schene, review of *Wild Horses*, p. 223; March, 2006, Carolyn Janssen, review of *Fantastic Farm Machines*, p. 212.

ONLINE

Boyds Mills Press Web site, http://www.boydsmillspress. com/ (September 9, 2003), "Cris Peterson."
Cris Peterson Home Page, http://www.crispeterson.com (October 6, 2006).
Peterson's Family Farm Web site, http://www. fourcubsfarm.com/ (October 6, 2006).
Transatlantic Literary Agency Web site, http://www.tla1. com/ (October 6, 2006), "Cris Peterson."

OTHER

Bridge (publicity newsletter of Boyds Mills Press), March, 1994, Cris Peterson, "Kissing Calves and Birthing Elephants: One Writer's Journey to a Book."

*   *   *

PICHON, Liz

Personal

Married; children: three. *Education:* Attended Middlesex Polytechnic (graphic design); attended Camberwell School of Art.

Addresses

Home and office—The Annex, Ground Floor Studios, Belmont St., Brighton BN1 6SE, England. *E-mail*—liz. pichon@virgin.net.

Career

Designer and illustrator. Jive Records, London, England, designer and art director; Freelance graphic designer.

Awards, Honors

National Book Parent Award (with Mary Joslin), for *Twilight Verses, Moonlight Rhymes.*

Writings

ILLUSTRATOR

Christina Goodings, *The Whizzy Bizzy Christmas Fun Book: Loads and Loads of Fun Things to Make and Do* (nonfiction), Lion (Colorado Springs, CO), 1999.

Lois Rock, *The Lord's Prayer for Children,* Lion (Colorado Springs, CO), 1999.
Mary Joslin, compiler, *Twilight Verses, Moonlight Rhymes* (poetry), Augsburg Fortress (Minneapolis, MN), 1999.
Mary Joslin, compiler, *God Bless the Moon: Rhymes and Blessings for Children,* Augsburg Fortress (Minneapolis, MN), 2000.
Mary Joslin, compiler, *Now the Day Is Over: Rhymes and Blessings for Children,* Augsburg Fortress (Minneapolis, MN), 2000.
Alison Boyle, *1, 2, 3, 4, 5, Once I Caught a Fish Alive!,* David & Charles (London, England), 2000.
Alison Boyle, *Twinkle, Twinkle, Little Star,* David & Charles (London, England), 2000.
Lois Rock, *The Ten Commandments for Children,* Lion Children's Books (Colorado Springs, CO), 2000.
Peter Patilla, *Starting off with Time,* Barron's (Hauppauge, NY), 2001.
Peter Patilla, *Starting off with Counting,* Barron's (Hauppauge, NY), 2001.
Peter Patilla, *Starting off with Shapes,* Barron's (Hauppauge, NY), 2001.
Peter Patilla, *Starting off with Adding and Subtracting,* Barron's (Hauppauge, NY), 2001.
Elizabeth Laird, *Beautiful Bananas,* Peachtree (Atlanta, GA), 2004.
Tasha Pym, *Colour Bears,* HarperCollins (London, England), 2005.
Melanie Joyce, *Let's Play Home Corner,* Ladybird (London, England), 2006.

SELF-ILLUSTRATED

The Very Ugly Bug, Little Tiger (London, England), 2004, Tiger Tales (Wilton, CT), 2005.
Bored Bill, Little Tiger (London, England), 2005.
Old MacDonald's Farm: Touch and Sing Playbook, Ladybird (London, England), 2005.
My Big Brother, Hippo (London, England), 2005.

Sidelights

After studying graphic design in her native England, Liz Pichon worked as a graphic artist and designer. Her art has appeared on a variety of products that have been distributed around the world, such as towels, fabrics, greeting cards, and calendars. Establishing herself as a designer, Pichon then moved on to illustrating children's books written by others, and eventually she decided to take over writer's duties for herself. The books Pichon has both written and illustrated include the humorous *The Very Ugly Bug* and *Bored Bill.*

The Very Ugly Bug centers on an unattractive bug who tries to fit in with her more-attractive insect friends. In her attempt to be more beautiful, the bug gussies herself up in attire she hopes will make her more like her friends. The ugly bug's plan backfires, however, when her disguise attracts a bird who sees the ugly bug as a mid-day snack. In the end, the ugly bug's natural appearance proves to save her from such bird attacks, and

Liz Pichon's quirky illustrations are paired with her humorous story about an insect seeking the key to bug beauty in **The Very Ugly Bug.** (Tiger Tales, 2004. Illustrations copyright © 2004 Liz Pichon. Reproduced by permission)

the quaint lesson makes *The Very Ugly Bug* "an entertaining picture-book take on self-acceptance" as *Bulletin of the Center for Children's Book* reviewer Hope Morrison explained. Discussing Pichon's illustrations, Morrison added that the artist's "bold palette and cartoonish characters add to the fun." *School Library Journal* critic Kathleen Simonetta claimed that Pichon's "large, cartoon-style paintings clearly show the different insects and their attributes," and concluded that "young children will be smiling as they discover the importance of being one's self."

As an illustrator, Pichon's artwork for Mary Joslin's poetry collection *Twilight Verses, Moonlight Rhymes* earned her England's National Parents Book Award.

The picture book, described as "uncommonly attractive" by a critic writing in *Publishers Weekly,* contains selections from contemporary writing as well as from English literature, all of which contain bedtime themes. In some cases the art is incorporated with Joslin's text, and the various selections blend in a way that is both "soothing and thoughtful," according to the reviewer. *School Library Journal* contributor Selene S. Vasquez predicted that children will find Pichon's bright, bold illustrations "warm and appealing," and both reviewers judged the book a likely bedtime favorite.

In *Beautiful Bananas,* written by Elizabeth Laird, Pichon creates art to complement a humorous story based on an African folktale about the traits of consideration and generosity. In Laird's tale, a girl named Beatrice takes a trip to her grandfather's house and plans to offer bananas as a gift. However, the girl's gift is ruined when a giraffe knocks the bananas out of her arms and they fall into a stream. The giraffe, in an apologetic gesture, offers Beatrice a bouquet of fresh flowers to replace the bananas. Unfortunately, the flowers are also ruined when a swarm of bees uses them for honeymaking. The bees make reparation to Beatrice by offering her some of their honey, continuing the story's cycle of apologies and gift-giving until an elephant offers the cluster of bananas that rounds out the tale. In *Publishers Weekly,* a critic reviewed *Beautiful Bananas* and remarked that "Pichon's pictures teem with energy, whether emanating from the comically expressive heroine or boisterous but eager-to-please animals." The reviewer also acknowledged the illustrator's use of color, adding that the story's "benevolently exotic setting glows with lemon yellow light and lime-green foliage." *Booklist* reviewer John Peters cited the book's "brightly lit cartoon scenes featuring a smiling, brown-skinned child" while Margaret R. Tassia acknowledged Pichon for creating "cheerful, bold artwork [that] complements the mood and setting of the story."

Biographical and Critical Sources

PERIODICALS

Booklist, December 15, 1999, Hazel Rochman, review of *Twilight Verses, Moonlight Rhymes,* p. 788.
Bulletin of the Center for Children's Books, May, 2005, Hope Morrison, review of *The Very Ugly Bug,* p. 399.
Publishers Weekly, July 26, 1999, review of *Twilight Verses, Moonlight Rhymes,* p. 83; March 15, 2004, review of *Beautiful Bananas,* p. 74; July 16, 1999, review of *Twilight Verses, Moonlight Rhymes,* p. 83.
School Library Journal, March, 2000, Selene S. Valquez, review of *Twilight Verses, Moonlight Rhymes,* p. 226; May, 2005, Kathleen Simonetta, review of *The Very Ugly Bug,* p. 94.

ONLINE

David Higham Associates Web site, http://www.davidhigham.co.uk/ (October 6, 2006), "Liz Pichon."
Liz Pichon Home Page, http://www.lizpichon.co.uk (October 6, 2006).*

*   *   *

POWELL, Consie

Personal

Married; husband a biologist; children: one daughter. *Education:* B.A.; M.S.T. (elementary education). *Hobbies and other interests:* Canoeing, hiking.

Addresses

Home—5208 Olive Rd., Raleigh, NC 27606; (May to August) 13348 Farm Lake Access Rd., Ely, MN 55731. *E-mail*—consbuff@earthlink.net.

Career

Illustrator and writer. Editor, designer, and illustrator of "North Carolina WILD Notebook" (young readers' section of *Wildlife in North Carolina* magazine); creator of illustrations for North Carolina Museum of Natural Sciences; North Carolina Zoo, visiting artist. *Exhibitions:* Work exhibited at North Carolina Museum of Natural Sciences Nature Gallery, North Carolina Botanical Garden, New York State Museum, Green Hill Center for North Carolina Art, and others.

Member

Society of Children's Book Writers and Illustrators, Guild of Natural Science Illustrators, Picture Book Artists Association, Writers and Illustrators of North Carolina.

Awards, Honors

American Association for the Advancement of Science Best Books designation, 1992-95, and Rocky Mountain Book Publishers Association Book Design Competition runner-up in Children's/Young Adult category, 1995, both for *A Bold Carnivore;* John Burroughs List of Nature Books for Young Readers inclusion, and Sigurd Olson Nature-Writing Award, 2006, both for *Leave Only Ripples.*

Writings

SELF-ILLUSTRATED

A Bold Carnivore: An Alphabet of Predators, Roberts Rinehart (Boulder, CO), 1995.
Old Dog Cora and the Christmas Tree, Albert Whitman (Morton Grove, IL), 1999.
Amazing Apples, Albert Whitman (Morton Grove, IL), 2003.
The First Day of Winter, Albert Whitman (Morton Grove, IL), 2005.
Leave Only Ripples: A Canoe Country Sketchbook, Raven Productions (Ely, MN), 2005.

ILLUSTRATOR

Roger A. Powell, *The Fisher,* University of Minnesota Press, 1982, 2nd edition, 1993.
S.W. Buskirk and others, editors, *Martens, Sables, and Fishers: Biology and Conservation,* Cornell University Press, 1994.

Roger A. Powell, *Ecology and Behaviour of the North American Black Bear: Home Ranges, Habitat, and Social Organization,* Chapman & Hall (London, England), 1997.

Jennifer Berry Jones, *Who Lives in the Snow?,* Roberts Rinehart (Boulder, CO), 1999.

Michael Elsohn Ross, *Baby Bear Isn't Hungry,* Yosemite Association (El Portal, CA), 1999.

Carolyn M. King and Roger A. Powell, editors, *The Natural History of Weasels and Stoats: Ecology, Behavior, and Management,* 2nd edition, Oxford University Press (New York, NY), 2007.

Illustrator for other scientific publications.

Sidelights

Nature illustrator and children's book author Consie Powell is passionate about her work and her love for animals and the natural world. Powell's interest in animals has found her raising porcupines, drawing weasels and lizards, and encouraging her daughter to keep toads as pets. Raised in California, Powell moved to Minnesota to attend college, and there she became interested in the winter habitats and habits of the region's animals. After graduating with a bachelor's degree in art and a master's degree in education, she developed a career path that has incorporated her talent as an artist, her love of teaching, and her interest in nature. As a writer and illustrator, Powell has produced several children's books, among them *A Bold Carnivore: An Alphabet of Predators, Old Dog Cora and the Christmas Tree, Leave Only Ripples: A Canoe Country Sketchbook,* and *The First Day of Winter.*

A holiday tale, *Old Dog Cora and the Christmas Tree* focuses on an elderly pup who breaks from her nap as her rural family bustles around the house in preparation for outdoor holiday activities. As the two younger dogs are harnessed in preparation for a jaunt into the woods in search of this year's Christmas tree, Cora is almost left at home because she is considered too old to pull the toboggan. The dog shows her human family that, although she may be old, she still has what it takes to be a good hauling dog, however. Praising Powell's graphic woodcut and watercolor illustrations, *Booklist* contributor Carolyn Phelan added that the "satisfying" story is "written with understanding and sympathy for" Cora's viewpoint. In *Publishers Weekly* a reviewer called Powell's artwork "slightly nostalgic" and deemed her story "sweet."

The rhyming text of *The First Day of Winter* plays off the familiar Christmas song "The Twelve Days of Christmas," encouraging readers to look for hidden images in each page, beginning with one tall tree that stays fresh all year and continuing on throughout the book. Powell introduces young readers to the changes brought by the winter season, such as what happens

Through her text and detailed illustrations, Consie Powell opens a window onto the natural world in **The First Day of Winter.** (Albert Whitman & Company, 2005. Illustrations copyright © 2005 by Constance Buffington Powell. Reproduced by permission)

when the weather turns cold, both above and below the snow-covered ground. Her watercolor and colored-pencil illustrations, characterized by Powell's use of strongly defined outlines and detail, feature a bounty of wild animals and plants. As Ilene Cooper wrote in *Booklist, The First Day of Winter* "brims with interesting information" and Powell's art features "handsomely portrayed" plants and animals that are strikingly positioned "against the white, bright snow." A *Kirkus Reviews* critic also enjoyed the book, noting that it provides "a wonderful seasonal activity that will have kids learning as they observe the wintry world around them."

Biographical and Critical Sources

PERIODICALS

Booklist, October 1, 1995, Leone McDermott, review of *A Bold Carnivore: An Alphabet of Predators,* p. 324; September 1, 1999, Carolyn Phelan, review of *Old Dog Cora and the Christmas Tree,* p. 150; November 15, 2001, Ellen Mandel, review of *Who Lives in the Snow?,* p. 577; January 1, 2006, Ilene Cooper, review of *The First Day of Winter,* p. 106.

Childhood Education, winter, 2004, Sherry Trotta, review of *Amazing Apples,* p. 108.

Kirkus Reviews, December 1, 2005, review of *The First Day of Winter,* p. 1279.

Publishers Weekly, May 22, 1995, review of *A Bold Carnivore,* p. 58; September 27, 1999, review of *Old Dog Cora and the Christmas Tree,* p. 56.

School Library Journal, October, 2003, Kathleen Simonetta, review of *Amazing Apples,* p. 155; January, 2006, Susan Weitz, review of *The First Day of Winter,* p. 112.

ONLINE

Consie Powell Home Page, http://www.consiepowell.com (October 10, 2006).

Picture Book Artists Association Web site, http://www.picturebookartists.org/ (October 10, 2006), "Consie Powell."

Writers & Illustrators of North Carolina Web site, http://www.wincbooks.com/ (October 10, 2006), "Consie Powell."

R

RIORDAN, Rick

Personal

Born in San Antonio, TX; married; children: two sons.

Addresses

Home—San Antonio, TX. *Agent*—Nancy Gallt Literary Agency, 273 Charlton Ave., S. Orange, NJ 07079.

Career

Writer. Middle-school English teacher in San Francisco, CA, 1990-98; middle-school social studies and American history teacher, St. Mary's Hall, San Antonio, TX, 1999-2004. Presenter at workshops for educational organizations.

Awards, Honors

Anthony Award for Best Original Paperback, and Shamus Award for Best First Private-Eye Novel, both 1997, both for *Big Red Tequila;* Anthony Award for Best Original Paperback, Edgar Allan Poe Award for Best Original Paperback, and Shamus Award nominee, all 1998, all for *The Widower's Two-Step;* Shamus Award nominee for Best Hardcover Private-Eye Novel, 2002, for *The Devil Went down to Austin;* Master Teacher Award, St. Mary's Hall, 2002; inducted into Texas Hall of Letters, 2003; Cooperative Children's Book Council Choice Award, and Notable Children's Book citation, National Council for Teachers of English, both 2006, both for *The Lightning Thief.*

Writings

"PERCY JACKSON AND THE OLYMPIANS" NOVEL SERIES; FOR YOUNG ADULTS

The Lightning Thief, Miramax/Hyperion (New York, NY), 2005.

The Sea of Monsters, Miramax/Hyperion (New York, NY), 2006.

The Titan's Curse, Miramax/Hyperion (New York, NY), 2007.

"TRES NAVARRE" MYSTERY NOVEL SERIES; FOR ADULTS

Big Red Tequila, Bantam (New York, NY), 1997.
The Widower's Two-Step, Bantam (New York, NY), 1998.
The Last King of Texas, Bantam (New York, NY), 2000.
The Devil Went down to Austin, Bantam (New York, NY), 2001.
Southtown, Bantam (New York, NY), 2004.
Mission Road, Bantam (New York, NY), 2005.

OTHER

Cold Springs (adult novel), Bantam (New York, NY), 2003.

Contributor to periodicals, including *Mary Higgins Clark Mystery Magazine* and *Ellery Queen's Mystery Magazine.*

Adaptations

The "Percy Jackson and the Olympians" books were recorded as audiobooks by Listening Library. *The Lightning Thief* was optioned for a feature film.

Sidelights

Rick Riordan is the award-winning author of the "Tres Navarre" mystery series as well as of several young-adult novels in the "Percy Jackson and the Olympians" series. His "Tres Navarre" mysteries begins with *Big Red Tequila.* Navarre is a San Antonio, Texas-based private detective with a Ph.D. in medieval studies, as well as a few degrees from the streets and an active interest in the martial art Tai Chi Chuan. Commenting in the *Chicago Tribune,* Dick Adler noted of this series that "Riordan writes so well about the people and topography of his Texas hometown that he quickly marks the territory as his own."

WINNER OF THE EDGAR, SHAMUS, AND ANTHONY AWARDS

RICK RIORDAN
AUTHOR OF *SOUTHTOWN*

MISSION ROAD

"IN RICK RIORDAN'S CASE,
BELIEVE THE HYPE.
HE REALLY IS THAT GOOD."
—Dennis Lehane

"RIORDAN HAS A KNACK
FOR SHOWING READERS A
CRAZY GOOD TIME."
—*New York Times Book Review*

Cover of Rick Riordan's 2005 novel Mission Road, *featuring popular P.I. Tres Navarre.* (Bantam Books, 2006. Cover photos © Michael Gesinger and Doug Plummer/Photonica/Getty Images)

Riordan spent eight years teaching English in a San Francisco middle school before following in his hero's footsteps and returning to his hometown of San Antonio in the summer of 1998. Riordan adopts a unique "Tex-Mex" style in describing the scenery, people, and popular places in south Texas. As a *Publishers Weekly* critic stated, the author's "dialogue is terse and the long first person descriptions show an unbeatable flair for detail. You can almost feel the summer storms rolling over south Texas."

In his work as a teacher in Texas schools, Riordan soon found himself with a dilemma. "When I first started writing adult mysteries, it never occurred to me that my middle-school students would ask if they could read them," he explained on his home page. Because he assesses the "Navarre" novels as inappropriate for pre-teen readers, Riordan told his students to wait until they were older. Meanwhile, the author's older son turned eight, and Riordan began retelling original Greek myths at the boy's request. "I'd taught mythology for years, so I began telling him myths for bedtime," the novelist explained to an interviewer for the Powells Web site. When Riordan moved from the classic myths to original tales featuring a modern demi-god, his son insisted that he write these stories down. "The next thing I knew, I was a children's novelist!"

In *The Lighting Thief* Riordan introduces Percy Jackson, a trouble-making middle schooler diagnosed with ADHD and dyslexia. In the story, Percy discovers that the things that have always made him feel "different" from his classmates are the result of the fact that he is actually a demi-god: His ADHD is needed to help him fight off monsters at a moment's notice and his dyslexia enables him to read ancient Greek. Pursued by monsters, Percy evades them, only to find himself at Camp Half-Blood, a summer camp for young demigods. Understanding his destiny, Percy soon finds himself embroiled in a quest to find Zeus's lightning bolt in order to prevent the Olympians from declaring war on Earth. Percy's friends Grover and Annabeth accompany him into the Underworld, where they discover that Kronos, the Titan who once ruled the Olympians, is plotting against all of Western civilization.

Diana Tixier Herald, reviewing the first "Percy Jackson and the Olympians" novel for *Booklist,* called *The Lightning Thief* a "clever mix of classic mythologies, contemporary teen characters, and an action-packed adventure" Despite the numerous references to Greek mythology incorporated into Riordan's tale, "one need not be an expert in Greek mythology to enjoy" the adventure, a *Kirkus Reviews* contributor maintained, "but those who are familiar . . . will have many an ah-ha moment." *School Library Journal* critic Patricia D. Lothrop dubbed the novel's references to Greek myth a "zippy review" of mythology and praised Riordan's story as "an adventure-quest with a hip edge." Chris Sherman, also writing in *Booklist,* called Percy "an appealing, but reluctant hero," adding that "the modernized gods are hilarious."

The Sea of Monsters continues Percy's adventures as he searches for the Golden Fleece in order to save Thalia's tree, which provides the magical border protecting Camp Half-Blood. To make matters worse, Percy is haunted by dreams in which friend Grover is in danger. In other plot developments, a homeless classmate at school turns out to be both a Cyclops and our hero's half-brother. "Percy has a sarcastically entertaining voice and a refreshing lack of hubris," wrote Anita L. Burkam in *Horn Book,* describing the preteen as "wry, impatient, [and] academically hopeless, with the sort of cut-to-the-chase bluntness one would wish for in a hero." A *Kirkus Reviews* contributor also enjoyed the character, writing that "Percy's sardonic narration and derring-do will keep the pages turning." Noting that the end of *The Sea of Monsters* baits readers for the happenings of the third book in the series, *The Titan's Curse,* a *Publishers Weekly* reviewer maintained that

Riordan's "cliffhanger leaves no question that Percy's high-stakes battle for Western Civilization will continue to surprise even himself."

The books in the "Percy Jackson" series have been complimented for their ability to engage even reluctant readers. "If you want a young person to read a book, take a lesson from Rick Riordan and start it by warning readers to close the book right away and go back to their uninformed lives," wrote Heather Rader in a *Kliatt* review of *The Lightning Thief*. Discussing *The Sea of Monsters*, fellow *Kliatt* contributor Paula Rohrlick deemed the novel "an entertaining retelling of Greek myths, and a good bet for adventure and fantasy fans as well as reluctant readers."

While Riordan enjoys writing for adults, creating fiction for a younger audience meshes nicely with his love of teaching. Along with visiting schools, he has also started a Web log called *Myth and Mystery*, where he provides updates about his "Percy Jackson" stories and discusses the writing process. When asked by *Edge of the Forest* online interviewer Camille Powell how the blog has affected his creative output, Riordan replied: "It is an interesting, informal way to share thoughts. It's sort of a cross between a diary, a travel journal, and an open letter to friends. What good is it? Darned if I know. But it is fun."

Biographical and Critical Sources

PERIODICALS

Booklist, December 1, 1999, Jenny McLarin, review of *The Last King of Texas,* p. 688; May 1, 2001, Jenny McLarin, review of *The Devil Went down to Austin,* p. 1640; March 15, 2003, Connie Fletcher, review of *Cold Springs,* p. 1279; April 15, 2004, Connie Fletcher, review of *Southtown,* p. 1428; May 1, 2005, Frank Sennett, review of *Mission Road,* p. 1534; September 15, 2005, Chris Sherman, review of *The Lightning Thief,* p. 59; July 1, 2006, Diana Tixier Herald, review of *The Sea of Monsters,* p. 52.

Bookseller, August 19, 2005, review of *The Lightning Thief.*

Chicago Tribune, July 6, 1997, p. 7.

Chronicle, April, 2005, Mike Jones, review of *The Lightning Thief,* p. 19.

Horn Book, July-August, 2005, Anita L. Burkam, review of *The Lightning Thief,* p. 479; May-June, 2006, Anita L. Burkam, review of *The Sea of Monsters,* p. 326.

Kirkus Reviews, April 1, 2003, review of *Cold Springs,* p. 503; May 15, 2005, review of *Mission Road,* p. 566; June 15, 2005, review of *The Lightning Thief,* p. 690; April 1, 2006, review of *The Sea of Monsters,* p. 355.

Kliatt, September, 2006, Heather Rader, review of *The Lightning Thief,* p. 34; March, 2006, Paula Rohrlick, review of *The Sea of Monsters,* p. 16.

Library Journal, December, 1999, Craig L. Shufelt, review of *The Last King of Texas,* p. 188; May 1, 2001, Rex Klett, review of *The Devil Went down to Austin,* p. 129; May 15, 2003, Ken St. Andre, review of *Cold Springs,* p. 132.

New York Times Book Review, June 7, 1998, p. 32; November 13, 2005, Polly Schulman, "Harry Who?," p. 42.

Publishers Weekly, April 28, 1997, p. 73; March 23, 1998, p. 96; December 20, 1999, review of *The Last King of Texas,* p. 58; April 30, 2001, review of *The Devil Went down to Austin,* p. 59; April 7, 2003, review of *Cold Springs,* p. 45; April 5, 2004, review of *Southtown,* p. 44; May 16, 2005, review of *Mission Road,* p. 40; July 18, 2005, review of *The Lightning Thief,* p. 207; April 24, 2006, review of *The Sea of Monsters,* p. 61.

School Library Journal, August, 2005, Patricia D. Lothrop, review of *The Lightning Thief,* p. 134.

Texas Monthly, July, 2005, Mike Shea, review of *Mission Road,* p. 64.

Times Educational Supplement, July 21, 2006, Fiona Lafferty, "Inspired by Mount Olympus," p. 29.

Voice of Youth Advocates, August, 2005, Dave Goodale, review of *The Lightning Thief,* p. 237.

ONLINE

Edge of the Forest, http://www.theedgeoftheforest.com/ (September, 2006), Camille Powell, interview with Riordan.

Myth and Mystery: The Official Blog of Rick Riordan, http://rickriordan.blogspot.com (November 3, 2006).

Powells Web site, http://www.powells.com/ (November 3, 2006), interview with Riordan.

Rick Riordan Home Page, http://www.rickriordan.com (November 3, 2006).*

*   *   *

RONG, Yu 1970-

Personal

Born December 16, 1970, in China; daughter of Li Chunpeng and Zhou Fengying; married Henning Sirringhaus (a professor at Cambridge University) July 3, 1997; children: Hannah, Moritz. *Ethnicity:* "Chinese." *Education:* Nanjing Normal University Art College, B.A. (Chinese art), 1993; Royal College of Art (London), M.A. (communication art and design), 2000. *Religion:* Christian.

Addresses

Home—Robindene, 79 Whitewell Way, Coton, Cambridge CB23 7PW, England. *Agent*—c/o Author Mail, Candlewick Press Inc., 2067 Massachusetts Ave. 3rd Fl., Cambridge MA 02140. *E-mail*—studio@yurong.co.uk.

Career

Author, artist, and illustrator. Formerly worked as a primary-school teacher. Designer; creates hand-painted lampshades featuring traditional Chinese designs.

Awards, Honors

Quentin Blake Award for Narrative Illustration, 1999; Folio Society Illustration Award, 1999; Sheila Robinson Drawing Prize, 2000.

Writings

SELF-ILLUSTRATED

A Lovely Day for Amelia Goose, Candlewick Press (Cambridge, MA), 2004.

Work in Progress

Tracks of a Panda, a self-illustrated picture book for Walker Books, 2007.

Biographical and Critical Sources

PERIODICALS

Booklist, May 1, 2004, Jennifer Mattson, review of *A Lovely Day for Amelia Goose,* p. 1564.
Kirkus Reviews, May 1, 2004, review of *A Lovely Day for Amelia Goose,* p. 447.
Publishers Weekly, May 3, 2004, review of *A Lovely Day for Amelia Goose,* p. 190.
School Library Journal, June, 2004, Maryann H. Owen, review of *A Lovely Day for Amelia Goose,* p. 118.

ONLINE

Yu Rong Home Page, http://www.yurong.co.uk (October 10, 2006).

*   *   *

ROOK, Sebastian
See JEAPES, Ben

*   *   *

ROTH, Matthue 1978(?)-

Personal

Born c. 1978; son of teachers; married; wife's name Itta (a photographer and sound artist). *Education:* Gratz College, teacher's certification (advanced Hebrew; with honors), 1996; George Washington University, B.A. (anthropological study of religion), 1999. *Religion:* Orthodox Jewish.

Addresses

Home—Philadelphia, PA. *Agent*—c/o Author Mail, Push/Scholastic, Inc., 557 Broadway, New York, NY 10012. *E-mail*—matthue@gmail.com.

Matthue Roth (Photograph courtesy of Matthue Roth)

Career

Novelist, performance poet, and musician. Precious Legacy Tours, Prague, Czech Republic, translator and secretary, 1999; Congregation Kesher Israel, Washington, DC, assistant to Rabbi Barry Freundel, 1999-2000; Coates & Jarratt Consulting, Washington, DC, researcher and writer, 1999-2001; Environmental Science Associates, San Francisco, CA, assistant librarian, 2001; Pacific Coast Associates, San Francisco, secretary, 2001-04. Poetry and arts editor for *Zeek* magazine, 2002-04, and *Blech!,* 2003—. Performer on stage tours of Deepak Chopra and Carlos Santana, and in national solo shows, festivals, and other assemblies. Appeared in films, including *The Waves,* 2004, and *Can't Touch This: Young Orthodox Jews and Sexuality.* Member of band Chibi Vision.

Writings

Never Mind the Goldbergs, PUSH/Scholastic (New York, NY), 2005.
Yom Kippur a Go-Go, Cleis Press (San Francisco, CA), 2005.
Candy in Action, Soft Skull Press (Brooklyn, NY), 2007.

Also author of *Platonic* (chapbook), 2001; *Bellybudding* (poetry), 2001; *A Child's Garden of Gender* (poetry), 2002; and *Sometimes I Throw Stuff at This House* (chapbook), illustrated by Phred Chao, 2002. Contributor to periodicals, including *San Francisco Bay Guardian, Bitch, Central Europe Review, Cherry Bleeds, Loop, Farbrengen, Forward, Response,* and *Zero;* contributor to books, including *This Is Push, Homewrecker, Bottoms Up,* and *Quirkyalone.* Co-author, with Mat Tonti, of graphic novel "Lost My Place," for *World Jewish Digest Online.*

Work in Progress

Philadelphia, a poetry memoir; *Out of Time,* a novel.

Sidelights

In marked contrast to his focus on punk and hip-hop music, sexuality, and other aspects of urban youth culture, Matthue Roth's Orthodox Jewish faith influences his career as a performance poet as well as his work as a writer. With a degree in the anthropology of religion and a proficiency in several languages, Roth spent several years touring the country, performing a variety of venues as a poet—including Home Box Office television's Def Poetry Jam—in addition to writing both poetry and prose. "I've always been a writer . . . ," he explained in an interview for *TeensReadToo.com.* "I used to make up stories with He-Man and Star Wars action figures. Then I started writing them down—and, yup, I never stopped." Roth's fiction, some of which is directed toward a young-adult audience, includes the novels *Never Mind the Goldbergs* and *Yom Kippur a Go-Go.* An autobiographical saga that follows the author's search for love and creative fulfillment via the writing life, *Yom Kippur a Go-Go* was described by *Tikkun* contributor Liz Winer as "exhilarating" due to its "frenetic pace," and "well worth the ride" due to Roth's effort to "wed tradition to the avant-garde."

Written for a younger audience than *Yom Kippur a Go-Go,* *Never Mind the Goldbergs* introduces Hava Aaronson, an independent-minded, hard-rocking, seventeen-year-old Orthodox Jew living in New York City and attending prep school. Hava's talent for acting reveals itself after she is cast in a local stage production and when a role in an upcoming Hollywood situation comedy is offered, she jumps at the chance. The role is that of a modern teen living in an Orthodox Jewish family, and although Hava's upbringing has prepared her for the role, it has not prepared her for life in Hollywood. After arriving in California to spend the summer as an actress, she is forced to deal with Hollywood culture and the pressure to alter her value system. "Hava tells her story in a vivid, funny, and distinguishable voice," commented *School Library Journal* reviewer Jack Forman, the critic praising Roth's novel for presenting an "irreverent, insider look into two cultures and a portrait of a character trying to define herself in these very different environments." A *Kirkus Reviews* critic stated that "readers will be both amused and intrigued by this lively teen struggling to amalgamate her religious and secular cultures without compromising either," while a *Children's Bookwatch* reviewer called *Never Mind the Goldbergs* a "lively" and "unusual story of a very modern punkish teen."

Biographical and Critical Sources

PERIODICALS

Children's Bookwatch, September, 2005, review of *Never Mind the Goldbergs.*
Kirkus Reviews, January 15, 2005, review of *Never Mind the Goldbergs,* p. 125.
Library Media Connection, August-September, 2005, Sarah Applegate, review of *Never Mind the Goldbergs,* p. 81.
Publishers Weekly, March 7, 2005, review of *Never Mind the Goldbergs,* p. 68.
School Library Journal, June, 2005, Jack Forman, review of *Never Mind the Goldbergs,* p. 168.
Tikkun, January-February, 2006, Liz Winer, review of *Yom Kippur a Go-Go,* p. 75.
Voice of Youth Advocates, June, 2005, review of *Never Mind the Goldbergs,* p. 136.

ONLINE

Matthue Roth Home Page, http://www.matthue.com (October 10, 2006).
PD Entertainment Web site, http://www.speakerspca.com/ (October 10, 2006), "Matthue Roth."
PUSH Web site, http://thisispush.com/ (October 10, 2006), "Matthue Roth."
Something Jewish Web site, http://www.somethingjewish.co.uk/ (October 20, 2003), Alexandra J. Wall, "Talking about It" (interview).
TeensReadToo, http://www.teensreadtoo.com/ (October 10, 2006), interview with Roth.
Zeek, http://www.zeek.net/ (October 10, 2006), interview with Roth."

* * *

ROWLING, J.K. 1965-
(Joanne Kathleen Rowling, Newt Scamander, Kennilworthy Whisp)

Personal

Surname pronounced "rolling"; born July 31, 1965, in Chipping Sodbury, England; married a journalist (divorced); married December 26, 2001; children: (first marriage) one daughter; (second marriage) one daughter, one son. *Education:* Exeter University, graduated, 1987.

Addresses

Home—Perthshire, Scotland. *Agent*—Christopher Little Literary Agency, Eel Brook Studios, 125 Moore Park Rd., London SW6 4PS, England.

Career

Children's book author. Amnesty International, former secretary; former teacher of English as a Foreign Language in Portugal; former teacher in Scotland. Writer, 1987—.

Awards, Honors

Scottish Arts Council grant, 1996; Children's Book of the Year, British Book Awards, and Gold Winner, Nestlé Book Prize, both 1997, and *Birmingham Cable* Chil-

J.K. Rowling (Photograph © Rune Hellestad/Corbis)

dren's Book Award, Young *Telegraph* Paperback of the Year, Sheffield Children's Book Award, *Guardian* Fiction Award shortlist, and Carnegie Medal, all for *Harry Potter and the Philosopher's Stone;* Anne Spencer Lindbergh Prize in Children's Literature, 1997-98, *Publishers Weekly* Best Book designation, *Booklist* Editor's Choice designation, American Library Association (ALA) Notable Book designation, New York Public Library Best Book of the Year designation, and *Parenting* Book of the Year Award, all 1998, ABBY Award, American Booksellers Association, 1999, and Rebecca Caudill Young Readers' Book Award, 2001, all for *Harry Potter and the Sorcerer's Stone;* Gold Award, Nestlé Smarties Book Prize, 1998, *Booklist* Editor's Choice designation, ALA Best Book for Young Adults designation, and *School Library Journal* Best Book of the Year designation, all 1999 and Whitbread Children's Book of the Year Award shortlist, all for *Harry Potter and the Chamber of Secrets;* Whitbread Prize for Children's Literature, Nestlé Smarties Gold Award, *Booklist* Editor's Choice designation, *Los Angeles Times* Best Book designation, and ALA Notable Book designation, all 1999, all for *Harry Potter and the Prisoner of Azkaban;* W.H. Smith Children's Book of the Year Award, 2000, and

Hugo Award for Best Novel, World Science Fiction Society, Scottish Arts Council Book Award, and Whitaker's Platinum Book Award, all 2001, all for *Harry Potter and the Goblet of Fire;* Prince of Asturias Concord Prize, 2003; Bram Stoker Award in Young Readers category, 2003, and W.H. Smith Book Award in fiction category, 2004, both for *Harry Potter and the Order of the Phoenix;* Doctor honoris causa, Edinburgh University, 2004; Quill Book Awards Book of the Year, 2005, and Royal Mail Award for Scottish Children's Book shortlist, and Book of the Year, British Book Awards, both 2006, all for *Harry Potter and the Half-Blood Prince;* Best Book award, Kids' Choice Awards, 2006, for "Harry Potter" series.

Writings

"HARRY POTTER" NOVEL SERIES

Harry Potter and the Philosopher's Stone, Bloomsbury (London, England), 1997, published as *Harry Potter and the Sorcerer's Stone,* Arthur A. Levine Books (New York, NY), 1998.

Harry Potter and the Chamber of Secrets, Bloomsbury (London, England), 1998, Arthur A. Levine Books (New York, NY), 1999.

Harry Potter and the Prisoner of Azkaban, Arthur A. Levine Books (New York, NY), 1999.

Harry Potter and the Goblet of Fire, Arthur A. Levine Books (New York, NY), 2000.

Harry Potter and the Order of the Phoenix, Arthur A. Levine Books (New York, NY), 2003.

Harry Potter and the Half-Blood Prince, Arthur A. Levine Books (New York, NY), 2005.

OTHER

(Under name Newt Scamander) *Fantastic Beasts and Where to Find Them,* special edition with a foreword by "Albus Dumbledore," Arthur A. Levine Books (New York, NY), 2001.

(Under name Kennilworthy Whisp) *Quidditch through the Ages,* Arthur A. Levine Books (New York, NY), 2001.

Rowling's "Harry Potter" books have been translated into sixty languages, including French, German, Italian, Dutch, Greek, Finnish, Danish, Spanish, and Swedish.

Adaptations

Five "Harry Potter" books have been adapted for film by Warner Bros.: *Harry Potter and the Sorcerer's Stone,* 2001, *Harry Potter and the Chamber of Secrets,* 2002, *Harry Potter and the Prisoner of Azkaban,* 2004, *Harry Potter and the Goblet of Fire,* 2005, and *Harry Potter and the Order of the Phoenix,* 2006. The "Harry Potter" books were adapted for audiocassette and CD-ROM, read by Jim Dale, Listening Library. The Harry Potter character is also featured in video games and has been licensed for use in hundreds of toys.

Work in Progress

The final novel in the "Harry Potter" series.

Sidelights

Her skill as a storyteller has propelled British fantasy novelist J.K. Rowling into illustrious company; she has been compared by critics to such classic children's authors as Roald Dahl, C.S. Lewis, and J.R.R. Tolkien. Because her works weave a substantial amount of humor and satire into their fantastic storylines, Rowling's "Harry Potter" novel series has also won broad popular appeal, wooing fans of all ages in addition to becoming a resounding hit among younger readers. The "Harry Potter" series—a seven-book sequence that includes *Harry Potter and the Sorcerer's Stone, Harry Potter and the Chamber of Secrets,* and *Harry Potter and the Half-Blood Prince*—focuses on a young boy who discovers he has a magical legacy and must attend a special school for witches and wizards. As Harry grows in knowledge, he also travels a path to self-discovery; the series traces his adventures from age eleven onward and details his battles with evil-doers as well as his experiences with friends, parents, schoolwork, and sports.

A former teacher, Rowling caused an overnight sensation when her first book, *Harry Potter and the Sorcerer's Stone*—first published in her native England as *Harry Potter and the Philosopher's Stone*—quickly sold out of its first edition, then broke U.S. publishing records: Scholastic, Inc. paid 100,000 dollars for publishing rights to the book, the highest ever for a first novel by a children's book author. Beginning a pattern that each of Rowling's popular series installments have followed in turn, *Harry Potter and the Sorcerer's Stone* quickly rose to the top of the U.S. children's best-seller lists before being adapted for audiobook and then for film by Warner Brothers. As she completed further books in her "Harry Potter" series, Rowling continued to make publishing news: *Harry Potter and the Chamber of Secrets* went to the top of the adult best-seller lists in England shortly after its 1998 release as the series' second installment, and demand for the book by U.S. readers brokered a new era in internet sales of books internationally. Collectively, the "Harry Potter" books, which have sold hundreds of millions of copies worldwide, eventually made their unsuspecting author into one of the wealthiest women in the world.

In her series, Rowling spins a magical blend of wit and fantasy, a surreal melange of "the dark juvenile novels of Roald Dahl and C.S. Lewis," according to *Newsweek* contributor Carla Power. In fact, the author's life makes for an interesting story in itself: a single mother, she wrote her first "Harry Potter" adventure while unemployed, working during her young daughter's nap time. Even after gaining publishing success and winning numerous awards, Rowling has taken her success in stride, changing her one-bedroom flat in Edinburgh for a comfortable house, but still continuing her habit of writing in cafés.

Rowling was born in July of 1965, in Chipping Sodbury, England. Her father is a retired aircraft factory manager, and her mother was a lab technician. Rowling and her younger sister grew up partly in Yate, just outside the city of Bristol, and then moved to nearby Winterbourne. Even as a child, Rowling had a penchant for storytelling, and many of her early tales involved rabbits, since she and her sister desperately wanted one as a pet. Her first written effort concerned a rabbit named Rabbit who contracted the measles and received visits from friends, including a large bee named Miss Bee. As Rowling once commented, "Ever since Rabbit and Miss Bee, I have wanted to be a writer, though I rarely told anyone so. I was afraid they'd tell me I didn't have a hope."

Two moves took the Rowling family to the town of Tutshill near Chepstow in the Forest of Dean, located at the border of England and Wales. This new home brought a long-time country-living dream to fruition for Rowling's parents, both Londoners, and the nine-year-old Rowling soon shared their love of the countryside. She and her sister could wander unsupervised in the fields near their new home and play along the River Wye. "The only fly in the ointment was the fact that I hated my new school," the author once noted. Tutshill Primary was an old-fashioned school with roll-top desks and a teacher who frightened Rowling.

From Tutshill Primary, Rowling moved to Wyedean Comprehensive School, where "I was quiet, freckly, short-sighted and rubbish at sports," as she recalled. English was her favorite subject and she created serial stories for her friends at lunchtime, each tale involving heroic deeds. Trading her eyeglasses for contact lenses lessened feelings of inferiority for Rowling as she entered her teens, and writing became more a compulsion and less a hobby. Attending Exeter University, she studied French, although she later found this course of study to be a mistake. Her parents had advised her that bilingualism would lead to a successful career as a secretary; "Unfortunately I am one of the most disorganised people in the world," she related, admitting that she had a significant disadvantage in the job market for budding secretaries. Eventually finding a job working at Amnesty International, Rowling discovered one positive aspect of life as a secretary: she could use the computer to type up her own stories during lulls at work.

In 1990, Rowling's mother died at age forty-five of multiple sclerosis, and Rowling lost her job soon afterward. This was not all her run of bad luck would provide, however; around this same time, Rowling's home in Manchester was burgled. To put things behind her, she moved to Portugal in September of that year, and taught English as a foreign language. In Portugal Rowling began a story that she thought might become a book, about a child who is sent off to wizard school. During her time in Portugal, she took notes for her story, slowly adding bits and pieces to the life of her protagonist, a boy named Harry Potter. In Portugal she also met and married, gave birth to a daughter, and got divorced.

Eventually returning to England, Rowling decided to settle in Edinburgh and set about raising her daughter as a single mother. Accepting a job as a French teacher, she also gave herself a goal: to finish her novel before her teaching job began. This was no easy task with an active toddler in hand. Rowling confined her writing to her daughter's nap time, much of it spent in coffeehouses where the understanding management allowed her space for her papers. She was able to send off her typed manuscript to two publishers before beginning her teaching post, and several months later the news arrived that Harry Potter would be brought to life between the covers of a children's book. A few months later, the U.S. rights were bought by Scholastic, allowing Rowling to say adieu to teaching.

When readers first meet Harry Potter in *Harry Potter and the Sorcerer's Stone,* he is an orphan who has been leading a miserable existence with the Dursley family, his maternal aunt and uncle. Ever since Harry arrived unannounced at their doorstep, the Dursleys have felt put upon, their vile son Dudley more so than even his parents. Harry is housed in a broom closet under the stairs, is bullied at school, and is and mistreated by the Dursleys. "Harry had a thin face, knobbly knees, black hair and bright green eyes," Rowling writes in her debut novel. "He wore round glasses held together with a lot of Scotch tape because of all the times Dudley had punched him in the nose." Small, skinny, and bespectacled, Harry is an unlikely hero; the only thing physically interesting about him is the lightning-shaped scar on his forehead.

When Harry turns eleven, he receives a letter. Although the Dursleys withhold it from him, a second letter manages to get through, and Harry learns he has been admitted to Hogwarts School of Witchcraft and Wizardry. For the first time, Harry learns that his parents were wizards who were killed by an evil sorcerer named Voldemort. Harry himself is something of a legend in wizard circles because of the fact that he survived Voldemort's attack, the same attack that left the unusual scar on his forehead. Before he fully understands what is happening, Harry is swept off into the sky by the giant Hagrid, keeper of the keys at Hogwarts, who is riding a flying motorcycle. Thus begins what Rayma Turton described in her *Magpies* review as "a ripping yarn" and a "school story with a twist." Instead of boring math and geography, Harry takes lessons in the history of magic and in charms, or defenses against the dark arts. He becomes something of a star at the school's athletic contest, quidditch, an aerial form of soccer that is played astride broomsticks. The new student soon forms friendships with Ron and Hermione and also encounters students who are far less pleasant, such as his nemesis, the sly Draco Malfoy. During his first year at Hogwarts, Harry investigates the secrets of

the school's forbidden third floor and battles evil in the form of Professor Snape, whom Harry fears intends to steal the sorcerer's stone and thus gain eternal life. Harry also discovers the secret behind his scar and, in the process, starts to become his own person.

"The language is witty, the plotting tight, the imagination soars," Turton commented in a review of *Harry Potter and the Sorcerer's Stone.* As a writer for the Associated Press observed, "Rowling has an unerring sense of what it means to be 11, and her arresting, brick-by-brick construction of Harry's world has turned a rather traditional plot into a delight." Hogwarts is a composite of the typical English public school (American readers will recognize it as a private school), yet turned on its head. Harry's rooms are in Gryffindor house, and as a resident there he is a rival of another campus dormitory, Slytherin. Rather than protractors and calculators, Harry's school supplies at Hogwarts include a message-bearing owl and a magic wand. "The light-hearted caper travels through the territory owned by the late Roald Dahl," observed a reviewer for *Horn Book,* the critic concluding that *Harry Potter and the Sorcerer's Stone* is a "charming and readable romp with a most sympathetic hero and filled with delightful magic details." A *Booklist* commentator called the book "brilliantly imagined and written," while a critic for *Publishers Weekly* noted that there "is enchantment, suspense and danger galore."

A classic tale of good versus evil, as well as a coming-of-age novel with a unique flavor, *Harry Potter and the Sorcerer's Stone* is not simply a novel about magic and wizardry. As Michael Winerip commented in the *New York Times Book Review,* "the magic in the book is not the real magic of the book." For Winerip, and countless other readers, it is the "human scale" Rowling gives her story that makes it work. "Throughout most of the book, the characters are impressively three-dimensional," Winerip noted, concluding that the author uses her own special "wizardry" to achieve "something quite special" with her first novel.

In *Harry Potter and the Chamber of Secrets* Harry returns to second term at Hogwarts in a flying car, and deals with old and new characters alike. One of these newcomers is Nearly Headless Nick, a poor creature upon whom an executioner made a messy cut; another is Moaning Myrtle, a ghost that inhabits Hogwarts' girls' bathrooms. Valerie Bierman, writing in *Carousel,* noted that the adventures comprising Harry's second outing are "brilliantly scary with horrible happenings, mysterious petrifyings and a terrifying conclusion." A reviewer in *Publishers Weekly* asserted that, "if possible," *Harry Potter and the Chamber of Secrets* "is even more inventive" than *Harry Potter and the Sorcerer's Stone* and Rowling's "ability to create such an engaging, imaginative, funny and, above all, heartpoundingly suspenseful yarn is nothing short of magical."

The title of *Harry Potter and the Prisoner of Azkaban* refers to the wizard prison, Azkaban, as Harry learns of the escape of the evil murderer Siruis Black. Black, Harry's godfather, is believed to have helped Voldemort murder the boy's parents, and with the man's escape Harry's life now appears threatened. As security is tightened at Hogwarts, ghastly robed and hooded dementors patrol the campus, but these beings have an especially strong affect on Harry, who hears unearthly, terrified voices whenever they draw near. Dark Arts Defense instructor Remus Lupin teaches Harry an advanced spell that repels the dementors. Werewolves, magic spells, and mysterious disappearances all find their way into Rowling's plot, as Harry and his friends find a way to rescue his friends and family from the soul-extracting dementors and rescue a surprising friend.

Harry Potter and the Prisoner of Azkaban again earned Rowling critical praise as well as Britain's prestigious Whitbread Prize for Children's Literature. *New Statesman* contributor Amanda Craig pointed out that while the novel follows the formula of its two predecessors, "there is comfort in formulas as good as this one and the inventiveness, the jokes, the characterization, and suspense are as enthralling as ever." In *Horn Book,* Martha V. Parravano deemed the new characters introduced in this outing "particularly interesting," and a *Publishers Weekly* reviewer described the conclusion of *Harry Potter and the Prisoner of Azkaban* "utterly thrilling."

In *Harry Potter and the Goblet of Fire* fourteen-year-old Harry faces his biggest challenge to date: battling evil Lord Voldemort to make friendship triumphant over discord. At Hogwarts, all are shocked when Harry's name is picked out of the magic Goblet of Fire to compete in the Triwizard Tournament. Surviving the first two challenges, Harry ties for the lead with fellow Howarts alum Cedric Diggory, but when the boys make a synchronized grab for the trophy after tying in the final challenge, they realize too late that it is a portkey—a device that can transport. Confronted by the evil Voldemort, Cedric is killed, Voldemort begins bringing to life a group of horrid Death Eaters, and Harry must face one of the biggest challenges of his life to survive.

Rowling "is highly inventive, funny, a fine plotter, and a superb narrator," wrote Brian Bethune in a *Maclean's* review of the fourth novel in Rowling's fantasy epic. "With *Harry Potter and the Goblet of Fire*," noted Kristen Baldwin in *Entertainment Weekly,* "the author gives her characters complex new dimensions—even exploring the chamber of secrets known as wizard puberty—without losing the whimsy that makes Potter fans long to ditch the Muggle world for a cottage in Hogsmeade." As *Entertainment Weekly* reviewer Kristen Baldwin observed, the novel "lulls the reader for so long with its lovely, meandering tale that when Rowling finally gets to the Harry/Voldemort showdown, the effect . . . is shocking." In *Newsweek* a contributor stated that, "for pure narrative power, this is the best Potter book yet," and Robert Papinchak concluded in his review for

People that "Rowling squeezes in more than a few good laughs as she moves toward the electrifying final confrontation," creating a novel that is "absolutely enchanting" and "the best of the series."

Fans had to wait three years for the publication of the next "Harry Potter" book. In the interim, Rowling published *Quidditch through the Ages,* a supplement to the "Harry Potter" series, under the pseudonym Kennilworthy Whisp. The slim paperback was made to look like a real tome from Hogwarts and was paired with a second Rowling book, *Fantastic Beasts and Where to Find Them,* published under the name Newt Scamander. "Harry Potter fans who pride themselves on knowing every minute bit of Hogwart's trivia will devour both books," noted Eva Mitnick in her *School Library Journal* review.

The ever-older adolescent Harry returns in *Harry Potter and the Order of the Phoenix,* which finds him ensconced with his muggle relatives, the Dursleys, during summer break from Hogwarts. When he returns to Hogwarts for his fifth year, he faces more than just an unpleasant Defense against the Dark Arts instructor, end-of-term Ordinary Wizarding Level exams, and a peevish house-elf. In addition to divisive political problems within the magical world, Harry also experiences the worst nightmare of his life. Critics and readers noted a change in Harry in this book: he is older, more serious, and angry at times. Steve Wilson, writing in *Book,* found that "finally, in this installment, Harry gets real" and his "believability as a teenager couldn't have come soon enough." Ilene Cooper, reviewing the novel for *Booklist,* praised the manner in which Rowling develops her protagonist "from the once downtrodden yet hopeful young boy to this new, gangly teenager showing all the symptoms of adolescence." While Mitnick described *Harry Potter and the Order of the Phoenix* as "a rich and compelling coming-of-age story," *January* online reviewer Sue Bursztynski went further, noting that, unlike earlier novels in the series, "this novel is no longer children's literature."As Bursztynski theorized, "Rowling has written on several levels for a wide variety of readers. It is a richly realized universe that becomes more complex with each book."

Rowling's sixth book in the "Harry Potter" series, *Harry Potter and the Half-Blood Prince,* was described as "the darkest and most unsettling installment yet" by *New York Times* reviewer Michiko Kakutani. In this novel Harry comes into possession of a book once owned by someone called the Half-Blood Prince, and the volume helps him earn top grades in his Potions class. Meanwhile, the evil Voldemort and his followers busy themselves in perpetrating a rash of murders, as well as an apparent hurricane and bridge collapse, while Harry's nemesis Draco Malfoy plots against someone at Hogwarts—but who? When Harry voices suspicion regarding Malfoy's nefarious activities, his warnings fall on deaf ears. Fortunately, working with Dumbledore he learns that Voldemort has placed pieces of his soul into six random objects or horcruxes; if these are destroyed the dark wizard will be vulnerable. The threat to both Harry and Dumbledore mounts, with tragic results, leaving a solemn Harry comprehending his destiny and the path his future life must take.

National Review contributor David J. Montgomery remarked of *Harry Potter and the Half-Blood Prince* that, "once again [Rowling] has spun an immensely enjoyable journey through the magical world of Harry Potter, a near breathless story of heroism, intrigue, and cowardly villainy." Kakutani noted that the novel "pulls together dozens of plot stands from previous volumes, underscoring how cleverly and carefully J.K. Rowling has assembled this giant jigsaw puzzle of an epic." Writing in the *Wall Street Journal*, Meghan Cox Gurdon concluded that "what leaps out from the [novel's] intricate storyline and wonderfully fresh prose . . . is the jaw-dropping scope of J.K. Rowling's achievement even before she publishes the last in the series." In *Horn Book* Anita Burkham noted that Rowling includes "plenty of engaging mystery and suspense" while also telling a strong coming-of-age story, adding that the "likable characters and thrilling situations" characteristic of the "Harry Potter" series are paired with "fresh novelties." "Rowling capably blends literature, mythology, folklore, and religion into a delectable stew," added *Booklist* reviewer Connie Tyrell Burns, the critic noting that *Harry Potter and the Half-Blood Prince* will leave fans enduring a "long and bittersweet wait for the final installment" in Rowling's epic fantasy.

Biographical and Critical Sources

BOOKS

Baggett, David, and Shawn E. Klein, editors, *Harry Potter and Philosophy: If Aristotle Ran Hogwarts,* Open Court (Chicago, IL), 2004.

Beacham's Guide to Literature for Young Adults, Volume 11, Beacham Publishing (Osprey, FL), 2001.

Beahm, George W., *Muggles and Magic: J.K. Rowling and the Harry Potter Phenomenon,* Hampton Roads Publishing, 2004.

Compson, William, *J.K. Rowling,* Rosen Publishing (New York, NY), 2003.

Fraser, Linda, *Conversations with J.K. Rowling,* Arthur A. Levine Books (New York, NY), 2001.

Granger, John, *The Hidden Key to Harry Potter: Understanding the Meaning, Genius, and Popularity of Joanne Rowling's Harry Potter Novels,* Zossima Press, 2002.

Heilman, Elizabeth, editor, *Harry Potter's World,* Routledge-Falmer (New York, NY), 2003.

Nel, Philip, *J.K. Rowling's Harry Potter Novels: A Reader's Guide,* Continuum (New York, NY), 2001.

Rowling, J.K., *Harry Potter and the Sorcerer's Stone,* Scholastic (New York, NY), 1998.

Shapiro, Marc, *J.K. Rowling: The Wizard behind Harry Potter,* St. Martin's Press (New York, NY), 2001.

Smith, Sean, *J.K. Rowling: A Biography,* Michael O'Mara (London, England), 2001.

Steffens, Bradley, *J.K. Rowling,* Lucent Books, 2002.

Wiener, Gary, *Readings on J.K. Rowling,* Greenhaven Press (San Diego, CA), 2004.

PERIODICALS

Book, September, 2000, Robert Allen Papinchak, review of *Harry Potter and the Goblet of Fire,* p. 74; September-October, 2003, Steve Wilson, review of *Harry Potter and the Order of the Phoenix,* p. 88.

Booklist, January 1, 1999, review of *Harry Potter and the Sorcerer's Stone,* p. 783; May 15, 1999, Sally Estes, review of *Harry Potter and the Chamber of Secrets,* p. 1690; April 15, 2001, Sally Estes, review of *Harry Potter and the Goblet of Fire,* p. 1561; May 1, 2001, Stephanie Zvirin, review of *Harry Potter and the Sorcerer's Stone,* p. 1611, Ilene Cooper, review of *Fantastic Beasts, and Where to Find Them,* p. 1683, and review of *Quidditch through the Ages,* p. 1683; July, 2003, Ilene Cooper, review of *Harry Potter and the Order of the Phoenix,* p. 1842.

Books for Keeps, September, 1997, review of *Harry Potter and the Philosopher's Stone,* p. 27; July, 1999, pp. 6-7.

Carousel, summer, 1998, Valerie Bierman, "Working from Home," p. 23.

Christianity Today, Michael G. Maudlin, review of *Harry Potter and the Goblet of Fire,* p. 117.

Christian Science Monitor, November 16, 2001, p. 15.

Chronicle of Higher Education, November 16, 2001, Edmund Kern, "Harry Potter, Stoic Boy Wonder," pp. B18-B19.

Daily Variety, December 22, 2004, Pamela McClintock, "In Hogwarts Heaven: Pubs' Stock Soars as 6th 'Potter' Tome Looms," p. 6.

Entertainment Weekly, July 21, 2000, Kristen Baldwin, "'Fire' Power," pp. 72-73; August 4, 2000, "Rowling Thunder," p. 44; August 11, 2000, "Hocus Focus," p. 28; November 30, 2001, p. 26; July 14, 2006, Missy Schwartz, "Will Harry Potter Die?," p. 19.

Europe Intelligence Wire, December 22, 2004, "July 16 Is Potter Magic Date."

Globe & Mail (Toronto, Ontario, Canada), July 16, 2005, Sandra Martin, review of *Harry Potter and the Half-Blood Prince.*

Guardian (London, England), February 16, 1999, p. EG4.

Horn Book, January, 1999, review of *Harry Potter and the Sorcerer's Stone,* p. 71; November, 1999, Martha V. Parravano, review of *Harry Potter and the Prisoner of Azkaban,* p. 744; January, 1999, review of *Harry Potter and the Sorcerer's Stone,* p. 71; November, 1999, Martha V. Parravano, review of *Harry Potter and the Prisoner of Azkaban;* November, 2000, Martha V. Parravano, review of *Harry Potter and the Goblet of Fire,* p. 762; September-October, 2003, Martha V. Parravano, review of *Harry Potter and the Order of the Phoenix,* p. 619; September-October, 2005, Anita

Burkham, review of *Harry Potter and the Half-Blood Prince,* p. 587.

Journal of Adolescent and Adult Literacy, November, 2002, review of *Harry Potter and the Goblet of Fire,* p. 215.

Kirkus Reviews, June 1, 1999, p. 888.

Kliatt, November, 2002, Paula Rohrlick, review of *Harry Potter and the Goblet of Fire,* p. 27; September, 2003, Paula Rohrlick, review of *Harry Potter and the Order of the Phoenix,* p. 12; September, 2005, Paula Rohrlick, review of *Harry Potter and the Half-Blood Prince,* p. 14.

Library Journal June 1, 2001, review of *Harry Potter and the Prisoner of Azkaban,* p. S53.

Maclean's, July 17, 2000, Brian Bethune, "Summer Books: Harry Potter Inc.," p. 42; November 26, 2001, p. 44.

Magpies, March, 1999, Rayma Turton, review of *Harry Potter and the Philosopher's Stone.*

National Review, October 11, 1999, "It's Witchcraft," p. 60; July 18, 2005, David J. Montgomery, review of *Harry Potter and the Half-Blood Prince.*

New American, July 28, 2003, "Potter-Mania's Dark Side," p. 5.

New Republic, November 22, 1999, "Harry Potter and the Spirit of Age: Fear of Not Flying," p. 40.

New Statesman, December 5, 1997, review of *Harry Potter and the Philosopher's Stone,* p. 64; July 12, 1999, Amanda Craig, review of *Harry Potter and the Prisoner of Azkaban,* pp. 47-49; July 17, 2000, Amanda Craig, review of *Harry Potter and the Goblet of Fire,* p. 54; July 7, 2003, Amanda Craig, review of *Harry Potter and the Order of the Phoenix,* p. 49.

Newsweek, December 7, 1998, Carla Power, "A Literary Sorceress," p. 79; August 23, 1999, Malcolm Jones, "Magician for Millions," p. 58; July 17, 2000, "Why Harry's Hot," p. 52; June 30, 2003, Malcolm Jones, review of *Harry Potter and the Order of the Phoenix,* p. 50.

New York Daily News, December 21, 2004, Paul D. Colford, "A Gift to Readers: *Harry Potter and the Half-Blood Prince*"; December 22, 2004, Paul D. Colford, "Next Harry Potter Book to Be Released in July."

New York Times, July 8, 2000, Alan Cowell, "All Aboard the Potter Express," pp. 1330-1332; November 16, 2001, p. E1; December 16, 2001, p. WK5; December 31, 2001, p. C6; July 16, 2005, Michiko Kakutani, "Harry Potter Works His Magic Again in a Far Darker Tale."

New York Times Book Review, February 14, 1999, Michael Winerip, review of *Harry Potter and the Sorcerer's Stone,* p. 26; September 5, 1999, Gregory Maguire, "Lord of the Golden Snitch," p. 12.

Papers: Explorations into Children's Literature, November, 2004, Andrew Burn, "Potterliteracy: Cross-Media Narratives, Cultures and Grammars," p. 5.

People, July 24, 2000, Robert Papinchak, review of *Harry Potter and the Goblet of Fire,* p. 52; December 31, 2001, p. 58; December 2, 2002, Samantha Miller, "Where's Harry? J.K. Rowling Has a Baby on the Way. Fine, but What about the Next Potter?," p. 211.

Publishers Weekly, July 20, 1998, review of *Harry Potter and the Sorcerer's Stone,* p. 220; December 21, 1998, p. 28; January 4, 1999, p. 30; January 11, 1999, p. 24;

February 15, 1999, Shannon Maughan, "The Race for Harry Potter," pp. 33-34; May 31, 1999, review of *Harry Potter and the Chamber of Secrets,* p. 94; July 19, 1999, Shannon Maughan, "The Harry Potter Halo," pp. 92-94; October 11, 1999, review of *Harry Potter and the Sorcerer's Stone* (audiobook), p. 30; November 1, 1999, Shannon Maughan, "Keeping Up with Harry," p. 36; July 24, 2000, "All Eyes on Harry," p. 31; October 15, 2001, p. 74; June 30, 2003, review of *Harry Potter and the Order of the Phoenix,* p. 79.

Reading Teacher, October, 1999, review of *Harry Potter and the Sorcerer's Stone,* p. 183.

Reading Time, February, 1999, p. 43.

Rolling Stone, December 6, 2001, p. 12.

School Librarian, August, 1997, review of *Harry Potter and the Philosopher's Stone,* p. 147; spring, 1999, p. 35.

School Library Journal, October, 1998, pp. 145-146; July, 1999, pp. 99-100; September, 1999, Roxanne Feldman, "The Truth about Harry," pp. 137-139; August, 2000, Eva Mitnick, review of *Harry Potter and the Goblet of Fire,* p. 188; September, 2000, Eva Mitnick, review of *Harry Potter and the Goblet of Fire,* p. 82; June, 2001, Eva Mitnick, review of *Quidditch through the Ages,* p. 155; August, 2003, Eva Mitnick, review of *Harry Potter and the Order of the Phoenix,* p. 165.

Science-Fiction Chronicle, December, 1999, review of *Harry Potter and the Sorcerer's Stone,* p. 42; September, 2005, Connie Tyrell Burns, review of *Harry Potter and the Half-Blood Prince,* p. 111, 212.

Teacher Librarian, December, 1999, review of *Harry Potter and the Sorcerer's Stone,* p. 48.

Telegraph (London, England), June 9, 2002, "A Kind of Magic," p. 2.

Time, April 12, 1999, "The Wizard of Hogwarts: A Novice Sorcerer's Exploits are Magical to Kids—and Adults," p. 86; July 26, 1999, "Abracadabra! J.K. Rowling's Magical Harry Potter Books Have Cast a Spell on Kids around the World," p. 72; July 17, 2000, review of *Harry Potter and the Goblet of Fire,* p. 70; December 17, 2000, Paul Gray, "The Magic of Potter"; June 30, 2003, Lev Grossman, review of *Harry Potter and the Order of the Phoenix,* p. 60; July 25, 2005, Lev Grossman, "J.K. Rowling Hogwarts and All," p. 60.

USA Today, October, 1998.

Variety, November 26, 2001, p. 5; November 29, 2004, Adam Dawtrey, "It's a Wand-erful Life: Rowling Transforms Kid Lit and Embodies Brit Grit," p. A1.

Wall Street Journal, July 19, 2005, Meghan Cox Gurdon, "Magical Prose."

Washington Post, November 2, 1999, p. A21; July 11, 2000, Jabari Asim, "Four's a Charm: The Steady Spell of Harry Potter," p. C1; November 5, 2001, p. A1.

World Literature Today, January-April, 2005, Kathy Howard Latrobe, "Ten English Authors for Young Adults," p. 69.

ONLINE

January Online, http://www.januarymagazine.com/ (October, 2000), Linda Richards, "J.K. Rowling"; (February

11, 2003) Linda Richards, "Harry's Real Magic"; (July, 2003) Sue Bursztynski, "Growing up with Harry."

Hoosier Times Online, http://www.hoosiertimes.com/ (November 29, 1998), "British Author Rides up Charts on a Wizard's Tale"

J.K. Rowling Official Web site, http://www.jkrowling.com (October 15, 2006).

Manchester Online, http://www.manchesteronline.co.uk/ (July 18, 2005), Cathy Winston, review of *Harry Potter and the Half-Blood Prince.*

Salon.com, http:// www.salon.com/ (March 31, 1999), "Of Magic and Single Motherhood."

USA Today, http://www.usatoday.com/ (September 10, 2003), Jacqueline Blais, "Not Everyone's Wild about Harry Potter."*

*   *   *

ROWLING, Joanne Kathleen
See ROWLING, J.K.

S

SAID, S.F. 1967-

Personal

Born May, 1967, in Beirut, Lebanon. *Education:* Cambridge University, Ph.D. (criminology).

Addresses

Home—London, England. *Agent*—c/o Children's Editorial Department, Random House Children's Books, 61-63 Uxbridge Rd., London W5 5SA, England. *E-mail*—feedback@varjakpaw.com.

Career

Journalist and writer. Former speechwriter for Crown Prince of Jordan; *Daily Telegraph,* London, England, journalist. Whitbread Children's Book Award, judge. Edinburgh Film Festival, programming consultant.

Awards, Honors

Nestlé Smarties Gold Book Prize, 2003, and Gateshead Children's Book Award, 2004, both for *Varjak Paw;* West Sussex Children's Book Award, 2005, for *The Outlaw Varjak Paw.*

Writings

Varjak Paw, illustrated by David McKean, Random House/David Fickling Books (New York, NY), 2003.
The Outlaw Varjak Paw, illustrated by David McKean, Random House/David Fickling Books (Oxford, England), 2005, Random House/David Fickling Books (New York, NY), 2006.

Sidelights

Journalist S.F. Said is the author of *Varjak Paw* and its sequel, *The Outlaw Varjak Paw,* a pair of illustrated novels featuring a Mesopotamian Blue cat with martial-arts skills. Born in Beirut, Lebanon, Said moved with his family to London, England, when he was two years old. Growing up with an interest in reading and writing, he has cited writers Richard Adams, Ursula Le Guin, and Rudyard Kipling as creative influences.

Said took a unique career path to becoming a novelist. He spent six years working as a speechwriter for the Crown Prince of Jordan, then attended Cambridge University, earning a Ph.D. in criminology. More recently, as a journalist for the London *Daily Telegraph,* Said interviewed several authors and illustrators, among them Philip Pullman and Quentin Blake.

Said's debut title, *Varjak Paw,* appeared in 2003. Varjak is the youngest member of the aristocratic Paw family, whose members live a pampered, privileged life in the house of an elderly contessa. Scorned by his siblings because his green eyes are not the mark of a true Mesopotamian Blue, Varjak longs for the grand, exciting life lived by his ancestor Jalal, a fierce hunter who traveled the world. When the contessa dies and her home is taken over by a mysterious gentleman and his two sinister black felines, Varjak escapes to the city. To survive on the dangerous streets, he befriends a pair of tough alley cats. One night Varjak has a dream about Jalal in which he is taught the Seven Skills of "The Way," a feline martial arts discipline that will enable the young cat to rescue his family. "Varjak is a spirited adventurer who evolves gradually and believably into a courageous protagonist," observed *Booklist* contributor Ed Sullivan.

Varjak Paw went through seventeen drafts and was rejected by forty publishers before finding a home. "Those seventeen drafts were about making the storytelling totally addictive, trying to give it the depth of a timeless, classic myth," Said commented on the Random House Web site. "For me, this is a book about being small in a big world, but learning that you're more than you think you are."

Several reviewers praised the complex interplay between Said's text and Dave McKean's artwork in *Varjak Paw.* The heroic feline's "world has a dreamlike qual-

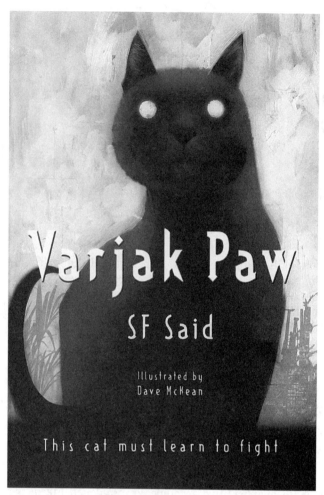

Cover of S.F. Said's **Varjak Paw,** *featuring artwork by illustrator Dave McKean.* (Dell Yearling, 2005. Illustrations copyright © 2003 by Dave McKean. Used by permission of Random House Children's Books, a division of Random House, Inc)

ity, both concretely familiar and creepily off-kilter, that's effectively reinforced by vivid ink sketches," noted a critic in *Kirkus Reviews.* Anita L. Burkam, writing in *Horn Book,* stated that McKean's "frequent black-ink illustrations of stylized, angular cats (and tangerine images behind the text in the dream sequences) give the book the edgy feel of a graphic novel."

The Outlaw Varjak Paw finds Varjak roaming the city streets together with his feline companions Holly and Tam and his canine friend Cludge. When Varjak learns that the evil Sally Bones and her warrior cats are terrorizing the free cats of the city, he takes action against the leader, only to find that Sally's powers with the Seven Skills are greater than his own. *The Outlaw Varjak Paw* received strong reviews. "Said's spare, taut writing effectively propels an increasingly grim plot, and makes Varjak's growing maturity and leadership appear both natural and admirable," observed a *Kirkus Reviews* critic. In the words of *School Library Journal* contributor Tasha Secker, "the unique combination of animal tale and martial arts is a winning one."

Asked if he had any advice for young writer, Said told an interviewer for *CBBC Newsround* online: "Try to imagine the story that you would most love to read, if you could have any story at all. Then sit down and write it yourself. Make it as good as it can possibly be, even if that means working and working and working. Don't ever give up, and never let anyone tell you that you can't do it—because if I can get there, anyone can!"

Biographical and Critical Sources

PERIODICALS

Booklist, June 1, 2003, Ed Sullivan, review of *Varjak Paw,* p. 1779; April 1, 2006, Ed Sullivan, review of *The Outlaw Varjak Paw,* p. 41.

Horn Book, July-August, 2003, Anita L. Burkam, review of *Varjak Paw,* p. 467.

Kirkus Reviews, May 1, 2003, review of *Varjak Paw,* p. 683; December 15, 2005, review of *The Outlaw Varjak Paw,* p. 1327.

Kliatt, September, 2004, Mary Purucker, review of *Varjak Paw* (audiobook review), p. 65.

School Library Journal, December, 2004, Tina Hudak, review of *Varjak Paw* (audiobook review), p. 76; February, 2006, Tasha Secker, review of *The Outlaw Varjak Paw,* p. 136.

New York Times Book Review, May 18, 2003, James Gorman, review of *Varjak Paw,* p. 30.

ONLINE

CBBC Newsround, http://news.bbc.co.uk/ (November 14, 2005), interview with Said.

Random House Web site, http://www.randomhouse.com/ (October 20, 2006), "S.F. Said."

Varjak Paw Web site, http://www.varjakpaw.com (October 20, 2006).*

* * *

SCAMANDER, Newt
See ROWLING, J.K.

* * *

SHATTUCK, Roger 1923-2005
(Roger Whitney Shattuck)

OBITUARY NOTICE— See index for *SATA* sketch: Born August 20, 1923, in New York, NY; died of prostate cancer December 8, 2005, in Lincoln, VT. Educator and author. Shattuck was a respected scholar and retired Boston University professor who wrote on topics ranging from the works of Marcel Proust to philosophical commentaries on literature and human knowledge.

Though he would hold several university positions over the years, Shattuck never earned a graduate degree. He initially was a pre-med student at Yale University, but left before earning a degree to enlist in the U.S. Army Air Forces. There he became a combat pilot, saw action in the Pacific theater, and, memorably, piloted a plane over Hiroshima not long after the atomic bomb was dropped. Returning to America, he went back to Yale, studied literature and was editor of the *Yale Review.* Graduating with a B.A. in 1947, he moved to Paris, where he worked for the United Nations Educational, Scientific, and Cultural Organization's film section. While in France, he met many of the expatriate literary community and other luminaries, such as Francis Bacon and Thornton Wilder. Back in New York City in 1949, he worked briefly as an assistant trade editor for Harcourt, Brace & Co. before becoming a member of the Society of Fellows at Harvard in 1950. From 1953 to 1956, he taught French at Harvard, then moved on to the University of Texas at Austin, where he was a professor of Romance languages through the 1960s and chaired that department from 1968 to 1971. A three-year period as a freelance writer was followed by fourteen years with the University of Virginia as Commonwealth professor of French. Finally, in 1988, Shattuck joined the Boston University faculty, where he was a professor until his 1997 retirement. Over the years, Shattuck developed a reputation for his thoughtful studies of Proust and Rousseau, as well as for works on literature, art, and society in general. In 1975 he won the prestigious National Book Award for his *Marcel Proust* (1974), and he also gained considerable attention for *Forbidden Knowledge: From Prometheus to Pornography* (1996) in which he posits whether some types of knowledge, such as nuclear weaponry, is best left unknown to human beings. Some critics misinterpreted his ideas, however, as supporting the possibility for government censorship. His *The Forbidden Experiment: The Story of the Wild Boy of Aveyron* (1980) is also notable for the author's insights into how intelligence develops in humans. As a critic, Shattuck gained attention for his criticism of such schools as deconstructionism, which he claimed stole the heart out of literature, and his deep concern that students were no longer being taught the classics. Among Shattuck's other books are *The Innocent Eye: On Literature and the Arts* (1984), *Candor and Perversion: Literature, Education, and the Arts* (1999), and *Proust's Way: A Field Guide to In Search of Lost Time* (2000). He also edited and coedited several books, most recently Helen Keller's *The Story of My Life and the World I Live In* (2003).

OBITUARIES AND OTHER SOURCES:

PERIODICALS

New York Times, December 10, 2005, p. A16.
Times (London, England), December 20, 3005, p. 53.
Washington Post, December 14, 2005, p. B6.

*   *   *

SHATTUCK, Roger Whitney
See SHATTUCK, Roger

SHERMAN, Pat

Personal
Female.

Addresses
Home—23 Rindge Ave., Cambridge, MA 02140.

Career
Children's book author.

Writings

The Sun's Daughter, illustrated by R. Gregory Christie, Clarion Books (New York, NY), 2005.

Sidelights
Pat Sherman's debut as a picture-book author came in 2005, with the publication of *The Sun's Daughter.* A porquoi tale, Sherman's story was inspired by a traditional Iroquois tale that focuses on a tribal figure known as the Corn Maiden. Food is plentiful when Maize, the Corn Maiden, walks the earth's surface. However, Maize is young and impressionable, and she ultimately ignores the warnings of her mother, the Sun. Lured by Silver, the Moon, to go beneath the earth, Maize leaves the fields and forests without nourishment. Now crops wither and die in the field, food grows scarce, and the

An inspiring picture book based on an Iroquois legend, Pat Sherman's **The Sun's Daughter** *features illustrations by R. Gregory Christie.*

people of Earth begin to starve. When the Sun realizes that Maize is missing, she scours the earth for her, burning the land in her search. Distraught over her daughter's loss, Sun then turns away, refusing to shine on Earth again. Ultimately, one tiny creature discovers the girl's whereabouts and Silver agrees to allow Maize to come above ground for half the year, marking the change from winter to spring.

Featuring "eloquent phrasing and vocabulary," *The Sun's Daughter* is enhanced by "energetic and exuberant" folk-style paintings by R. Gregorie Christie, according to *School Library Journal* reviewer Cris Riedel. A *Publishers Weekly* critic also praised Sherman's debut, writing that "Maize's tale will sow the seeds for discussions about myths and the role they play." Jennifer Mattson, reviewing the work for *Booklist,* called *The Sun's Daughter* "evocative," while a *Kirkus Reviews* critic deemed it an "original story."

Biographical and Critical Sources

PERIODICALS

Booklist, March 15, 2005, Jennifer Mattson, review of *The Sun's Daughter,* p. 1292.
Horn Book, May-June, 2005, Joanna Rudge Long, review of *The Sun's Daughter,* p. 314.
Kirkus Reviews, March 1, 2005, review of *The Sun's Daughter,* p. 295.
Publishers Weekly, March 21, 2005, review of *The Sun's Daughter,* p. 51.
School Library Journal, June, 2005, Cris Riedel, review of *The Sun's Daughter,* p. 144.

ONLINE

Houghton Mifflin Books Web site, The Sun's Daughter, http://www.houghtonmifflinbooks.com/ (October 10, 2006).
Western New York Family Magazine Online, http://www.wnyfamilymagazine.com/ (October 10, 2006), Donna Phillips, "Legends and Traditional Tales: There's a Lesson to Be Learned."*

*   *   *

SHIELDS, Carol Diggory

Personal

Female; married. *Education:* Trained in therapeutic recreation.

Addresses

Home—Salinas, CA. *Office*—Salinas Public Library, 350 Lincoln Ave., Salinas, CA 93901.

Career

Writer and librarian. Salinas Public Library, Salinas, CA, coordinator of children's services and children's librarian.

Member

Society of Children's Book Writers and Illustrators.

Awards, Honors

Please Touch Museum Award, c. 1997, for *Saturday Night at the Dinosaur Stomp.*

Writings

FOR CHILDREN

I Am Really a Princess, illustrated by Paul Meisel, Dutton Children's Books (New York, NY), 1993.
Lunch Money, and Other Poems about School, illustrated by Paul Meisel, Dutton Children's Books (New York, NY), 1995.
Saturday Night at the Dinosaur Stomp, illustrated by Scott Nash, Candlewick Press (Cambridge, MA), 1997.
I Wish My Brother Was a Dog, illustrated by Paul Meisel, Dutton Children's Books (New York, NY), 1997.
Day by Day a Week Goes 'Round, illustrated by True Kelley, Dutton Children's Books (New York, NY), 1998.
Month by Month a Year Goes 'Round, illustrated by True Kelley, Dutton Children's Books (New York, NY), 1998.
Lucky Pennies and Hot Chocolate, illustrated by Hiroe Nakata, Dutton Children's Books (New York, NY), 2000.
Colors, paintings by Svjetlan Junakovic, Handprint Books (Brooklyn, NY), 2000.
Music, paintings by Svjetlan Junakovic, Handprint Books (Brooklyn, NY), 2000.
Martian Rock, illustrated by Scott Nash, Candlewick Press (Cambridge, MA), 2000.
Homes, paintings by Svjetlan Junakovic, Handprint Books (Brooklyn, NY), 2001.
Sports, paintings by Svjetlan Junakovic, Handprint Books (Brooklyn, NY), 2001.
On the Go, paintings by Svjetlan Junakovic, Handprint Books (Brooklyn, NY), 2001.
Patterns, paintings by Svjetlan Junakovic, Handprint Books (Brooklyn, NY), 2001.
Food Fight!, illustrated by Doreen Gay-Kassel, Handprint Books (Brooklyn, NY), 2002.
The Bugliest Bug, illustrated by Scott Nash, Candlewick Press (Cambridge, MA), 2002.
American History, Fresh Squeezed!: 41 Thirst-for-Knowledge-Quenching Poems, illustrated by Richard Thompson, Handprint Books (Brooklyn, NY), 2002.
Science, Fresh Squeezed!: 41 Thirst-for-Knowledge-Quenching Poems, illustrated by Richard Thompson, Handprint Books (Brooklyn, NY), 2003.

Almost Late to School, and More School Poems, illustrated by Paul Meisel, Dutton Children's Books (New York, NY), 2003.

English Fresh Squeezed!: 40 Thirst-for-Knowledge-Quenching Poems, illustrated by Tony Ross, Handprint Books (Brooklyn, NY), 2004.

Sidelights

With over a dozen publications to her credit, Carol Diggory Shields has established herself within the children's-book world, an accomplishment Shields did not initially anticipate. Originally trained in therapeutic recreation, Shields had a hard time finding a job within in her field after moving with her husband to Salinas, California in the mid-1980s. She was finally offered a position in the Salinas Public Library's children's department, and it was there that Shields recognized and cultivated her love for children's literature. Her subsequent writing career has produced picture books such as *Saturday Night at the Dinosaur Stomp* and *The Bugliest Bug,* as well as the poetry collection *English Fresh Squeezed!: 40 Thirst-for-Knowledge-Quenching Poems.*

As a novice children's writer, Shields initially had difficulty finding a publisher for her books. Determined, she wrote diligently for eight years before joining the Society of Children's Writers and Illustrators and began attending writing workshops. The workshops Shields attended helped to strengthen her writing and in 1993 she published her first children's title, *I Am Really a Princess* with Dutton Children's Press.

In an online interview with Laurie Saurborn for California's *Monterey County Weekly,* Shields noted that one of her main goals in writing is to "help kids laugh at real situations," adding that the best children's books "speak to the child's experiences, not to the adult's experience." Shields' efforts to relate to children can be seen in her creation of engaging titles such as *Food Fight!, I Wish My Brother Was a Dog, Lunch Money, and Other Poems,* and *Almost Late to School, and More School Poems.*

Regarded as a "pun-tastical midnight ramble," by a *Kirkus Reviews* writer, *Food Fight!* is an imaginative tale about what happens inside a refrigerator after the light goes off. In penning *Food Fight!* Shields utilizes fun and humorous verses: "'Lettuce have a party!' said the salad greens. . . . The coffee perked up and the beets started thumping,/ The bread made a toast and the jello was jumping." "Readers' appetite for Shields' delicious puns will keep them glued to the food frenzy," noted a reviewer for *Publishers Weekly.* Likewise, *School Library Journal* reviewer Maryann H. Owen claimed that the author's "humorous rhyming text, which dips and swirls over vividly colored backgrounds, begs to be read aloud."

In *I Wish My Brother Was a Dog* a little boy, who is annoyed by his baby brother, imagines how his life would change if his younger brother were a dog. The young

Cover of Carol Diggory Shields' **English Fresh Squeezed,** *featuring forty gramatically enlightening poems paired with illustrations by Tony Ross.* (Handprint Books, 2004. Illustrations copyright © 2004 by Tony Ross. Reproduced by permission)

boy rationalizes that if his baby brother was in fact a dog then there would be no stinky diapers, squeaky cribs, or messy toys. The young boy furthers his fantasy by imagining his baby brother eating out of a dog bowl, sleeping outside, and entering dog shows and eventually being sold. Once the young boy's fantasy reaches its peak, he concludes that he would rather have an annoying brother around than no brother at all. A *Publishers Weekly* critic, in an assessment of *I Wish My Brother Was a Dog,* acknowledged Shields for humorously capturing "the sometimes intense and angry feelings children can have toward siblings, wishing a brother or sister might just disappear." *Booklist* contributor Hazel Rochman noted that the silly notions of the narrator will cause young readers to "laugh at the unbridled anger of the older sibling, as well as the sweet innocence of the baby."

In *Lunch Money, and Other Poems* Shields includes a series of comical poems which describe the everyday activities that children experience in school. She recounts a variety of goings on, including arriving too late to ride the morning schoolbus, struggling with homework, and trading lunches with friends. Hazel Rochman, writing in *Booklist,* explained that the majority of situations found in Shields' book are "social, though there are some dreamers lost in a book or walking on a moon or hooked up to the Nintendo."

Following in the tradition of *Lunch Money, and Other Poems!, Almost Late to School* also incorporates hilarious rhyming verses that describe the daily events of school, such as science-fair projects, oral reports, jealousy among classmates, and the joy of a finding a new best friend. "Students will relate to the situations presented and the emotions that are expressed," observed *School Library Journal* critic Helen Foster James. *Almost Late to School* not only addresses common issues that children experience but also allows young readers to explore the realms of poetry. In addition to providing situational experiences that children can relate to, Shields also includes twenty-two poems that explore a variety of poetic forms—such as the concrete form and the two-voice form—and allow readers to experience the full range of the poetic muse. Gillian Engberg, writing in *Booklist,* deemed *Almost Late to School* an entertaining read "with plenty of substance to lighten up poetry units."

Biographical and Critical Sources

BOOKS

Shields, Carol Diggory, *Food Fight!,* illustrated by Doreen Gay-Kassel, Handprint Books (Brooklyn, NY), 2002.

PERIODICALS

Booklist, November 15, 1995, Hazel Rochman, review of *Lunch Money, and Other Poems about School,* p. 562; November 15, 1995, Hazel Rochman, review of *I Wish My Brother Was a Dog,* p. 1722; August, 2003, Gillian Engberg, review of *Almost Late to School, and More School Poems,* p. 1994.
Kirkus Reviews, July 1, 2002, review of *Food Fight!,* p. 963.
Publishers Weekly, April 29, 2002, review of *Food Fight!,* p. 17; May 19, 1997, review of *I Wish My Brother Was a Dog,* p. 76.
School Library Journal, October, 2002, Maryann H. Owen, review of *Food Fight!,* p. 130; August, 2003, Helen Foster James, review of *Almost Late to School, and More School Poems,* p. 152.

ONLINE

Monterey County Weekly Online, http://www.montereycountyweekly.com/ (December 20, 1998), Laurie Saurborn, "Salinas Children's Librarian Also Writes for Her Young Audience."*

*   *   *

SITOMER, Alan Lawrence

Personal

Born in NY. *Education:* University of Southern California, B.A. (English), 1989; M.A. (cross-cultural language arts education).

Alan Lawrence Sitomer (Photograph courtesy of Alan Sitomer)

Addresses

Office—Milk Mug Publishing, 9190 W. Olympic Blvd., Ste. 253, Beverly Hills, CA 90212. *E-mail*—AlanLawrenceSitomer@yahoo.com.

Career

Educator and writer. Lynwood High School, Los Angeles, CA, teacher of English; Milk Mug Publishing, Beverly Hills, CA, founder; Loyola Marymount University, Los Angeles, professor. Has worked as a screenwriter, playwright, and greeting-card author.

Awards, Honors

Teacher of the Year Award, California Literacy Program, 2003; Award for Classroom Excellence, Southland Council Teachers of English, 2004.

Writings

FOR YOUNG ADULTS

The Hoopster, Milk Mug Publishing (Los Angeles, CA), 2002.
(With Michael Cirelli) *Hip Hop Poetry and the Classics,* Milk Mug Publishing (Los Angeles, CA), 2004.
Hip Hop High School, Hyperion Books for Children (New York, NY), 2006.

Adaptations

The Hoopster was adapted for audiocassette, read by J.D. Jackson, Recorded Books, 2005.

Work in Progress

Homeboyz, for Jump at the Sun, expected 2007.

Sidelights

Alan Lawrence Sitomer is the author of a group of young-adult books that are aimed at urban teens. A high-school English teacher as well as a writer, Sitomer was working in a Los Angeles inner-city high school when he penned his first novel, *The Hoopster*. The book—about a high-school basketball star—was written in order to give his more reading-averse students a literature they could identify with. In an interview with the University of Southern California' *Trojan Family Magazine,* Sitomer recounted of his students' introduction to literary classics: "We were asking them to read *Pride and Prejudice, The Scarlet Letter* . . . they didn't have anything they could relate to." To solve the problem, Sitomer created a contemporary novel that focuses on the issues of modern teens.

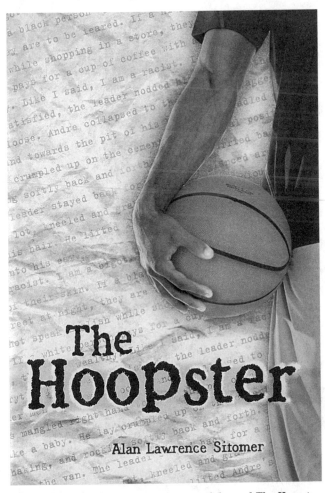

Cover of Alan Lawrence Sitomer's young-adult novel The Hoopster, *which finds a young man's accomplishments threatened by gang violence.* (Reprinted by permission of Hyperion Books For Children and Corbis. All rights reserved)

The popularity of Sitomer's unpublished novel spread throughout the high school where he worked and it soon prompted the writer to market his novel through his own publishing company, Milk Mug Publishing. In the published version of *The Hoopster,* Sitomer also included a teacher's study guide. His first novel caught the attention of educators as well as publishers. In 2003 the California Literacy Program named Sitomer Teacher of the Year; Disney also recognized Sitomer's appeal and offered the author a three-book publishing deal.

Critics have acknowledged *The Hoopster* for its straightforward approach to racial issues and for its ability to engage young, reluctant readers. John Peters, writing for *Booklist,* regarded the novel as "unvarnished" and noted that Sitomer's tale "will engage unpracticed older readers, and . . . may prompt them to reexamine some of their own racial attitudes."

The Hoopster focuses on talented young athlete Andre Anderson. Besides being the high school basketball star at his school, Andre is also a skillful journalist. The teen's writing skills are put to the test, however, when the editor of the magazine where Andre is interning assigns the high schooler to write an article about racism. Andre's articles stir the public's attention, so much so that a local hate group attacks the teen for voicing his opinions. *The Hoopster* follows Andre as he struggles to overcome his racist attitudes and reveals the effect of that racism not only on Andre, but also on his family and friends. Sitomer utilizes lively dialogue and exciting scenes to engage teen readers, and a *Kirkus Reviews* critic observed Sitomer's "strong prose, humor and well-described basketball scenes [that] support a larger tale of a writer who, even after his injuries to his hand says, 'I will type with my goddamned nose if I have to.'" *School Library Journal* reviewer Francisca Goldsmith acknowledged Sitomer's use of "gritty images, clever banter, and a genuine consideration of the facets of race and racism." Goldsmith also deemed *The Hoopster* "good literature, and a stellar read [that] . . . is bound to attract both student and teacher fans."

Biographical and Critical Sources

BOOKS

Sitomer, Alan Lawrence, *The Hoopster,* Hyperion Books for Children (New York, NY), 2005.

PERIODICALS

Booklist, June 1, 2005, John Peters, review of *The Hoopster,* p. 1792.
Kirkus Reviews, March 1, 2005, review of *The Hoopster,* p. 296.
School Library Journal, November, 2005, Francisca Goldsmith, review of *The Hoopster,* p. 75.

ONLINE

Alan Lawrence Sitomer Home Page, http://www.alanlawrencesitomer.com (October 6, 2006).
USC Trojan Family Web site, http://www.usc.edu/ (October 6, 2006).*

SLATE, Joseph 1928-
(Joseph Frank Slate)

Personal

Born January 19, 1928, in Holiday's Cove, WV; son of Frank Edward (a contractor) and Angela (Palumbo) Slate; married Patricia Griffin (a director of research), September 11, 1954. *Education:* University of Washington, B.A., 1951; Yale University, B.F.A., 1960; studied printmaking in Tokyo, Japan, 1955-56, and sumi-e painting in Kyoto, Japan, 1975.

Addresses

Home—15107 Interlachen Dr. No. 701, Silver Spring, MD 20906-5632. *Agent*—William Reiss, John Hawkins & Associates, 71 W. 23rd St., Ste. 1600, New York, NY 10010. *E-mail*—Jslate28@aol.com.

Career

Journalist, educator, and artist. *Seattle Times,* Seattle, WA, reporter, 1951-54; editor for Foreign Broadcast Information Service, 1955-59; Kenyon College, Gambier, OH, began as instructor, 1962, professor of art, 1969-88, chair of art department, 1963-75, 1981-82; presently professor emeritus. Consultant in psychology of art to Dr. Irvin Child, Yale University, 1960-66; National Endowment for the Arts, consultant, 1977-78, and originator of Fiction in Newspaper program, 1983—. *Exhibitions:* Paintings and graphics have been exhibited in numerous group and one-man shows, 1960-88.

Member

University of Washington Fir Tree Club (honorary member), Oval Club (honorary member).

Awards, Honors

University of Washington Top-Flight Award for journalism, 1951; Yale University alumni fellowship, 1960; painting award from Ohio Expositions, 1962; grants from Carnegie Foundation and Danforth Foundation, both 1968; Ford-Kenyon Faculty Awards grant, 1970-71; grant from Great Lakes Colleges Association, 1975; named Kenyon Outstanding Educator of America, 1973; honorary D.F.A., Kenyon College, 1988; Ohioana Library Association award, 1988, for distinguished service in the field of children's literature; Delaware Blue Hen Award, 1997, for *Miss Bindergarten Gets Ready for Kindergarten;* Notable Children's Book selection, American Library Association, 2000, for *The Secret Stars;* Outstanding Maryland Author Award, Association for Childhood Education International, 2001.

Writings

PICTURE BOOKS

The Star Rocker, illustrations by Dirk Zimmer, Harper & Row (New York, NY), 1982.

Joseph Slate (Photograph by Patricia Slate. Reproduced by permission of Joseph Slate)

How Little Porcupine Played Christmas, illustrations by Felicia Bond, Crowell (New York, NY), 1983, published as *Little Porcupine's Christmas,* Laura Geringer Books (New York, NY), 2001.

Mean Clean Giant Canoe Machine, illustrations by Lynn Munsinger, Crowell (New York, NY), 1983.

Lucky Lula Cat, illustrations by Bruce Degen, Harper & Row (New York, NY), 1984.

Lonely Lula Cat, pictures by Bruce Degen, Harper & Row (New York, NY), 1985.

Who Is Coming to Our House?, illustrated by Ashley Wolff, Putnam (New York, NY), 1988.

Miss Bindergarten Gets Ready for Kindergarten, illustrated by Ashley Wolff, Dutton (New York, NY), 1996.

Miss Bindergarten Celebrates the 100th Day of Kindergarten, illustrated by Ashley Wolff, Dutton (New York, NY), 1998.

The Secret Stars, illustrated by Felipe Davalos, Marshall Cavendish (New York, NY), 1998.

Miss Bindergarten Stays Home from Kindergarten, illustrated by Ashley Wolff, Dutton (New York, NY), 2000.

Miss Bindergarten Takes a Field Trip with Kindergarten, illustrated by Ashley Wolff, Dutton (New York, NY), 2001.

Story Time for Little Porcupine, illustrated by Jacqueline Rogers, Marshall Cavendish (New York, NY), 2001.

Miss Bindergarten Plans a Circus with Kindergarten, illustrated by Ashley Wolff, Dutton (New York, NY), 2002.

The Great Big Wagon That Rang: How the Liberty Bell Was Saved, illustrated by Craig Spearing, Marshall Cavendish (New York, NY), 2002.

Miss Bindergarten Has a Wild Day in Kindergarten, illustrated by Ashley Wolff, Dutton (New York, NY), 2005.

Miss Bindergarten Celebrates the Last Day of Kindergarten, illustrated by Ashley Wolff, Dutton (New York, NY), 2005.

What Star Is This?, illustrated by Alison Jay, Putnam (New York, NY), 2005.

OTHER

(With Martin Garhart) *Poetry and Prints,* Pothanger Press, 1974.

Crossing the Trestle (young-adult novel), Marshall Cavendish (New York, NY), 1999.

Contributor of short stories, articles, and interviews to periodicals, including *Contempora, New Yorker, Saturday Review, Kenyon Review,* and *Art Journal.*

Sidelights

Joseph Slate is the author of award-winning picture books for children. He is perhaps best known for his works featuring Miss Bindergarten, a canine kindergarten teacher whose students include an alligator and a zebra. A painter and educator in addition to being an author, Slate had a fascination for illustrated books long before he decided to learn more about them by writing one himself. As he once remarked, "I've always liked the short form in literature—poetry and short stories—so it was natural I'd gravitate to the picture book. As an artist, I am very visual in my writing."

Slate published his first picture book, *The Star Rocker,* in 1982. The story is a reworking of the tale of Cassiopeia in Greek mythology. In the Greek version, Cassiopeia was a queen who was raised onto a chair of stars in the sky, where she became a constellation. Slate's Cassie is instead an elderly African-American woman who smokes a corncob pipe while sitting in a rocking chair on a raft, calming the animals of the woods when they become frightened by the noises of the night.

Slate examines a dramatic piece of American history in *The Great Big Wagon That Rang: How the Liberty Bell Was Saved.* Based on both historical accounts and legend, his story details how a Pennsylvania farmer transported the famous bell in his horse-drawn wagon from Philadelphia to the Zion Reformed Church in Allentown, covering the bell with hay and thus hiding it from the British soldiers who intended to melt it down and use its metal for ammunition. "Rhythmic and rhyming without the rumpety-thump that characterizes too much of children's poetry, [Slate's] . . . natural-sounding verse conveys a good, pithy story," observed Carolyn Phelan in *Booklist.*

What Star Is This? uses a rhyming text to retell the Nativity story. Slate imagines the celestial body seen by the wise men as a comet streaking across the sky, "and its particular mission is spreading good will as it lights

A Christmas story with its roots in Mexican tradition, Joseph Slate's **The Secret Stars** *features illustrations by artist Felipe Davalos.* (Marshall Cavendish, 1998. Reproduced by permission)

the way for those seeking 'the One,'" according to a critic in *Kirkus Reviews.* In the words of *Booklist* critic Diane Foote, *What Star Is This?* "offers a fresh take on the traditional Christian account" of the Christmas story.

In 1996, Slate published *Miss Bindergarten Gets Ready for Kindergarten,* the first work in his highly regarded "Miss Bindergarten" series. The inspiration for the book came from members of Slate's own family, as he noted on his home page. "My niece was getting ready to teach one year, and my nephew was getting ready to go to kindergarten," Slate explained. "I wondered if they were preparing in the same way. I wondered if they were nervous about that first day." Slate has since published several other works in the series, including *Miss Bindergarten Plans a Circus with Kindergarten* and *Miss Bindergarten Celebrates the 100th Day of Kindergarten.* In each of the "Miss Bindergarten" books readers are introduced to the border-collie instructor and her alphabetically arranged students, including Christopher the cat and Ian the iguana. Critics have lauded Slate's efforts. Reviewing *Miss Bindergarten Celebrates the Last Day of Kindergarten* in *School Library Journal,* for example, Martha Topol praised the "cooperative good cheer of this tightly knit class."

In addition to his works for children, Slate has a young-adult novel to his credit: *Crossing the Trestle.* Set in

1944 in West Virginia, the work concerns young siblings Petey and Loni as they struggle in the aftermath of a car accident that has left their father dead and Loni disfigured. With the help of a troubled World War I veteran, the children learn to deal with their grief, and Petey conquers his fear of crossing the trestle bridge on the path to his new school. "Slate has created an entire cast of thoroughly likable, believable characters," noted *Booklist* reviewer Chris Sherman, who also complimented the author's "vivid descriptions of wartime conditions" in the book's rural locale.

Though Slate has enjoyed his greatest success with picture books, he views novel-writing as a continued goal. As he remarked on his home page, "It's hard to know what one will be good at unless one tries. I enjoy writing, although I have never been at ease with grammar and vocabulary. That puzzles me, but that is true of many writers. We struggle to carve out our words. Maybe that struggle contributes to the originality in our work."

Biographical and Critical Sources

PERIODICALS

Booklist, September 15, 1998, Hazel Rochman, review of *The Secret Stars,* p. 240; January 1, 2000, Chris Sherman, review of *Crossing the Trestle,* p. 927; October 15, 2000, Shelley Townsend-Hudson, review of *Story Time for Little Porcupine,* p. 446; October 1, 2001, Ilene Cooper, review of *Miss Bindergarten Takes a Field Trip with Kindergarten,* p. 327; November 1, 2002, Carolyn Phelan, review of *The Great Big Wagon That Rang: How the Liberty Bell Was Saved,* p. 509; December 1, 2005, review of *What Star Is This?,* p. 57; February 15, 2006, Julie Cummins, review of *Miss Bindergarten Celebrates the Last Day of Kindergarten,* p. 105.

Horn Book, May-June, 2006, Martha V. Parravano, review of *Miss Bindergarten Celebrates the Last Day of Kindergarten,* p. 304.

Kirkus Reviews, September 15, 2001, review of *Little Porcupine's Christmas,* p. 1368; August 15, 2002, review of *The Great Big Wagon That Rang,* p. 1237; November 1, 2005, review of *What Star Is This?,* p. 1196.

Publishers Weekly, November 25, 2002, review of *Miss Bindergarten Celebrates the 100th Day of Kindergarten,* p. 71; September 26, 2005, review of *What Star Is This?,* p. 1196.

School Library Journal, November, 2000, Sheilah Kosco, review of *Miss Bindergarten Stays Home from Kindergarten,* p. 134; November, 2002, Robin L. Gibson, review of *The Great Big Wagon That Rang,* p. 138; December, 2002, Carolyn Janssen, review of *Miss Bindergarten Plans a Circus with Kindergarten,* p. 108; July, 2004, Lisa G. Kropp, review of *Miss Bindergarten Celebrates the 100th Day of Kindergarten,* p. 44; February, 2005, Christine E. Carr, review of *Miss*

Bindergarten Has a Wild Day in Kindergarten, p. 109; March, 2006, Martha Topol, review of *Miss Bindergarten Celebrates the Last Day of Kindergarten,* p. 202.

Teaching Children Mathematics, December, 1999, Joanne L. Parent, review of *Miss Bindergarten Celebrates the 100th Day of Kindergarten,* p. 267.

ONLINE

Joseph Slate's Home Page, http://www.josephslate.com (October 15, 2006).

*   *   *

SLATE, Joseph Frank
See SLATE, Joseph

*   *   *

SOTO, Gary 1952-

Personal

Born April 12, 1952, in Fresno, CA; son of Manuel and Angie Soto; married Carolyn Sadako Oda, May 24, 1975; children: Mariko Heidi. *Education:* California State University, Fresno, B.A., 1974; University of California, Irvine, M.F.A., 1976.

Addresses

Home—Berkeley, CA.

Career

University of California, Berkeley, assistant professor 1979-85, associate professor of English and ethnic studies, 1985-91, part-time senior lecturer in English department, 1991-93; full-time writer, 1992—; University of California, Riverside, Distinguished Professor of Creative Writing. University of Cincinnati, Cincinnati, OH, Elliston Poet, 1988; Wayne State University, Detroit, MI, Martin Luther King/Cesar Chavez/Rosa Parks Visiting Professor of English, 1990. Young People's Ambassador for California Rural Legal Assistance and United Farm Workers of America.

Awards, Honors

Discovery-Nation prize, 1975; United States Award, International Poetry Forum, 1976, for *The Elements of San Joaquin;* Bess Hokin Prize, *Poetry,* 1978; Guggenheim fellowship, 1979-80; National Endowment for the Arts fellowships, 1981, 1991; Levinson Award, *Poetry,* 1984; American Book Award, Before Columbus Foundation, 1985, for *Living up the Street;* California Arts Council fellowship, 1989; Beatty Award, California Library Association, 1991, Reading Magic Award, *Parent-*

Gary Soto (Photograph by M.L. Marinelli. Chronicle Books. Reproduced by permission)

ing magazine, and George G. Stone Center Recognition of Merit, Claremont Graduate School, 1993, all for *Baseball in April, and Other Stories;* Carnegie Medal, 1993 for *The Pool Party;* National Book Award, and *Los Angeles Times* Book Prize finalist, both 1995, both for *New and Selected Poems;* Literature Award, Hispanic Heritage Foundation, 1999; Author-Illustrator Civil Rights Award, National Education Association, 1999; PEN American Center West Book Award, 1999, for *Petty Crimes;*;Tomás Rivera Prize Silver Medal, Commonwealth Club of California.

Writings

FOR CHILDREN

The Cat's Meow, illustrated by wife, Carolyn Soto, Strawberry Hill (San Francisco, CA), 1987.

A Fire in My Hands (poems), Scholastic (New York, NY), 1990, revised edition, Harcourt (Orlando, FL), 2006.

Baseball in April, and Other Stories, Harcourt (San Diego, CA), 1990.

Taking Sides, Harcourt (San Diego, CA), 1991.

Neighborhood Odes (poems), Harcourt (San Diego, CA), 1992.

Pacific Crossing, Harcourt (San Diego, CA), 1992.

The Skirt, illustrated by Eric Velasquez, Delacorte (New York, NY), 1992.

Too Many Tamales, illustrated by Ed Martinez, Putnam (New York, NY), 1992.

Local News (short stories), Harcourt (San Diego, CA), 1993.

The Pool Party (also see below), Delacorte (New York, NY), 1993.

Crazy Weekend, Scholastic (New York, NY), 1994.

Jesse (young-adult novel), Harcourt (San Diego, CA), 1994.

Boys at Work, Delacorte (New York, NY), 1995.

Canto Familiar/Familiar Song (poetry), Harcourt (San Diego, CA), 1995.

The Cat's Meow, Scholastic (New York, NY), 1995.

Chato's Kitchen, illustrated by Susan Guevara, Putnam (New York, NY), 1995.

Summer on Wheels, Scholastic (New York, NY), 1995.

The Old Man and His Door, Putnam (New York, NY), 1996.

Snapshots from the Wedding, Putnam (New York, NY), 1996.

Off and Running, illustrated by Eric Velasquez, Delacorte (New York, NY), 1996.

Buried Onions, Harcourt (San Diego, CA), 1997.

Novio Boy (play; also see below), Harcourt (San Diego, CA), 1997.

Petty Crimes (stories), Harcourt (San Diego, CA), 1998.

Big Bushy Mustache, illustrated by Joe Cepeda, Knopf (New York, NY), 1998.

Chato and the Party Animals, illustrated by Susan Guevara, Putnam (New York, NY), 1999.

Nerdlandia (play), Putnam (New York, NY), 1999.

Jessie de la Cruz: Profile of a United Farm Worker (nonfiction), Persea (New York, NY), 2000.

(With Molly Fisk) *100 Parades,* California Poets in the Schools, 2000.

If the Shoe Fits, illustrated by Terry Widener, Putnam (New York, NY), 2002.

Fearless Fernie: Hanging out with Fernie and Me (poems), illustrated by Regan Dunnick, Putnam (New York, NY), 2002.

Cesar Chavez: A Hero for Everyone (nonfiction), illustrated by Lori Lohstoeter, Aladdin (New York, NY), 2003.

The Afterlife (young-adult novel), Harcourt (Orlando, FL), 2003.

Marisol, Pleasant Company (Middleton, WI), 2005.

Worlds Apart: Traveling with Fernie and Me (poems), illustrated by Greg Clarke, Putnam (New York, NY), 2005.

Help Wanted: Stories, Harcourt (Orlando, FL), 2005.

Chato Goes Cruisin', illustrated by Susan Guevara, Putnam (New York, NY), 2005.

My Little Car/Mi carrito, illustrated by Pam Paparone, Putnam (New York, NY), 2006.

Accidental Love (young-adult novel), Harcourt (Orlando, FL), 2006.

Chato's Day of the Dead, illustrated by Susan Guevara, Putnam (New York, NY), 2006.

Mercy on These Teenage Chimps (young-adult novel), Harcourt (Orlando, FL), 2007.

POETRY; FOR ADULTS

(With Michael Peich) *Heaven,* Aralia Press, 1970.

The Level at Which the Sky Begins, University of California (Irvine, CA), 1976.

The Elements of San Joaquin, University of Pittsburgh Press (Pittsburgh, PA), 1977.

The Tale of Sunlight, University of Pittsburgh Press (Pittsburgh, PA), 1978.

(With Ernesto Trejo) *Como arbustos de Niebla,* Editorial Latitudes (Mexico City, Mexico), 1980.

Father Is a Pillow Tied to a Broom, (Pittsburgh, PA), 1980.

Where Sparrows Work Hard, University of Pittsburgh Press (Pittsburgh, PA), 1981.

Black Hair, University of Pittsburgh Press (Pittsburgh, PA), 1985.

Who Will Know Us?, Chronicle Books (San Francisco, CA), 1990.

Home Course in Religion, Chronicle Books (San Francisco, CA), 1991.

Afternoon Memory, Lagniappe Press, 1994.

New and Selected Poems, Chronicle Books (San Francisco, CA), 1995.

The Sparrows Move South: Early Poems, Bancroft Library Press, 1995.

(With John Digby) *Super-Eight Movies,* Lagniappe Press (Tuscaloosa, AL), 1996.

Junior College, Chronicle Books (San Francisco, CA), 1997.

A Natural Man, Chronicle Books (San Francisco, CA), 1999.

Shadow of the Plum: Poems, Cedar Hill Publications (San Diego, CA), 2002.

One Kind of Faith, Chronicle Books (San Francisco, CA), 2003.

Contributor of poems to *Nation, Ploughshares, Iowa Review, Ontario Review,* and *Poetry.*

SHORT FILMS

The Bike, Gary Soto Productions, 1991.

The Pool Party, Gary Soto Productions, 1993.

Novio Boy (based on Soto's play), Gary Soto Productions, 1994.

OTHER

Living up the Street: Narrative Recollections (prose memoirs), Strawberry Hill (San Francisco, CA), 1985.

Small Faces (prose memoirs), Arté Público (Houston, TX), 1986.

Lesser Evils: Ten Quartets (memoirs and essays), Arté Público (Houston, TX), 1988.

(Editor) *California Childhood: Recollections and Stories of the Golden State,* Creative Arts Book Company (Berkeley, CA), 1988.

A Summer Life (autobiography), University Presses of New England (Hanover, NH), 1990.

(Editor) *Pieces of the Heart: New Chicano Fiction,* Chronicle Books (San Francisco, CA), 1993.

(Editor) *Everyday Seductions,* Ploughshare Press (Sea Bright, NJ), 1995.

Nickel and Dime (novel), University of New Mexico Press (Albuquerque, NM), 2000.

The Effects of Knut Hamsun on a Fresno Boy: Recollections and Short Essays, Persea (New York, NY), 2000.

Poetry Lover (novel), University of New Mexico Press (Albuquerque, NM), 2001.

Amnesia in a Republican County (novel), University of New Mexico Press (Albuquerque, NM), 2003.

Contributor to textbooks, including *Scholastic Read XL, Grade 7,* Scholastic (New York, NY), 2001.

Adaptations

Soto's works have been adapted to audiocassette and videocassette.

Work in Progress

A book of poetry for middle graders.

Sidelights

Gary Soto, born in Fresno, California, is an American writer who is influenced by his working-class Mexican-American background. An award-winning author, he is best known for his poetry, short stories, and novels for young adults. Soto brings the sights and sounds of the barrio, the urban, Spanish-speaking neighborhood where he was raised, vividly to life within the pages of his books. In his writing, as Raymund Paredes noted in the *Rocky Mountain Review,* "Soto establishes his acute sense of ethnicity and, simultaneously, his belief that certain emotions, values, and experiences transcend ethnic boundaries and allegiances."

In his first volume of poetry, *The Elements of San Joaquin,* Soto offers a grim portrait of Mexican-American life. His poems depict the violence of urban life, the exhausting labor of rural life, and the futility of trying to recapture the innocence of childhood. In *Chicano Poetry,* Juan Bruce-Novoa likened Soto's poetic vision to early twentieth-century British writer T.S. Eliot's bleak portrait of the modern world in *The Waste Land.* Soto uses wind-swept dust as a dominant image, and he also introduces such elements as rape, unflushed toilets, a drowned baby and, as Bruce-Novoa quoted him, "men/ Whose arms/ Were bracelets/ Of burns."

Soto's skill with the figurative language of poetry has been noted by reviewers throughout his career, and in *Western American Literature* Jerry Bradley praised the metaphors in *The Elements of San Joaquin* as "evocative, enlightening, and haunting." Though unsettled by the negativism of the collection, Bruce-Novoa noted that the work nonetheless "convinces because of its well-wrought structure, the craft, the coherence of its totality." Moreover, he thought, because it brings such a vivid portrait of poverty to the reading public, *The Elements of San Joaquin* is "a social as well as a literary achievement."

In the poems in *Black Hair* Soto focuses on his friends and family. He portrays fondly the times he shared with his friends as an adolescent as well as the more recent moments he has spent with his young daughter. Ellen Lesser, writing in *Voice Literary Supplement,* was charmed by Soto's poetic tone, "the quality of the voice, the immediate, human presence that breathes through the lines." The critic claimed that Soto's celebration of innocence and sentiment is shaded with a knowledge of "the larger, often threatening world." In the *Christian Science Monitor,* Tom D'Evelyn hailed Soto's ability to go beyond the circumstances of his own life and write of "something higher," concluding: "Somehow Gary Soto has become not an important Chicano poet but an important American poet. More power to him."

When Soto discusses American racial tensions in the prose collections *Living up the Street: Narrative Recollections* and *Small Faces,* he uses vignettes drawn from his own childhood. One vignette reveals the anger the author felt upon realizing that his brown-skinned brother would never be considered an attractive child by conventional American standards. Another shows Soto's surprise at discovering that, contrary to his family's advice to marry a Mexican, he was falling in love with a woman of Japanese ancestry. In these deliberately small-scale recollections, as Paredes noted, "it is a measure of Soto's skill that he so effectively invigorates and sharpens our understanding of the commonplace." With these volumes Soto acquired a solid reputation as a prose writer as well as a poet; *Living up the Street* earned him an American Book award.

Soto's autobiographical prose continued with *Lesser Evils: Ten Quartets* and *A Summer Life,* the first of which reflects the poet's experience with Catholicism—in the same interview Soto declared himself a reconciled Catholic. *A Summer Life* consists of thirty-nine short essays. According to Ernesto Trejo in the *Los Angeles Times Book Review,* these pieces "make up a compelling biography" of Soto's youth. As he had done in previous works, Soto here "holds the past up to memory's probing flashlight, turns it around ever so carefully, and finds in the smallest of incidents the occasion for literature." Writing in the *Americas Review,* Hector Torres compared *A Summer Life* with Soto's earlier autobiographical texts and asserted that the later book "moves with greater stylistic elegance and richer thematic coherence."

Soto's fictional exploration of Latino-American culture continues in the novel *Nickel and Dime.* The work recounts the lives of three adult men: Roberto and Gus, both security guards at a local bank, and Silver, a poet. One of the guards loses his job and finds himself plummeting into an economic free fall; another character also becomes homeless. Silver reminds his audience at an open-mike poetry night that poetry should not concern itself with mundane, self-absorbed matters; it should be about "people who suffer," he rails. Through the plight of the men, Soto attempts to show that even

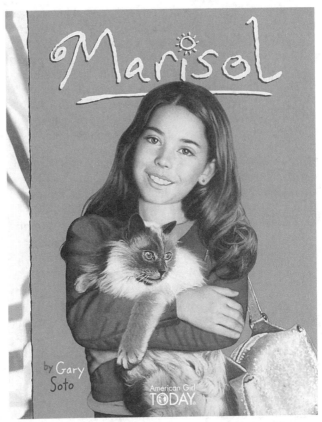

Soto's teen novel **Marisol** *is part of the "American Girl" novel series published by Pleasant Company.* (American Girl, 2005. Copyright © 2005 by American Girl, LLC. Reproduced with permission of Pleasant Company Publications)

the best intentions cannot help those on the lower rungs of the economic ladder make it past "working poor" status, even in good times. A *Publishers Weekly* review of *Nickel and Dime* called its author "a versatile, unsentimental and clear storyteller, and his range of talents converge to illuminate the lives of these three Chicano men living in the shadows."

During the early 1990s Soto turned his attentions in a new direction: children's literature. A first volume of short stories for young readers, *Baseball in April, and Other Stories,* was published in 1990. The eleven tales depict Mexican-American boys and girls as they enter adolescence in Hispanic California neighborhoods. In the *New York Times Book Review,* Roberto Gonzalez Echevarria called the stories "sensitive and economical," then praised Soto: "Because he stays within the teenagers' universe . . . he manages to convey all the social change and stress without bathos or didacticism. In fact, his stories are moving, yet humorous and entertaining." In the *Americas Review,* Torres suggested that *Baseball in April, and Other Stories* is "the kind of work that could be used to teach high school and junior high school English classes."

One of Soto's juvenile characters, a boy named Lincoln Mendoza, appears as a protagonist in two works: *Taking Sides* and *Pacific Crossing.* As a Mexican-American eighth-grader in *Taking Sides,* Lincoln is confronted with challenges and insecurities when he and his mother move from San Francisco's Mission District to a predominantly Anglo suburb, and he must work to keep his heritage intact in his new environment. *Pacific Crossing* finds Lincoln and one of his friends facing cultural challenges in another context: they embark on a voyage to Japan as exchange students. Writing in the *Multicultural Review,* Osbelia Juarez Rocha called *Pacific Crossing* "cleverly crafted" and "entertaining."

Soto has also written poetry for younger readers, most notably the volumes *A Fire in My Hands* and *Neighborhood Odes,* both of which focus on growing up in the Mexican neighborhoods of California's Central Valley. Maeve Visser Knoth described Soto's verse as "simple poems of childhood, adolescence, and adulthood . . . about ordinary events and emotions made remarkable by Soto's skilled use of words and images," in her review for *Horn Book.* In *A Fire in My Hands,* the poet prefaces each selection with a brief paragraph providing background information on both the events described in the poem and the process by which the work was written, thus aiding younger readers' comprehension of his work. *Neighborhood Odes* glorifies the small celebrations in a child's life. While Soto's setting remains the barrios of Fresno, as a *Horn Book* reviewer noted, "other than the small details of daily life—peoples' names or the foods they eat—these poems could be about any neighborhood."

Fearless Fernie: Hanging out with Fernie and Me and its companion volume *Worlds Apart: Traveling with Fernie and Me* are told in verse. The works feature the misadventures of two middle school boys, best friends since they could crawl. In the former work, the pair navigate such familiar adolescent situations as learning to dance and trying to impress a teacher, and in the latter they take an imaginary trip around the globe. According to Hazel Rochman, reviewing *Worlds Apart* in *Booklist,* "It's the friendship story, both silly and affectionate, that is the real subject."

Soto has ventured as well into the arena of children's picture books. *Too Many Tamales* depicts the story of Maria, a young girl who misplaces her mother's wedding ring in tamale dough while helping to prepare a Christmastime feast. Maria—with her cousins' help—embarks on a futile effort to recover the ring by consuming vast quantities of tamales. A little girl gets a shiny new lowrider pedal car for her birthday in *My Little Car/Mi carrito,* "an enjoyable foray into Mexican-American culture," according to *School Library Journal* contributor Maria Otero-Boisvert. Teresa loves her new present, but when she neglects the toy and it falls into disrepair, her grandfather helps her restore it to mint condition. "Soto's pithy text uses a mix of Spanish and English to great effect," noted a reviewer in *Publishers Weekly,* and a critic in *Kirkus Reviews* deemed the work "a multicultural lesson with lots of zip."

Chato's Kitchen introduces a cat whose efforts to entice the local "ratoncitos"—little mice—lead him to prepare abundant portions of fajitas, frijoles, enchiladas, and other foods. Soto continued the adventures of the indomitable feline in *Chato and the Party Animals* and *Chato Goes Cruisin'.* In *Chato and the Party Animals* Chato learns that his pal Novio Boy has never had his own birthday party. The fellow feline doesn't even know when he was born, because he came from the pound. Chato decides to throw him a party—but then forgets to invite the guest of honor. The assembled party becomes a search operation, and when they cannot find Novio Boy, the guests turn mournful. The missing Novio Boy turns up with new adventures to tell, and the party becomes celebratory once again. "Rollicking language—a completely integrated and poetic combination of barrio slang, Spanish, and colloquial English—carries the story along," remarked *School Library Journal* reviewer Ann Welton, while in *Booklist* Gillian Engberg praised the book's "startlingly expressive animals, symbols of Latino culture, and winged-cat angels [that] form dynamic, wild compositions." In *Chato Goes Cruisin'* Chato wins a sweepstakes cruise for two and invites Novio Boy to join him. Once on the ship, however, the pair discover that the other guests are all dogs, and the food and festivities are geared to a canine clientele. When the dogs fall ill and require medical assistance, Chato and Novio Boy come to their rescue. According to *School Library Journal* Angela J. Reynolds, "the 'homecats' endear themselves to readers with charm and humor."

In the young-adult novel *Buried Onions,* Eddie is trying to escape the poverty and gang violence of the Fresno barrio by taking vocational classes. When his cousin Chuy is stabbed to death, he is urged by his aunt to find the killer and avenge the death of his relative, but Eddie just wants to find a way out of this claustrophobic world. Meanwhile, a job in an affluent suburb goes awry when his boss's truck is stolen while in his care. Finally, with a gang member looking for him and with his money gone, Eddie opts to join the U.S. military in hopes that he can find a better life. "In bleak sentences of whispered beauty, Eddie tells how he dropped out of vocational college and is attempting to get by with odd jobs," remarked a critic for *Kirkus Reviews.* The same reviewer noted that this "unrelenting portrait is unsparing in squalid details," concluding that the book is a "valuable tale" and "one that makes no concessions."

The Afterlife, a sequel of sorts to *Buried Onions,* looks at many of the same events from a different perspective: that of Chuy's ghost. After the stabbing incident, Chuy's spirit rises from his body and visits the people and places that were most important to him. "Chuy's death has placed him in a position to view life philosophically, especially his own lost life," wrote James Blasingame in the *Journal of Adolescent & Adult*

Cover of the short-story collection **Local News,** *in which thirteen Chicano teens come to life through Soto's text and illustrations by Peter Fiore.* (Scholastic Inc., 1994. Illustration copyright © 1994 by Scholastic Inc. Reprinted by permission of Scholastic Inc)

Literacy. Chuy then meets Crystal, a girl who has just committed suicide; according to *Booklist* critic Ilene Cooper, "their relationship is beautifully evoked, with Chuy grasping every thread of love he can as he slowly disappears." "Soto sends the couple floating toward the afterlife with poetic metaphors of autumn," stated *Horn Book* reviewer Lauren Adams, "defining the book not as tragic reality but ghostly romance."

An angry, indifferent high school girl finds romance with a loveable nerd in *Accidental Love,* a "warm-hearted, humorous novel," wrote Miranda Doyle in *School Library Journal.* After a scuffle in an elevator, Marisa realizes she has grabbed the wrong cell phone. When she returns the phone to its rightful owner, Rene, a geeky chess player, Marisa is captivated. She transfers to Rene's magnet school, loses weight, and even lands a role in the school play. Marisa and Rene's "efforts to changes themselves and each other are touching and

funny," noted a *Kirkus Reviews* contributor. Not everyone is happy with the situation, however; Marisa's former classmates, as well as Rene's mother, disapprove of the relationship. "Soto deepens this gentle romance between opposites with subtle, authentic glimpses of an uncertain world," remarked *Booklist* critic Gillian Engberg.

Soto's shorter works are included in several collections, among them *The Effects of Knut Hamsun on a Fresno Boy: Recollections and Short Essays.* While some of the selections in this volume were previously published, the book includes five new essays in which Soto focuses on his life as a writer. Soto's lyrical style emerges even when recounting incidents from his childhood, *Booklist* critic Hazel Rochman stated, adding: "The poet is always here, not portentous, but in the cadences of how we talk."

Rochman also commended Soto's biography of a well-known California Latina union activist, *Jessie de la Cruz: Profile of a United Farm Worker,* terming it "stirring American history" and predicting that "teens will be caught by the facts of her hardship and struggle." As Soto noted on his home page, he met de la Cruz and felt immediately drawn to tell her story. The longtime union activist had become an agricultural laborer as a very young child, and was intensely involved in the industry's struggles in California during the 1950s and 1960s. Soto himself once worked in the San Joaquin Valley as a fruit picker when he was younger, and was familiar with the backbreaking nature of the work. He interviewed those who knew de la Cruz and sought to infuse her story with a certain sense of drama. He examines the life of another famous activist in *Cesar Chavez: A Hero for Everyone.* Chavez, a Mexican-American laborer, co-founded the National Farm Workers Association, which later became the United Farm Workers. In the biography, "Soto clearly shows how Chavez's outlook and determination were rooted in his boyhood experiences with poverty, injustice, and prejudice," observed *Booklist* critic Carolyn Phelan.

Soto's ability to tell a story, to recreate moments of his own past in a manner that transcends the boundaries of race or age, to transport his reader to the world of his own childhood is felt within each of his written works. "Soto's remembrances are as sharply defined and appealing as bright new coins," wrote Alicia Fields in the *Bloomsbury Review.* "His language is spare and simple yet vivid." But it is his joyful outlook, strong enough to transcend the poverty of the barrio, that makes his work so popular. The optimism with which he views his own life radiates from each of his young characters—Soto views life as a gift and his talent for expression is his gift to his readers. As he told Hector Avalos Torres in the *Dictionary of Literary Biography,* Writing "is my one talent. There are a lot of people who never discover what their talent is . . . I am very lucky to have found mine."

Biographical and Critical Sources

BOOKS

Bruce-Novoa, Juan, *Chicano Poetry: A Response to Chaos,* University of Texas Press (Austin, TX), 1982.

Children's Literature Review, Volume 38, Thomson Gale (Detroit, MI), 1996.

Contemporary Literary Criticism, Thomson Gale (Detroit, MI), Volume 32, 1985, Volume 80, 1994.

Dictionary of Literary Biography, Volume 82: *Chicano Writers,* Thomson Gale (Detroit, MI), 1989.

Hispanic Literature Criticism, Thomson Gale (Detroit, MI), 1994.

PERIODICALS

American Book Review, July-August, 1982.

Americas Review, spring, 1991, Hector Torres, review of *A Summer Life,* pp. 111-115.

Bloomsbury Review, January-February, 1987, Alicia Fields, "Small but Telling Moments," p. 10.

Booklist, April 1, 1992, Hazel Rochman, review of *A Fire in My Hands,* pp. 1437-1438; September 15, 1993, Hazel Rochman, review of *Too Many Tamales,* p. 151; June 1, 1995, review of *Boys at Work,* p. 1773; October 1, 1995, Hazel Rochman, review of *Canto Familiar,* p. 312; March 15, 1998, Hazel Rochman, review of *Petty Crimes,* p. 1245; October 1, 1999, Annie Ayres, review of *Nerdlandia: A Play,* p. 349; November 1, 1999, Karen Harris, review of *Pacific Crossing,* p. 549; February 15, 2000, James O'Laughlin, review of *Nickel and Dime,* p. 1085; August, 2000, Gillian Engberg, review of *Chato and the Party Animals,* p. 2150; November 1, 2000, Hazel Rochman, review of *The Effects of Knut Hamsun on a Fresno Boy: Recollections and Short Essays,* p. 512; November 15, 2000, Hazel Rochman, review of *Jessie de la Cruz: Profile of a United Farm Worker,* p. 633; August, 2003, Ilene Cooper, review of *The Afterlife,* p. 1981; December 15, 2003, Carolyn Phelan, review of *Cesar Chavez: A Hero for Everyone,* p. 748; March 15, 2005, Hazel Rochman, review of *Worlds Apart: Traveling with Fernie and Me,* p. 129; May 1, 2005, Linda Perkins, review of *Help Wanted,* p. 1581, and Gillian Engberg, review of *Chato Goes Cruisin',* p. 1593; January 1, 2006, Gillian Engberg, review of *Accidental Love,* p. 86; March 1, 2006, Jennifer Mattson, review of *My Little Car/Mi carrito,* p. 99; April 1, 2006, Hazel Rochman, review of *A Fire in My Hands,* p. 31.

Bulletin of the Center for Children's Books, April, 1990, Roger Sutton, review of *Baseball in April and Other Stories,* p. 199.

Christian Science Monitor, March 6, 1985, Tom D'Evelyn, review of *Black Hair.*

Denver Quarterly, summer, 1982.

Horn Book, March, 1992, review of *A Fire in My Hands,* p. 216; May, 1992, review of *Neighborhood Odes,* p. 352; November-December, 1992, Ellen Fader, review of *Pacific Crossing,* pp. 725-726; July-August, 2002, Nell D. Beram, review of *If the Shoe Fits,* p. 451, and

Roger Sutton, review of *Fearless Fernie: Hanging out with Fernie and Me,* p. 480; November-December, 2003, Lauren Adams, review of *The Afterlife,* p. 755; May-June, 2005, Peter D. Sieruta, review of *Help Wanted,* p. 333, and Roger Sutton, review of *Worlds Apart,* p. 344; July-August, 2005, Christine M. Heppermann, review of *Chato Goes Cruisin',* p. 459.

Journal of Adolescent and Adult Literacy, November, 2003, James Blasingame, review of *The Afterlife,* p. 269.

Kirkus Reviews, April 1, 1993, review of *Local News,* p. 464; June 15, 1993, review of *The Pool Party,* p. 792; April 1, 1997, review of *Buried Onions,* p. 1229; March 1, 1998, review of *Petty Crimes,* p. 345; October 15, 2000, review of *The Effects of Knut Hamsun on a Fresno Boy,* pp. 1469-1470; April 15, 2005, review of *Chato Goes Cruisin',* p. 482; May 1, 2005, review of *Help Wanted,* p. 547; December 15, 2005, review of *Accidental Love,* p. 1327; March 1, 2006, review of *My Little Car/Mi carrito,* p. 240.

Kliatt, September, 2003, Michele Winship, review of *The Afterlife,* p. 13.

Library Journal, December, 1999, Harold Augenbraum, review of *Nickel and Dime,* p. 190.

Los Angeles Times Book Review, August 5, 1990, Ernesto Trejo, "Memories of a Fresno Boyhood," pp. 1, 9; August 15, 1993, Suzanne Curley, "A Better Place to Live," p. 8.

Magazine of Fantasy and Science Fiction, May, 2004, Michelle West, review of *The Afterlife,* p. 32.

Multicultural Review, June, 1993, Osbelia Juarez Rocha, review of *Pacific Crossing,* pp. 76, 78.

Nation, June 7, 1993, pp. 772-774.

NEA Today, November, 1992, p. 9.

New York Times Book Review, October 11, 1981, Alan Cheuse, "The Voices of Chicano," pp. 15, 36-37; August 20, 1990, Roberto Gonzalez Echevarria, "Growing up North of the Border," p. 45.

Parnassus, fall-winter, 1979, Peter Cooley, review of *The Tale of Sunlight.*

Poetry, March, 1980, Alan Williamson, "In a Middle Style," pp. 348-354; June, 1985.

Publishers Weekly, march 4, 1988, review of *Lesser Evils,* p. 102; March 23, 1992, review of *Neighborhood Odes,* p. 74; April 12, 1993, review of *Local News,* p. 64; August 16, 1993, p. 103; January 31, 1994, review of *Crazy Weekend,* p. 90; August 24, 1992, review of *The Skirt,* p. 80; February 6, 1995, review of *Chato's Kitchen,* pp. 84-85; January 20, 1997, review of *Snapshots from the Wedding,* p. 401; December 8, 1997, review of *Off and Running,* p. 74; April 26, 1999, Joanne M. Hammond, review of *Pacific Crossing,* p. 55; February 14, 2000, review of *Nickel and Dime,* p. 175; April 24, 2006, review of *My Little Car/Mi carrito,* p. 60.

Revista Chicano-Riqueña, summer, 1983.

Rocky Mountain Review, Volume 41, numbers 1-2, 1987, Raymund Paredes, "Recent Chicano Fiction," pp. 126-128.

San Francisco Review of Books, summer, 1986, Geoffrey Dunn, review of *Living up the Street,* p. 11.

School Library Journal, November, 1991, Bruce Anne Shook, review of *Taking Sides,* p. 124; March, 1992,

Barbara Chatton, review of *A Fire in My Hands*, p. 264; May, 1992, Renee Steinberg, review of *Neighborhood Odes*, p. 128; June, 1995, Rosie Peasley, review of *Boys at Work*, p. 113; July, 1995, review of *Chato's Kitchen*, p. 69; July, 2000, Ann Welton, review of *Chato and the Party Animals*, p. 88; November, 2003, Francisca Goldsmith, review of *The Afterlife*, p. 148; January, 2004, John Sigwald, review of *Cesar Chavez*, p. 123; March, 2005, Nina Lindsay, review of *Worlds Apart*, p. 234; May, 2005, Diane P. Tuccillo, review of *Help Wanted: Stories*, p. 139; June, 2005, Angela J. Reynolds, review of *Chato Goes Cruisin'*, p. 128; July, 2005, Coop Renner, review of *Taking Sides*, p. 45; January, 2006, Miranda Doyle, review of *Accidental Love*, p. 143; June, 2006, Maria Otero-Boisvert, review of *My Little Car/Mi carrito*, p. 145.

Voice Literary Supplement, September, 1985, Ellen Lesser, review of *Black Hair*.

Voice of Youth Advocates, April, 1995, Maura Bresnahan, review of *Summer on Wheels*, pp. 27-28.

Western American Literature, spring, 1979, Jerry Bradley, review of *The Elements of San Joaquin*; May, 1989, Gerald Haslam, review of *Lesser Evils*, pp. 92-93.

OTHER

Official Gary Soto Home Page, http:// www.garysoto.com (October 15, 2006).*

* * *

STURGES, Philemon

Personal

Married; wife's name Judy Sue; children: three daughters. *Hobbies and other interests:* Cooking.

Addresses

Home—Boston, MA; Princeton, MA.

Career

Architect and children's writer. *Military service:* U.S. Navy, served four years.

Writings

FOR CHILDREN

The Gift of Christmas, illustrated by Holly Berry, North-South Books (New York, NY), 1995.

Ten Flashing Fireflies, illustrated by Anna Vojtech, North-South Books (New York, NY), 1995.

Rainsong/Snowsong, illustrated by Shari Halpern, North-South Books (New York, NY), 1995.

What's That Sound, Woolly Bear?, illustrated by Joan Paley, Little, Brown (Boston, MA), 1996.

(Reteller, with Anna Vojtech) *Marushka and the Month Brothers: A Folktale*, illustrated by Anna Vojtech, North-South Books (New York, NY), 1996.

Bridges Are to Cross, illustrated by Giles Laroche, G.P. Putnam (New York, NY), 1998.

Crocky Dilly, illustrated by Paige Miglio, Museum of Fine Arts (Boston, MA), 1998.

(Reteller) *The Little Red Hen Makes a Pizza*, illustrated by Amy Walrod, Dutton Children's Books (New York, NY), 1999.

I Love Trucks!, illustrated by Shari Halpern, HarperCollins (New York, NY), 1999.

Sacred Places, illustrated by Giles Laroche, G.P. Putnam (New York, NY), 2000.

(With Bonnie Lass) *Who Took the Cookies from the Cookie Jar?*, illustrated by Ashley Wolff, Little, Brown (Boston, MA), 2000.

I Love Trains!, illustrated by Shari Halpern, HarperCollins (New York, NY), 2001.

I Love Planes!, illustrated by Shari Halpern, HarperCollins (New York, NY), 2003.

I Love School!, illustrated by Shari Halpern, HarperCollins (New York, NY), 2004.

She'll Be Comin' 'round the Mountain, Little, Brown (Boston, MA), 2004.

Down to the Sea in Ships, illustrated by Giles Laroche, G.P. Putnam (New York, NY), 2004.

I Love Bugs!, illustrated by Shari Halpern, HarperCollins (New York, NY), 2005.

This Little Pirate, illustrated by Amy Walrod, Dutton Children's Books (New York, NY), 2005.

Waggers, illustrated by Jim Ishikawa, Dutton Children's Books (New York, NY), 2005.

I Love Tools!, illustrated by Shari Halpern, HarperCollins (New York, NY), 2006.

Adaptations

She'll Be Comin' 'round the Mountain, was adapted as a video, Nutmeg Media, 2005.

Sidelights

Philemon Sturges left behind his career as an architect so he could focus all his energies on writing children's books. "Everything is new to kids," Sturges noted on his home page. "It is an honor to introduce them to things—plus, it's fun." In one of his first books, *Ten Flashing Fireflies*, Sturges tells the story of a little boy and girl catching fireflies and putting them in a glass jar. The book enables the young reader to count from one to ten as each firefly is captured. At the end of the story the young children count down as they watch the fireflies fly away. In a review in *Booklist*, Lauren Peterson commented that "this most unusual counting book captures the charm and innocence of a favorite summertime activity." A *Publishers Weekly* contributor called the book "a memorable entry in a heavily populated picture-book category."

Sturges focuses on the holiday season in *The Gift of Christmas,* which a *Publishers Weekly* contributor noted "catalogues with delight the sights, sounds and smells" of Christmas. In *Rainsong/Snowsong* the author tells various stories through rhyme as a boy and a girl marvel at the rain and snow. "The fun of it all is captured in the buoyant double-page illustrations," noted Leone McDermott in *Booklist.*

What's That Sound, Woolly Bear? guides young readers through a list of various insects. "A final spread gives interesting additional information on each insect, including a way to tell temperature by counting chirps," noted Susan Dove Lempke in *Booklist.* A *Publishers Weekly* contributor also commented that the "final spread successfully blends succinct information and colorful fun facts."

The author mines the folklore of Czechoslovakia in *Marushka and the Month Brothers: A Folktale.* Like the tale of Cinderella, the story revolves around a young girl living with her evil stepmother and stepsister. As the story progresses, the girl is sent out into a blizzard to retrieve food and is only able to make it back safely through the help of the twelve Month brothers. Eventually, the evil stepmother and stepsister disappear into a storm conjured up by the brothers. Hazel Rochman, writing in *Booklist,* called the book "a freshly told version" of the tale, while a *Publishers Weekly* contributor noted the story's "lyrical narrative."

Sturges describes amazing bridges from around the world, such as the rope suspension bridge in the Andes mountains of Peru, in *Bridges Are to Cross.* "In just two or three sentences, Sturges . . . explains how each particular bridge works within its environment," noted a contributor to *Publishers Weekly.* Susan Dove Lempke,

writing in *Booklist,* commented that the book "is guaranteed to make most readers look at bridges with new eyes."

Sturgess is also the author of a series of rhyming books that began with *I Love Trucks!,* a work *Booklist* contributor Carolyn Phelan commended for its inclusion of women truck drivers, noting that the "text is as direct and purposeful as its subject." In *I Love Trains!* a little boy describes the various trains he watches passing by on the tracks. "Toddlers will enjoy making the hoot, roar, and rumble sounds and identifying the various cars," noted Hazel Rochman in *Booklist. I Love Planes!* includes descriptions of technical terms associated with planes and flying as a little boy talks about flying in planes, gliders, and balloons. "Young flight enthusiasts will soon be taking off on solo reading jaunts," wrote a *Kirkus Reviews* contributor. Julie Cummins, writing in *Booklist,* called the book "a high-flying treat for children."

Sturges takes on education in *I Love School!* as he leads readers through a day at school as described by a group of children. A *Kirkus Reviews* contributor called the book "a soothing, bright-as-noon introduction to school that ought to help chase away any shim-shams" felt by young children who may be going to school for the first time. *School Library Journal* contributor Phyllis M. Simon deemed the work a "a good choice for family sharing." *I Love Bugs!* follows a little boy on a safari in his backyard and was called "engaging as well as informative," by *Booklist* contributor Connie Fletcher.

Sturges presents a new take on another old story in *The Little Red Hen Makes a Pizza,* which recounts a hen's hankering for a pizza and her recruitment of other animals to help her assemble the ingredients and prepare one. A *Publishers Weekly* contributor noted that the

Philemon Sturges has produced picture books as well as board books designed to appeal to the toddler set, one of which is the Shari Halpern-illustrated **I Love Trains!,** (HarperFestival, 2006. Cover art © 1989 by Shari Halpern. Used by permission of HarperCollins Publishers)

Marushka and the Month Brothers, *a folk tale from Eastern Europe, is retold by Sturges and illustrator Anna Vojtech.* (North-South Books, 1996. Illustrations copyright © 1996 by Anna Vojtech. Used with permission of North-South Books, Inc., New York)

book "exudes charm, thanks to conversational narration." In *Who Took the Cookies from the Cookie Jar?* the author tells the story of a search for the animal that snatched the cookies. "Children will enjoy the challenge of solving the mystery and astute observers will notice the clues provided on the front cover and title page," noted Tim Wadham in *School Library Journal.*

Nautical themes are the basis for *Down to the Sea in Ships* and *This Little Pirate. School Library Journal* contributor Teresa Pfeifer called the first "a seamless collection of finely honed but telling histories," while Linda Staskus commented in the same periodical that *This Little Pirate* is a "wacky, imaginative nautical tale . . . filled with action and adventure."

In *Waggers,* Sturges recounts an old folk tale about dogs sniffing each other. As the story goes, the practice is left over from bygone days when dogs misplaced their tails after hanging them up during a meeting on how to get rid of cats once and for all. Unknown to the dogs, a cat also attended the meeting. When it dispersed by calling out "Fire!," the dogs ran for their lives, grabbing whatever tail they could, and have spent the rest of their days checking to see if they have the right ones. "Sturges's saucy rhyme and imaginative plot will tickle the fancy of children," wrote Marge Loch-Wouters in *School Library Journal.*

On a more serious note, Sturges addresses a timely topic in his book *Sacred Places,* as he talks about different religions and religious practices around the world. "The text is simple and stately," noted *Booklist* contributor Ilene Cooper. Patricia Lothrop-Green, writing in *School Library Journal,* called the book a "striking tour of 28 religious sites around the world" and also noted that "Sturges's open-minded view of religious aspirations is a worthy one."

Sturges • teams up with writer Bonnie Lass in writing **Who Took the Cookies from the Cookie Jar?,** *featuring illustrations by Ashley Wolff.* (Little, Brown and Company, 2000. Text copyright © 2000 by Bonnie Lass and Philemon Sturges. Illustrations copyright © 2000 by Ashley Wolff. Reproduced by permission of Little, Brown, and Company, Inc. To purchase copies of this book, please call 1.800.759.0190)

Biographical and Critical Sources

PERIODICALS

Appleseeds, March, 2002, Sheila Wilensky, review of *Sacred Places*, p. 32.

Booklist, June 1, 1995, Lauren Peterson, review of *Ten Flashing Fireflies*, p. 1789; November 1, 1995, Leone McDermott, review of *Rainsong/Snowsong*, p. 478; April 15, 1996, Susan Dove Lempke, review of *What's That Sound, Woolly Bear?*, p. 1447; October 15, 1996, Hazel Rochman, review of *Marushka and the Month Brothers: A Folktale*, p. 429; December 15, 1998, Susan Dove Lempke, review of *Bridges Are to Cross*, p. 747; February 1, 1999, Carolyn Phelan, review of *I Love Trucks!*, p. 978; April 1, 1999, Susan Dove Lempke, review of *Crocky Dilly*, p. 1422; November 15, 1999, Marta Segal, review of *The Little Red Hen Makes a Pizza*, p. 639; October 1, 2000, Ilene Cooper, review of *Sacred Places*, p. 360; October 15, 2000, Todd Morning, review of *Who Took the Cookies from the Cookie Jar?*, p. 445; July, 2001, Hazel Rochman, review of *I Love Trains!*, p. 2022; February 1, 2003, Julie Cummins, view of *I Love Planes!*, p. 1002; August, 2004, Hazel Rochman, review of *I Love School!*, p. 1949; August, 2004, Jennifer Mattson, review of *She'll Be Comin' 'round the Mountain*, p. 1940; March 1, 2005, Connie Fletcher, review of *I Love Bugs!*, p. 1206; May 15, 2005, Gillian Engberg, review of *Down to the Sea in Ships*, p. 1655; June 1, 2005, Hazel Rochman, review of *This Little Pirate*, p. 1824.

Horn Book, March-April, 1997, Ann A. Flowers, review of *Marushka and the Month Brothers*, p. 207.

Kirkus Reviews, February 1, 2003, review of *I Love Planes!*, p. 240; June 15, 2004, review of *I Love School!*, p. 582; March 1, 2005, review of *Waggers*, p. 296; April 1, 2005, review of *I Love Bugs!*, p. 426; April 15, 2005, review of *Down to the Sea in Ships*, p. 483; May 15, 2005, review of *This Little Pirate*, p. 596.

Publishers Weekly, June 5, 1995, review of *Ten Flashing Fireflies*, p. 61; September 18, 1995, review of *The Gift of Christmas*, p. 98; April 29, 1996, review of *What's That Sound, Woolly Bear?*, p. 71; November 11, 1996, review of *Marushka and the Month Brothers*, p. 74; November 9, 1998, review of *Bridges Are to Cross*, p. 74; August 16, 1999, review of *The Little Red Hen Makes a Pizza*, p. 83; October 2, 2000, review of *Who Took the Cookies from the Cookie Jar?*, p. 83; October 30, 2000, review of *Bridges Are to Cross*, p. 78; June 25, 2001, review of *I Love Trucks!*, p. 75; December 16, 2002, review of *I Love Planes!*, p. 69; June 28, 2004, review of *I Love School!*, p. 52; February 28, 2005, review of *Waggers*, p. 65.

School Library Journal, October, 2000, Tim Wadham, review of *Who Took the Cookies from the Cookie Jar?*, p. 128; December, 2000, Patricia Lothrop-Green, review of *Sacred Places*, p. 136; June, 2001, Melinda Piehler, review of *I Love Trains!*, p. 130; March, 2003, Bina Williams, review of *I Love Planes!*, p. 208; July, 2004, Bina Williams, review of *She'll Be Comin' 'round the Mountain*, p. 96; August, 2004, Phyllis M. Simon, review of *I Love School!*, p. 96; December, 2004, Ginny Gustin, review of *She'll Be Comin' 'round the Mountain*, p. 59; March, 2005, Marge Loch-Wouters, review of *Waggers*, p. 188; April, 2005, Be Astengo, review of *I Love Bugs!*, p.113; June, 2005, Teresa Pfeifer, review of *Down to the Sea in Ships*, p. 187; July, 2005, Linda Staskus, review of *This Little Pirate*, p. 82; June, 2006, JoAnn Jonas, review of *I Love Tools!*, p. 128.

Teacher Librarian, March, 1999, Shirley Lewis, review of *Bridges Are to Cross*, p. 44.

ONLINE

BookLoons, http://www.bookloons.com/ (August 22, 2005), Hilary Williamson, review of *She'll Be Comin' 'round the Mountain*.

Philemon Sturges Home Page, http://www.philemonsturges.com (October 16, 2006).*

T

THOMAS, Margaret
See THOMAS, Peggy

* * *

THOMAS, Peggy
(Margaret Thomas)

Personal

Born in Buffalo, NY; daughter of Howard F. (a teacher) and Margery (an author; maiden name, Metz) Facklam; married; children: two. *Education:* State University of New York College at Buffalo, B.A. (anthropology), M.A. (anthropology).

Addresses

Home—5 Francis St., Middleport, NY 14105.

Career

Author. *Buffalo News,* Buffalo, NY, freelance writer. Institute of Children's Literature, West Redding, CT, instructor.

Member

Society for Children's Book Writers and Illustrators, Rochester Area Children's Book Writers and Illustrators.

Awards, Honors

New York Public Library Best Book for the Teen Age selection, 1993, for *Kid's World Almanac of Amazing Facts about Numbers, Math, and Money,* and 1997, for *Medicines from Nature;* Outstanding Science Trade Book for Children, National Science Teachers Association/Children's Book Council, 2001, for *Marine Mammal Preservation.*

Peggy Thomas (Photograph courtesy of Peggy Thomas)

Writings

NONFICTION

Volcano!, Crestwood House (New York, NY), 1991.

(With mother, Margery Facklam) *Kid's World Almanac of Amazing Facts about Numbers, Math, and Money,* illustrated by brother, Paul Facklam, Pharos Books (New York, NY), 1992.

Talking Bones: The Science of Forensic Anthropology, Facts on File (New York, NY), 1995, revised edition published as *Forensic Anthropology: The Growing Science of Talking Bones,* Facts on File (New York, NY), 2003.

Medicines from Nature, Twenty-first Century Books (New York, NY), 1997.

Bacteria and Viruses, Lucent Books (San Diego, CA), 2004.

Artificial Intelligence, Lucent Books (Farmington Hills, MI), 2005.

(With Margery Facklam) *New York: The Empire State,* illustrated by Jon Messer, Charlesbridge (Watertown, MA), 2007.

"SCIENCE OF SAVING ANIMALS" SERIES

Big Cat Conservation, Twenty-first Century Books (Brookfield, CT), 2000.

Bird Alert, Twenty-first Century Books (Brookfield, CT), 2000.

Marine Mammal Preservation, Twenty-first Century Books (Brookfield, CT), 2000.

Reptile Rescue, Twenty-first Century Books (Brookfield, CT), 2000.

FICTION

Joshua the Giant Frog, illustrated by Cat Bowman Smith, Pelican Publishing (Gretna, LA), 2005.

Snow Dance, illustrated by Paul Facklam, Pelican Publishing (Gretna, LA), 2007.

Contributor to *Cricket* and *Hopscotch for Girls.*

Sidelights

Peggy Thomas is the author of highly regarded nonfiction books for children, among them *Talking Bones: The Science of Forensic Anthropology, Medicines from Nature,* and *Big Cat Conservation.* She has also penned *Joshua the Giant Frog,* a tall tale inspired by folklore about the Erie Canal.

Though Thomas grew up in a literary household—her mother is respected children's author Margery Facklam—she initially chose a different career path. "Although I loved to write and read, I dreamt of being a scientist," Thomas noted on her home page. "But I could never decide what kind of scientist to be. I went to college and got my master's degree in anthropology (the study of people and cultures). I loved to dig in the dirt looking for archaeological artifacts. I didn't start writing until after my daughter was born." Thomas made her publishing debut in 1991 with *Volcano!*

In *Talking Bones,* a 1995 book, Thomas examines the world of forensic scientists. The author presents a number of case studies of real life murders and recounts the investigative methods used to solve the crimes. "Each of the cases is interesting," noted Paul Joseph Cohen in a review for *Science Activities,* the critic adding that "the details of how the police scientists did their work are equally fascinating." "Although not for the faint-hearted, perhaps . . . the information is intriguing, unusual fare and highly readable in style," remarked *Booklist* contributor Anne O'Malley.

Thomas looks at the healing powers of the natural world in *Medicines from Nature.* In this 1997 title she examines how scientists search for and test the medicinal properties of insects, animals, and plants, among them taxol, an extract from the bark of the Pacific yew that is used to fight cancer. "Thomas' account is fascinating," commented *Booklist* reviewer Frances Bradburn of the nonfiction title.

In Joshua the Giant Frog *Peggy Thomas teams up with illustrator Cat Bowman Smith to create a humorous tale of life along the Erie Canal.* (Pelican Publishing Company, 2005. Illustrations copyright © 2005 by Cat Bowman Smith. Reproduced by permission)

In 2000 Thomas published four works in the "Science of Saving Animals" series. *Big Cat Conservation* looks at programs designed to protect panthers, cheetahs, tigers, and other creatures, and *Reptile Rescue* features conservation efforts involving crocodiles, tortoises, and snakes. In her review of both titles, *School Library Journal* contributor Cynthia M. Sturgis praised the "well-written texts" and "easy-to-read page design." *Bird Alert* and *Marine Mammal Preservation* complete the series.

In 2005 Thomas published her debut picture book, *Joshua the Giant Frog.* After finding a giant polliwog swimming in the Erie Canal, young Red McCarthy decides to bring the creature home. As Joshua the polliwog grows into an enormous frog, however, he wreaks havoc on the town, shaking the ground with every hop. Just as the townspeople decide to banish Joshua, Red finds a way to make his supersized pet a hero to the community. Linda Staskus, reviewing the work in *School Library Journal,* called *Joshua the Giant Frog* a "wonderful read-aloud."

Thomas finds her work as an author both challenging and rewarding. "The best part of being a nonfiction writer is that I don't have to choose just one field of science to concentrate on," she commented on her home page. "I can learn about all of them. I can spend a year learning about bones and bodies from forensic anthropologists, and then hang out with marine mammal veterinarians, reptile rehabilitators or virus hunters."

Biographical and Critical Sources

PERIODICALS

Booklist, October 15, 1995, Anne O'Malley, review of *Talking Bones: The Science of Forensic Anthropology,* p. 393; September 15, 1997, Frances Bradburn, review of *Medicines from Nature,* p. 231; June 1, 2000, Shelle Rosenfeld, reviews of *Big Cat Conservation* and *Reptile Rescue,* p. 1888.

Kirkus Reviews, March 15, 2005, review of *Joshua the Giant Frog,* p. 359.

School Library Journal, January, 1996, Jeanette Larson, review of *Talking Bones,* p. 137; August, 1997, Ann G. Brouse, review of *Medicines from Nature,* p. 176; July, 2000, Cynthia M. Sturgis, reviews of *Big Cat Conservation* and *Reptile Rescue,* p. 123; December, 2000, Cynthia M. Sturgis, review of *Bird Alert,* p. 166; January, 2001, Cynthia M. Sturgis, review of *Marine Mammal Preservation,* p. 157; April, 2005, Linda Staskus, review of *Joshua the Giant Frog,* p. 113.

Science Activities, summer, 1996, Paul Joseph Cohen, review of *Talking Bones,* p. 45.

Voice of Youth Advocates, April, 1996, review of *Talking Bones,* p. 61.

ONLINE

Peggy Thomas Home Page, http://www.peggythomas. smartwriters.com (October 20, 2006).

*   *   *

THOMPSON, Lauren 1962-

Personal

Born November 7, 1962, in Eugene, OR; daughter of David A. (a professor of psychology) and Ruth M. (a psychiatric nurse; maiden name, Flynn) Stevens; married Robert E. Thompson (a college English teacher), May 21, 1994; children: Owen R. *Education:* Mount Holyoke College, B.A. (math), 1984; Clark University, M.A. (English), 1991. *Religion:* "Buddhist studies." *Hobbies and other interests:* Nature, religion.

Addresses

Home—Brooklyn, NY. *Agent*—c/o Author Mail, Simon & Schuster, 1230 Avenue of the Americas, New York, NY 10020.

Career

Children's book author. Editor, 1988-2006; former senior editor at a New York children's book publishing company; full-time writer, beginning 1999.

Member

Society of Children's Book Writers and Illustrators.

Lauren Thompson (Photograph by JuAnne Ng. Courtesy of Lauren Thompson)

Awards, Honors

Children's Choice selection, International Reading Association, 2001, for *One Riddle, One Answer,* 2003, for *Little Quack,* and 2004, for *Polar Bear Night;* Oppenheim Toy Portfolio Best Book designation, 2003, for *A Christmas Gift for Mama;* New York Times Best Book designation, and CCBC Charlotte Zolotow Honor designation, both 2004, both for *Polar Bear Night.*

Writings

Mouse's First Christmas, illustrated by Buket Erdogan, Simon & Schuster (New York, NY), 1999.

(Reteller) *Love One Another: The Last Days of Jesus,* illustrated by Elizabeth Uyehara, Scholastic (New York, NY), 2000.

Mouse's First Halloween, illustrated by Buket Erdogan, Simon & Schuster (New York, NY), 2000.

One Riddle, One Answer, illustrated by Linda S. Wingerter, Scholastic (New York, NY), 2001.

Mouse's First Valentine, illustrated by Buket Erdogan, Simon & Schuster (New York, NY), 2002.

Little Quack, illustrated by Derek Anderson, Simon & Schuster (New York, NY), 2003.

Mouse's First Day of School, illustrated by Buket Erdogan, Simon & Schuster (New York, NY), 2003.

A Christmas Gift for Mama, illustrated by Jim Burke, Scholastic (New York, NY), 2003.

Thompson's story of a tiny mouse looking forward to his first holiday is enhanced by Buket Erdogan's paintings in **Mouse's First Christmas.** (Aladdin Paperbacks, 2003. Illustrations copyright © 1999 by Buket Erdogan. Reprinted with the permission of Simon & Schuster Books for Young Readers, an imprint of Simon & Schuster Children's Publishing Division)

Mouse's First Summer, illustrated by Buket Erdogan, Simon & Schuster (New York, NY), 2004.

Little Quack's Hide and Seek, illustrated by Derek Anderson, Simon & Schuster (New York, NY), 2004.

Polar Bear Night, illustrated by Stephen Savage, Scholastic (New York, NY), 2004.

Mouse's First Spring, illustrated by Buket Erdogan, Simon & Schuster (New York, NY), 2005.

Mouse's First Snow, illustrated by Buket Erdogan, Simon & Schuster (New York, NY), 2005.

Little Quack's Bedtime, illustrated by Derek Anderson, Simon & Schuster (New York, NY), 2005.

Mouse's First Fall, illustrated by Buket Erdogan, Simon & Schuster (New York, NY), 2006.

Little Quack's New Friend, illustrated by Derek Anderson, Simon & Schuster (New York, NY), 2006.

The Apple Pie That Papa Baked, illustrated by Jonathan Bean, Simon & Schuster (New York, NY), 2007.

Ballerina Dreams: A True Story, photographs by James Estrin, Feiwel & Friends (New York, NY), 2007.

Sidelights

Lauren Thompson, the author of several critically acclaimed picture books for younger readers, is perhaps best known for her "Mouse" and "Little Quack" stories. She has garnered particular praise for her "Mouse" books, each of which start with a very simple premise and, with the help of illustrator Buket Erdogan, become something truly memorable, according to reviewers. In her debut work, *Mouse's First Christmas,* Thompson plays with the rhythms and borrows some of the language of the famous poem "'Twas the Night before Christmas," then turns Mouse's first experiences of the sights, sounds, textures, and tastes of the holiday into a celebration of the senses. The overall experience of sharing Mouse's first Christmas with Thompson's character is cozy, familiar, and gently humorous, reviewers noted. A contributor to *Publishers Weekly,* remarking on how well the author's text, illustrator's paintings, and designer's design interact, claimed that together they "make much from a simple premise." A contributor to the *Children's Book Review Service* called *Mouse's First Christmas* "a perfect read-aloud for classrooms and libraries."

Mouse's First Christmas has been followed by *Mouse's First Halloween,* a gentle, rhyming rendition of Mouse's first experience with the daunting aspects of one of the

One of Thompson's most popular picture-book characters is the feisty little duckling brought to life in Derek Anderson's illustrations for **Little Quack.** (Simon & Schuster Books for Young Readers, 2003. Illustrations copyright © 2003 Derek Anderson. Reprinted with the permission of Simon & Schuster Books for Young Readers, an imprint of Simon & Schuster Children's Publishing Division)

With Persian-influenced illustrations by Linda S. Wingerter, Thompson's One Riddle, One Answer *poses a mathematical riddle within its folktale-like story.* (Scholastic Press, 2001. Illustration copyright © 2001 by Linda S. Wingerter. Published by Scholastic Press, an imprint of Scholastic Inc. Reprinted by permission of Scholastic Inc)

scariest holidays. As Mouse steps outside to join the special day's after-dark festivities, he is overcome by fear. With effective use of page turns and repetition, *Mouse's First Halloween* becomes a reassuring litany of things that may seem frightening but turn out not to be. As *Booklist* reviewer Carolyn Phelan remarked, the book "is a fine Halloween read-aloud for young children who like the idea of a scary book, but need plenty of reassurance along the way." Again, text and illustrations were found to work well together. "This author and illustrator make a superb team," enthused Karen Land in *School Library Journal*, the critic recommending *Mouse's First Halloween* for young fans of Thompson's other "Mouse" books.

Mouse explores another popular American holiday in *Mouse's First Valentine*. Here, the rodent spies on big sister Minka as she secretively gathers such mysterious items as red paper, ribbon, lace, and paste from around the house, and then assembles them into a valentine for Mouse. Reviewers had come to expect a heartwarming story and richly colored illustrations from the pair, and the publication of *Mouse's First Valentine* was greeted by a contributor to *Kirkus Reviews* with the statement: "Thompson and Erdogan pair up yet again for a delightful dose of holiday cheer."

Mouse experiences a familiar rite of passage in *Mouse's First Day of School,* "a bouncy, appealing read-aloud for soothing apprehensive day care and preschool jitters," according to *Booklist* contributor Gillian Engberg. In this story, Mouse slips into an open backpack and winds up in a busy classroom where he discovers toys, games, crayons, snacks, and new friends. Mary Ann Carcich, reviewing the work in *School Library Journal*, praised Thompson's "expressive and playful text," and a critic in *Kirkus Reviews* called *Mouse's First Day of School* "an enjoyable jaunt."

Other "Mouse" books find the title character learning about the seasons. In *Mouse's First Summer*, Mouse and Minka enjoy a picnic lunch, fly a kite, and play on the green grass. Thompson's "poetic, spare text dabbles in alliteration," remarked *School Library Journal* contributor Gay Lynn Van Vleck. In *Mouse's First Spring*, Mouse and his mother discover a butterfly, a bird, a frog, and several other creatures while out on a springtime jaunt. A gust of wind eventually carries each creature away, including Mouse, who lands in his mother's arms. "This gentle story is just right for toddlers who . . . are encountering new things," observed Elaine Lesh Morgan in *School Library Journal*. Mouse spends a wintry day sledding and skating with his father in *Mouse's First Snow.* "For all the ice and snow depicted, this picture book continually radiates warmth," stated Phelan. Mouse and his big sister Minka celebrate the fun of autumn leaves in *Mouse's First Fall,* a book praised as a "solid choice" by Phelan.

Thompson introduces another of her popular creations in *Little Quack,* a read-aloud about a tiny duckling and his four sprightly siblings who, at their mother's urgings, leave the nest to take their first swim in the big pond. "With a judicious use of repetition and an ear for both Mama's mellifluous pleadings and the squawkings of her recalcitrant crew, Thompson's text trips off the tongue," noted a reviewer in *Publishers Weekly. Little Quack's Hide and Seek,* a counting tale, uses a "Quack-u-lator" to help young readers track the ducklings, and *Little Quack's Bedtime* focuses on Mother Duck's efforts to get her offspring to sleep.

Little Quack's New Friend addresses themes of inclusion and acceptance. When his siblings shy away from Little Ribbit, who is too tiny and too green for their tastes, Little Quack takes the opportunity to splash around with the young frog, making a pal in the process. "Filled with unequivocally positive energy, this exuberant tale shows children the joy of making new friends," wrote Martha Topol in *School Library Journal*.

In Thompson's *A Christmas Gift for Mama* a work inspired by O. Henry's famous holiday story "The Gift of the Magi," a girl and her mother trade their most prized possessions to obtain Christmas gifts for one another. As the author once told *SATA:* "In my picture books for older children, such as *Love One Another: The Last*

Cover of Thompson's award-winning picture book **Polar Bear Night,** *featuring illustrations by Stephen Savage.* (Scholastic Press, 2004. Illustrations copyright © 2004 by Stephen Savage. Reprinted by permission of Scholastic Inc)

Days of Jesus, my aim is to honor the deep feelings that the bonds of love invoke. In every case, on some level, I am really writing for the child I was."

In *One Riddle, One Answer*, a book for early readers, a Persian girl is granted permission to choose her own husband from among those who correctly answer a riddle of her own devising. The riddle is a mathematical one, and reviewers noted that, along with the Persian motif, which is echoed in Linda S. Wingerter's fanciful illustrations, Thompson's folktale-like story provides an interesting segue into math units. The author "chooses her riddle wisely, since it presents a challenge for her audience, yet perspicacious readers can

solve it by themselves," remarked a contributor to *Publishers Weekly.* In *Booklist* Carolyn Phelan similarly praised Thompson's effort, concluding of *One Riddle, One Answer* that the tale "joins a growing number of enjoyable picture-book tales with mathematical themes."

Featuring illustrations by Stephen Savage, *Polar Bear Night*, a bedtime tale, is considered one of Thompson's most highly regarded works. Beckoned by the moonlight, a bear cub wakes and leaves her warm den to trek across the arctic landscape. When she reaches a snowdrift, she receives her reward: the sky is alight with a brilliant meteor shower. *Polar Bear Night* "harks back to an earlier, more technologically constrained era of bookmaking, when enduring classics were born of well-honed writing and thoughtful design," remarked *Booklist* critic Jennifer Mattson. The book was selected as a Best Illustrated Book and a Best Book of the Year by the *New York Times,* and also received a Charlotte Zolotow Honor designation in recognition of Thompson's text.

"When I was in grade school my family spent two years in the Netherlands, where I attended school, made friends, and became fluent in Dutch," Thompson once told *SATA.* "Unfortunately, I can now barely count in Dutch, but I suspect that the experience of living in two different cultures when I was so young still influences the way I see the world. In the same way, loving two very different subjects, literature and math, continues to shape my work.

"I was interested in almost every subject when I was young, but especially reading and writing my own stories—and math," Thomson explained. "I focused on the latter up through college. Yet when it came time to imagine life in the real world, I changed my course away from numbers toward my other love, words. But it seems inevitable that eventually I would write about math."

"My experience as a children's book editor has taught me a lot about structure and pacing in stories, about the importance of concision, and in picture books, leaving something of the tale for the illustrations. But I draw on my childhood rather than adult experiences when I am plumbing for book ideas. In my books for very young children, such as *Mouse's First Christmas* or *Mouse's First Halloween,* I try to put in words for them that sense of wonder and excitement they bring to everything, for everything is still new to them. I try to celebrate that sense of wonder and foster it."

Biographical and Critical Sources

PERIODICALS

Booklist, September 1, 1999, Carolyn Phelan, review of *Mouse's First Christmas,* p. 151; February 1, 2000, Shelley Townsend-Hudson, review of *Love One Another: The Last Days of Jesus,* p. 1027; September 1, 2000, Carolyn Phelan, review of *Mouse's First Halloween,* p. 135; February 1, 2001, Carolyn Phelan, review of *One Riddle, One Answer,* p. 1058; February 1, 2003, Connie Fletcher, review of *Little Quack,* p. 1002; November 15, 2005, Carolyn Phelan, review of *Mouse's First Snow,* p. 54; September 15, 2006, Carolyn Phelan, review of *Mouse's First Fall,* p. 68.

Children's Book Review Service, November, 1999, review of *Mouse's First Christmas,* p. 28; August, 2003, Gillian Engberg, review of *Mouse's First Day of School,* p. 1995; September 1, 2003, Ilene Cooper, review of *A Christmas Gift for Mama,* p. 133; November 15,

2004, Jennifer Mattson, review of *Polar Bear Night,* p. 585; March 1, 2005, Carolyn Phelan, review of *Mouse's First Spring,* p. 1206; November 15, 2005, Carolyn Phelan, review of *Mouse's First Snow,* p. 54.

Horn Book, November-December, 2004, Lauren Adams, review of *Polar Bear Night,* p. 703.

Instructor, November-December, 2001, Judy Freeman, review of *One Riddle, One Answer,* p. 16.

Kirkus Reviews, December 15, 2001, review of *Mouse's First Valentine,* p. 1763; December 15, 2002, review of *Little Quack,* p. 1858; June 15, 2003, review of *Mouse's First Day of School,* p. 865; November 1, 2003, review of *A Christmas Gift for Mama,* p. 1320; January 15, 2004, review of *Little Quack's Hide and Seek,* p. 90; October 15, 2004, review of *Polar Bear Night,* p. 1014; January 15, 2005, review of *Little Quack's Bedtime,* p. 126; December 15, 2005, review of *Little Quack's New Friend,* p. 1329.

Publishers Weekly, September 27, 1999, review of *Mouse's First Christmas,* p. 55; February 21, 2000, Elizabeth Devereaux, review of *Love One Another,* p. 55; February 19, 2001, review of *One Riddle, One Answer,* p. 91; November 11, 2002, review of *Little Quack,* p. 62; September 22, 2003, review of *A Christmas Gift for Mama,* p. 71; November 22, 2004, review of *Polar Bear Night,* p. 59.

School Library Journal, October, 1999, Maureen Wade, review of *Mouse's First Christmas,* p. 71; March, 2000, Patricia Pearl Dole, review of *Love One Another,* p. 232; August, 2000, Karen Land, review of *Mouse's First Halloween,* p. 166; April, 2001, Barbara Scotto, review of *One Riddle, One Answer,* p. 123; September, 2003, Mary Ann Carcich, review of *Mouse's First Day of School,* p. 192; October, 2003, Susan Patron, review of *A Christmas Gift for Mama,* p. 68; June, 2004, Gay Lynn Van Vleck, review of *Mouse's First Summer,* p. 120; November, 2004, Jane Marino, review of *Polar Bear Night,* p. 118; February, 2005, Lisa Gangemi Kropp, review of *Little Quack's Bedtime,* p. 110; April, 2005, Elaine Lesh Morgan, review of *Mouse's First Spring,* p. 113; February, 2006, review of *Little Quack's New Friend,* p. 111; April, 2006, Piper L. Nyman, review of *Mouse's First Snow,* p. 119; October, 2006, Susan Lissim, review of *Mouse's First Fall,* p. 128.

Washington Post Book World, February 6, 2005, Elisabeth Ward, review of *Polar Bear Night,* p. 12.

*   *   *

THONG, Roseanne

Personal

Born in Fullerton, CA; married; husband's name Francis; children: Maya. *Education:* California State University, Fullerton, B.A. (journalism, history, and American studies), M.A. (American studies, TESOL); California State University, Long Beach, earned teaching credential; Leicester University, Doctorate of Education.

Addresses

Home—Hong Kong, China. *Agent*—c/o Author Mail, Henry Holt & Co., 175 5th Ave., New York, NY 10010. *E-mail*—rosghk@gmail.com.

Roseanne Thong (Photograph courtesy of Roseanne Thong)

Career

Educator and writer. Hong Kong University School of Continuing and Professional Education, teacher of English. Worked variously as a journalist, elementary and secondary school teacher in California, Guatemala, Hong Kong, Taiwan and Vietnam.

Awards, Honors

Negative Capability's Short Fiction Contest honorable mention, 1996; Pushcart Prize for Fiction nomination, 1998; *Potato Eyes Literary Magazine* award, 1999, for short fiction; *South China Morning Post* Best Nonfiction Title of the Year listee, 2000, for *Round Is a Mooncake;* Cooperative Children's Book Center Best-of-the-Year Award, 2002, for *Red Is a Dragon; Hunger Mountain* Howard Frank Mosher Short-Story Fiction Prize finalist, 2005; *Skipping Stones* Honor Award in Multicultural Understanding, 2006, for *The Wishing Tree.*

Writings

FOR CHILDREN

Round Is a Mooncake: A Book of Shapes, illustrated by Grace Lin, Chronicle Books (San Francisco, CA), 2000.

Red Is a Dragon: A Book of Colors, illustrated by Grace Lin, Chronicle Books (San Francisco, CA), 2001.

One Is a Drummer: A Book of Numbers, illustrated by Grace Lin, Chronicle Books (San Francisco, CA), 2004.

The Wishing Tree, illustrated by Connie McLennan, Shen's Books (Fremont, CA), 2004.

Tummy Girl, illustrated by Sam Williams, Henry Holt (New York, NY), 2007.

Gai See: What You Can See in Chinatown, illustrated by Yangsook Choi, Harry Abrams (New York, NY), 2007.

FOR ADULTS

Fruit Dreams, and Other Asian Stories, Chameleon Press (Hong Kong), 2006.

Contributor to literary journals, including *American Studies Journal, Asian Pacific American Journal, Dalhousie Review, Dimsum, Evansville Review, Fiction International, Louisville Review, Lullwater Review, Northwoods Review, Poetry L.A., Potato Eyes,* and *Timber Creek Review.*

Work in Progress

Ten Friendly Fireflies, for Piggley Toes Press; *The Worst New Year,* for Lee & Low.

Sidelights

Roseanne Thong grew up in Fountain Valley, California, but has been a resident of Asia for more than fifteen years. As a teacher of English overseas, she has had the opportunity to work with students of many ages and from a number of countries, among them Guatemala, Hong Kong, Taiwan, and Vietnam. When Thong's daughter, Maya, was two years old, the family was living in Hong Kong. When Thong attempted provide Maya with English-language books about common shapes, colors, numbers, and themes found in Asia, she was unsuccessful. Her decision to write children's books to fill this need resulted in her first picture book, *Round Is a Mooncake: A Book of Shapes.*

Described by *Booklist* reviewer Connie Fletcher as an "enchanting book [that] provides a gentle lesson in shapes . . . as well as culture," *Round Is a Mooncake* features simple shapes such as circle, square, and rectangle through Thong's rhyming verse. The narrator of the book, a young Chinese girl, describes a number of items from her everyday life that contain these shapes, including "squares of dim sum and radish cakes, circles of rice bowls, and a rectangular Chinese abacus," as noted by *School Arts* reviewer Ken Marantz. Thong also includes a glossary in which she describes Chinese words and the unusual Chinese items she features throughout the book. Linda M. Kenton, reviewing *Round Is a Mooncake* for *School Library Journal,* considered the book a "useful purchase for young patrons interested in Chinese culture." A similar book by Thong, *One Is a Drummer: A Book of Numbers* was praised by *Booklist* contributor Carolyn Phelan as an "appealing counting book" that will be valuable to American children of Chinese ancestry "who want to learn a little about their heritage."

In *Red Is a Dragon: A Book of Colors* Thong creates an award-winning concept book that focuses on colors. Similar to *Round Is a Mooncake, Red Is a Dragon* contains rhyming verses that detail the colors seen in the environment of a young Chinese-American girl. Thong describes the colors of a red dragon, a jade bracelet, and a blue wishing pool with "rhymes that bounce along quite effortlessly, buoyed by the vivid colors that echo each verse," according to a *Kirkus Reviews* writer. While *School Library Journal* reviewer Marian Drabkin commented that Thong's rhymes "sometimes outweigh

A young Chinese girl's discovery of color is the subject of Roseanne Thong's **Red Is a Dragon,** *featuring illustrations by Grace Lin* (Chronicle Books, 2001. Illustrations © 2001 by Grace Lin. Used with permission of Chronicle Books, LLC, San Francisco. Visit ChronicleBooks.com)

the regard for exact description," she concluded that "concept books are always needed and this one offers a peek at Chinese-American culture." Critics have also acknowledged *Red Is a Dragon* for its universal appeal, Kay Weisman commenting in *Booklist* that the book should be a "welcome addition to preschool story hours for children of all backgrounds."

Thong moves away from the concept format in her 2005 book, *The Wishing Tree.* Depicted as a "deftly woven" picturebook by a *Children's Bookwatch* contributor, *The Wishing Tree* takes place in Hong Kong and tells the story of Ming and Ming's grandmother as they carry out the yearly tradition of visiting the Wishing Tree to make wishes for the New Year. Although Ming wishes for the recovery of his grandmother's health, the elderly woman eventually passes away, whereupon Ming ceases visiting the Wishing Tree. Many years later he resumes his visit, showing that he has come to terms with the woman's death. Corrina Austin, reviewing *The Wishing Tree* for *School Library Journal,* noted that Thong's "narrative voice has a gentle and musical quality that will lure readers into the book's pages, as well into the landscape of this lovely little corner of China." In *Booklist,* Gillian Engberg deemed *The Wishing Tree* "sentimental without being saccharine," and added that Thong's story "illustrates how traditions can help us voice our deepest wishes and emotions."

Biographical and Critical Sources

PERIODICALS

Booklist, December 1, 2000, Connie Fletcher, review of *Round Is a Mooncake: A Book of Shapes,* p. 723; No-
vember 15, 2001, Kay Weisman, review of *Red Is a Dragon: A Book of Colors,* p. 584; June 1, 2004, Carolyn Phelan, review of *One Is a Drummer;* February 1, 2005, Gillian Engberg, review of *The Wishing Tree,* p. 966.

Kirkus Reviews, September 15, 2001, review of *Red Is a Dragon,* p. 1369.

School Arts, April, 2000, Ken Marantz, review of *Round Is a Mooncake,* p. 73.

School Library Journal, August, 2000, Linda M. Kenton, review of *Round Is a Mooncake,* p. 166; January, 2002, Marian Drabkin, review of *Red Is a Dragon,* p. 111; August, 2005, Corrina Austin, review of *The Wishing Tree,* p. 107.

ONLINE

Paddy Field Web site, http://www.paddyfield.com.hk/ (October 6, 2006).

Roseanne Thong Home Page, http://www.greenfield-thong.com (October 6, 2006).*

*   *   *

TINGLE, Rebecca

Personal

Born in UT; married Bryce Tingle (an attorney); children: Miranda, Afton. *Education:* University of Utah, B.A. (English); Brigham Young University, M.A. (English with a medieval specialization); attended Oxford University.

Addresses

Home—Calgary, Alberta, Canada. *Agent*—Kraas Literary Agency, 13514 Winter Creek Ct., Houston, TX 77077.

Career

Writer. Ballet West, Salt Lake City, UT, former ballerina; Brigham Young University, Provo, UT, member of admissions committee.

Writings

FOR YOUNG ADULTS

The Edge on the Sword, G.P. Putnam's (New York, NY), 2001.
Far Traveler, G.P. Putnam's (New York, NY), 2005.

Adaptations

The Edge on the Sword was adapted for audiocassette, read by Emily Gray, Recorded Books, 2002.

Sidelights

Becoming immersed in the Anglo-Saxon past while attending Oxford University as a Rhodes Scholar in Old English literature, Rebecca Tingle has since incorporated her understanding of British history into her fictional works for young adults, which include the novels *The Edge on the Sword* and *Far Traveler.* Critics have acknowledged Tingle's novels for their historical accuracy as well as for the author's ability to engage readers through her mastery of plot development. She is also credited with possessing a knack for creating empathetic characters, many of which are strong young women.

In her first novel, *The Edge on the Sword,* Tingle spins a fictional account of Æthelflaed, the Anglo-Saxon queen who conquered the Danes in ninth-century England. *Kliatt* reviewer Sally M. Tibbetts commented that *The Edge on the Sword* is "an exciting look into medieval history, women's role and life choices, military strategies and the constant strife that was part of life." Continuing her story in *Far Traveler,* Tingle continues her saga by centering on Æthelflaed's daughter, Æfwyn.

In reviewing *The Edge on the Sword,* a *Publishers Weekly* contributor noted that "medieval history buffs will be enthralled" by the book. In the novel, fifteen-year-old Æthelflaed—the eldest daughter of King Alfred—submits to a political betrothal to King Ethelred, a man nearly twice her age. The impending marriage of Æthelflaed and Ethelred also symbolizes a union between northern and southern England, and the young bride-to-be now finds herself in an influential position.

In an effort to protect his daughter from threats to her life, King Alfred appoints Red as a bodyguard to protect the young woman until her marriage. After the wedding, Æthelflaed first rebels against Red and yearns for her independence, but with the man's help the young woman eventually develops into the leader she is meant to become. *School Library Journal* critic Starr E. Smith claimed that Tingle's "story is filled with exciting action, interesting characters, and convincing historical details of the late ninth-century that bring life to this distant and violent time in Britain." In a similar fashion, Sally Estes commented in *Booklist* that the author's "research is obvious, and her graceful, tightly plotted narrative is steeped in a tangible sense of time and place—of the culture as well as the unrest, danger, and violence."

With *Far Traveler* Tingle centers her focus on Ælfwyn, the daughter of Queen Æthelflaed. Ælfwyn, a bookish and shy sixteen year old, is very unlike her mother, who was renowned for her prowess in battle and in politics. Ælfwyn's inner strength is put to the test when her mother dies suddenly, leaving the teen alone to fend against an uncle who demands that she marry or enter a convent. Ælfwyn rebels against her uncle by disguising herself as a boy and running away. Later, she finds herself forced to choose between a new life and the security of her family. A *Kirkus Reviews* contributor, in a critique of *Far Traveler,* noted that "Tingle wears her erudition lightly, yet every detail . . . rings absolutely authentic. More importantly, her characters think and act like real Anglo-Saxons, rather than moderns in fancy dress." Ginny Gustin, reviewing the novel for *School Library Journal,* regarded *Far Traveler* as a "compelling novel . . . filled with well-researched details, an action-packed plot, and well-drawn and sympathetic characters."

Biographical and Critical Sources

PERIODICALS

Booklist, April 15, 2001, Sally Estes, review of *The Edge on the Sword,* p. 1551.
Kliatt, July, 2002, Sally M. Tibbetts, review of *The Edge on the Sword,* p. 50.
Kirkus Reviews, February 15, 2005, review of *Far Traveler,* p. 236.
Publishers Weekly, July 2, 2002, review of *The Edge on the Sword,* p. 77.
School Library Journal, July, 2001, Starr E. Smith, review of *The Edge on the Sword,* p. 114; February, 2005, review of *Far Traveler,* p. 142.

ONLINE

Penguin Group Web site, http://www.penguingroup.com/ (October 6, 2006), "Rebecca Tingle."*

TURNER, Megan Whalen 1965-

Personal

Born November 21, 1965, in Fort Sill, OK; daughter of Donald Peyton (in the U.S. military) and Nora Courtenay (Green) Whalen; married Mark Bernard Turner (a professor of English), June 20, 1987; children: John Whalen, Donald Peyton. *Education:* University of Chicago, B.A. (English language and literature; with honors), 1987. *Hobbies and other interests:* Cooking, traveling.

Addresses

Agent—c/o Greenwillow Press, 1350 Avenue of the Americas, New York, NY 10019. *E-mail*— MeganWhalenTurner@harpercollins.com.

Career

Writer. Harper Court Bookstore, Chicago, IL, children's book buyer, 1988-89; Bick's Books, Washington, DC, children's book buyer, 1991-92.

Member

Authors Guild.

Awards, Honors

Dorothy Canfield Fisher Children Book Award master listee, 1996-97, for *Instead of Three Wishes;* Newbery Honor Book Award, Notable Book and Best Book for Young Adults designations, American Library Association, Young Adult Library Services Association Best Books for Young Adults designation, New York Public Library Best Books for the Teen Age selection, and *Horn Book* Fanfare listee, all 1997, all for *The Thief;* Parents' Choice Fiction Gold Award, 2000, and Cooperative Children's Book Center Choice designation, New York Public Library Books for the Teen Age selection, and *Booklist* Top-Ten Fantasy Books for Youth listee, all 2001, all for *The Queen of Attolia.*

Writings

FICTION; FOR YOUNG ADULTS

Instead of Three Wishes (short fiction), Greenwillow Books (New York, NY), 1995.
The Thief (novel), Greenwillow Books (New York, NY), 1996.
The Queen of Attolia (novel), Greenwillow Books (New York, NY), 2000.
The King of Attolia (novel), Greenwillow Books (New York, NY), 2006.

Contributor of short fiction to anthologies, including *Firebirds: An Anthology of Original Fantasy and Science Fiction,* edited by Sharyn November, Penguin Putnam, 2003.

Megan Whalen Turner (Photograph by Alex Madonik. Reproduced by permission of Megan Whalen Turner)

Author's works have been translated into several languages, including Danish and Japanese.

Sidelights

Grounding her award-winning young-adult fiction in myth and fantasy, Megan Whalen Turner has also earned comparisons to such writers as Joan Aiken and E.L. Konigsburg due to her sense of whimsy and humor. Her acknowledgment as a talented writer came early in her career; in 1997 Turner's second published book and first novel, *The Thief,* was one of only four books to be named Newbery Honor books that year. The success of *The Thief* came as no surprise to readers who had dipped into Turner's first book, the short-story collection *Instead of Three Wishes;* the seven tales included in that book showcase her light, yet deliberate touch and ability to create likeable, realistic characters who confront the fantastic in their lives by drawing on down-to-earth common sense.

Born in Oklahoma in 1965, as the youngest of four children, Turner sampled life in several states while growing up. "When I was ten I read a lot of great books," she once recalled, "and when I couldn't easily find more, I decided I would be a writer and write stories of my own, even though it didn't sound as exciting as reading. The only impediment to beginning my career right then was that I couldn't think of anything to write."

For inspiration, the young Turner looked to her favorite writers. "Joan Aiken said she saw stories all around her, prompted by everyday events. . . . She'd been telling stories since birth and completed her first novel in Latin class when she was seventeen. And there I was ten years old without a rag of a story to call my own. Roald Dahl said he kept a notebook in which he scribbled his ideas so that he wouldn't forget them." While the young Turner recognized that "this sounded sensible," when she attempted the same strategy "the idea just sat there on the page. It did not magically turn into a story the way it was supposed to. So much for Roald Dahl."

Attending the University of Chicago after high school, Turner studied Greek history, a required course for freshmen. There she was particularly influenced by a reading of Thucydides' history of the Peloponnesian war. Then, during her junior year, Turner's love of writing resurfaced. "I had to choose a field and begin a senior project," she recalled. "I thought that writing had to be easier than sitting down to read, say, *The Mill on the Floss,* and I proposed to study children's literature and write some of my own."

Frustrated by her college writing efforts, Turner got a job as a children's book buyer after graduation, and spent seven years in that career, first in Chicago and then again in Washington, DC. Meanwhile, she married Mark Turner, a professor of English at the University of Maryland. Because of her husband's research, the couple traveled extensively, spending time in Princeton, New Jersey, as well as to several colleges in California. 1992 found the couple in Del Mar, California, where Mark Turner was serving a year-long Guggenheim fellowship. Having left her buyer's job, Turner decided to start writing again, penning several of the stories that would appear in her first published work. "I was pregnant with my first child and my schedule was not so full then," the author explained in an interview for *Authors and Artist for Young Adults.* "After Jack came along, Mark agreed to take him for long stretches so that I could write, but that was all I was supposed to do. NO DISHES."

Aimed at middle-grade readers, *Instead of Three Wishes* contains seven stories in which unexpected magic alters the lives of ordinary people. In the title story a little girl repeatedly refuses the offer of three wishes from an elf dressed in a business suit, while "Aunt Charlotte and the NGA Portraits" finds a young girl stepping into a painting in order to find a missing object. Other tales in Turner's imaginative debut introduce readers to a New Hampshire town in the throes of a leprechaun hunt, a ghost who haunts a factory and snares the heart of a young worker, and a modern-day boy named Leroy, who is transported back to the Viking heyday to save a frustrated monarch from an infestation of cockroaches.

The intersection between the everyday and the fantastic in *Instead of Three Wishes* impressed reviewers and readers like. Turner's prose style "helps the reader easily suspend disbelief," noted a *Book Report* critic, while a *Publishers Weekly* reviewer cited the author's "expansive" style and her ability to salt her mix of realistic background details and magic with a dash of wit. In *School Library Journal* Jane Gardner Connor wrote that the author's "mild humor . . . will elicit gentle chuckles and smiles," and Sarah Guille noted in *Horn Book* that Turner "combines a shrewd wit with an eye for the endearingly absurd." While each story resonates with history and the "eternal truths" echoing throughout much of literature, Carolyn Phelan maintained in *Booklist* that the "real magic" of *Instead of Three Wishes* is its author's "ability to convince readers that the realms of fairy tales can intersect with contemporary life."

Published the year after *Instead of Three Wishes,* Turner's debut novel *The Thief* was inspired by a vacation she and her husband took to Greece, where they became steeped in the history and landscape of the

Cover of Turner's 1996 middle-grade novel The Thief, *a Newbery Honor Book featuring artwork by Walter Gaffney-Kessell.* (Greenwillow Books, 1996. Jacket art © 1996 by Walter Gaffney-Kessell. Used by permission Harper-Collins Publishers)

Mediterranean. The intricately plotted novel introduces readers to the enigmatic Gen. An expert thief, Gen—short for Eugenides—lives in Eddis, a country very similar to ancient Greece, where life is overseen by a pantheon of gods. Imprisoned after boasting that he can steal anything, even if it belongs to the king, Gen is unexpectedly released from his dungeon cell on the orders of a scholarly man who is magus to the greedy King of Sounis. As readers soon discover, the magus's interest in the boastful thief stems from his own desire to gain possession of a legendary stone known as Hamiathes' Gift, which will give to its owner control of a neighboring kingdom. Ordered to seek out this stone, Gen is joined on his quest by the magus, several soldiers, and a group of aristocrats. The travelers eventually reach their goal: a temple maze that remains hidden under water for all but two days each year, whereupon readers discover what a *Publishers Weekly* reviewer called "one of the most valuable treasures of all—a twinkling jewel of a surprise ending."

Along with several awards came heaps of critical praise for *The Thief.* In *School Library Journal,* for example, Patricia A. Dollisch praised the novel's clever protagonist, writing that Turner "does a phenomenal job of creating real people to range through her well-plotted, evenly paced story." Citing the book's "believable characters" and "well-realized setting," Phelan called *The Thief* "a refreshing change of pace for readers who enjoy adventure stories with a touch of magic." In *Horn Book,* Martha V. Parravano added special praise for Turner's hero, writing that Gen "is simply superb: she lets the reader know so much about him—his sense of humor, his egotism, his loyalty, his forthrightness, his tendency to sulk," all the while "manag[ing] to hide the most essential information" to keep the denouement in shadow. A *Kirkus Reviews* contributor maintained that, in reading of the young man's adventures, "no adolescent will be able to ignore Gen's resentment, embarrassment, and pain, made palpable through Turner's compassion and crystalline prose."

The Thief proved to be the first volume in a trio of novels that feature Gen. In *The Queen of Attolia* the young man shows that he has well-honed his survival skills when he finds himself a pawn in the war between the queens of Attolia and Eddis (the latter being his cousin). Having previously incurred the animus of the queen of Attolia, Gen suffers when he is captured by her troops: she order his hand cut off before casting him out and leaving him to make his way back to Eddis. Surviving this ordeal, Gen becomes involved in a plan to kidnap the queen, but the complex plan backfires when he recognizes his love for her and ultimately becomes her king. Calling *The Queen of Attolia* a "spellbinder of a sequel" to *The Thief,* a *Publishers Weekly* writer praised Turner's second novel as "every bit as devilishly well plotted and grandly conceived" as her first, and also praised the author's dramatic flair and "engrossing" storyline. Although Bruce Anne Shook described the battle scenes as "lengthy and tedious" in her *School Li-*

A thief faces one of his greatest challenges in Turner's spellbinding fantasy novel **The Queen of Attolia.** (Eos, 2006. Jacket art © 2006 by Vince Natale. Used by permission of HarperCollins Publishers)

brary Journal review, she also deemed the novel "a story of love and war in which love wins out." While noting that *The Queen of Attolia* requires a familiarity with *The Thief* in order to follow its complicated intrigue, *Booklist* critic Sally Estes wrote that Turner "maintains her well-created world and believable characterizations."

Gen has risen to the level of ruler by the time readers open the first pages of *The King of Attolia,* which *Horn Book* reviewer Deirdre F. Baker praised as "one of the most fascinating and original children's fantasies to appear in years." Unfortunately for Turner's hero, Gen's assumption of the Attolian throne upon marriage to the kingdom's queen has not won the slippery thief many friends. The soldier Costis counts himself among King Eugenides' many enemies, and balks when he is ordered to serve as the novice monarch's bodyguard. Costis's antipathy mellows into a grudging affection, however, as he begins to understand Gen's complex character. Within her story Turner inserts "well-constructed puzzles and intrigues," as a *Kirkus Reviews* writer noted, the critic adding that readers can also enjoy her inclusion of "characteristic secrets and subtle revelations."

Focusing more on relationships between characters than on the ongoing battle between Eddis and Attolia, *The King of Attolia* centers on "the amazingly charismatic and beguiling character of Eugenides," according to *School Library Journal* contributor Sharon Rawlins. Continuing the admonition of past critics, Rawlings added that to best enjoy Turner's series the three novels should be read in order. As with her other works, Turner "excels in intrigue," Claire Rosser explained in *Kliatt*, and tantalizes readers by slowly revealing that "people and situations [are] not . . . what they appear to be." Predicting that fans of the series will "devour" *The King of Attolia*, a *Publishers Weekly* reviewer dubbed Turner's third novel a "complex tapestry" richly woven with "ample detail."

Biographical and Critical Sources

PERIODICALS

Booklist, October 1, 1995, Carolyn Phelan, review of *Instead of Three Wishes,* p. 309; January 1, 1997, Carolyn Phelan, review of *The Thief,* p. 863; April 15, 2000, Sally Estes, review of *The Queen of Attolia,* p. 1543; January 1, 2006, review of *The King of Attolia,* p. 86.

Book Report, December, 1995.

Horn Book, May-June 1996, Sarah Guille, review of *Instead of Three Wishes,* p. 337; December 1996, Martha V. Parravano, review of *The Thief,* p. 747; March-April, 2006, Deirdre F. Baker, review of *The King of Attolia,* p. 195.

Kirkus Reviews, June 15, 1996, review of *The Thief;* December 15, 2005, review of *The King of Attolia,* p. 1329.

Kliatt, March, 2000, Claire Rosser, review of *The Queen of Attolia;* January, 2006, Claire Rosser, review of *The King of Attolia,* p. 14.

Locus, September, 2003, review of *Firebirds: An Anthology of Original Fantasy and Science Fiction.*

New York Times Book Review, November 5, 1995, review of *Instead of Three Wishes,* p. 31.

Publishers Weekly, July 24, 1995, p. 66; October 21, 1996, review of *The Thief,* p. 84; May 1, 2000, review of *The Queen of Attolia,* p. 71; January 16, 2006, review of *The King of Attolia,* p. 65.

School Library Journal, September 1995, Jane Gardner Connor, review of *Instead of Three Wishes,* p. 204; October 1996, Patricia A. Dollisch, review of *The Thief,* p. 150; May, 2000, Bruce Anne Shook, review of *The Queen of Attolia,* p. 176; February, 2006, Sharon Rawlins, review of *The King of Attolia,* p. 138.

ONLINE

Megan Whalen Turner Home Page, http://home.att.net/~mwturner (November 2, 2006).*

U-V

UHLBERG, Myron 1933-

Personal

Born 1933, in Brooklyn, NY; married; wife's name Karen; children: three.

Addresses

Home—Palm Springs, CA. *Agent*—c/o Author Mail, Peachtree Publishers, 1700 Chattahoochee Ave., Atlanta, GA 30318.

Career

Children's writer. Formerly worked in business; retired.

Awards, Honors

Comstock Book Award, Livingston Lord Library, and Schneider Family Book Award, both 2006, both for *Dad, Jackie, and Me.*

Writings

CHILDREN'S BOOKS

Flying over Brooklyn, illustrated by Gerald Fitzgerald, Peachtree (Atlanta, GA), 1999.
Mad Dog McGraw, illustrated by Lydia Monks, G.P. Putnam (New York, NY), 2000.
Lemuel, the Fool, illustrated by Sonja Lamut, Peachtree (Atlanta, GA), 2001.
The Printer, illustrated by Henri Sorensen, Peachtree (Atlanta, GA), 2003.
Dad, Jackie, and Me, illustrated by Colin Bootman, Peachtree (Atlanta, GA), 2005.

Sidelights

Myron Uhlberg, a retired businessman, writes children's books that are sometimes based on his own experiences as a youth growing up in Brooklyn, New York. For ex-
ample, his first book, *Flying over Brooklyn,* is based partially on Uhlberg's memory of the Great Blizzard of 1947, which dropped several feet of snow on the New York metropolitan area. Told through the eyes of a child narrator, the story follows the boy as he is suddenly swept away from a snow bank by a gust of wind and then flies over the snow-covered rooftops and streets, past Ebbets Field, and on to Coney Island. The experience turns out to be a dream, but when the boy awakes he is greeted by the real snowstorm and the dreary city streets have been transformed into a winter wonderland. A *Publishers Weekly* contributor called the story "more lyrical than plot-driven" and added that the author and illustrator "create an enchanted vision of Brooklyn transformed but ever itself." Writing in *Booklist,* GraceAnne A. DeCandido commented that the illustration pairs with Uhlberg's "poetic text [to] make this a satisfying winter read-aloud."

In *Mad Dog McGraw* Uhlberg tells the story of a young boy who eventually wins over a dog that is terrorizing his neighborhood. Initially the boy tries various ways of getting around the dog, even to the point of offering up a cat appropriately named Bait. But in the end, on the advice of his mother, the boy offers the dog a biscuit, leading to a new friendship. In a review for *School Library Journal,* Joy Fleishhacker commented that "the story is told in short, action-filled sentences that perfectly suit a child's voice." *Booklist* contributor Linda Perkins wrote that, "warm but never sappy," *Mad Dog McGraw* "rates 'two paws up.'"

Lemuel, the Fool is based on an old Yiddish folk tale and tells the story of a man who dreams of the magical city he believes is located beyond the horizon of his fishing village. The man eventually leaves behind his wife and children and sails off to find his dream city. Through careful navigation, he arrives at his destination and is wonderstruck that everything seems to be the same, down to a house just like his own and a woman who looks exactly like his wife and who shares the same name. The adventurer never realizes he has actually sailed in a circle and returned to his own home,

Myron Uhlberg's memories of time spent with his father inspired Dad, Jackie, and Me, *featuring illustrations by Colin Bootman.* (Peachtree Publishers, 2005. Illustrations © 2005 by Colin Bootman. Reproduced by permission)

and his wife and family never tell him differently when he sets sail once again, desirous of returning home. Martha Link, writing in *School Library Journal,* noted that "story and pictures combine to form a fine choice for most collections," while *Booklist* contributor Hazel Rochman commented that "the fun is in the straight-faced comedy and lively pictures."

Uhlberg draws once gain on his own experience, this time as the son of deaf parents, for his book *The Printer.* The story revolves around a young boy who recounts the tale of his father, a man who, because of his deafness, is largely ignored by his coworkers at the printing press of a large city newspaper. However, when fire breaks out, their special skills enable the boy's father and his other deaf coworkers to warn their colleagues and save lives, thus earning coworkers' eternal gratitude

and a newfound appreciation for the value of sign language. "The simplicity of the story gives the text its drama, and its message of caring for one's fellow humans is powerful," wrote Nancy Menaldi-Scanlan in *School Library Journal.*

In *Dad, Jackie, and Me* Uhlberg revisits his childhood and recounts how his deaf father was affected by the signing of Jackie Robinson playing for the Brooklyn Dodgers baseball team. Robinson was the first African American to play major-league baseball, and Uhlberg's father identified with the athlete as someone who was looked at unfavorably by much of the rest of society. At first, the boy in the story feels ashamed by his father's unabashed support of Robinson, but he soon accepts the ballplayer just as his father does. In a climatic ending, the father catches a ball thrown straight to him by Robinson, in the player's thanks for the man's garbled cheers throughout the season. "The endpapers, an actual scrapbook of old newspaper articles about Robinson, provide a satisfying context for this ultimately upbeat, multi-dimensional story," wrote a *Kirkus Reviews* contributor, while in *Booklist* Bill Ott praised the book's "moving finale" as well as the "evocative watercolors" by Colin Bootman. According to Marilyn Taniguchi, in her review for *School Library Journal*, the "strength" of Uhlberg's story "lies in its depiction of the bond between father and son."

Biographical and Critical Sources

PERIODICALS

Booklist, December 1, 1999, GraceAnne A. DeCandido, review of *Flying over Brooklyn,* p. 707; August, 2000, Linda Perkins, review of *Mad Dog McGraw,* p. 2150; April 15, 2001, Hazel Rochman, review of *Lemuel, the Fool,* p. 1567; September 1, 2003, Hazel Rochman, review of *The Printer,* p. 131; August, 2005, Bill Ott, review of *Dad, Jackie, and Me,* p. 2036.

Kirkus Reviews, August 1, 2003, review of *The Printer,* p. 1025; March 1, 2005, review of *Dad, Jackie, and Me,* p. 297.

Publishers Weekly, October 4, 1999, review of *Flying over Brooklyn,* p. 74; February 7, 2005, review of *Dad, Jackie, and Me,* p. 59.

School Library Journal, August, 2000, Joy Fleishhacker, review of *Mad Dog McGraw,* p. 166; August, 2001, Martha Link, review of *Lemuel, the Fool,* p. 164; December, 2003, Nancy Menaldi-Scanlan, review of *The Printer,* p. 129; May, 2005, Marilyn Taniguchi, review of *Dad, Jackie, and Me,* p. 103.

ONLINE

Educational Paperback Association Web site, http://www.edupaperback.org/ (November 2, 2006), "Myron Uhlberg."*

*   *   *

van ROSSUM, Heleen 1962-

Personal

Born November 8, 1962, in Utrecht, Netherlands; immigrated to England, 1990, then United States, 1995; married; children: two. *Education:* University of Amsterdam, degree (modern history), 1989; University London, studied archive studies, 1991-92.

Addresses

Home—NJ. *E-mail*—heleen@hvanrossum.com.

Career

Author and illustrator, beginning c. 1998. Formerly worked as an archivist in Oxford, England, then Princeton, NJ.

Awards, Honors

Listed among Ten Best Picture Books in the Netherlands, 2004, and Book Sense Children's Picks listee, 2005, both for *Will You Carry Me?*

Writings

Goedemorgen, Meneer Stukjes, illustrated by Tijn Snoodijk, Zirkoon (Amsterdam, Netherlands), 2003.

Wil je me Dragen?, illustrated by Peter van Harmelen, Zirkoon (Amsterdam, Netherlands), 2004, translated as *Will You Carry Me?,* Kane/Miller (La Jolla, CA), 2005.

Tim doeth het niet, illustrated by Peter van Harmelen, Zirkoon (Amsterdam, Netherlands), 2005.

Author's works have been translated into Italian.

Biographical and Critical Sources

PERIODICALS

Children's Bookwatch, April, 2005, review of *Will You Carry Me?*

Kirkus Reviews, January 15, 2005, review of *Will You Carry Me?,* p. 126.

Margriet (Netherlands), September 29-October 6, 2006, interview with Van Rossum.

Publishers Weekly, April 4, 2005, review of *Will You Carry Me?,* p. 58.

School Library Journal, June, 2005, Marge Loch-Wouters, review of *Will You Carry Me?,* p. 130.

ONLINE

Heleen Van Rossum Home Page, http://www.hvanrossum.com (October 10, 2006).

Kane/Miller Book Publishers Web site, http://kanemiller.com/ (October 10, 2006), "Heleen van Rossum."

Zirkoon Web site, http://www.zirkoon.nl/ (October 10, 2006), "Heleen van Rossum."

*   *   *

VEGA, Denise B.

Personal

Born December 10, in CO; married; children: Zachary, Jesse, Rayanne. *Education:* University of California, Los Angeles, B.A. (motion-picture television); Harvard University, Ed.M. *Hobbies and other interests:* Fishing, hiking, camping, swimming, watching movies, reading.

Addresses

Home—P.O. Box 101596, Denver, CO 80250-1596. *E-mail*—readermail@denisevega.com.

Career

Children's book author; former technical writer.

Member

Authors Guild, Colorado Authors League, International Reading Association (member, Colorado Council), Society of Children's Book Writers and Illustrators (Rocky Mountain chapter, co-regional advisor).

Awards, Honors

Lee & Low Books New Voices Honor Award for unpublished manuscript, 2001, for *Superhombre;* Top-Shelf Fiction for Middle-School Readers designation, *Voice of Youth Advocates,* 2005, for *Click Here (To Find Out How I Survived Seventh Grade).*

Writings

JUVENILE FICTION

Click Here (To Find out How I Survived Seventh Grade) (middle-grade novel), Little, Brown (New York, NY), 2005.

Contributor of short fiction to periodicals, including *Pockets.*

NONFICTION

WordPerfect for Legal Professionals, Version 5.1, CFMS (Jacksonville, FL) 1992.
Groupwise for Windows 3.1 on the Job Essentials, Que Corporation (Indianapolis, IN), 1996.
Groupwise for Windows 3.1 on the Job Essentials Instructor's Manual, Que Corporation (Indianapolis, IN), 1996.
WordPerfect 101 for the Law Office: A Guide to Basic Document Production, ABA Section of Law Practice Management (Chicago, IL), 1996.
WordPerfect 201 for the Law Office: A Guide to Advanced Document Production, ABA Section of Law Practice Management (Chicago, IL), 1996.
Discover WordPerfect Suite 8, IDG Books Worldwide (Foster City, CA), 1997.
WordPerfect 7 for Windows '95 Essentials, Level II, Que E & T (Indianapolis, IN), 1997.
WordPerfect 7 for Windows '95 Essentials Level III, Que E & T (Indianapolis, IN), 1997.
(With Shelley O'Hara and Julia Kelly) *Discover Office '97,* IDG Books Worldwide (Foster City, CA), 1997.
Learning the Internet for Kids: A Voyage to Internet Treasures, DDC (New York, NY), 1998.
Word Processing for Kids, illustrated by Ryan Sather, DDC (New York, NY), 1999.

Work in Progress

Two multicultural toddler books; a sequel to *Click Here.*

Sidelights

Although Coloradoan Denise B. Vega wrote her first novel when she was fifteen years old, she had to wait for many years to see her first work of fiction published. By the time that book, the middle-grade novel *Click Here (To Find Out How I Survived Seventh Grade),* reached bookstore shelves, Vega was no stranger to the publishing process; she had already made a success out of writing instructional books for popular computer programs, and had even penned a few computer books for young readers.

"I always wanted to be a writer and I always wrote," Vega explained on her home page, "but I started out writing a lot of magazine articles, computer books, and other stuff like that for adults to help keep our family in toilet paper and chocolate chip cookies." In *Click Here* she focuses on a preteen protagonist who shares Vega's

Cover of Denise Vega's novel **Click Here,** *a humorous middle-grade saga written in secret-diary format.* (Little, Brown, and Company, 2006. Cover photography © Lucky Pix. Other photos courtesy of Getty Images. Reproduced by permission)

own interest in computers. Self-conscious Erin Swift thinks her feet are too big; in evaluating her life she believes the only thing she is good at is working on the computer and writing on her secret Web log. Entering middle school, she immediately encounters disappointment when she realizes that best friend Jilly is in another class. To make matters worse, Erin is forced into a dreaded confrontation with her arch nemesis, a classmate named Serena. As romance develops and jealousy and heartache follow, Erin vents her rollercoaster emotions on her blog, but when the confidential e-diary is accidentally posted online for friends and classmates to see, her honesty threatens the relationships she values most.

In a review of *Click Here* for *School Library Journal*, Linda L. Plevak commented that Vega's "characters and situations are believable, and readers will relate to and sympathize with Erin's dilemmas." A *Publishers Weekly* contributor called the story "a heartfelt book about a girl becoming her own person," while in *Kirkus Reviews* a critic praised the "the blog segments and first-person narration" as "immediate and funny." Hillary Williamson, in an online review for *BookLoons*, commended Vega's novel "for its excellent portrayal of the self-conscious vulnerability of the early teens, and of a girl growing out of a friend's shadow into her own strength of character." Angela Etheridge called *Click Here* "one of the funniest, most entertaining novels I have read in a long time" in her online review for the *Romance Readers Connection*, and added that Vega's story "will keep all readers laughing and begging for more!"

Biographical and Critical Sources

PERIODICALS

Girls' Life, April-May, 2005, review of *Click Here (To Find Out How I Survived Seventh Grade),* p. 36.

Kirkus Reviews, March 1, 2005, review of *Click Here,* p. 297.

Publishers Weekly, April 4, 2005, review of *Click Here,* p. 60.

School Library Journal, May, 2005, Linda L. Plevak, review of *Click Here,* p. 140.

Voice of Youth Advocates, June, 2005, Arlene Garcia, review of *Click Here,* p. 140.

ONLINE

BookLoons, http://www.bookloons.com/ (August 24, 2005), Hilary Williamson, review of *Click Here.*

Denise Vega Home Page, http://www.denisevega.com (October 24, 2006).

Lee & Low Books Web site, http://www.leeandlow.com/ (October 10, 2006), "Denise Vega."

Romance Readers Connection, http://www.theromancereadersconnection.com/ (August 24, 2005), Angela Etheridge, review of *Click Here.*

Society of Children's Book Writers and Illustrators: Rocky Mountain Chapter Web site, http://www.rmcscbwi.org/ (October 10, 2006), "Denise Vega."

Time Warner Bookmark Web Site, "Denise Vega," http://www.twbookmark.com/ (October 10, 2006).

W-Y

WAITE, Judy

Personal
Born in England; children: two daughters.

Addresses
Home—Southhampton, England. *Agent*—c/o Author Mail, Atheneum Books for Young Readers/Simon & Schuster, 1230 Avenue of the Americas, New York, NY 10020. *E-mail*—judy@judywaite.com.

Career
Teacher in Hampshire, England, including at Locks Heath Junior High School; South Wonston School, writer-in-residence, 2002; Southhampton University, tutor in creative-writing program; visiting author and leader of writing workshops and clubs.

Awards, Honors
Best Picture Book designation, English Association, 1998, and Nevada Young Readers Award, and Children's Book Award, Florida Reading Association, both 2001, all for *Mouse, Look Out!*; Children's Book Federation Award, 1999, for translation of *Laura's Star* by Klaus Baumgart.

Writings

PICTURE BOOKS

Mouse, Look Out!, illustrated by Norma Burgin, Dutton Children's Books (New York, NY), 1998.
The Storm Seal, illustrated by Neil Reed, Crocodile Books (New York, NY), 1998.
The Stray Kitten, Crocodile Books (New York, NY), 2000.
Nanuark: A Bear in the Wilderness, illustrated by Norma Burgin, Little Tiger (London, England), 2003.

Look out the Window Picture Book, Big Book Rigby (Oxford, England), 2003.
Digging for Dinosaurs ("Flying Foxes" series), illustrated by Garry Parsons, Crabtree Publishing (New York, NY), 2004.

Also author of *Fox Beware* and *I Wish I Had a Monster.*

"HORSE HEALER" NOVEL SERIES

Eclipse, Hippo (London, England), 1999.
Puzzle, Hippo (London, England), 1999.
Sapphire, Hippo (London, England), 1999.
Starlight, Hippo (London, England), 2000.

YOUNG-ADULT NOVELS

Shopaholic, Oxford University Press (Oxford, England), 2001, Atheneum Books for Young Readers (New York, NY), 2003.
Shadow, Walker (London, England), 2002.
A Trick of the Mind, Oxford University Press (Oxford England), 2003, Atheneum Books for Young Readers (New York, NY), 2005.
Forbidden, Oxford University Press (Oxford, England), 2004, Atheneum Books for Young Readers (New York, NY), 2006.

MIDDLE-GRADE READERS

Cheat!, Heinemann Educational (Oxford, England), 1999.
Star Striker, Heinemann Educational (Oxford, England), 1999.
Deep Water, Heinemann Educational (Oxford, England), 1999.
The Singing Princess, Rigby Literacy (Oxford, England), 2000.
(With Andrew Melrose) *Foul Play,* Rigby Literacy (Oxford, England), 2000.
A Mammoth Mistake, Rigby Literacy (Oxford, England), 2000.

Tiger Hunt, Rigby Literacy (Oxford, England), 2000.

A Prince among Donkeys, Rigby Literacy (Oxford, England), 2000.

Eerie Encounters, Rigby Literacy (Oxford, England), 2000.

Pet Rescue, Heinemann Educational (Oxford, England), 2000.

Animal Heroes, Heinemann Educational (Oxford, England), 2000.

Robbie in the River, Ginn & Company (Oxford, England), 2000.

TRANSLATOR

Klaus Baumgart, *Laura's Secret,* Tiger Tales (Wilton, CT), 2003.

Klaus Baumgart, *Laura's Christmas Star,* Tiger Tales (Wilton, CT), 2003.

Also translator of picture books *Laura's Star* and *Too Scary* by Baumgart, both both published by Magi Publications.

OTHER

Contributor of poems and short stories to anthologies, including *Essentail Texts,* Heinemann Educational, 1998; *Phenomenal Future Stories,* Corgi Books, 1999; *The Hairy Hamster Hunt,* edited by Tony Bradman, 1999; and *Werewolf Granny,* Bloomsbury Publishing, 1999.

Sidelights

British children's writer Judy Waite has produced picture books, intermediate-level readers, and teen fiction. Born in England and raised in Singapore, she began writing picture books when her daughters were young and now writes for children at all levels. Waite's popular "Horse Healer" novel series for middle-graders follows the adventures of a gypsy boy who has a gift for healing horses, while her young-adult novels focus on teens challenged in their search for autonomy by unusual and often restrictive circumstances. Waite has also written many educational books for England's early elementary school curriculum. In addition, she has translated from the German several children's books written and illustrated by Klaus Baumgart.

Featuring illustrations by Norma Burgin, Waite's award-winning picture book *Mouse, Look Out!* is about a mouse being stalked by a black cat in a spooky abandoned house. Waite keeps the stalking just short of scary as the mouse hides in ivy-covered walls, the bristles of a broom, an old shoe, and assorted other nooks and crannies. In each scene, the mouse is warned that "there's a cat about" on pages that display the eyes of an owl. Cobwebs, autumn leaves, and other darker accents are balanced with a teddy bear and a straw hat. As the story continues, it becomes evident that there is also a dog about. A *Publishers Weekly* contributor noted that these "layers of one watching the other, reader, owl and cat, heighten the suspense, and the surprise ending" in Waite's unique picture book.

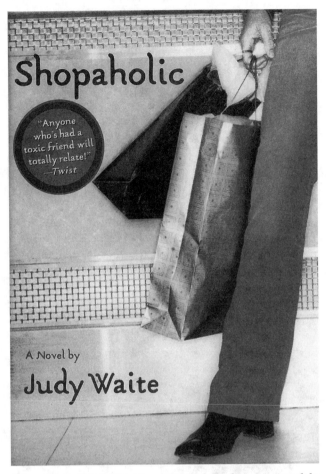

Cover of Judy Waite's 2001 YA novel Shopaholic, *featuring artwork by Raquel Jaramillo.* (Simon Pulse, 2004. Cover photograph copyright © 2003 by Leland Bobbe/Getty Images)

The Storm Seal presents the tale of an injured seal pup that, rescued from a net by a compassionate sailor, is nursed back to health. When the kindly sailor becomes ill, the neighborhood children take over the little seal's care, but they get carried away, dressing it and trying to teach the sea creature tricks. Ultimately, the sailor explains to the children that this is wrong; the seal is a wild animal that must be returned to the sea when its strength returns. Reviewing the book for *School Library Journal,* Marianne Saccardi wrote that "Waite's sometimes lyrical text takes readers from the 'exploding night' of the storm to the satisfying moment of the seal's return to the sea."

Waite's first young-adult novel, *Shopaholic* focuses on fourteen-year-old Taylor, a British teen who feels responsible for the drowning death of her younger sister. In response, she takes over most of the household chores, hoping to relieve the burden placed on her still-grieving mother. When Taylor's childhood friends Sophie and Sam begin drifting away, the teen soon finds a new friend in Kat, a beautiful but troubled girl who aspires to be a model. Desperate to maintain this new friendship, the lonely Taylor dips into the weekly household allowance provided by her grandfather for family support and uses the funds to pay for Kat's self-indulgent shopping sprees. Taylor's mother begins to see Kat's manipulation of her daughter after she is put on a new medication for her depression, and she helps Kat explore the facts surrounding her sister's death and begin the healing process.

Deborah Stevenson, reviewing *Shopaholic* for the *Bulletin of the Center for Children's Books,* noted that, despite the fact that shopping is an integral part of most teen's lives, there are "few books that really address it." In addition to successfully avoiding "heavy-handedly hammering home the moral of responsibility, Waite captures the pleasures and temptations of the mall," the critic added. In *School Library Journal,* Catherine Ensley called the book "an engaging, emotionally wrenching read," while a *Publishers Weekly* contributor concluded that, although "dark in places," *Shopaholic* "winds to a brighter and satisfying close."

Erin and Matt, the teen protagonists of Waite's YA novel *A Trick of the Mind,* are outsiders who each struggle to

Waite spins a futuristic story about a teen questioning her secluded world in the novel Forbidden, *featuring cover artwork by Sammy J. Yuen.* (Atheneum Books For Young Readers, 2006. Photograph of girl copyright © 2006 by Lisa Kimmell/Photonica/Getty Images. Reproduced by permission of Atheneum Books For Young Readers, an imprint of Simon & Schuster Macmillan)

come to terms with their fatherless childhoods and their personal identity. Erin is an amateur magician, while Matt is considered strange and a troublemaker. The couple meet when Erin begins hanging out with her friends Kristy and Billy; while Erin falls for Matt, he becomes infatuated with Kristy. When Matt does pay attention to Erin, she misinterprets his admiration and desire for friendship as something more. *Kliatt* reviewer Janis Flint-Ferguson wrote of Waite's compelling novel that, "in the end, Matt develops an identity and a cause, while Erin continues to struggle between reality and illusion."

Among Waite's other works for teen readers is *Forbidden,* a dark story about young people caught up in a cult. Featuring a shocking conclusion, the story finds fifteen-year-old Elinor forced to stay focused on dictates of the True Cause. However, she becomes distracted by her attraction to Jamie, one of the people called "Outsiders," with whom she is forbidden to have contact. In *Kliatt,* Ferguson called the novel "a compelling look at the inside workings of a religious cult," while Jack Forman concluded in *School Library Journal* that Waite's story "moves quickly to a message-laden climax that readers will not soon forget." In a *Kirkus Reviews* appraisal, a critic deemed *Forbidden* "gripping and memorable," and featuring an "absorbing inside perspective" narrated by Waite's troubled protagonist.

Biographical and Critical Sources

PERIODICALS

Booklist, October 1, 1998, Lauren Peterson, review of *Mouse, Look Out!,* p. 337; May 1, 2003, Francisca Goldsmith, review of *Shopaholic,* p. 1589; March 15, 2005, Debbie Carton, review of *Trick of the Mind,* p. 1288.

Bulletin of the Center for Children's Books, June, 2003, Deborah Stevenson, review of *Shopaholic,* p. 425.

Kirkus Reviews, May 1, 2003, review of *Shopaholic,* p. 685; January 1, 2005, review of *Trick of the Mind,* p. 58; December 15, 2005, review of *Forbidden,* p. 1329.

Kliatt, January, 2005, Janis Flint-Ferguson, review of *Trick of the Mind,* p. 11, and Amanda MacGregor, review of *Shopaholic,* p. 18; January, 2006, Janis Flint-Ferguson, review of *Forbidden,* p. 14.

Publishers Weekly, August 17, 1998, review of *Mouse, Look Out!,* p. 72; May 5, 2003, review of *Shopaholic,* p. 222; January 31, 2005, review of *Trick of the Mind,* p. 69.

School Library Journal, December, 1998, Marianne Saccardi, review of *The Storm Seal,* p. 94; September, 2000, Jody McCoy, review of *The Stray Kitten,* p. 210; July, 2003, Catherine Ensley, review of *Shopaholic,* p. 135; January, 2004, Sally R. Dow, review of *Laura's Secret,* p. 87; June, 2005, Christine McGinty, review of *Trick of the Mind,* p. 172; March, 2006, Jack Forman, review of *Forbidden,* p. 232.

ONLINE

Judy Waite Home Page, http://www.judywaite.com (October 30, 2006).
Word Pool Web site, http://www.wordpool.co.uk/ (March 7, 2005), "Judy Waite."*

*   *   *

WASSERSTEIN, Wendy 1950-2006

OBITUARY NOTICE— See index for *SATA* sketch: Born October 18, 1950, in New York, NY; died of lymphoma, January 30, 2006, in New York, NY. Actress and author. Wasserstein was a Tony Award-and Pulitzer Prize-winning playwright best known for writing *The Heidi Chronicles.* Growing up as the daughter of well-to-do Jewish parents, she initially intended to study either law or medicine for a career after leaving Mount Holyoke College, where she graduated with a degree in intellectual history in 1971. A writing course at Smith College during one summer changed her mind, however. She studied creative writing at the City College of New York, taking classes from such renowned figures as Joseph Heller and Israel Horvitz. In 1973, she had her first success with the play *Any Woman Can't,* which was produced Off-Broadway. Completing her master's degree that same year, she then went to Yale University, graduating with an M.F.A. in 1976. Writing while holding down a job delivering scripts for the Eugene O'Neill Theater, her next success came with *Uncommon Women and Others,* which was produced by Playwrights Horizons in 1977. Noticing that not many authors were writing scripts about the kinds of people she knew and had grown up with—middle-class, Jewish, liberal women— Wasserstein felt that someone should write plays about them. Her 1983 play, *Isn't It Romantic,* earned her a grant, which she used to travel to London and write her best-known work, *The Heidi Chronicles* (1988). The Pulitzer Award-winning play, which chronicles the decades of the 1960s through the 1980s, was praised for offering a unique feminist view of those years. This was followed by another play with similarly strong female characters, *The Sisters Rosensweig,* which won an Outer Critics Circle award and a Tony nomination when produced at Lincoln Center in 1992. Her last plays include *Psyche in Love* (2004) and *Third* (2005). In addition to her dramas, Wasserstein also penned scripts for television, including an adaptation of her own work, *Uncommon Women and Others* (1978); a children's book titled *Pamela's First Musical* (1996); and the autobiographical *Shiksa Goddess; or, How I Spent My Forties* (2001). Her last publication was 2005's *Sloth.*

OBITUARIES AND OTHER SOURCES:

BOOKS

Wasserstein, Wendy, *Shiksa Goddess; or, How I Spent My Forties,* Knopf (New York, NY), 2001.

PERIODICALS

Chicago Tribune, January 31, 2006, section 1, pp. 1, 6.
Los Angeles Times, January 31, 2006, pp. A1, A14.
New York Times, January 31, 2006, pp. A1, A20.
Times (London, England), February 2, 2006, p. 61.
Washington Post, January 31, 2006, p. B6.

*   *   *

WATTENBERG, Jane

Personal

Married; children: three sons. *Hobbies and other interests:* Travel, beekeeping, raising poultry.

Addresses

Office—80 Putnam St., San Francisco, CA 94110. *E-mail*—jane@janewattenberg.com.

Career

Photographer, writer, and illustrator.

Awards, Honors

Bulletin of the Center for Children's Books Blue Ribbon designation, 2000, for *Henny Penny;* Children's Choice designation, International Reading Association/ Children's Book Council, 2006, for *Never Cry Woof!*

Writings

SELF-ILLUSTRATED PICTURE BOOKS

Mrs. Mustard's Baby Faces, Chronicle Books (San Francisco, CA), 1989.
Mrs. Mustard's Beastly Babies, Chronicle Books (San Francisco, CA), 1990.
Mrs. Mustard's Name Games: Including the Common and the Curious, the Famous and the Infamous, the Long and the Short of It, Chronicle Books (San Francisco, CA), 1993.
Henny-Penny, Scholastic Press (New York, NY), 2000.
Never Cry Woof!: A Dog-U-Drama, Scholastic Press (New York, NY), 2005.

ILLUSTRATOR

Lola M. Schaefer, *This Is the Rain,* Greenwillow Books (New York, NY), 2001.

Sidelights

A lifelong love of photography has inspired San Francisco native Jane Wattenberg to establish a career as a picture-book author and illustrator. Her energetic col-

Cover of Jane Wattenberg's quirky self-illustrated picture book Never Cry Woof!, *which takes a dog's-eye view of a traditional tale.* (Scholastic Press, 2005. Copyright © 2005 by Jane Wattenberg. Reprinted by permission of Scholastic Inc)

lage art and quirky texts have come together in such works as *Henny-Penny,* a playful retelling of the classic folktale, and the rambunctious *Never Cry Woof!: A Dog-U-Drama,* a retelling of one of Aesop's most time-honored tales. In addition, Wattenberg's creative talents were paired with Lola M. Schaefer's descriptive text for the 2001 picture book *This Is the Rain.* Praised by *School Library Journal* contributor Adele Greenlee for her "interesting" photographic collage art, Wattenberg was also cited by a *Kirkus Reviews* writer who appreciated the "glowing photographic collage illustrations" featured in Schaefer's "striking" picture book.

Featuring illustrations a *Publishers Weekly* reviewer described as "pulsating to a high-energy beat," *Henny-Penny* introduces readers to a classic story-book character. A chicken, Henny-Penny becomes convinced that the sky is falling after she is hit on the noggin by a falling acorn. Setting off to warn the king of the impending disaster, the flustered fowl travels around the world, trying to locate her monarch's king. During her travels, she picks up a gaggle of colorful characters that accompany her on her search, among them the ultra-glamorous Goosey Loosey and the sly Foxy-Loxy. Wattenberg pairs her colorful collage art with an original hip-hopping rhyming story, producing a "waggish" take on the original tale, according to the *Publishers Weekly* critic. Marlene Gawron also had praise for Wattenberg's tale, writing in *School Library Journal* that *Henny-Penny* "has surefire appeal, especially to reluctant readers."

Retelling yet another traditional story in her unique fashion, Wattenberg recasts Aesop's fable about the boy who cried "wolf!" as *Never Cry Woof!* As the title suggests, dogs take center stage, particularly Bix, a hyperactive hound with a nose for excitement. Joining a group of guard dogs hired to watch over a pack of sheep, Bix stirs things up with a howl that proves to be a false alarm. As folk-tale followers will anticipate, Bix ultimately finds himself alone when the predatory wolf finally does make an bold, memorable appearance, and Bix's career as a watchdog plays out with, alas, humorous but unfortunate results. Cheryl Stritzel McCarthy wrote in her Cleveland *Plain Dealer* review that "swinging rhyme, loads of puns and . . . energetic photo collages" all contribute to the book's "high-octane story." In *School Library Journal* Marilyn Taniguchi noted that Wattenberg's "hip-hop banter moves along at a brisk clip" and the text's wealth of puns is balanced by the "sight gags" incorporated into the author/illustrator's humorous collage art.

Biographical and Critical Sources

PERIODICALS

Booklist, December 15, 2001, Todd Morning, review of *This Is the Rain,* p. 741.
Kirkus Reviews, January 15, 2005, review of *Never Cry Woof!: A Dog-U-Drama,* p. 127.
New York Times, May 14, 2000, Sam Swope, review of *Henny Penny.*
Plain Dealer (Cleveland, OH), February 27, 2005, Cheryl Stritzel McCarthy, review of *Never Cry Woof!*
Publishers Weekly, April 10, 2000, review of *Henny-Penny,* p. 98; July 23, 2001, review of *This Is the Rain,* p. 76.
School Library Journal, April, 2000, Marlene Gawron, review of *Henny-Penny,* p. 128; September, 2001, Adele Greenlee, review of *This Is the Rain,* p. 205; March, 2005, Marilyn Taniguchi, review of *Never Cry Woof!,* p. 189.

ONLINE

Jane Wattenberg Home Page, http://www.janewattenberg. com (October 10, 2006).
Scholastic Web site, http://books.scholastic.com/ (October 10, 2006), "Jane Wattenberg."

*   *   *

WHISP, Kennilworthy
See ROWLING, J.K.

*   *   *

WILSON, Karma

Personal

Born October 8; married; husband's name Scott; children: Michael, David, Chrissy.

Addresses

Home—Bonner's Ferry, ID. *Agent*—c/o Steven Malk, 21 W. 26th St., New York, NY 10010.

Career

Writer.

Awards, Honors

Children's Resource Gold Award, and Capitol Choices Noteworthy Book for Children designation, both 2002, and National Parenting Publications, Oppenheim Toy Portfolio Platinum Book Award, American Library Association Notable Book designation, Charlotte Zolotow Highly Commended designation, New Hampshire Ladybug Book Award nomination, and Children's Book of the Year finalist, International Reading Association, all 2003, Wyoming Buckaroo Book Award nomination, 2002-03, New York Charlotte Award nomination, Great Lakes Great Books Award nomination, Maryland Children's Book Award nomination, Wisconsin Wema Golden Archers Award nomination, Arizona Young Readers Award nomination, and Virginia Young Readers Award nomination, all 2004, and Washington Children's Choice Picture Award nomination, and Michigan Reader's Association Book Award nomination, both 2005, all for *Bear Snores On;* Texas 2x2 Book Award nomination, 2003, and Missouri Building Block nomination, 2004, both for *Frog in the Bog.*

Writings

FOR CHILDREN

Bear Snores On, illustrated by Jane Chapman, Margaret K. McElderry Books (New York, NY), 2001.

Frog in the Bog, illustrated by Joan Rankin, Margaret K. McElderry Books (New York, NY), 2003.

Cattle Drive, illustrated by Karla Firehammer, Little, Brown (Boston, MA), 2003.

Bear Wants More, illustrated by Jane Chapman, Margaret K. McElderry Books (New York, NY), 2003.

Sweet Briar Goes to School, illustrated by LeUyen Pham, Dial Books for Young Readers (New York, NY), 2003.

Grandmother's Whopper Birthday Cake, Margaret K. McElderry Books (New York, NY), 2003.

Bear Stays up for Christmas, illustrated by Jane Chapman, Margaret K. McElderry Books (New York, NY), 2004.

Dinos on the Go!, illustrated by Laura Radar, Little, Brown (New York, NY), 2004.

Hilda Must Be Dancing, illustrated by Suzanne Watts, Margaret K. McElderry Books (New York, NY), 2004.

Never, Ever Shout in a Zoo, illustrated by Doug Cushman, Little, Brown (New York, NY), 2004.

Mr. Murray and Thumbkin, illustrated by Ard Hoyt, Little, Brown (New York, NY), 2004.

Sweet Briar Goes to Camp, illustrated by LeUyen Pham, Dial Books for Young Readers (New York, NY), 2005.

Dinos in the Snow!, illustrated by Laura Radar, Little, Brown (New York, NY), 2005.

Bear Hugs: Romantically Ridiculous Animal Rhymes, illustrated by Suzanne Watts, Margaret K. McElderry Books (New York, NY), 2005.

Sakes Alive!: A Cattle Drive, illustrated by Karla Firehammer, Little, Brown (New York, NY), 2005.

Mortimer's Christmas Manger, illustrations by Jane Chapman, Margaret K. McElderry Books (New York, NY), 2005.

Mama Always Comes Home, illustrated by Brooke Dyer, HarperCollins (New York, NY), 2005.

Sleepyhead, illustrated by John Segal, Margaret K. McElderry Books (New York, NY), 2006.

Animal Strike at the Zoo, illustrated by Margaret Spengler, HarperCollins (New York, NY), 2006.

Moose Tracks!, illustrated by Jack E. Davis, Margaret K. McElderry Books (New York, NY), 2006.

Bear's New Friend, illustrated by Jane Chapman, Margaret K. McElderry Books (New York, NY), 2006.

How to Bake an American Pie, illustrations by Raul Colon, Margaret K. McElderry Books (New York, NY), 2007.

Bear Feels Sick, illustrated by Jane Chapman, Margaret K. McElderry Books (New York, NY), 2007.

Give Thanks to the Lord: Celebrating Psalm 92, illustrated by Amy Bates, Zonderkidz (Grand Rapids, MI), 2007.

I Will Rejoice!, Zonderkidz (Grand Rapids, MI), 2007.

Let's Make a Joyful Noise!: A Celebration of Psalm 100, Zonderkidz (Grand Rapids, MI), 2008.

Sidelights

Karma Wilson made an impressive debut with the publication of her first children's title, *Bear Snores On.* The book won several accolades, including the Oppenheim Toy Portfolio Platinum Book Award, and was signified as an American Library Association notable book. Wilson's signature style involves using rhythmic texts; as she noted in an online interview for *Suite 101,* "rhyme gives me this basic set of rules to conform to. I have to think of whatever 'form' I've chosen and there are only so many choices." For Wilson, writing is the easiest aspect of her work. As she admitted in her interview, "a good story is the hardest part for me to come up with."

Wilson's stories—often humorous and light hearted— are intended primarily to entertain and captivate young readers and listeners. *Bear Snores On,* for example, is the first installment in a picture-book series that features the mis-adventures of a forest bear. In the story, while Bear is fast asleep in his cozy cave, safely protected from the cold winter, other forest animals take refuge in Bear's cave. First Mouse arrives and builds a warm fire. Then Hare appears, bringing pop corn and tea, while Badger offers nuts to the growing gathering. Soon, the cozy cave is filled with forest animals and a party ensues. A contributor to *Kirkus Reviews* acknowledged the book for its "lyrical text," while *Booklist* reviewer Ellen Mandel cited the "snappy rhythm . . . [that] beckon[s] youngsters into the story."

Karma Wilson's simple picture-book texts have been paired with artwork by illustrators such as Jane Chapman, who collaborated with Wilson on the humorous **Bear Snores On.** (Little Simon, 2005. Illustrations copyright © 2002 by Jane Chapman. Reprinted with the permission of Margaret K. McElderry Books, an imprint of Simon & Schuster Children's Publishing Division)

Bear Wants More is Wilson's follow-up to *Bear Snores On,* and once again, Bear's forest animal friends appear. Bear has just awoken from his hibernation and immediately begins foraging for food in order to satiate his voracious hunger. Bear's friends attempt to help Bear find food: Mouse brings offerings of berries, while Hare brings clover. However, nothing can satisfy the large creature's hunger as, as Wilson repetitively notes, "Bear wants more." Bear's friends then prepare a feast that they feel sure will quell Bear's hunger, and when Bear returns from ransacking the forest he finds a huge feast ready and waiting for him in his den. The only problem is that Bear is now too fat to fit through his den's door.

Booklist reviewer Connie Fletcher characterized *Bear Wants More* as "an appealing romp about springtime and friendship." The author's "use of repetitive refrain" teases readers' appetites for more," "neatly building to the anticipation of the tale's surprise ending," observed a *Kirkus Reviews* writer, the critic concluding that Wilson's "sing-song" paired rhymes "lend . . . sprightliness to the ebullient tale." Likewise, *School Library Journal* critic Amy Lilien-Harper noted that Wilson's "rollicking, rhyming text flows smoothly, and the repeated refrain will have youngsters chiming right in."

Another highly recognized title written by Wilson, *Frog in the Bog* incorporates Wilson's trademark rhymes, and features a hungry frog that counts as it eats: one tick, two fleas, three flies, and so on. As the frog of the title grows heavier as a result of his large lunch, a

Featuring Wilson's characteristic breezy rhyme, **Sakes Alive! A Cattle Drive** *is illustrated in lighthearted fashion by Karla Firehammer.* (Little, Brown, and Company, 2005. Illustrations copyright © 2005 by Karla Firehammer. Reproduced by permission of Little, Brown and Co., Inc)

nearby alligator takes notice of the greedy amphibian and contemplates a meal of his own. *Frog in a Bog* counts from one up to five snails, making the book "especially suitable for the youngest beginning counters," according to a *Kirkus Reviews* writer. According to a *Publishers Weekly* critic, Wison's book successfully melds "early learning concepts, humor and wordplay" into "a jaunty read-aloud." *School Library Journal* reviewer Linda L. Walkins called *Frog in the Bog* an "imaginative counting book [that] will keep children laughing."

Biographical and Critical Sources

BOOKS

Wilson, Karma, *Bear Snores On,* Margaret McElderry Books (New York, NY), 2001.
Wilson, Karma, *Bear Wants More,* Margaret McElderry Books (New York, NY), 2003.

PERIODICALS

Booklist, January 1, 2002, Ellen Mandel, review of *Bear Snores On,* p. 868; April 15, 2003, Connie Fletcher, review of *Bear Wants More,* p. 1479.
Kirkus Reviews, November 15, 2001, review of *Bear Snores On,* p. 161; December 1, 2002, review of *Bear Wants More,* p. 1776; August 1, 2003, review of *Bear Wants More,* p. 1025.
Publishers Weekly, October 20, 2003, review of *Frog in the Bog,* p. 52.
School Library Journal, February, 2003, Amy Lilien-Harper, review of *Bear Wants More,* p. 124; December, 2003, Linda L. Walkins, review of *Frog in the Bog,* p. 130.

ONLINE

Hachette Book Group Web site, http://www.twbookmark.com/ (October 6, 2006).
Karma Wilson Home Page, http://www.bearsnoreson.com (October 6, 2006).
Suite 101 Web site, http://www.suite101.com/ (October 6, 2006), Sue Reichard, "Children's Author Karma Wilson Writes On."*

*   *   *

YOO, Paula 1969(?)-

Personal

Born c. 1969; married. *Ethnicity:* "Asian." *Education:* Yale University, B.A. (English), 1991; Columbia University, M.S. (journalism), 1992; Warren Wilson College, M.F.A. (creative writing), 2002. *Hobbies and other interests:* Music, films, reading.

Addresses

Home—Los Angeles, CA. *Agent*—Writers House, 21 W. 26th St., New York, NY 10010.

Career

Writer, educator, screenwriter, and musician. Former journalist with *Detroit News* other periodicals; *People* magazine, former entertainment correspondent; Glendale Community College, Glendale, CA, instructor in English. Professional violinist; member of rock band Random AOK.

Member

Society of Children's Book Writers and Illustrators.

Awards, Honors

Society of Children's Book Writers and Illustrators grant, 2000; Lee & Low New Voices Award, 2003, Children's Books of the Year designation, Bank Street College Children's Book Committee, Notable Social Studies Trade Books for Young People, National Council of Social Studies/Children's Book Council, International Reading Association Children's Book Award Notable designation, and Comstock Book Award Honor, Minnesota State University Moorhead, all 2006, and North Dakota Library Association Flicker Talk Children's Book Award finalist, 2007, all for *Sixteen Years in Sixteen Seconds.*

Writings

Sixteen Years in Sixteen Seconds: The Sammy Lee Story, illustrated by Dom Lee, Lee & Low Books (New York, NY), 2005.

Also screenwriter for television programs, including segments of series *The West Wing,* 2002-03, *Tru Calling,* 2004, and *Angel.*

Sidelights

When she began her writing career, Paula Yoo chose journalism because, as she told *Asian Week Online* contributor Terry Hong, "I thought being a journalist would be a great way to hone my writing skills, live life, and have great adventures." In fact, Yoo did have great adventures, and has since moved from journalism to working in Hollywood as a television scriptwriter, all the while continuing to add to her performance credits as a violinist and rock musician. Now teaching writing in addition to working for television, she has also added "children's book writer" to her resume with the publication of *Sixteen Years in Sixteen Seconds: The Sammy Lee Story.*

Yoo was inspired to write about Olympic Gold Medal winner Sammy Lee while researching Korean-American history for her M.F.A. at Warren Wilson College. Not-

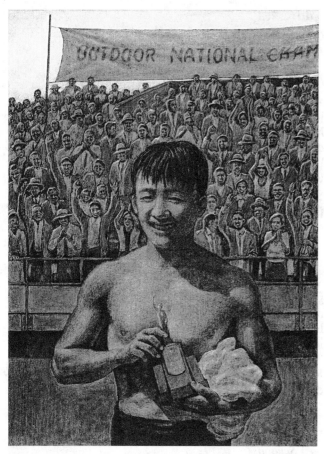

Paula Yoo tells the story of noted Korean-American swimmer Sammy Lee in Sixteen Years in Sixteen Seconds, *featuring illustrations by Dom Lee.* (Lee & Low Books, Inc., 2005. Illustrations copyright © 2005 by Dom Lee. Reproduced by permission of Lee & Low Books, Inc)

ing that, despite the hurdles prejudice and family expectations put before him, in 1948 Lee became the first Asian American to win the Olympic gold. As Yoo told a Lee & Low *Booktalk* online interviewer, "I found myself distracted from my M.F.A. research and began spending time researching Sammy Lee instead of working on my thesis!" In the course of her research, Yoo had the opportunity to interview Lee, whom she described to Hong as "a delightful man" who is both "feisty" and "colorful."

Sixteen Years in Sixteen Seconds follows Lee's life, and illustrates the passion the athlete felt for swimming. As a child growing up in California, Lee faced racial discrimination in the form of restrictions placed on non-whites at public swimming pools; meanwhile, to further

complicate things, his father was determined that his son become a doctor. Dedication and determination ultimately propelled Lee to the Olympic trials, and after his historic win he continued to achieve successes in life.

Yoo's "elegantly told" story, with "soft, semi-impressionistic style artwork" by Dom Yee, was praised by a *Children's Bookwatch* critic as "an inspirational testimony for young readers about [each person's] . . . infinite potential." *Horn Book* critic Susan Dove Lempke also lauded Yoo's writing debut, stating that in *Sixteen Years in Sixteen Seconds* the author "smoothly incorporates the historical context" of early twentieth-century American society, and "creates a picture of a person who succeeded through determined hard work—not a larger-than-life hero, but an ordinary person of great achievement." Blair Christolon, in *School Library Journal*, deemed *Sixteen Years in Sixteen Seconds* an "inspirational biography."

Biographical and Critical Sources

PERIODICALS

Booklist, March 15, 2005, Gillian Engberg, review of *Sixteen Years in Sixteen Seconds: The Sammy Lee Story*, p. 1287.
Children's Bookwatch, August, 2005, review of *Sixteen Years in Sixteen Seconds*.
Horn Book, July-August, 2005, Susan Dove Lempke, review of *Sixteen Years in Sixteen Seconds*, p. 493.
Kirkus Reviews, March 15, 2005, review of *Sixteen Years in Sixteen Seconds*, p. 361.
Publishers Weekly, April 4, 2005, review of *Sixteen Years in Sixteen Seconds*, p. 59.
School Library Journal, April, 2005, Blair Christolon, review of *Sixteen Years in Sixteen Seconds*, p. 128.

ONLINE

Asian Week Online, http://news.asianweek.com/ (May 13, 2005), Terry Hong, "The Patiently Tenacious Paula Yoo."
Lee & Low Booktalk, http://www.leeandlow.com/ (October 10, 2006), interview with Yoo.
Paula Yoo My Space Page, http://profile.myspace.com/ paulayoo (October 10, 2006).*

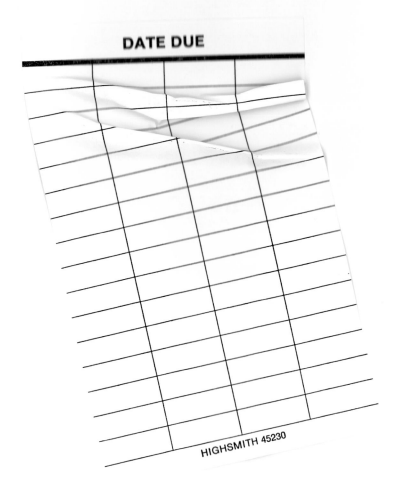

DATE DUE

HIGHSMITH 45230